THE COMING

1763-1775 OF THE

REVOLUTION

harper ⚜ torchbooks

A reference-list of Harper Torchbooks, classified by subjects, is printed at the end of this volume.

THE NEW AMERICAN NATION SERIES

Edited by HENRY STEELE COMMAGER *and*
RICHARD B. MORRIS

* *In preparation*

THE COMING

1763-1775 # OF THE

REVOLUTION

BY LAWRENCE HENRY GIPSON

❧ HARPER TORCHBOOKS
The University Library
HARPER & ROW, Publishers
New York

Contents

15256

Illustrations and Maps

These illustrations, grouped·in a separate section, will be found following page 144.

MAPS

Editors' Introduction

DURING the past half century the lapse of time and the uncovering of much new evidence have made it possible for scholars to pursue their investigations into the causes of the American Revolution in an atmosphere far less partisan than had prevailed in earlier generations. As a result of this more objective handling of the period of mounting tension that preceded the War of Independence, the rights on both sides of the controversy are more generally conceded.

Most historians agree today that the British government was justified in calling upon the colonies for a larger contribution to the imperial program than they had made prior to the Peace of Paris of 1763, but affirm the correctness of the colonial position in labeling the government's program after that year an infringement of that substantial measure of self-government which the colonists had achieved for themselves over a period of a century and a half. No longer is George III portrayed as a wicked, designing man. However, by establishing himself at the center of British politics and breaking with the Old Whigs, the monarch is viewed as having failed to serve as a symbol of imperial unity. British-American relations foundered on the rock of the conservatism of the King and his supporters, but this conservatism provided the ultimate base for a new Tory party.

The complex and varied aspects of imperial relations on the eve of the Revolution are carefully explored by Dr. Lawrence H. Gipson in this volume. His multivolume study, *The British Empire Before the American Revolution,* has abundantly demonstrated the author's profound knowledge of the sources, his insights into the complex issues of the day, and his ability to treat these events with balance and objectivity. To Dr. Gipson the Revolution marks the culmination in America of the twin forces of federalism and nationalism. The author sees no basic clash between England and her colonies over commerce or church policy or westward expansion. To him the forces of federalism and nationalism were irreconcilable with the outmoded system of imperial relationships upon which the old British Empire had been founded.

This volume is one of *The New American Nation Series,* a comprehensive co-operative survey of the history of the area now known as the United States, from the days of discovery to the mid-twentieth century. Since the publication a half century ago by the House of Harper of the *American Nation* series under the editorship of the distinguished historian, Albert Bushnell Hart, the scope of history has been broadened and a new approach has been developed to deal with the problems of historical interpretation and presentation. The time has now come for a judicious appraisal of the new history, a cautious application of the new techniques of investigation and presentation, and a large-scale effort to achieve a synthesis of the new findings with the traditional facts, and to present the whole in attractive literary form.

To this task the New American Nation Series is dedicated. Each volume is part of a carefully planned whole, and co-ordinated with other volumes in the series; at the same time each volume is designed to be complete in itself. Some overlapping is doubtless inevitable, but it has seemed to the editors that overlapping is less regrettable than omissions, and from time to time the same series of events and the same actors will be seen from different points of view. While for the most part the series follows a chronological organization, separate volumes or groups of volumes will be devoted to cultural history, constitutional history, and foreign affairs.

HENRY STEELE COMMAGER
RICHARD BRANDON MORRIS

Preface

THIS volume is concerned with the revolutionary movement within the thirteen American continental colonies during the period that extended from the Peace of Paris of 1763 to the outbreak of open hostilities between Great Britain and these colonies in 1775. Other volumes in The New American Nation Series will treat the social and cultural aspects of the period, as well as colonial culture and trans-Appalachian developments, which have not been covered herein. The controversy over the project to appoint an American bishop for the colonial Anglican establishment has been treated rather fully in Alice M. Baldwin's *The New England Clergy and the American Revolution* (Durham, N.C., 1928) and in the late Arthur Lyon Cross's *The Anglican Episcopate and the American Colonies* (New York, 1902). Neither study provides any evidence that the controversy contributed measurably toward arousing colonial hostility against the government of Great Britain, which was in fact opposed to the appointment of an American bishop. Nonetheless, many of the New England clergy continued to lash what was really a dead horse. As to the West, I have at length reached the same conclusion that Professor Abernethy set forth in his *Western Lands and the American Revolution* (Charlottesville, 1937), namely, that the fundamental causes for the American Revolution are not to be found specifically in the Proclamation of 1763 or in the activities of various groups either seeking to lay their hands on western lands or hoping to erect new western colonies, or in the measures taken by the Crown in an effort to control the western Indian tribes—far-reaching as was the indirect influence of these developments upon British colonial policy.

It is the argument of this book that the causes of the Revolution stem first from the effort of the British Government, faced with vast territorial acquisitions in North America at the end of the Great War for the Empire, along with an unprecedented war debt, to organize a more efficient administration on that continent and to make the colonies contribute directly to the support of the enlarged Empire amounts over and beyond the indefinite and indirect contributions already provided through the operation of the old colonial system of controls. Secondly, the causes of the breach can be traced to the radically altered situation of the colonies after 1760, by which date they were at long last relieved of the intense pressure previously exerted along their borders by hostile nations. Thus, at the very time when their dependence upon the mother country had largely disappeared and they felt impelled to demand greater autonomy than ever, the colonials found, instead, that their sphere of freedom of political action was seriously circumscribed by the government at home. Inevitably this led, first of all, to a re-examination by colonial leaders of the implications of the complicated British imperial system; then to challenging the doctrine of the supremacy of Parliament throughout the Empire; finally, to setting forth the counterdoctrine that the assemblies of the colonies were alone the ultimate judges of the extent of authority that the Crown and Parliament of Great Britain would be permitted to exercise within their borders. All this occurred between the years 1761 and 1775.

The progression in American political ideas just described was indubitably revolutionary in nature, as John Adams, who played a leading part in it, affirmed. This phase of the American Revolution may be characterized as the period of political maneuver—in contrast to the period of actual fighting between 1775 and 1781. It is this earlier period of the Revolution—marked at its worst by the disorder of mobs rather than by armed insurrection—with which the present volume is concerned.

By 1763 English civilization had been in existence along the eastern Atlantic seaboard of North America for over a century and a half. It had, however, been modified profoundly in the course of the passing generations, and not only by the isolation of the New World from the Old World through the lack of any ready means of communication and intercourse between the peoples so widely separated by the Atlantic. The impact on the settlers mode of life of the continuous battle with the American wilderness, of religious divergency, and of the presence, particularly in the middle and southern colonies, of tens of thousands of people of non-English stock fostered the rise of an American nationalism.

Indeed, one can speak, not inaccurately, of the emergence by 1763 of an American civilization: a blend of many ancient English and non-English transplanted mores to which were added those newer mores that a strange environment and unprecedented conditions for human survival had molded. Here then was a modified European civilization that responded to, that symbolized, the complex material, social, and spiritual needs of the settlers. Therefore, where the peculiar ideals embodied in this New World civilization actually clashed with those of the mother country, colonials would be inclined to repudiate older loyalties for the newer. Moreover, in so far as the self-interest of colonials—irrespective of ideals—diverged basically from the self-interest of the people of Great Britain, there was bound to be conflict between the two. That no deep schism developed between the English colonials and the English at home before 1763—in spite of differences in point of view over particular issues that arose from time to time prior to this period—is indicative of the existence of certain ideals and interests that were recognized by both to be more vital than any which made for conflict and for the lessening of the bonds that held them together. This was not true after the close of the Great War for the Empire and for reasons that have already been suggested earlier in this preface.

Since Professor Howard published his *Preliminaries of the American Revolution* (New York, 1905), as one of the American Nation Series, much additional original source material relating to this period of history has been made available to Americans. Numerous important monographic studies have also appeared. These and other sources still abroad have been drawn upon liberally in the writing of this volume. The author therefore hopes that the reader will find in it new approaches as well as a clarification of those that are traditional. The Bibliography will, I trust, also be helpful to those seeking more specialized knowledge of the period.

I am under particular obligation to the following depositories for special assistance in gathering materials that I have here sought to utilize: the Library of Congress, the Canadian Archives at Ottawa, the Public Record Office in London, the British Museum, the Clements Library at Ann Arbor, the Huntington Library at San Marino, the Massachusetts Archives, the Massachusetts Historical Society, the Historical Society of Pennsylvania, the Manuscript Division of the New York Public Library, the New York Historical Society, the New York State Archives at Albany, the Virginia Historical Society, the Virginia State Library, the South Carolina Archives, the Georgia State Library, the Library of Princeton University, and the Lehigh University Library. I must also acknowledge my indebtedness to Lehigh University and the Lehigh Institute of Research for providing both the financial resources and freedom from other duties that alone made it possible to write this volume. Further, I must mention that a portion of Chapter 1 was used in the Inaugural Lecture that I delivered at the University of Oxford as the Harmsworth Professor of American History and that was published in 1952 by the Clarendon Press under the title *The British Empire in the Eighteenth Century: Its Strength and Its Weakness*. Finally, thanks are due to Mr. James D. Mack, Lehigh University Librarian, for aiding me in checking the titles of works included in the Bibliography, to Mr. John F. Roche of Fordham University for valued editorial assistance, and to my wife, Jeannette Reed Gipson, for constant aid in the research involved in this volume and in preparing it for publication.

L. H. G.

"Rotha"
Rydal, Pennsylvania

CHAPTER 1

The British Empire in 1763

THE GREAT War for the Empire fought by Great Britain and the American colonies against the French and later the Spaniards between the years 1754 and 1763 had at last, after nine agonizing years, come to an end. The peace that concluded it, signed on February 10, 1763, at Paris, not only brought a recognition of British claims in North America to all the land east of the Mississippi River, outside of New Orleans and its environs, but also gathered within the folds of the Empire both Canada and Florida, as well as certain of the so-called "Neutral Islands" of the West Indies, and at least political control of Bengal in India. Therefore, along the Atlantic seaboard from Hudson Bay to the Florida Keys the Union Jack could now wave without a rival; soon it would wave, too, over all those former symbols of French power in the interior of the continent: Detroit, Michilimackinac, Vincennes, Fort Chartres, and Mobile, as well as over Pensacola and the walls of once Spanish St. Augustine. The conquest of these hitherto hostile territories gave the inhabitants of the older British colonies a new sense of security and excited within their breasts the sense of mission and destiny.

In 1763 all colonials were Britons—at least those who were white and either born within the Empire or naturalized. The Empire was their own and they were proud of membership in it. There were good reasons for this pride. Its government rested fundamentally on law and not on men. Both in Great Britain and the colonies in the

1

eighteenth century the law of the land that bound all men, even the King, was a mixture of common and statutory law; that is, law based upon judicial interpretation of common custom, on the one hand, and on formal legislative enactment, on the other. Despite the striking contrasts in the seventeenth century between the codes enforced within some of the colonies and the legal system of the mother country, in the course of the eighteenth century colonial law and British law were in substantial harmony by 1763. This degree of uniformity was reached not only as a result of the adoption of English law by colonial assemblies, particularly Pennsylvania, but by reason of the exercise by the King's Privy Council of the power both to disallow colonial legislation and to review colonial judicial decisions. In substance, the colonies acquiesced in the exercise of these supervisory powers.[1] Further, although all the older and more mature colonies legislated for themselves, by 1763 many statutes of Parliament extended throughout the Empire by express enactment and covered a multiplicity of subjects, from such external matters as the regulation of imports and exports and the naturalization of foreigners to such internal matters as the regulation of currency, the operations of stock companies, and the cutting of timber.

The instrumentalities of lawmaking and enforcement within the colonies were about as similar to those of Great Britain as could be expected under differing conditions. Indeed, the colonial assemblies not only consciously adopted as far as was possible the forms and procedures of the House of Commons but constantly sought to acquire its powers. With respect to the electorate that selected the lawmakers, everywhere, as was true in England, there existed what might be called a political aristocracy made up of qualified males who enjoyed the right of franchise and a monopoly of public offices—as against the great mass of the disfranchised, whose persons and property were subject to regulation and taxation without true representation.

In short, the popular branches of the colonial assemblies were consciously evolving from the earlier purely dependent ordinance-making bodies, and in structure and powers approaching the like-

[1] See R. B. Morris, *Studies in the History of American Law* (New York, 1930), chap. 1; J. H. Smith, *Appeals to the Privy Council from the American Plantations* (New York, 1950).

ness of the House of Commons. Moreover, other features of the colonial governments were just as consciously patterned after the institutions of the mother country. The colonial governor was regarded as one who, to a greater or less extent, represented the King, either directly under royal commission and royal instruction, as in the royal colonies, or less directly, as in the proprietary and the corporate colonies. At least, in every instance this official as the chief executive was under heavy bond to see that imperial regulations were enforced; he also had an advisory council not unlike the King's Cabinet Council. Likewise, the English offices of sheriff and of justice of the peace, county or parish courts, courts of oyer and terminer, and courts of appeal had made their appearance in the colonies. In fact, these and other institutions transplanted from the mother country were so well adapted to meet the divergent needs of Americans that, even with the establishment of their independence from Great Britain, they were, with some modifications, preserved and are still regarded as among the most cherished possessions of most North Americans.

Not only were the inhabitants of the Empire bound together by similar, if not identical, systems of law and institutions of government but the religious, ethical, intellectual, and social conceptions of the mother country were still largely those of the English-speaking colonials and increasingly those of the non-English transplanted elements. An important factor in producing this broad uniformity, with infinite variations, was the fact that the British people of both the Old and New World were by and large not only literate but were eager readers of weekly newspapers and pamphlets concerned with contemporary world developments; most of them also read the King James version of the Holy Scriptures, thus drawing their religious inspiration from the same source. Then, too, large numbers of colonials perused the works of British theologians, philosophers, scientists, essayists, poets, novelists, and dramatists. Further, English etiquette, dress, architecture, and home furnishings, as well as other English practices, exerted a profound influence, especially on the more settled communities of the eastern Atlantic seaboard.[2]

[2] Louis B. Wright, *The Atlantic Frontier: Colonial American Civilization* (New York, 1947); Michael Kraus, *International Aspects of American Culture* (New York, 1928), and *Atlantic Civilization* (Ithaca, N.Y., 1950).

Moreover, one must take into account the connections existing between Anglicans, Quakers, Baptists, Presbyterians, and other religious groups in the colonies and the parent organizations in Great Britain.

While these common conceptions, common legal and social codes, and common institutions produced a very great degree of cultural homogeneity within the British Empire, there were, nevertheless, divergencies that are equally important to recognize.

The American frontier was creating a new type of Briton—the American—one who was less and less, as time elapsed, under the influence of tradition and inherited cultural patterns and more and more shaped by his contest with nature and the necessity to improvise if he were to survive. The King, the Privy Council, the ministers of state, and the Parliament, established as they were beyond the intervening forest and the rushing rivers and across the wide Atlantic, were quite lost to his view. Indeed, only in time of great emergency, when things were beyond his and his fellow pioneers' control—as in the face of the threat of annihilation in the early years of the late war—did the wilderness dweller heed the existence of or value of the imperial connections that still bound him to Great Britain. His recognized leader was not, as a rule, even the colonial governor of the colony in which he had his isolated western home, or even the sheriff or lieutenant of his county, but rather the most enterprising and daring of his wilderness companions. In other words, the form of social structure that the backwoodsman knew and the only one that to him had significance was a rude but true type of democratic society, with authority, such as it was, exercised by those who by common consent had shown superior capacity to face the hard conditions of life on the frontier.

Even along the settled Atlantic seaboard, where conditions of living were far less fluid and primitive than those of the wilderness, there were likewise deviations from the institutions of England. While here an aristocracy of wealth enjoying political and social domination was firmly planted, there was no aristocracy of title, nor was there a hereditary body clothed with legislative and judicial power as was the case in the British Isles. In contrast, while the status of slavery was not recognized in English law, a substantial percentage of the population in the southern provinces and at least a small percentage in every colony were slaves whose status was recognized and defined by local law. These cultural variations sprang largely from differences in environment.

To Englishmen at home a titled aristocracy was inextricably woven into the texture of their long history. Moreover, with the disappearance of the old feudal baronage, as the result of the War of the Roses and the calculated policy of the Tudors, a new nobility had arisen that had its roots in the upper middle class of country gentry and city merchants and remained closely associated with these groups. But slightly privileged, this new nobility was highly respected and provided leadership in almost all great enterprises. Where it lacked the genius for leadership demanded by a peculiar situation in public affairs, it readily supported an able commoner as a rule, as in the case of William Pitt during the course of the late war. Hence, Englishmen would accept a hereditary order of nobility clothed with political power as a stabilizing element in the British polity, but looked upon the institutions of slavery in America as running counter to traditional English liberties.

In America, a pioneer outlook combined with a Puritan tradition ran counter to the setting up of a hereditary titled class—and this in spite of the existence in some of the colonies of such feudal institutions as primogeniture and entail, which in England had helped create and preserve a hereditary landed aristocracy. However, the institution of slavery had fastened itself on American life, not only by reason of the activities of British slavers—at first directed toward the carrying of Africans to the Spanish possessions—but primarily because it offered to colonials an easy and profitable means of rolling back the North American wilderness and thereby laying out and exploiting plantations, and staffing the households of the wealthy with permanent servants. So between the years 1763 and 1775 fiery advocates of liberty—planters, merchants, lawyers, and even ministers of the Gospel—saw apparently no moral inconsistency in openly offering rewards in newspapers for the return into captivity of some runaway black, while at the time denouncing as "slavery" restrictions that the mother country had seen fit to place upon their freedom of action.

Indeed, the sharp accent upon colonial rights after 1763, the rapid development of sectionalism within the Empire, the armed revolt of the thirteen colonies, the declaration of American independence, and, finally, the creation of a new nation followed one after the other with almost breath-taking speed. All were accomplished facts twenty-five years after Great Britain and the colonies had in closest association won the most spectacular and also by far the most important military successes in the history of the old Empire.

This overwhelming victory doubtless seemed to most people to portend that the Empire, for more than a century to follow, would by the utilization of its varied talents and vast material resources be not only dominant on the seas but also a most potent force in two hemispheres, both in peace and in war. It was an empire without an emperor, setting an example to the rest of mankind as to how liberty could be reconciled with law, even within physical boundaries as widespread as those of the autocratic Spanish Empire and much more extended than those of imperial Rome at the height of its glory—a living testimony that there could exist in the midst of a world of despotisms the unity of a great, free, and enlightened society, where men could worship, speak and write, and mold their own lives with remarkably few restraints and with a sense of personal security and dignity. Where else in the contemporary world of the eighteenth century, people could ask, had a whole literature flowered, based upon conceptions of the rights and privileges of the individual? Where else could men point with pride to a series of great constitutional documents, stemming from past centuries, as the symbols of their liberties?

As tokens of their common sense of security and freedom from fear, the inhabitants of the Empire in 1763 could point to the fact that they were protected not only by a victorious army but, what was of greater assurance, by the most powerful fleet that had ever sailed the seas. Their merchant marine was also vastly larger than that of any other nation, and in its bottoms they exported to foreign ports a greater surplus of cereals and meat products than was exported by all the rest of the world combined, obtaining in return a bewildering variety of commodities to add to the satisfactions of life. They ranked first in the iron industry and in shipbuilding, as well as in other fields. In fact, despite squalor and poverty to be found here and there and especially in the British Isles, in the eyes of contemporaries most of King George III's subjects enjoyed an enviable standard of living: they were, by and large, better fed, better clothed, better sheltered, better rewarded for their efforts, than any other people with the possible exception of the Dutch. This was particularly true of those freemen dwelling in the American colonies.

Men, however, do not live by bread alone. What of the higher satisfactions of life and the evidences of civilized living within the Empire? By any standard that might be applied, the epoch now under consideration was indubitably one of the greatest in the history of the English-speaking people; indeed, the pages of its annals were crowded with the achievements of men of commanding capacity. Consider the statesman William Pitt, the Great Commoner, who by his superb organizing ability and dynamic qualities of leadership in the late war had brought victory to the Empire; Edmund Burke, who as an orator surpassed him in profundity; and Charles James Fox, Burke's brilliant and radical political rival. There were David Hume, the philosopher, and Samuel Johnson, the writer and lexicographer, each an intellectual colossus in his own field—men would later refer to "the age of Johnson" and could with equal reason refer to "the age of Hume." There were the historians, such as William Robertson and Edward Gibbon, the latter to leave to the world his *Decline and Fall of the Roman Empire,* a historical work still to be eclipsed by any other yet produced in the English-speaking world. There were the distinguished jurist William Blackstone and equally distinguished political economist Adam Smith, both to publish in this era the results of massive learning: the one in his classic *Commentaries on the Laws* and the other in his equally classic *The Wealth of Nations.* John Wesley, the most outstanding English religious reformer since the days of John Wycliffe, was still active in his Christian ministry, with a message destined to transform the lives of countless people and to inject into the harsh criminal law of both the Old and the New World a new humanitarian spirit; and George Whitefield, a former colleague in the Methodist movement, and the most powerful field evangelist that England has ever produced or America has ever heard, was still going from city cross to village cemetery speaking with a voice of deep conviction to even tens of thousands of forgotten men, drawn together and held spellbound by his burning exhortations. There were Thomas Gray, the poet; Oliver Goldsmith, the dramatist; James Boswell, greatest of all British biographers; David Garrick, perhaps the first among a galaxy of Shakespearean actors; and Sir Joshua Reynolds, George Romney, and Thomas Gainsborough, three of the most gifted of portrait painters, together with William Hogarth, whose inimitable caricatures of his own age have amused and sobered generations of people. Samuel Richardson, the father of the English novel, died only in 1761 and his successor, Tobias Smollett, not until 1771. Nor must one forget the brothers Robert and James Adam, great architects and designers of furniture, who together with Thomas Chippendale and young Thomas Sheraton were to leave a lasting influence on the beauty of living and good taste of the English-speaking world. Finally, there were James Watt, who gave to his generation the improved steam engine in 1764—shortly followed by James Hargreaves's spinning jenny and a little later by Richard Arkwright's spinning water frame—and the young scientist, Henry Cavendish, already embarked upon his remarkable series of investigation into the properties of gases and electricity. All four were heralds of a new age of science and technology.

Although the overseas English-speaking peoples up to 1763 had been largely preoccupied with conquering the wilderness, they, too, could point to some notable personalities. Jonathan Edwards, theologian and metaphysician, whose treatise on the *Freedom of the Will* has been called "the one large contribution that America has made to the deeper philosophic thought of the world," died only in 1758; the fame of Benjamin Franklin, whose impressive achievements in many fields were to gain for him world-wide recognition, had already spread to Great Britain, where he had received not only the gift of the freedom of the city from the corporation of Edinburgh but honorary degrees from the ancient universities of St. Andrews and Oxford; and his friend John Bartram, distinguished as one of the leading eighteenth-century naturalists and a tireless collector of New World flora, was in the midst of his life work. Further, the eve of the Revolution ushered in a new generation of American political philosophers and statesmen—such men as John Dickinson, John Adams, Thomas Jefferson, and young James

Madison—who would leave a lasting imprint on the institutions and political ideals of the Western Hemisphere. Finally, living in quiet retirement in Virginia, was the planter George Washington, destined to display such wisdom, such patience, such strength of character and purpose, such utter self-dedication to the fulfillment of the tasks that he was to undertake both in war and in peace, that by the universal verdict of mankind he would be accorded a place among the world's greatest men.

Only in Ireland—cursed for two centuries with strife engendered by the interfusion of religious, ecclesiastical, and political issues—was there within the Empire in 1763 any noticeable discontent among the people with their lot, and rightly so. Yet before the outbreak of the American Revolution even this unhappy land was to find in Henry Flood and Henry Grattan not unworthy champions of Irish rights, and was thus to see the beginnings of the long travail that would ultimately bring about the birth of a free nation.

In short, the British Empire in 1763 was perhaps more economically self-contained and more prosperous than any other that had ever before existed. Nor is this all. No better testimony to its enlightened character can be offered than the fact that between 1763 and 1775 there existed not simply one religion, as was the case within the French, Spanish, and Portuguese empires, but four different Christian faiths which were established by law in various areas: the Anglican, the Presbyterian, the Congregational, and the Roman Catholic; while many other faiths were quietly tolerated. In addition there were even colonies with no religious establishment. These varied achievements together with the spirit of enlightenment stamped the old Empire as truly the wonder of the world. Yet within a decade it was to be torn asunder by internecine strife.

CHAPTER 2

America Waxes Rich and Strong

L ET US now consider the internal situation in the American
colonies in 1763. While there are no accurate population
figures for the thirteen colonies for that year, it would appear that
they numbered at least 1,750,000 and perhaps as many as
2,000,000, including blacks as well as whites.[1] They were scattered
along the Atlantic seaboard from upper Maine to the borders of
Florida and had penetrated points far inland, following as a rule
either the course of rivers or, in the case of such colonies as Pennsylvania and Massachusetts Bay, such artificial means of communication as Indian paths and roads. However, they were not
evenly distributed. In some of the colonies, such as Connecticut, the
population was fairly dense and had already settled the lands most
suitable for cultivation, with the result that many families were rest-
lessly seeking new homes beyond their bounds; in other colonies, as
was true of New York, much of the good land was still held by great
families either for speculative purposes or for tenantry, and these
areas were therefore avoided by people seeking to acquire farms.

While most colonials dwelt either in the open country, particularly in the South, or in small towns and villages, after the pattern
of New England, there were also some seaports that indicated the

[1] E. B. Greene and V. D. Harrington, *American Population before the Federal
Census of 1790* (New York, 1932), p. 6. For estimates of the numbers of whites
and blacks in the American colonies before the outbreak of the Great War for
the Empire, see the author's *The British Empire Before the American Revolution* (8 vols., Caldwell, Ida., and New York, 1936–54), II, III.

presence of a real concentration of wealth and of people, such as Boston with a population of some 22,000 inhabitants, Newport with perhaps 10,000, New York City with about 18,000, Philadelphia surpassing Boston in size, and Charles Town (Charleston), the metropolis of the South,[2] with some 10,000. As the result of huge demands for provisions at high prices paid by the British army contractors for supplying the armed forces, the late war had brought added prosperity to the colonies. Nowhere was there manifest the type of squalor that marked the low standard of living of people in many parts of the Old World. For, rude as were the conditions under which many, if not most, frontier families lived, these were accepted as an inevitable part of the task of subduing the wilderness and were lightened by the ever-present anticipation of future rewards for present hardships. Colonials in 1763 were, by and large, self-confident, resourceful, energetic, and positive, and they displayed a forthrightness born of these qualities. This forthrightness had its expression even in religious matters. The homogeneity that had distinguished, for example, both New England and Virginia in 1663 no longer existed a century later. Both the established Congregational Church of New England and the Anglican Church of Virginia had suffered heavy blows to their prestige from the Great Awakening and the resultant secessions from the local churches. In 1763 such heterodox groups as the Baptists were boldly challenging the older religious establishments, and outside of the organized churches there were other movements, such as deism, that appealed to the more intellectually inclined. Further, by 1763 the weekly press all along the Atlantic seaboard constituted a formidable threat to the position that clergymen had long enjoyed in America as oracles on social as well as religious and ethical issues, and exerted a powerful influence along secular lines.

To repeat, the great wilderness of North America was slowly helping to create a new kind of Briton—the American. But the American was not shaped from any one mold. Certainly the ranchers of the western Carolinas, who tended the great herds of cattle that roamed and fattened upon the marshy uplands about the sources of

[2] Accuracy is unattainable in this matter; see Greene and Harrington, *American Population,* pp. 22, 97, 117–118, 177; and also the author's *British Empire,* I, 182; II, 4–6, 66, 120–121, 185–187.

the Santee and other rivers, were by 1763 as distinct in pattern of living as were the cowboys of the western plains in the nineteenth century. Quite distinct were the western traders and trappers, who lived a life not unlike that of the Indians and one very different from other frontiersmen primarily interested in husbandry and homebuilding. In the more settled parts of the colonies, not only the wealthy tobacco and rice planters of the South but the merchant princes of the North had become as dissimilar from their prototypes in England as were American farmers, sailors, fishermen, small tradesmen, and mechanics. Moreover, the woodsmen, both of Maine and New Hampshire and of the pine barrens of the Carolinas, represented types that had no counterpart in the mother country. There were also extensive communities of German-speaking people in Pennsylvania, western Maryland, and western Virginia who preserved much of the culture of their ancestral homeland, as did the Ulster Scots—more familiarly known as Scotch-Irish—who remained a border people much like their ancestors in northern Ireland and earlier in the Lowlands of Scotland. Finally, there were the Negroes, probably numbering by 1763 almost 175,000.[3] The impact of their mores, as well as their mere presence as slaves, upon the English civilization of the New World was clearly evident and as much as any other social institution distinguished it sharply from that of the mother country.

In short, many distinct groups were jostling one another in the British North America of 1763. Some were pacifistic like the Quakers, the Mennonites, and Dunkards in Pennsylvania, and others decidedly militant, like the Presbyterian Ulster Scots and the New England Congregationalists; many were devout communicants and others were apparently disassociated from any church or religion; most of them used the tongue of England, and yet thousands spoke some other language. Thus, there was a vital need of the spirit of tolerance in the colonies, were conditions of living not to be rendered unbearable. That this spirit of toleration was growing cannot be doubted; that it still fell far short of the present Ameri-

[3] James Abercrombie in 1752 estimated the number of slaves in the continental colonies to be 150,000 (Abercrombie's Examination, p. 30, in Huntington Library); see also the author's *British Empire,* II, III, for statistics on the various colonies.

can ideal is not to be denied. In 1763, Roman Catholics as well as non-Christians, including Jews, were denied the franchise and other rights of citizenship even in Rhode Island, that colony of "soul freedom." [4] Nor was religious freedom of Catholics protected in Massachusetts Bay under its charter, while in the province of Maryland a harsh code directed toward the complete suppression of their religion still remained on the statute books.[5] In Connecticut men were being haled into court and fined or imprisoned for the crime of separatism; [6] neither "unitarians" nor "deists" were capable of holding any office.[7] In Virginia, Baptist and other dissenting preachers were liable to persecution for carrying on their activities, and so late as 1768[8] many of them were actually imprisoned as disturbers of the peace. Nevertheless, the spirit of the times was hostile to this intolerance, under whatever name it presented itself, and such popular leaders as Patrick Henry came powerfully to the defense of those who suffered for their nonconformity.[9]

It is quite evident, in surveying their progress in the eighteenth century, that the American continental colonies had attained a large measure of maturity by 1763. Since this maturity had a very direct bearing upon their ultimate relationship to the rest of the British Empire and particularly to the mother country, it is important to indicate its characteristics with some clearness.

Economically, no colonial people had ever made such progress in the course of half a century. Although the American iron industry had its real beginnings only with the opening of the eighteenth century, it had by 1750 reached such proportions as bade fair to drive the iron manufactures of England from the markets of the Empire. In face of the danger of unemployment at home, an attempt was made in that year, with the passage by Parliament of the Iron Act, to curb colonial competition.[10] The act placed restrictions on the

---

[4] *Acts and Laws of the Colony of Rhode Island* (Boston, 1719), p. 3.

[5] Thomas Bacon (ed.), *Laws of Maryland* (Annapolis, 1765), for 1704, chap. LIX; for 1715, chap. XXXVI; for 1716, chap. V; for 1717, chap. X.

[6] See the *Connecticut Journal,* Mar. 26, 1777, and *Laws of Connecticut* (Hartford, 1750), p. 139.

[7] *Ibid.,* p. 69.

[8] William Wirt Henry, *Patrick Henry* (3 vols., New York, 1891), I, 117–119.

[9] *Ibid.*

[10] 23 George II, c. 29, *Statutes at Large* (C. Eyre and A. Strahan printers,

manufacturing of American iron by positive prohibitions against the erection in the New World of additional slitting, plating, or steel mills, while at the same time it encouraged the increased production of American pig iron and bar iron in the vain hope that these products would be sent in large quantities to the mother country.[11] Not only was no effective check placed upon colonial iron production and manufacturing by the act, but expansion of the industry in open violation of it continued. By the time of the outbreak of the American Revolution there were actually more furnaces and forges in operation in the continental colonies than in England and Wales, and the amount of both pig iron and bar iron flowing from them was larger than the total output of Great Britain.[12] Moreover, the quality of American steel and iron manufactures was excellent.

The explanation of this phenomenon lies in the fact that sufficient capital had accumulated in the colonies to finance these costly undertakings; that managerial and technical skill of high order was available to conduct them successfully; and that the American iron industry was free of many handicaps facing English ironmasters. Virgin forests of hardwood provided at low cost an apparently inexhaustible supply of essential charcoal, an article that in England could be secured only in measured quantities upon the basis of the most careful planning well in advance of the need; iron ore of high quality was also abundant; and, finally, markets for all the iron and steel produced in America were close at hand, involving no such expensive carrying charges as those facing the British ironmaster who sought to compete in the markets of the New World. While this industry had its chief concentration in Pennsylvania, it was at the same time widely spread throughout the colonies and the prosperity that it enjoyed was therefore broadly distributed.

Not only was British North America by 1763 one of the world's leading centers for iron production; it had acquired too a leading

---

10 vols., London, 1786), VI, 490–492. Unless otherwise indicated, this edition of the British statutes will be cited throughout this volume.

[11] For a discussion of this act, see Gipson, *British Empire,* III, chap. VIII.

[12] A. C. Bining, *The Rise of American Economic Life* (New York, 1943), p. 93; see also, by the same author, *British Regulation of the Colonial Iron Industry* (Philadelphia, 1933), and *Pennsylvania Iron Manufacture in the Eighteenth Century* (Harrisburg, 1938).

position in shipbuilding. Although ships were built in most of the colonies, the largest and the best constructed in the New World came from the shipyards of New England and, particularly, Massachusetts Bay. The building of good sailing vessels demanded both a high degree of skill and proper facilities. Where else within the Empire were these so happily combined as in New England where shipways were scattered along the coasts at places favorable for launching? The beginning of this industry goes back to the seventeenth century: its foundation rested in the Navigation Act of 1660,[13] which provided that ships flying the merchant flag of England and entitled to the privileges therein stated must not only have crews that were chiefly of English nationality, but must be of English or colonial construction. As a result, early in the eighteenth century as many as 140 ships were being launched each year by the Massachusetts Bay shipyards alone.[14] By the year 1715 some forty or fifty of these were being sold annually to merchants in England,[15] and by 1775 it was estimated that some 30 per cent of all the ships employed in the commerce of the mother country had been built in America.[16] In this industry, as in iron production, the colonials had a tremendous advantage over their competitors in Great Britain. Not only was the oak of New England unsurpassed in quality, but the quantity—unlike the limited supply available in the mother country—could be measured only by the ability of loggers to float it down the rivers to the sawmills of the coastal towns. In that area was also the great white-pine belt, the trees of which were ideal for masts, bowsprits, and yardarms, which English shipwrights had to import at high cost. Moreover, naval stores, such as pitch for calking, tar and turpentine, anchors, chains, and other ship metal, sails and cordage, were all being produced in abundance in America by the year 1763.[17] In fact, it was estimated that it cost

[13] 12 Charles II, c. 18, *Statutes at Large* (C. Eyre and A. Strahan edition), III, 166–169.

[14] A. P. Usher in *The Commonwealth History of Massachusetts,* ed. A. B. Hart (New York, 1928), II, 399–400.

[15] V. S. Clark, *History of Manufactures in the United States* (3 vols., New York, 1916–29), I, 95.

[16] C. P. Nettels, *The Roots of American Civilization* (New York, 1938), p. 435.

[17] Gipson, *British Empire,* III, chap. II and p. 217; A. C. Bining, *Rise Am. Econ. Life,* pp. 75–6.

about twice as much to build a merchant ship in England as in Massachusetts Bay—the difference being from £15.5 to £16.5 sterling per ton as against £8 per ton.[18]

Although many of these ships were sold in Great Britain, they were built principally for colonial needs. A large proportion of them were at all times employed in the fisheries. As early as the seventeenth century the men of Massachusetts Bay had appropriated the great cod and mackerel beds in the Gulf of Maine at the expense of the fishermen of western England, and in the next century they came to dominate the still more important cod fisheries to the south of the Strait of Canso in Nova Scotia, also in competition with the fishing fleets of the mother country. By 1750 some six hundred New England vessels were engaged in this activity and by 1771, including the whalers, they numbered over a thousand,[19] and gave profitable employment to thousands of people during the open season. There was, indeed, deep apprehension in England even before the middle of the eighteenth century that English ships would be driven from the Banks of Newfoundland by this competition, just as they had earlier been driven from the Gulf of Maine and by 1750 from the Canso fisheries.[20] There was good reason for this fear. The cod caught by New Englanders was cured under conditions much more favorable than was possible for the English "bankers" to enjoy, obliged as they were to dry their catch on the damp, foggy southeastern coast of Newfoundland. As a result the New England cod early commanded a much higher price in the Portuguese markets than did that carried there by the English sack ships from the port of St. John's.[21]

Nor does this tell the whole story of the successful competition of American businessmen with those of the mother country. The carrying trade as well had an importance to Great Britain equal to, if not surpassing, the fisheries in providing sources of revenue and in the training of men to a seafaring life who would be available in times of emergency to man the great Royal Navy

[18] A. P. Usher in *Hist. of Mass.*, II, 400.

[19] W. B. Weeden, *Economic and Social History of New England* (2 vols., Boston, 1890), II, 641, 644.

[20] Gipson, *British Empire*, III, 17.

[21] *Ibid.*, 258; C. P. Nettels, *The Money Supply of the American Colonies Before 1720* (Madison, Wis., 1934), p. 78.

and thus protect England and her possessions. But the carrying trade that involved the continental colonies was in the course of the eighteenth century gradually taken over not only by colonial-made ships but by those with colonial registration. In 1753, of 496 vesels that legally cleared from Boston harbor, according to its port records, all but sixty-four were constructed within the province of Massachusetts Bay itself, only five carried a London registration, and only seven others that of an English or Scottish outport.[22] By 1775, three quarters of all the commerce of the continental colonies, it has been estimated, was carried on in ships belonging to them.[23] It is thus clear that the enterprise of American shipmasters and ship captains was gradually driving the ships of Great Britain from the waters of the New World outside of the West Indies.

In other fields the people of the colonies were indicating by 1763 that they were very well able to compete with those at home—for example, in the production of pottery and stoneware and even glassware. From American distilleries there came an immense volume of rum, the drink of the common people and an article of high esteem to those employed in the Indian trade, in the purchase of Negro slaves off the coast of Guinea, and in supplying the demands of the loggers and those engaged in the fisheries. As much as 2,000,000 gallons of this heady potation were being exported by the sixty-three distilleries of Massachusetts Bay alone in 1750,[24] and in 1764 the merchants of Rhode Island asserted that not all of the molasses produced in the British West Indies was sufficient to meet the demands of their distilleries, which required at least 15,000 hogsheads each year.[25] Other colonies, such as Pennsylvania and New York, were also heavily involved in this activity. In this connection, it is clear that the spirits produced in England, such as gin, could not compete in the New World with this beverage either in popularity or in price, nor could these compete easily even along the

[22] See a critique presented by the author at the December, 1941, meeting of the American Historical Association on papers relating to the background of the American Revolution (*Canadian Historical Review*, XXIII, 37–38).

[23] Nettels, *Roots of Amer. Civiliz.*, p. 435.

[24] G. R. Minot, *Continuation of the History . . . of Massachusetts Bay* (2 vols., Boston, 1798), I, 155–161; C. W. Taussig, *Rum, Romance and Rebellion* (New York, 1928), p. 16.

[25] Edward Channing, *History of the United States* (6 vols., New York, 1912–25), III, 41.

African coast where rum was brought in great quantity by Rhode Island slavers.[26]

If American colonials were driving hard and successfully against their competitors in the British Isles in many fields of industry and in commerce, the same was true in agriculture, in milling, and in the meat-packing industry. This was especially the case of the men of the middle colonies and Virginia, who shipped great surpluses of wheat, flour, bread, beef, and pork as well as horses to the West Indies and elsewhere. In fact, it was asserted by Governor Morris of Pennsylvania in 1755 that that colony alone was able to export each year enough food to sustain a 100,000 people.[27] By 1775 its people were annually sending abroad some 350,000 barrels of flour [28] and other commodities in like proportions. It is clear that there was no difficulty in disposing of these food supplies profitably in the West Indian and other markets in competition with English flour and pork and Irish beef, and equally clear is it that in 1763 agriculture in these colonies was riding on a crest of prosperity. This was also true of the rice-producing colonies, especially South Carolina, which faced no competition from the British Isles where rice could not be raised. In competing with Mediterranean rice in the markets of Europe, the American product was so superior in quality as to obtain premium prices.[29] In 1740 some 90,000 barrels of this commodity were exported from Charleston.[30] In view of the abundance of other foods, such as vegetables and fruits, eggs, and poultry, that were consumed locally rather than exported, it is needless to point out that American colonials were not only a well-nourished people but were able to provide from their own fertile lands practically all the food that sustained them.

From the continental colonies also came enormous crops of tobacco, a great deal of indigo, and some silk; from the southern pine belt, abundant naval stores, such as pitch, resin, tar, and turpentine; and from the northern hardwood areas, large amounts of lumber,

[26] C. F. Adams, et al. (eds.), Commerce of Rhode Island, 1726–1800, Coll. Mass. Hist. Soc., 7th Ser., IX, 46–47.

[27] Morris to General Braddock, March 12, 1755, Pa. Arch., 4th ser., II, 372.

[28] Bining, Rise of Amer. Econ. Life, p. 59.

[29] Gipson, British Empire, II, 185. Only in the poverty-stricken area of the Mediterranean was the local rice able to compete with Carolina rice.

[30] Ibid., p. 169.

pearl ash, and potash—none of these articles in competition with the products of the mother country and all of them, in fact, enjoying special encouragement by Parliament in the way of either tariff protection or bounties. Indeed, not only did North American tobacco—the great staple of the Chesapeake Bay—enjoy a virtual monopoly of the markets of the British Isles through the early discrimination against foreign-grown tobacco by means of very high tariffs, but it was able in the century under consideration to dominate those of all northern Europe as well. This was owing to its high quality and reasonable price and to the fact that shipping was adequate to maintain a constant flow in quantity of the aromatic weed from British ports to those of the Continent. Upon its culture was largely based the impressive prosperity of both Virginia and Maryland, a prosperity that in the final analysis was, as a rule, only seriously affected by the careless business methods and extravagant tastes of the planters and the tendency at times to increase the area of tobacco culture within these and neighboring colonies more rapidly than the demand would warrant without a fall in price.[31]

Finally, from the North American interior there moved to the coast in times of peace a great volume of furs and skins, secured in trade with the natives, which were thereupon exported to Great Britain, chiefly from the ports of New York, Philadelphia, and Charleston. From Charleston, for example, in 1748 deerskins to the value of £252,000 South Carolina currency were shipped and, between 1739 and 1759, an annual average of 200,000 pounds of buckskin.[32]

These trade statistics attest the fact that the British colonials of North America in 1763 were among the most fortunate people in the world and also among the most enterprising. Their chief cities reflected this tide of prosperity. Boston, in the middle of the century, was the greatest commercial and shipping center within the British Empire beyond the British Isles—a town of great docks,

[31] *Ibid.*, pp. 118–139, 148–155, 170–174. It is true that all foreign-grown tobacco was never eliminated from the English market, even by high tariffs. It appears, however, that this tobacco thus imported was never great in quantity and doubtless was designed for the making of special blends or was brought in to round out cargoes (C. M. Andrews, *The Colonial Period of American History* [4 vols., New Haven, 1938], IV, 88–89).

[32] Gipson, *British Empire,* IV, 53.

extensive warehouses, with exclusive shops and many mansions, the heart of a commercial empire of its own. One traveler was led to remark with surprise that "considering the bulk of the place, they outdo London." [33] Although New York City was less populous than Boston, it was already a cosmopolitan, opulent seaport as well as a pleasant place of residence, with attractive, tall buildings and shaded streets that delighted the Swedish traveler Per Kalm in 1750.[34] The same gentleman, upon viewing Philadelphia—second only to Boston in commerce and with an even greater population—was impelled to record in his journal its "grandeur and perfection," and to affirm that "its fine appearance, good regulations, agreeable situation, natural advantages, trade, riches and power, are by no means inferior to those of any, even of the most ancient, towns of Europe" and that it was the capital of a province which "now vies with several kingdoms in Europe in the number of inhabitants." [35] Nor was Charleston in South Carolina inferior to Boston, New York, or Philadelphia in the appearance of its homes and in display of wealth, with its people clothed on Sundays and gala days in expensive laces from Flanders, finest Dutch linens, French cambrics, chintzes, and gold and silver fabrics, and with the streets crowded on such occasions with liveried coaches, chariots, and chaises.[36]

In addition to these principal seaports and provincial capitals, there were dozens of colonial towns smaller in size, but hardly less attractive to the traveler, such as Portsmouth in New Hampshire, Newport in Rhode Island, New Haven, Norwich, New London, and Hartford in Connecticut, Albany in New York, Lancaster in Pennsylvania, and Annapolis in Maryland. In the South, outside of South Carolina, people did not, however, congregate in towns, as a rule, and those of wealth were almost always to be found residing on their plantations. There many of the tobacco planters lived in almost

[33] J. Winsor (ed.), *The Memorial History of Boston* (4 vols., Boston, 1880–81), II, 440–441.

[34] A. B. Benson (ed.), *Per Kalm's Travels in North America* (2 vols., New York, 1937), I, 131.

[35] *Ibid.*, p. 33. Philadelphia's population was probably about 25,000 in 1763 (Green and Harrington, *American Population*, pp. 117–118).

[36] Journal of the South Carolina Commons House of Assembly, 23:250; Shelburne Papers, 45:144–146, in Clements Library. Its estimated population of some 13,000 or 14,000 in 1765 places it somewhat below New York City in size (Greene and Harrington, *American Population*, pp. 97, 102, and 178).

regal fashion, with their broad estates operated by scores and frequently hundreds of slaves; their refinements of living were not to be surpassed in many parts of the world. In contrast with this splendor was the more sober manner of life of such people as the inhabitants of New Jersey, who, living on their wonderfully fertile farms, were described in 1742 as "the most easie and happy people of any Collony in North America." [37]

Here then, briefly, is a picture of life in the thirteen continental British colonies in 1763. That it was possible to have achieved so much—to have built so solidly, to have gained so many economic advantages, and to have attained to such prosperity—was due to the fact that up until the outbreak of war in 1754 most of the settlers had been able for generations to devote their entire energies to peaceful activities, with a sense of profound security (outside of the alarm in Georgia when the War of Jenkin's Ear broke out in 1739). Not since Queen Anne's War at the beginning of the century had any part of these older colonies before 1754 suffered serious devastation at the hands of an enemy, and merchant ships flying the merchant flag of Great Britain felt free to sail the seas with an equal sense of security when bound on truly lawful trade. That this security had been paid for at a price is indubitable; that it flowed from the power that the British armed forces could apply at any time to an enemy nation or to pirates that sought to disturb the tranquillity of the Empire is equally axiomatic.

From the latter part of the sixteenth century until the age of air power, the security and prosperity of England depended upon sea power—upon the capacity of the Royal Navy to defend the shores of the island from invasion and to enable the merchant marine freely to engage in trade. Moreover, the growth of the British Empire was only made possible by this emphasis upon maritime strength. There would doubtless have been no United States of America without this, for it is not likely that there could have been any English colonies in the eighteenth century. The fate in the seventeenth century of the Swedish and the Dutch colonial establishments in North America and of the Portuguese empire in the Far East is sufficient proof of what would surely have befallen the

[37] *Papers of Governor Lewis Morris* (Ed. W. A. Whitehead, New York, 1852), p. 147.

English had they attempted to colonize in the New World without this massive strength. Anything that threatened the ability to protect the Kingdom and its overseas possessions was therefore a matter of great moment to those responsible for governmental policy as well as to English colonizers. Herein lies the explanation for the first of the English Navigation Acts.

The act of 1651 was passed after the Dutch not only had seized the possessions of Portugal, England's ally, but had shown their ability to drive English shipping from the ports of Virginia and the English West Indies in sharp competition with it. In these and other ways they gave evidence of advancing "toward a monopoly of trade and to a supremacy on the sea. . . ." [38] Under the terms of this law, which became invalid with the restoration of the Stuarts, and a series of binding statutes that subsequently were passed in 1660 and thereafter, and, in particular, under the comprehensive statute of 1696,[39] all commerce involving England and the English possessions was placed under regulation. This involved certain broad principles designed to make England the trade entrepôt for the American colonies and to aid in maintaining the English and English colonial shipping on the high seas. Therefore, no ship that was not owned and commanded by an English subject, and that did not have a crew at least three fourths of which was English or colonial, could import into any English colony or export from it goods of whatsoever nature. Again, ships that sought to carry the products of Europe, as well as those of the Far East, to the New World were expected, with but few exceptions, to bring these first of all to England and to pay such duties as were levied upon them; whereupon, under certificate and with the enjoyment of such drawbacks of customs as were granted, they could then be carried in British Empire bottoms across the Atlantic to their destination. Further, the exportation of certain staple commodities produced in the English colonies was canalized. These could not be carried to any

[38] C. M. Andrews, *Colonial Period of Amer. Hist.*, IV, 32.
[39] The principal Navigation Acts, not including the Commonwealth Act of Oct. 19, 1651, were 12 Charles II, c. 18; 14 Charles II, c. 11; 15 Charles II, c. 7; 25 Charles II, c. 7; and 7 and 8 William III, c. 22, *Statutes at Large* (C. Eyre and A. Strahan edition), III, 166-169, 216-223, 246-249, 357-359, 584-589). For a detailed examination of these, see L. A. Harper, *The English Navigation Acts* (New York, 1939).

foreign country but only to England, if not shipped to another colony. The first list of so-called "enumerated" articles, outside of tobacco, largely affected the island possessions of England rather than the continental plantations. But the original list that included sugar, cotton, indigo, ginger, and dyewoods, as well as tobacco, was gradually extended to embrace many other commodities. Rice, molasses, and rum were enumerated in 1704; tar, pitch, resin, turpentine, hemp, masts, yards, and bowsprits in 1705; copper, beaver, and other furs in 1721; and, finally, iron, coffee, pimento, cacao, hides, skins, whale fins, raw silk, pot and pearl ashes, and lumber in 1764.[40]

Again, the commerce of the continental colonies with the foreign West Indies was placed under restraint by Parliament in 1733,[41] whereby the import duties on the rum, molasses, and sugar of these islands were made sufficiently high, it was felt, to provide an adequate advantage to the British West Indies in their disposal of these same products on the mainland. Moreover, the parliamentary restrictions were not limited to colonial commerce, but were extended to colonial industry as well. The Woolen Act of 1699 [42] prohibited the export out of any colony of raw wool, woolen yarn, and cloth; the Hat Act of 1732 [43] also forbade the exportation of beaver hats out of the colony where they were made and limited to two the number of apprentices that a colonial hatter might employ; the Iron Act of 1750 [44] sought to limit iron manufacturing; and the Paper Money Act of 1751 [45] rigidly regulated the issue of bills of credit by the colonies of New England by requiring that provision should be made for their redemption within a period of five years after they were placed in circulation. Nor, under terms of a series of Parliamentary statutes, could white-pine trees suitable for the use of the

[40] 3–4 Anne c. 5, Par. xii, and c. 10, Par. viii; 8 George I, c. 18, Par. xxii; and 4 George III, c. 15, Par. xxvi and xxvii, *Statutes at Large* (C. Eyre and A. Strahan edition), IV, 170, 176–177, V, 275, and VI, 462); Andrews, *Colonial Period of Amer. Hist.,* IV, 85–107; Harper, *Eng. Navig. Acts,* pp. 57, 197–198, 396–400.

[41] 6 George II, c. 13, *Statutes at Large,* V, 616–9.

[42] 10 and 11 William III, c. 10, *ibid.,* IV, 7–11.

[43] 5 George II, c. 22, *ibid.,* V, 594–595.

[44] 23 George II, c. 29, *ibid.,* VI, 490–492.

[45] 24 George II, c. 53, *ibid.,* VI, 580.

Royal Navy be harvested without certificate,[46] nor could colonial lands be legally sold to foreigners without consent of the Crown,[47] nor could stock companies and business undertakings that were unlawful in England be carried on in the colonies.[48]

Thus over the course of a century many regulations had been passed by Parliament designed to channel, and in some cases sharply restrict, the business activities of colonials. It should, however, be emphasized that in view of the fact that some of these regulations might cause real embarrassment in the colonies, the government of Great Britain fully realized both the exigency and the justice of granting compensation. With respect to the enumerated commodities, not only was provision made for their protection in the British market from outside competition, but, in the case of such commodities as indigo, pot and pearl ashes, naval stores, and ship timber, substantial premiums in the way of bounties were provided for colonial articles imported into Great Britain.

The degree to which this regulatory system actually checked colonial development is not easy to determine. The colonial producers of such enumerated articles as rice, naval stores, indigo, tobacco, iron, pot and pearl ashes, and ship timber seemed to have found their activities, all in all, highly profitable. It is clear that the Navigation Act of 1660 was the basis for the prosperous shipbuilding industry in America, and that the prohibition of the presence of foreign merchant ships in colonial seaports was largely responsible for the existence in the eighteenth century of a flourishing and extensive American colonial merchant marine. In fact it was estimated in 1752 that it required the services of three thousand ships to care for the vast British colonial trade,[49] and most of these vessels not only had been built by Americans but were owned by them. It should, in this connection, be kept in mind that large numbers of articles exported from North America, especially from the middle and northern colonies, were not on the enumerated list and therefore could freely be carried direct to foreign markets. Among these were fish, beef, pork, horses, mules, grain, flour, bread, fruits dried and fresh, vegetables, and wood products such as bar-

[46] 3 and 4 Anne, c. 10, Par. 6; 9 Anne, c. 17; 8 George I, c. 12, Par. 5; and, 2 George II, c. 35, *ibid.*, IV, 177, 450, V, 259-260, 521-525.

[47] 7 and 8 William III, c. 22, Par. 16, *ibid.*, III, 588.

[48] 14 George II, c. 37, *ibid.*, VI, 164-166.

[49] James Abercrombie's Examination (Huntington Library).

rels, staves, and home furnishings. Indeed, if one were to compare
the circumstances of British colonials with those of other countries
in the New World, the conclusion might well accord with the observations of the Pennsylvanian, John Bartram, in his *Travels* published in 1751:

> In vain do we look for an equal prosperity among the plantations of
> other European Nations, because every power has transplanted its
> constitution with its people. This surprising increase of people [in
> British North America] is a foundation that will bear a mighty super-
> structure. . . . [50]

It should be understood that fundamentally the elaborate system
of economic controls that were supposed to bind the British Empire
in 1763 was in essence not only a protectionist system but one
designed to make the Empire as nearly as possible economically
self-contained.[51] In other words, as least from about the middle of
the seventeenth century the government of England sought to realize
in the planting of colonies the ideal of having each new establishment supplement rather than supplant the gainful activities of the
people of the mother country and those of the other possessions.
Nor, on the other hand, were the inhabitants of England permitted
to depress the condition of Englishmen overseas who had discovered
profitable means of gaining a livelihood in harmony with this objec-

[50] *Observations on the Inhabitants, Climate, etc., Made by Mr. John Bartram
in His Travels . . .*" (London, 1751), pp. iii and iv. Professor O. M. Dickerson,
in his recent book, *The Navigation Acts and the American Revolution* (Philadelphia, 1951), strongly supports the thesis that the acts were beneficial to the
colonies. Professor Harper, while insisting that the system was burdensome, adds
that under it both Britain and the colonies flourished (*Pennsylvania Magazine
of History and Biography*, LXXVI, 226).

[51] Andrews (*Colonial Period of Amer. Hist.*, IV, 425–428) presents the idea
that until 1763 British mercantilism was, as a politico-economic system, in the
ascendant, but that after that date imperialism as a system relegated mercantilism to a secondary place. L. M. Hacker, in his *Triumph of American Capitalism* (New York, 1940), on the other hand, sees the struggle of the American
Revolution as one designed to free colonials from restrictions of a still pre-
dominantly mercantile system. However, G. N. Clark, in his *The Wealth of
England from 1496 to 1760* (London, 1946), significantly, in describing the
British system of controls, avoids the use of the term mercantilism in favor of
that of protectionism. This certainly eliminates a great deal of confusion, in
view of the fact that mercantilism, as R. L. Schuyler has emphasized in his *The
Fall of the Old Colonial System: A Study in British Free Trade, 1770–1870*
(London, 1945), pp. 3–37, has meant different things to those who have at-
tempted to define it.

tive. Therefore, those in southwestern England who in the seventeenth century had established tobacco plantations were compelled by law and the use of force to cease activities. Consistent with this conception, when, in 1663, Carolina was established, it was hoped by those close to King Charles II that the new colony would devote itself to providing many commodities not as yet produced in England and the other English colonies rather than compete in established fields, and this also was true when Georgia was founded in 1732.

The steady growth of the Empire brought about not only an increasing realization of the goal of economic self-containment, but a vast increase in the cost of military and naval security. Even in times of peace the charges upon the government steadily rose. By 1700 these charges averaged over £3,750,000 a year, including debt retirement; between 1715 and 1739 they averaged about £5,750,000; and between 1750 and 1755 they reached over £6,500,000.[52] Moreover, the wars in which England had been engaged since the days of William III, and upon the successful outcome of which the welfare, if not the fate, of the colonies depended, had been very costly. Between 1693 and the end of 1749, over £144,649,000 had been spent on them alone.[53] Yet the national debt in 1755, as the result of steady, heavy taxation of the people of England, stood at a sum but slightly over £75,000,000.[54] This result could only have been achieved by an England permitted to prosper. Therefore, the restrictive system that sought not only to make the mother country the center of the commercial life of the Empire, but also to protect it from competition in such special fields as the manufacturing of woolen and iron commodities, upon which English economic stability so largely depended, was designed to serve this end. Furthermore, by means of this system the colonies were able to make an indirect contribution to the end of sustaining both the public credit of England and the means of their own security. While it is true that much has been written against the system, it is difficult to vizualize one that would under given conditions have been better adapted to serve the ends of preserving and

---

[52] H. E. Fisk, *English Public Finance from the Revolution of 1688* (New York, 1920), p. 138; Stephen Dowell, *A History of Taxation and Taxes in England* (4 vols., London, 1884), II, chap. V.

[53] *Annual Register, 1763* (London, 1764), pp. 174–175.

[54] Dowell, *Hist. of Taxation*, II, 130.

nurturing the colonies embraced within the old British Empire before 1763. That they themselves were among its chief beneficiaries can hardly be questioned in view of the impressive evidence of their unprecedented development in the course of the eighteenth century.

But by 1763 the old British continental colonies were arriving not only at economic maturity, but at political maturity as well. It may be questioned whether in any other part of the world, including Great Britain, there was to be found so high a percentage of the inhabitants versed in the art of government. Though most of this political activity took place on the level of local government, and while the right of franchise was strictly limited in most of the colonies,[55] American colonials by and large had a degree of awareness respecting matters of public interest and a degree of understanding of the problems of statecraft that would have been a matter of surprise to most of the peoples of continental Europe. Only too late did those responsible for British imperial policy come to appreciate that awareness and understanding. For the ability of the colonists to manage their own governmental affairs with competence and economy is indicated on every hand by a study of local and provincial records. When consideration is taken of the maturity of American social patterns, of modes of social expression in daily living—diverging as these patterns did from those of the mother country in so many respects and, among some groups, quite radically—the formidable problem of a continuing supervision of the activities of the colonials of North America by the government of Great Britain after the conclusion of the war with France becomes self-evident.

Self-interest before 1763 had with good reason operated to bind the old continental colonies to the mother country; but would self-interest still operate to that end under fundamentally altered conditions in the New World brought about by the Treaty of Paris? There were ominous signs that this was not destined to be. In fact, even before the conclusion of hostilities, portents appeared in Massachusetts Bay and Virginia of a new sense of colonial freedom from ministerial and parliamentary control that arose over issues which must now be analyzed.

[55] A. E. McKinley, *The Suffrage Franchise in the Thirteen English Colonies in America* (Philadelphia, 1905).

CHAPTER 3

Writs of Assistance, 1761

TWO YEARS before the close of the Great War for the Empire an issue arose in the Superior Court of Massachusetts Bay which anticipated the constitutional crises of the years ahead. This controversy revolved about the writs of assistance requested by the customs officials for the purpose of seizing goods that there was reason to believe had been imported not only illicitly but also from enemy sources.

Before the war the smuggling of foreign West Indian products into the colonies was so common a practice in New England and in some other northern colonies that it caused little stir, although the practice placed the fair trader at an obvious disadvantage. But with the beginning of hostilities in North America in 1754 it was generally recognized, at least by men of character, to be an act totally out of harmony with the duty of a patriotic citizen, especially where it involved trade with the enemy. Unfortunately, much, if not most, of the smuggling activities involved just that. For example, on March 15, 1755, Deputy Governor Robert Hunter Morris of Pennsylvania wrote to General Braddock that as many as forty ships, chiefly from New York, Rhode Island, and Boston, had been seen at one time in the harbor of Louisbourg carrying provisions to the French.[1] Morris also at this same period, in referring to trade with the enemy, expressed the fear to Lieutenant Governor de Lancey of New York that by this means the French troops in North America

[1] *Pennsylvania Archives,* 4th ser., II, 373–374.

had been provided with sufficient food to meet their needs for the coming campaign.[2] Reprehensible as was the practice, it was especially difficult to check by reason of the fact—as Morris pointed out to the Pennsylvania Assembly in June of that year—that ships could ostensibly sail to Newfoundland with supplies from American ports, but actually traded with the French on Cape Breton Island.[3] On that island there were available, in exchange for flour and meat, large quantities of French West India products, which, in view of the silence of the customhouse records, were evidently smuggled into the colonies. The gravity of the situation is set forth in a "Letter from New England" found among the Newcastle Papers:

It is certain that the Inhabitants of Canada do at no time raise Provisions sufficient to their Support, and that were it not for the great Supplies thrown in from several Neighbouring English Colonies on private Account as well as by Contracts with the French Governor, the King [of France] could not maintain his Troops in that wretched Country so that these People in their Marches to Destroy one English Province, are actually supported by the Bread raised in another.[4]

Despite formal action taken by the colonial assemblies to eliminate this evil, the illicit trade still flourished. On May 27, 1756, an order in council was issued by the King's Privy Council to provide all colonial governors with an instruction "to hinder all correspondence between His Majesty's Subjects and the Subjects of the French King, and to prevent any of the Colonies and Plantations belonging to the Enemy in America being supplied, either by Land or by Sea, from any of His Majesty's Colonys, with Provisions, or Warlike

[2] New York Provincial Papers, 14:25, in New York State Archives.

The reader is referred to an interesting study by Walton E. Bean entitled "War and the British Colonial Farmer: A Reevaluation in the Light of New Statistical Methods," *Pacific Historical Review*, XI (1942), 439–447, which takes the position that only a relatively small part of the total amount of grain produced in the colonies could have found its way to the enemy during the war under consideration, with Virginia and Maryland then the leading grain producers rather than Pennsylvania, and other middle colonies as had been the case earlier in the eighteenth century. The important point in the eyes of the British military authorities was, however, not the total quantity of food supplies reaching the enemy, but the fact that what was reaching them was giving them effective aid in their war effort.

[3] *Pennsylvania Archives*, 4th ser., II, 416–417.

[4] Newcastle Papers, in British Museum, Additional Mss., 33029, fol. 322.

Stores of any kind." [5] Later that year a royal embargo was laid on all ships bound for neutral ports loaded with provisions and was reinforced by an act of Parliament.[6] There was need of this. For it now became the practice of unscrupulous traders to carry their products intended for the enemy to some neutral port and thereupon to arrange for the transfer of goods. Henry Livingston, writing from Jamaica to Henry Holland of New York on January 20, 1757, told of a ship loaded at Philadelphia with thirteen hundred barrels of flour that left that city bound for South Carolina, supposedly in ballast. The ship was actually transferred with its cargo to a Santo Domingo firm that sought to bring it into the French port of Cap François in the West Indies, but it was captured by a British privateer and carried to Jamaica where it was condemned.[7] In June of that year Isaac Sears, commanding the privateer *Catherine,* was given a commission to cruise to the eastward of Long Island in order to capture vessels engaged in this commerce. It stated that "an illegal and pernicious Trade is carried on between Rhode Island and the French settlements in Hispaniola for supplying His Majesty's enemies." [8] In fact, Lord Loudoun, the commander in chief of his Majesty's forces, writing to Pitt in May, charged that the traders of that colony were "a lawless set of smugglers, who continually supply the Enemy with What Provisions they want, and bring back their goods in Barter for them." [9]

From available evidence it is abundantly clear that illicit trade with the American colonies sustained and prolonged the French military and naval effort. For instance, when the powerful fleet of the French Admiral de Beaufremont was at anchor in the harbor of Cap François in the French West Indies, it was provisioned so adequately that it was enabled to sail in the spring of that year to the defense of Cape Breton and thereby help checkmate Lord

[5] Public Record Office, C.O. 323: 13, O. 136.

[6] E. B. O'Callaghan (ed.,) *Documents Relating to the Colonial History of the State of New York* (Albany, 1853–87), VII, 126.

[7] Loudoun Papers, No. 2686, in Huntington Library.

[8] The owners of this vessel, Evert Byrank and Cornelius van Raust, both of New York, gave a bond of £2,000 in order to be permitted to let Sears take the ship out of the blockade (New York Historical Society Mss.).

[9] Loudoun to Pitt, May 30, 1757, Public Record Office, C.O. 5:48.

Loudoun's attempt to capture the island.[10] Nor was there a cessation of these lawless activities, although less daring spirits resorted to the device of sending supplies to the enemy by means of so-called flag-of-truce ships which carried a few prisoners on board for exchange along with produce of the French West Indies clandestinely landed.[11] According to Deputy Governor Hamilton of Pennsylvania, writing to Pitt from Philadelphia in November, 1760, William Denny, his predecessor, brazenly sold flags of truce at a high price. As the result of this "iniquitous conduct," Hamilton affirmed, he had found "a very great part of the principal merchants of this City, engaged in a trade with the French Islands in the West Indies." [12] Most of this traffic was carried on by way of either the small Dutch island of St. Eustatius or the Spanish port of Monti Cristi on the island of Hispaniola where vessels flying French and British flags jostled one another.[13] William Vassall, writing from Boston in March, 1759, declared:

> The Colonies on the Continent carry on a prodigious great and very pernicious Trade to Monte Christo on Hispaniola . . . so that the markets in the Colonies are so glutted with French Sugars, that the fair Trader cannot import Sugars from the English West India Islands but at a great disadvantage and loss.[14]

Vice Admiral Thomas Cotes on December 6 of that year, while at his station in the West Indies, declared that the "vile Illicit Trade that has been carried on here ever since the commencement of the present War is really and still remains infamous and barefaced." [15] On February 18, 1760, George Colebrooke, addressing the Lords Commissioners of the Treasury after returning to London from the West Indies, affirmed that, as the result of an investigation, he was able to report that as many as a hundred vessels flying the British

[10] J. S. Corbett, *England in the Seven Years' War* (2 vols., New York, 1907), I, 168.

[11] Richard Pares, *War and Trade in the West Indies, 1739–1763* (Oxford, 1936), pp. 446–455.

[12] G. S. Kimball (ed.), *Correspondence of William Pitt* (2 vols., New York, 1906), II, 351–352.

[13] Pares, *War and Trade,* pp. 456–468.

[14] Chatham Mss., Public Records Office, Bundle 96 (Canad. Arch. Trans.).

[15] Public Record Office, C.O. 323 (Board of Trade Papers, Plant. Gen., 1760, p. 20.4. Hist. Soc. of Pa. Trans.).

flag were to be found at one time at Monti Cristi, all heavily insured at high premiums "as imply consciousness of the great hazard attending these illegal activities."[16]

Evidence against those concerned in the unpatriotic business of supplying the French with provisions—so desperately needed by them to continue the war in America—was for obvious reasons very difficult to obtain. On occasion, however, it was forthcoming. In September, 1759, Lieutenant Governor de Lancey of New York issued a proclamation for the arrest of one William Heysham, master of the ship *Speedwell,* charging him with high treason in giving aid and comfort to the enemy by boldly sailing into the French port of Cap François with a load of provisions.[17] The fact was that the enemy trade was big business; the participants were usually men of wealth and influence in public affairs, often acting in concert, and could count upon a body of seamen to do their bidding.

The power wielded by the illicit traders is demonstrated by the case of George Spencer, who in the spring of 1760 sent a communication to a local New York paper setting forth facts about this trade with the enemy. The printer flatly refused to publish it. Spencer was set upon by a mob and pelted with filth, and even thrown into jail on a false charge. Writing from jail to General Amherst on May 29, he made clear that he would have been freed long ago had he not implicated two of the justices of the New York Supreme Court of Judicature, and were it not for the fear that he would go to England and be the cause of regulations "as would Effectually Prevent any Illicit Contraband Commerce for the Future and Especially Stores or Ammunition, either directly or indirectly to the Enemy, which Practice hitherto hath been of the Utmost Ill."[18]

The illegal practices of merchants and their abettors and accomplices in the leading northern colonial seaports were brought home to Pitt and his fellow ministers busy with the great task of bringing the war in North America to a victorious conclusion. On August 23, 1760, Pitt sent a circular letter to all the colonial governors in which he declared:

[16] Public Record Office, C.O. 323 (Plant. Gen., 1760, p. 17).
[17] New York Historical Society Mss.
[18] New York State Archives, Mss. 89:30.

The Commanders of His Majesty's Forces, and Fleets, in North America, and the West Indies, having Transmitted repeated and certain Intelligence of an illegal and most pernicious Trade, carried on by the King's Subjects, in North America, and in the West Indies, as well as to the French Islands, as to the French Settlements on the Continent of America, and particularly to the Rivers Mobile, and Mississippi, by which the Enemy is, to the greatest Reproach & Detriment of Government, supplyed with Provisions, and other Necessities whereby they are, principally, if not alone, enabled to sustain, and protract, this long and expensive War. . . . It is His Majesty's express will and Pleasure, that you do forthwith make the strictest and most diligent Enquiry into the State of this dangerous and ignominious Trade . . . and that you do take every Step, authorized by Law, to bring all such heinous ˙Offenders to the most exemplary and condign Punishment. . . .[19]

So determined was this combination against law and order that Jeffrey Amherst, the commander in chief of the British forces in North America, felt obliged to notify Governor Bernard on May 6, 1762, that de Lancey in New York had issued his warrant to seize certain Frenchmen who had actually come to New York

sent on purpose to Establish Such a Commerce with the enemy that not only their Settlements in the West Indies, but their Fleets & Troops were to be Supplied with Provisions from this Continent. As . . . papers seized belonging to a Monsieur Comte mention Some People at Boston concerned with him, I think it proper to Send You the Originals . . . that You may take such Steps as you judge best for bringing the guilty to condign punishment.[20]

The general also wrote to both Governor Fitch of Connecticut and Governor Ward of Rhode Island that merchants of these colonies, he had discovered, were deeply involved. In his letter to Ward dated May 7 he declared that from the seized papers it appeared that

[19] *Corresp. of Pitt*, II, 320–321. Josiah Tucker, in his *A Letter to Edmund Burke* published in 1775, emphasized the futility of Pitt's circular letter directing colonials "to desist from the infamous and traitorous Practices of supplying the Enemy with Provisions and Military Stores during a War, undertaken at their Request, and for their immediate Protection." R. S. Schuyler, *Josiah Tucker* (New York, 1931), p. 376.

[20] P.R.O., War Office, 34. 27:481–483, Lib. of Cong., Trans.

Rhode Island is one of the principal colonies upon which they [the French] depend; and that several of the Merchants of Newport, are deeply concerned in this iniquitous trade, which is not only infamous in itself, by supporting the avowed enemies of the King, but occasions great difficulty in procuring necessary supplies for carrying on His Majesty's service.[21]

Such was the background of the famous Writs of Assistance case. Now for the immediate facts leading up to it. In November, 1760, an officer of the customhouse at Salem, a Mr. Cockle, petitioned the justices of the Superior Court to grant him a "writ of assistants" (more generally known as a "writ of assistance") in order that he might be duly authorized to make a search for goods that he had reason to believe had been smuggled into the port of Salem. It happened that Stephen Sewall was Chief Justice of the court and —according to John Adams, a young lawyer in attendance at the court sessions at this period—as

a zealous friend of liberty expressed some doubts of the legality and constitutionality of the writ, and of the power of the court to grant it. The court ordered the question to be argued at Boston in February Term, 1761. In the meantime Mr. Sewall died; and Mr. Hutchinson, then lieutenant-governor, a councillor and judge of probate for the country of Suffolk, etc. was appointed, in his stead, Chief Justice. The first vacancy on that bench had been promised in two former administrations [those of Shirley and Pownall], to Colonel James Otis, of Barnstable. This event produced a dissention between Hutchinson and Otis which had consequences of great moment.[22]

The above explanation given by Adams in his *Autobiography*, while substantially correct in the light of available evidence, does not tell the whole story. The real reason that Hutchinson received without solicitation the appointment of Chief Justice was Bernard's conviction that he could be depended on to cooperate fully in carrying out Pitt's recent instructions respecting law enforcement. On the other hand, Bernard held serious misgivings as to Colonel Otis's attitude on this issue and was determined not to appoint him even

[21] Conn. Hist. Soc., *Coll.*, XVIII, 202; *R. I. Col. Rec.*, VI, 317-318.

[22] C. F. Adams (ed.), *Works of John Adams* (10 vols., Boston, 1850-56), II, 124.

if Hutchinson refused that high judicial office.[23] As to the hostility now directed against the administration by the Otises, it would appear that this was in evidence even before the opening of the February session of the Superior Court. Writing to his friend Colonel Israel Williams on January 21, 1761, Hutchinson stated: "Upon the Governor's nominating me to Office, one of the Gentleman's sons who was sollicitous for it swore revenge." [24]

The first act in the unfolding drama played by the Otises concerned, not the writs of assistance, but the old Molasses Act of 1733, providing for the payment of sixpence a gallon on molasses imported from foreign places. Charles Paxton, collector of customs at Boston, it appears, had been accustomed to paying considerable sums for information which informers secured from others and which led to the conviction of some of those guilty of smuggling. In fact, the informers received not only one third the amount of the forfeiture by action of the vice-admiralty court, as provided by law, but also a portion of the forfeiture that under its terms the province was entitled to receive. Otis, who had been advocate general of this court but who had, with Hutchinson's appointment to the Superior Court, resigned his post, agreed to represent the merchants in a suit they now decided to institute against both the officers of the vice-admiralty court and Paxton to recover the sums thus paid out. Since the Assembly was drawn into the matter, it resolved that the Treasurer of the province should bring the suit before the Superior Court with this end in mind. Hutchinson, as the Chief Justice, took the view that the true remedy lay in an appeal to the Court of High Admiralty in Great Britain and not in a suit in civil court. The jury under his instructions gave a verdict for the defendants. The disposition of the case hardly enhanced his popularity. "But it is not a farthing's matter what principle I acted from, so long as I oppose a popular measure the clamour will be against me," [25] he wrote Colonel Williams.

As might be anticipated, the council chamber of the Boston Town House was crowded when the Superior Court met to consider

[23] Mr. [Thomas] Hutchinson, *The History of the Province of Massachusetts Bay from the Year 1750, until June 1774* (London, 1828), pp. 86–88.
[24] Israel Williams Mss., 2:155, Massachusetts Historical Society.
[25] *Ibid.;* see also Hutchinson, *History of Mass. Bay,* pp. 89–91.

the issue of writs of assistance. Such writs had been granted by this court in 1755, 1758, 1759, and 1760 to various customs officials. The purpose of the writ was to provide against the abuse of power on the part of the customs official, who was by his commission ordered to search for smuggled goods. It authorized him to require a court officer to accompany him to any place where he had reason to believe such goods were stored and to assist him in gaining access to the place. Apparently first authorized in England in the days of Charles II (12 Car. II, c. 19 and 23, and 14 Car. II, c. 11), it had been extended by Parliament to the colonies in the days of William III (7 and 8, Wm. III, c. 23). The writ was very general in form and, when granted, was only limited in time by the life of the reigning sovereign and six months thereafter, when it would lapse and must be renewed.[26] Therefore, with the death of George II on October 25, 1760, it was necessary to apply for new writs both in Great Britain and the colonies. In Massachusetts Bay this was done by Thomas Lechmere, Surveyor General of the Customs in America, not only for himself but for other customs officers when acting within the province.

The Massachusetts Bay merchants, having determined to oppose the granting of further writs, sought to secure the services of the learned Benjamin Pratt of that province; but the latter, having received an appointment as Chief Justice of the Superior Court of New York, was unwilling to serve. Otis and Oxenbridge Thacher, however, readily agreed to act in their behalf; they were opposed by Jeremiah Gridley, a distinguished lawyer, who, in fact, had prepared Otis for the bar in his own office. While both Thacher and Gridley argued quietly on points of the law, Otis, when his turn came, according to the recollections of John Adams, who was pres-

---

[26] For a broad and interesting discussion of the writs of assistance, see O. M. Dickerson, "Writs of Assistance as a Cause of the Revolution," in R. B. Morris (ed.), *The Era of the American Revolution: Studies Inscribed to Evarts Boutell Greene* (New York, 1939), pp. 40–75. G. W. Wolkins, in his "Writs of Assistance in England," Massachusetts Historical Society *Proceedings*, LXVI (1942), 357–64, makes clear how mistaken many American writers have been respecting the limitations placed in England on the use of general writs of assistance. General warrants, when specifically authorized by Parliament, as in the case of the custom services, are and always have been considered perfectly legal in England, in spite of assertions to the contrary by those who have failed to study with care the history of these warrants.

ent, poured forth a torrent of eloquence extending over a period of four hours. Writing in later years Adams declared:

> Otis was a flame of fire . . . he hurried away all before him. . . . Every man of an immense crowded audience appeared to me to go away, as I did, ready to take arms against Writs of Assistance. Then and there, was the first scene of the first act of opposition, to the arbitrary claims of Great Britain. Then and there, the child Independence was born.[27]

In his *Autobiography* Adams describes this speech, which to his dying day he considered as perhaps the most remarkable he had ever heard. It is indeed now possible to be reasonably sure of what took place by referring not only to notes that he as a young lawyer apparently took in the course of the hearing and that are printed in his *Works,* but to the résumé of the speeches of Gridley and Otis recorded in the commonplace book of Joseph Hawley, another Massachusetts Bay lawyer.[28] According to these sources Gridley insisted that constables, in distraining the property of a man who did not pay his rates or taxes, were acting even more inconsistently with English rights and liberties than those using writs of assistance, and that necessity authorized both. "Everybody knows," he declared, "that the subject has the privilege of house only against his fellow subjects, and not versus the King either in matters of crime or fine." Thacher, on the other hand, contended that by such a writ any private person might, when accompanied by a sheriff and constable, go into any shop or store and seize property. Otis went much farther than his colleague. He insisted that such a writ was "against the fundamental principles of law"; that an act of Parliament "against the Constitution is void; an act against natural equity is void; and if an act of Parliament should be made, in the very words of this petition, it would be void. The executive Courts must pass such acts into disuse." [29] Adams's account indicated the impact that this doctrine had upon that young attorney.

[27] William Tudor, *The Life of James Otis* (Boston, 1823), pp. 56–62, 88.

[28] It is clear from these notes that Hawley, a leader of the Northampton bar, was present when Gridley and Otis spoke. "I have omitted many Authorities," he wrote, "also many fine touches in the order of reasoning, and numberless Rhetorical & popular flourishes" (Commonplace Book, Joseph Hawley Papers, II, Manuscript Division, New York Public Library).

[29] *Works of John Adams,* II, 521–523. According to Hawley, Otis declared:

He [Otis] asserted, that every man, merely natural, was an independent sovereign, subject to no law, but the law written on his heart, and revealed to him by his Maker, in the constitution of his nature, and the inspiration of his understanding and his conscience. His right to his life, his liberty, no created being could rightfully contest. Nor was his right to his property less incontestable. . . . Young as I was, and ignorant as I was, I shuddered at the doctrine he taught; and I have all my life shuddered, and still shudder, at the consequences that may be drawn from such premises.[30]

Extremely difficult as it is to discover a consistent political philosophy in Otis's writings, it would, nevertheless, appear that while at times he was prepared to make on paper the greatest theoretical admissions respecting the sovereignty of Parliament throughout the Empire—even with respect to the *right* of taxation of the colonials without representation in that body—[31] in practice he continued to hold so many mental reservations regarding the practical limitations on the exercise of that legally unlimited authority as utterly to nullify its admitted powers. His astuteness as a lawyer and as an agitator before the dimming of his mental powers is nothing less than amazing. He seemed to shift from time to time from one extreme to the other; protecting himself from charges of high treason for some bold assertion by another equally bold, in fact so

---

"I will to my dying day oppose . . . all such instruments of slavery on the one hand & villany on the other as this writ of Assistance is. . . . And as it is in opposition to a kind of power . . . which in former periods of English history, cost one King of England his head and another his throne—I have taken more pains in this cause than ever I will take again. . . . No acts of parliament can establish such a writ; tho it should be made in the very words of the petition 'twould be void. An act against the constitution is void" (Commonplace Book, Hawley Papers). Otis, it would seem, took his stand in line with views occasionally expressed in the seventeenth century that there existed a fundamental law above Parliament that bound it. This law was the law of reason or nature that lay behind the common law. See Horace Gray on Otis's argument in *Massachusetts Bay Reports, 1761–1772*, compiled by Josiah Quincy, Jun. (Boston, 1865), Appendix I. For a broad discussion of fundamental law in the eighteenth century, the student should consult C. F. Mullett's *Fundamental Law and the American Revolution* (New York, 1933).

[30] Tudor, *Life of Otis*, pp. 68–69.

[31] See, for example, Otis's extreme concessions as to the powers of Parliament over the colonies in his *A Vindication of the British Colonies Against the Aspersions of the Halifax Gentleman, in His letter to a Rhode Island Friend* (Boston, 1765).

extreme as few supporters of the royal prerogative in America would have dared express.

As to the outcome of the issue of the writs, Chief Justice Hutchinson at the end of the arguments declared:

> The Court has considered the subject of writs of assistance, and can see no foundation for such a writ, but as the practice in England is not known, it has been thought best to continue the question to the next term, that in the mean time opportunity may be given to know the result.[32]

After consulting the Massachusetts Bay colonial agent in England, the legality of the issuance of these writs by the Massachusetts Bay Superior Court was upheld and in 1767, with the passing of the Townshend Revenue Act, the exercise of this authority was expressly affirmed.[33] But never again was it possible to make effective use of them in Massachusetts Bay. And, in most of the other colonies, the courts declared that the provision of the Townshend Act authorizing their use was unconstitutional.[34]

To recapitulate, Otis in his attack upon the writs of assistance helped to lay the foundation for the breach between Great Britain and her continental colonies. In denouncing as unconstitutional and *ultra vires* the statute of Parliament that legalized these writs in the New World, he not only denied the competence of that body to place all people owing allegiance to the King under an equal obligation to assist in upholding the law, but raised the fundamental question as to the extent to which Parliament could exercise sovereign powers within the Empire.

[32] Tudor, *Life of Otis*, p. 86.

[33] Hutchinson, *History of Mass. Bay*, p. 94. Hutchinson wrote to the colony's London agent, William Bollan, to secure information as to the writs; this was done and thereupon the Superior Court issued them as legally valid (Massachusetts Historical Society *Proceedings*, LIX, 220–221). The issue over them did not again become acute until late in 1766 an attempt to use them to search the premises of Captain Daniel Malcom in Boston for uncustomed brandy and wines was unsuccessfully made. For the legal aspects of this case, see G. G. Wolkins's "Daniel Malcom and Writs of Assistance," *ibid.*, LVIII, 5–84, sharply modified by his later study "Writs of Assistance in England," *ibid.*, LXVI, 357–364, previously referred to in note 26 of this chapter.

[34] Professor Dickerson ("Writs of Assistance") had made clear the nature of the obstacles that were set up in the various colonies to the use of the writs, especially after 1767.

CHAPTER 4

Planter Debts

THE NEW issues that arose with the conclusion of the Great War for the Empire prompted radical leaders in other colonies to invoke constitutional rights. Just as in Massachusetts Bay James Otis in 1761 had denied the authority of Parliament to extend to the colonies by statute a law permitting the issuing of writs of assistance, so in Virginia Patrick Henry in 1763 called into question the right of the King's Privy Council to declare void the so-called Twopenny Act passed by the Assembly of Virginia in 1758. While in the long run constitutional issues such as these were to rend the empire, it is perhaps significant that at the time the pronouncements of neither Otis nor Henry seemed to have created much of a stir. Nevertheless, each of these men, largely as a result of a flaming speech of defiance of the British Government made in open court, was elected to a seat in his colonial assembly and there came to exercise an extraordinary influence upon the attitudes and decisions of his fellow members.

The intimate connection between the King's Privy Council and England's overseas possessions became especially significant with the establishment of a royal government in Virginia in 1624 when that body was given direct responsibility for the government of the colony.[1] Especially after the Restoration in 1660 was the mechanism regularized and expanded for maintaining control over the Empire.

---

[1] A. P. Newton, "The Great Emigration, 1618–1648," in *The Cambridge History of the British Empire* (8 vols., Cambridge, 1929–40), I, 167.

The principle was established that all laws passed by the Virginia Assembly must be sent home for ratification or disallowance, and this principle was ultimately applied to all other colonies save for the proprietary of Maryland and the corporate colonies of Connecticut and Rhode Island.[2] Further, in all the colonies, irrespective of rights claimed by them under royal patents, the ultimate right of appeal by individuals from decisions of the local courts to the King in Council was affirmed.[3]

During the colonial period over 8,500 laws were submitted by the continental colonies to the Privy Council for action, and out of this large number but somewhat over 5 per cent were disallowed;[4] slightly more than 4 per cent of Virginia's laws met a like fate.[5] The grounds for disallowance of colonial laws were various: they might be held to violate the rights of the Crown or of Parliament; they might be in conflict with the common law, with the statutes of Parliament, with the provisions of the charter, or with the instructions of the governor; they might infringe individual liberty or the rights to private property; finally, they might involve the vital interests of the inhabitants of a neighboring colony. There were inconveniences involved in this procedure of sending colonial legislation to England for approval. The average length of time required before a law could be finally disposed of was some three years and five months. But if the law officers needed more information, the time lag might be very much greater.

When a law had been submitted to the Privy Council for confirmation, this was automatically referred to its own committee, known as the Lords of the Committee; the latter in turn, in the eighteenth century, referred the same to the Lords Commissioners for Trade and Plantations, a group with large advisory powers and popularly known as the Board of Trade. This body, after gathering what light it could respecting the propriety of the law from such

---

[2] C. M. Andrews, "The Royal Disallowance," *Proceedings of the American Antiquarian Society* (1914); E. B. Russell, *The Review of American Colonial Legislation by the King in Council* (New York, 1915).

[3] A. M. Schlesinger, "Colonial Appeals to the Privy Council," *Political Science Quarterly*, XXVIII, 279–297, 433–450; and J. H. Smith, *Appeals to the Privy Council from the American Plantations* (New York, 1950).

[4] Russell, *Rev. of Amer. Colon. Legis.*, p. 221.

[5] *Ibid.*

sources as were available, particularly from the accredited London agent of the colony, and also after submitting the measure, as a rule, either to the observation of the Attorney and Solicitor General or to its special legal adviser, prepared a so-called "representation" or report upon it. With this report in hand the Lords of the Committee were then prepared in most instances after deliberation to recommend to the Council either approval, allowance, or repeal.

It goes without saying that were all laws held in suspense and deemed without effect until the pleasure of the Privy Council could be known, incalculable hardship would have been caused to colonials. In fact, the only laws that did not go into effect immediately upon passage were those that sought to alter an act already approved by the King's Council; under the instructions given to the governor, these could not be signed by him without a clause suspending their taking effect until approved at home. Yet even with respect to this latter requirement, there was a good deal of indulgence displayed on occasions. For example, in Virginia, during the years 1746–48, a revision of the statutes was carried out by the Assembly and a body of eighty-nine acts transmitted to London. As this code had the effect of repealing or amending the former laws, the governor, technically, should only have approved it with a suspending clause. But the Board of Trade in its representation stressed the point that as "there was a necessity and expediency of having these Laws take place as soon as possible, We shall not propose to Your Majesty to repeal any of them," except ten which, it was pointed out, were "liable to many Objections." [6]

It may be noted in passing that the present arrangements for testing the constitutionality of state laws in the United States are open to all the objections respecting delay that were raised against the colonial procedure of disallowance. What is more, the voiding of a state law by the Supreme Court, even though the law may have been in operation for some years, is not unlikely to affect the property rights of those who acted in good faith in conformity with the state enactment. With respect to the colonial laws automatically referred to England, it is apparent that in most cases they received an objective consideration. As E. B. Russell, in his *The*

[6] James Munro (ed.), *Acts of the Privy Council of England, Colonial Series* (6 vols., London, 1908–12), IV, 138.

Review of American Colonial Legislation by the King in Council (New York, 1915), has stated:

The process of review, complex and dilatory as it was, certainly afforded the colonists ample opportunity for presenting their case. Both the Board of Trade and the committee of the Council were essentially fair in their attitude toward colonial affairs, willing to take advice and anxious to gather all available information before pronouncing judgment.[7]

As has been true of the United States Supreme Court, so the Privy Council—in light of "the importance which English law accorded to the preservation of personal security and freedom [and] to the protection and security of rights in private property"—was very critical of "unseemly infringements" of these rights, and did not hesitate to disallow laws violative of them.[8] It was this protection accorded property rights that was the target of attack in Virginia in 1763.

To understand clearly what was involved in the Twopenny Act, one must go back to the year 1749, when Lieutenant Governor Gooch gave his assent to "An Act Declaring the Law Concerning Executions and for the Relief of Insolvent Debtors." According to the twenty-ninth section, all executions for debts in terms of sterling money were to be levied in current Virginia money at 25 per cent advance upon sterling for the difference in exchange value; this was to go into force after June 10, 1751.[9] The law struck at the

[7] P. 218.

[8] *Ibid.*, pp. 150, 152.

[9] W. W. Hening, *Statutes at Large, 1619–1792* (13 vols., New York, Richmond, and Philadelphia, 1810–23), V, 526–540; *Journals of the House of Burgesses, 1742–1749* (ed. H. R. McIlwaine, Richmond, 1909), p. 400. The term "sterling money" has reference to the money of Great Britain. In contrast to this, there was "proclamation money," fixed by Queen Anne's royal proclamation and confirmed by act of Parliament, which was supposed to represent the minimum value of money permitted to circulate in the colonies; and "current money," that is, the currency of the individual colony, which might or might not approximate the value of proclamation money. It was customary in the eighteenth century to think of the Spanish milled dollar or piece of eight that commonly circulated within the Empire as the standard of value. In relation to it sterling money passed in exchange, as a rule, at about 4*s.* 6*d.*; proclamation money at 6*d.*; while current money might, as in the case of the Rhode Island inflated bills of credit, be rated so low in value as to require 140*s.* in exchange for it.

large debts in sterling owed by Virginians to British creditors. As a result memorials were forwarded to the Board of Trade by groups of London, Bristol, and Liverpool merchants denouncing the act as confiscatory. In connection with their argument, it should be borne in mind that in 1751, at the time of these memorials, the rate of exchange was at least 33 per cent, instead of 25 per cent; in 1757 it stood at 37½ per cent; in 1759, at 65 per cent.

The embarrassing fact, however, was that the law embodying this significant clause had been confirmed by the Privy Council upon the basis of a representation of the Board of Trade. Nevertheless, after Lieutenant Governor Dinwiddie had failed to secure through tactful means a repeal of the law, a formal royal instruction was sent to him in 1754 to secure the elimination of the clause at issue. This was laid before the House of Burgesses in May, 1755. The colony was then engaged in hostilities with the French and had appealed to the mother country for aid for the purpose of freeing the Ohio Valley from the enemy; it was manifestly no time to defy the home authorities. Therefore, while unwilling to rescind the law in question, the Assembly after much discussion agreed on a bill that offered some protection to British creditors. Under its terms the local courts were empowered to settle the rate of exchange in each case that should come before them.[10]

In 1732, as Josiah Tucker pointed out, Parliament came to the assistance of British creditors to protect them from unfair legislation. For the latter were placed at a serious disadvantage in attempting to collect debts owed in Virginia; not only were they compelled to make an appearance at great expense in the local courts of law to prove the debt, but found when they did so that the lands, houses, and slaves of the planters were not liable to the payment of commercial or book debts because these were not regarded technically as "assets" (R. L. Schuyler (ed.), *Josiah Tucker*, New York, 1931, p. 387). The British merchants therefore petitioned Parliament for redress; this was supplied in 5 George II, c. 7. Thereafter not only could debts be proved on oath before a magistrate in Great Britain, but lands, houses, and Negroes belonging to the debtor in the colony were made liable to and chargeable with all such just debts owed by him. In this connection, it may be pointed out that in 1705 a law had been passed by the Virginia Assembly that made slaves real property for most purposes (Hening, *Statutes at Large*, III, 338), and in 1727 it had been provided also by law that slaves could be entailed with the lands (*ibid.*, IV, 224)—a device that, while it kept the plantation system intact, gave to the heir of the entailed estate special protection of his property in Negroes.

[10] Hening, *Statutes at Large*, VI, 478–483. For a discussion of this issue, see L. H. Gipson, *British Empire Before the American Revolution* (8 vols., Caldwell, Ida., and New York, 1936–54), II, 58–63.

However, in 1757 the Assembly, still in the midst of war, passed "An Act for Granting an Aid to His Majesty for the better protection of this Colony and for other Purposes therein mentioned," which provided for the issuing of bills of credit that were to pass as a legal tender. Again memorials were received by the King from London and Bristol merchants that the act was in the nature of an *ex post facto* law, since "it depreciates the value of such debts owing in Sterling money of certain and fixed Value and subjects them to be discharged in paper Notes of a local, uncertain Value. . . ."[11] Then there came, in 1762, "An Act for the Relief of Insolvent Debtors and for the Effectual Discovery and more equal Distribution of their Estates," which in the view of British creditors likewise placed them at a serious disadvantage.[12]

By 1764 the Assembly had placed in circulation some £250,000 of paper money. Although the amount was not in excess of the need, the issues, unlike the bills of credit of Pennsylvania and New Jersey, were made legal tender for the payment of *all* debts except the royal quitrents. Once again in that year there were strongly worded memorials from the London, Liverpool, and Glasgow merchants against this practice. In their protest the Glasgow merchants pointed out that the power of making paper notes legal tender assumed by the Virginia Assembly was without precedent in the mother country. They asserted

that the Notes or Bills of the Bank of England, whose foundation and credit is far Superior to any one Colony in America, never were made a legal tender in Britain or any where else—And the extending this emission to Debts Contracted before making the Law Authorizing thereof, is a stretch of the power never practiced in any free Commercial Country.[13]

As the result of these protests Parliament passed that year a colonial currency act (4 Geo. III, c. 34) forbidding the making of the bills of credit of any colony a legal tender; it also extended to all the colonies the provisions of the New England currency act of 1750 (24 Geo. II, c. 53).

The passage of the legal tender act, combined with the refusal

[11] *Acts of the Privy Council,* Col. Ser., IV, 389–393.
[12] *Ibid.,* pp. 563–565.
[13] *Ibid.,* pp. 641–645.

of the Virginia Assembly to rescind the insolvency act of 1749 relating to contracts, constitute abundant evidence both of the extent to which the debtor elements had assumed control of the House of Burgesses as well as of their attitude toward royal interference in provincial financial matters. Here then is the setting for a consideration of the issue of the Twopenny Act of 1758.

The regulation of the salary of the clergy went back to 1696. In that year the Assembly had fixed the annual salary of the Virginia clergy, paid by the parish vestries out of taxes collected, as 16,000 pounds of tobacco, a commodity that by reason of its relatively stable value had already become a legal tender for the payment of private and public debts. When the codification of the laws of the province took place in 1748 and 1749, this specification of the law of 1696 was retained in the new law;[14] the latter was confirmed by the Privy Council, as were most of the other laws embodied in the revised statutes.[15] However, in 1753, in view of a threatened shortage in the tobacco crop in some parts of Virginia, two of the counties—Princess Anne and Norfolk—were permitted to meet their obligations by paying the sum of £100 in local currency instead of in the prescribed amount of tobacco,[16] and in 1755 the same counties were also allowed to settle their dues in money, the amount of which was to be left to the determination of the justices of the county court.[17] Later in that same year, a law was passed to run for ten months that gave all taxpayers in the province the opportunity to commute their tobacco levies in money fixed by the Assembly itself at the rate of twopence on the pound;[18] finally, in 1758, again in view of prospective tobacco shortage, an act was passed in October authorizing for the period of a year the payment in local currency, at the same rate as was fixed by law in 1755, of all debts contracted and taxes due upon a tobacco basis.[19] In other

[14] Hening, *Statutes at Large,* III, 151; VI, 88.
[15] *Acts of the Privy Council,* IV, 137.
[16] Hening, *Statutes,* VI, 369.
[17] *Ibid.,* p. 502.
[18] *Ibid.,* p. 568.
[19] *Ibid.,* VII, 240. Before Governor Fauquier gave his assent to this statute he asked the advice of his Council, the members of which—mostly great tobacco planters—pointed out that the act did not alter the quantity of tobacco allowed to the clergy by law but simply made it subject to a compensation by ascertaining "the Price thereof to be paid in Money for all Dues, as well to Officers as

words, while the tax on tithables could still be paid in tobacco, the taxpayer was given the choice of paying either in this medium or in currency at the prescribed rate. For obvious reasons he chose the latter, since tobacco was soon selling locally at the rate of about 6*d*. a pound. What this really involved was a cut in taxes by two thirds.

As early as 1755 the clergy were alerted to this situation, and even appealed to the Bishop of London.[20] However, it was not until after the passage of the Act of 1758 that they were made fully to feel the full impact of such legislation. Denied by custom as well as experience the opportunity to make additional money on the side, the clergy pointed out that the law bore unfairly upon them since others in the province "have different ways of gain, and if they lose by the bill one way, they may gain in another." [21] In a letter to the Bishop of London in 1756 the ten clerical signers stated that the clergy were kept in a perpetual state of debt by reason of the fact that their salaries were always paid at least a year after the pastoral work had been performed and frequently not until after the lapse of at least a year and a half or even longer. They were therefore obliged to purchase the necessities of life on credit in England and to remit the tobacco received as salary to cover their indebtedness. But under the new law, they declared, they could make no remittances in tobacco to cover these debts, having been offered no tobacco by the collectors of the rates. The local currency tendered to them, now rapidly depreciating in value, could not be used to settle these debts because of the prohibitive exchange rates. What is more, were they to seek to purchase the necessities of life with this money in Virginia, it was necessary to pay "at least double the first cost," they contended.[22]

For the clergy to resort to litigation over pay may well seem un-

---

to the Clergy" (*Journals of the House of Burgesses, 1761–1765,* xlix-l). However, the payment in money was hardly intended to be equivalent for the tobacco. In fact, in 1759 an act was passed explaining the statute of 1758. In this it was stated that nothing in the statute in question should be construed as applying to any sheriff or other collectors of levies and office fees who had received such levies and fees [in tobacco] and had not paid them into the public treasury (Hening, *Statutes at Large,* VII, 277).

[20] W. S. Perry, *Historical Collections Relating to the American Colonial Church* (4 vols., Hartford, 1870), I, 434.

[21] *Ibid.,* 436.

[22] *Ibid.,* p. 440.

dignified to us today. The fact is, however, this was not an un-common practice in eighteenth-century America and was resorted to perhaps as frequently by the Congregational clergy of New England as by the Anglicans of Virginia.[23] In view of their des-perate financial plight, it is not surprising that the Virginia clergy should have gone into court and been championed by the Reverend John Camm, Professor of Divinity at William and Mary College and pastor of the parish of York-Hampton, who agreed to go to England to lay their grievances before the Bishop of London.[24]

In fairness to the clergy, it may be pointed out that they had avowed in 1756 that were it a matter simply of

compassion for the poor . . . none are more ready and willing to promote charitable designs, than the clergy are here, according to their abilities. . . . Had the Law had a respect to the poor and them only, the clergy would have cheerfully acquiesced in it, but we think it hard that the whole Burden should be laid upon us; nay, that near half a Salary should be taken from us by law and distributed among the rich and the great (which is really the case here), and not among the Poor.[25]

They had also pointed out that in Maryland, where the clergy were also paid in tobacco and where "there are as short crops made there as here and tho' the Maryland Clergy receive yearly, near twice as

[23] See, for example, the suits instituted by both the Reverend Joseph Noyes and the Reverend Samuel Bird in the April term of the New Haven County Court in 1773 (New Haven County Court Records, V, 197, 349, 356). In 1759 came the most notorious litigation involving a New Haven clergyman when Mr. Noyes sued his own ecclesiastical society to recover £150 that he claimed was due him (F. B. Dexter (ed.), Itineraries . . . of Ezra Stiles (New Haven, 1916), p. 582).

[24] Mr. Camm was dismissed from his professorship by the college authorities for his support of the cause of the clergy. He asked for a writ of mandamus in order to be restored to his post. On Oct. 10, 1759, the General Court presided over by Governor Fauquier ordered the writ to be quashed. Camm then ap-pealed to the Privy Council, which, on Mar. 16, 1763, sustained him (Acts of the Privy Council, IV, 530).

[25] Perry, Historical Collections, pp. 440–443. It was argued that the advantage given to the wealthy planter who had a hundred or more tithables —white males over sixteen years and all Negroes above that age—on his plantation was disproportionately greater than that to the poor man who could employ no one on his land. It was the latter who might reasonably be the recipient of this relief but not the former (ibid.).

much Tobacco as we do in Virginia, yet there is no Option Law in that Govt nor any attempt made to Subvert their Establishment." [26]

In fact, the student will search in vain for any overpowering economic ground to support either the Twopenny Act or the act of 1749 for the relief of debtors. It is clear that the Assembly wielded the threat to withhold appropriations to protect its own frontiers in the midst of the war as a club over the head of the governor to force him to sign the bill in 1758.[27] It is equally clear that among poor and rich alike the law was extremely popular. Had Virginia given all-out support to this war effort, some argument might have been made to justify the measure. But, despite the wealth and lavish manner of living of the Virginia planters, that colony—with resources at its command in the form of the export of some 50,000 to 60,000 hogsheads of tobacco, together with grain, pork, bar iron, lumber, and indigo—did not make a war contribution comparable with the much less opulent colony of Connecticut. The widely publicized view that the Virginia planters were not well off was challenged in the following terms by the author of *American Husbandry*, published in 1775:

The tobacco planters live more like country gentlemen of fortune than any other settlers in America; all of them are spread about the country, their labour being mostly by slaves, who are left to overseers; and the masters live in a state of emulation with one another in buildings . . . furniture, wines, dress, diversions etc. and this to a degree, that is rather amazing they should be able to go on with their plantations at all, than that they should not make additions to them. . . . The poverty of the planters here . . . is much talked of, and from thence there has arisen a notion that their husbandry is not profitable: this false idea [prevails because of] the general luxury, and extravagant way of living which obtains among [them] . . . for men without some rich article of product cannot afford, even with the assistance of credit, to live in such a manner . . . that will support such luxury, and pay eight per cent on their debts. What common culture in Europe will do this? [28]

---

[26] *Ibid.*

[27] Andrew Burnaby, *Travels Through the Middle Settlements in North America in the Years 1759 and 1760* (London, 1775), p. 22.

[28] The full title of this volume is *American Husbandry. Containing an account of the soil, climate, productions, and agriculture of the British colonies in North-America and the West-Indies; with observations on the advantages and*

To return to the Twopenny Act of 1758 and the appeal against it. On May 14, 1759, the Lords of the Committee on Appeals of the Privy Council transmitted to the Board of Trade a memorial of the Virginia clergy together with another drawn up by the Reverend Mr. Camm, their agent. The Lords Commissioners, desiring all available light on the problem, in turn sent the papers, including the law itself, to Thomas Sherlock, Bishop of London,[29] requesting an opinion. Sherlock on June 14 replied:

I have considered the Act from Virginia, referred to me: It seems to be the Work of Men conscious to themselves that they were doing wrong; for, though it is very well known that the Intention of the Act is to abridge the Maintenance of the Clergy, yet the Framers of the Act have studiously avoided naming them, or properly designating them, throughout the Act; so that it may be doubted whether, in a legal Construction, they are included or not. But, to take the Act as they meant it, and as everybody understands it, we must first consider by what Authority the Assembly acted, in passing such a Law; and, in the next Place, how inconsistent the Provision of the Act was with Justice and Equity: The Subject-Matter of the Act, as far as the Clergy are concerned, was settled before by the Act of Assembly; which Act has the Royal Assent and Confirmation, and could not be repealed by a lesser Power than made it; and, to make an Act to suspend the Operation of the Royal Act, is an attempt which in some Times would have been called Treason, and I do not know any other Name for it in our Law.[30]

Then, on the 26th of the same month, the issue was argued before the Board, with Camm representing the clergy and James Abercromby, the London agent of the government of Virginia, representing the colony.[31] With the facts before them, the Lords

---

disadvantages of settling them, compared with Great Britain and Ireland. By an American (London, 1775).

There is nothing in Washington's correspondence that would indicate poverty of the people, in spite of the short crop of tobacco. For in 1759, the latter was selling at high prices. Washington's orders upon Robert Cary and Company for the year, including a supply of luxuries, underscores the affluence of the great planters. J. C. Fitzpatrick (ed.), *Writings of Washington* (39 vols., Washington, 1931-44), II, 320-336.

[29] *Board of Trade Journal, 1759-1763,* p. 39.

[30] Perry, *Historical Collections,* I, 461.

[31] *Board of Trade Journal, 1759-1763,* p. 46.

Commissioners thereupon drafted a representation to the Lords of the Committee recommending the repeal of the act, a step which was accordingly taken by the Privy Council on August 10.[32] In fact, Lord Hardwicke is reputed to have declared before the Council "that there was no Occasion to dispute about the authority by which the act was passed, for that no court in the judicature whatever could look upon it to be law by reason of its manifest injustice alone."[33] Moreover, not only was the act in question disallowed but the earlier acts of 1753 and 1755 were also rendered nugatory.

The disallowance did not meet the problem full square, as in the case of laws enacted for limited periods whose operation would be terminated before the Privy Council could possibly pass on their validity. In practice this meant that without a suspending clause even statutes of manifest injustice were considered valid until the news of their disallowance had been officially received.[34] Camm urged the Privy Council to declare the legislation under review "absolutely null and void" with "no force or Authority at the time of making or otherwise"; but that body, adhering strictly to time-honored practice, refused to go that far.[35] Fauquier, nevertheless, was threatened with recall should he again put his signature to such legislation.[36]

In view of the protection now accorded to the clergy, it would doubtless have been far wiser had they let the matter rest and suffered their losses in silence. Instead, they attempted to recover their back pay by instituting new legal proceedings.[37] In no instance, however, did their suits meet with success.[38] When the Reverend John Camm brought suit for his salary as the pastor of the parish

---

[32] Smith, *Appeals to the Privy Council,* pp. 611–615; A. P. Scott, "The Constitutional Aspects of the 'Parson's Cause,' " *Political Science Quarterly,* XXXI, 560–561.

[33] Perry, *Historical Collections,* I, 510.

[34] Hening, *Statutes at Large,* V, 435; Scott, "Parson's Cause," 562–563; J. H. Smith, *Appeals,* p. 614.

[35] Perry, *His. Coll.,* I, 488 and 510; Scott, "Parson's Cause," p. 564; and especially Smith, *Appeals to the Privy Council,* pp. 618–623.

[36] L. W. Labaree, *Royal Instructions to British Colonial Governors* (2 vols., New York, 1935), I, No. 210.

[37] The Reverend Andrew Burnaby, who was in the colony at the time, was quite critical of the conduct of the clergy in pressing their case. *Travels,* p. 22.

[38] For the cases of Thomas Warrington and Alexander White, see Perry, *Historical Collections,* I, 413, 430, 496, 513.

of York-Hampton, the House of Burgesses passed an order that, in case of appeal, the cost of defending the parish collectors would be borne by the public.[39] His case originated in the General Court in October 1759—since Williamsburg was located within his parish— and was not terminated until April 1764, when, by a vote of five to four, with two abstentions, that body decided against recovery.[40] Camm thereupon appealed to the Privy Council, where his case was finally dismissed,[41] not on its merits, but simply on the technical ground that the original suit should have been brought for debt instead of trespass. The endorsement penned by the Secretary of the Council on the brief for the respondents read:

Judgement affirmed for the Respondents (the action being mis-conceived) . . . no determination, as to the disallowance of the Act of Assembly 1758, whether it avoided the *Act* ab initio, or whether it was void in Law as being against natural Justice.[42]

The most famous of the cases arising out of the statute of 1758 was that instituted on April 1, 1762, by the Reverend James Maury, the learned and respected, if pugnacious, pastor of Fredericksville Parish in Hanover County, who had interested himself in the education of Jefferson as a youth. This suit was argued on November 5, 1763, in the county court, which, significantly, decided that the act in question was null and void as beyond the competence of the Assembly to enact.[43] All therefore that remained to be done was for a jury to ascertain the extent of the damage that Maury was entitled to receive. Considering the case lost, the lawyer, John Lewis, who had defended the collectors of the parish rates, now retired from the case and Patrick Henry was appointed in his place. The jury trial was held on December 1 and attracted a large number of people, many from out of the county. From those who had assembled the sheriff selected a jury panel composed of what was declared to be the rougher type of people living in the county. Peter Lyons, a

[39] *Ibid.*, 511.
[40] Scott, "Parson's Cause," pp. 567-568; Smith, *Appeals to the Privy Council*, p. 619.
[41] *Ibid.*, pp. 621-624; *Acts of the Privy Council*, IV, 699.
[42] *Ibid.*
[43] W. W. Henry, *Patrick Henry* (New York, 1891), I, 35; Scott, "Parson's Cause," pp. 566-567.

lawyer of distinction, who was to become President of the Virginia Court of Appeals, represented Maury. In opening the case he introduced evidence not only to prove that the collectors were under bond in 1759 to make a levy under the terms of the law to provide for the minister's salary but also that the vestry had ordered them to do so; he also presented as witnesses the two largest tobacco dealers in the county, who testified that in the year in issue the price of tobacco was 50s. per one hundred pounds, that is, 6d. a pound rather than 2d.[44]

Patrick Henry then arose to address the jury. This sharp-featured young man, with deep-set, piercing eyes, aquiline nose, heavy eyebrows, hollow cheeks, and a mouth that never really wreathed a smile, was on this day to emerge from the status of a petty county lawyer to that of the leading advocate of Virginia rights. In his address to the jury in the presence of his own father, the presiding judge, Henry, as had Otis in 1761, rested his plea upon natural rights and stressed the existence of a conditional compact, composed of mutual and dependant covenants between the King and the people over whom he ruled. He is reputed by Maury to have argued:

That the act of 1758 had every characteristic of a good law; that it was a law of general utility, and could not, consistently with what he called the original compact between the King and the people, stipulating protection on the one hand and obedience on the other, be annulled. [He, then proceeded to affirm] that a King, by annulling or disallowing Acts of so salutary a nature, from being the Father of his people degenerated into a Tyrant, and forfeits all right to his subjects' Obedience. . . . [45]

At this point, still following Maury's account, Lyons cried out, "That the gentleman had spoken treason," and expressed his astonishment that the judges "could hear it without emotion, or any mark of dissatisfaction." At the same time there was a confused murmur from the spectators of "Treason, Treason!" [46] Not to be stopped, the orator next launched into a bitter attack upon the

[44] Henry, *Patrick Henry*, I, 37–38.
[45] James Maury to John Camm, December 12, 1763, *Journal of the House of Burgesses, 1761–1765*, pp. lii–liii.
[46] *Ibid.*

clergy and, even in the face of the high regard in which Mr. Maury had been held in his parish by the people at large, denounced him and his fellow clerics, according to Captain Trevilian, as

rapacious harpies [who] would . . . snatch from the hearth of their honest parishioner his last hoe-cake, from the widow and her orphan children their last milch cow! the last bed, nay, the last blanket from the lying-in woman! [47]

Finally, addressing himself to the issue of the royal government's supervisory authority, he attacked "the bondage of the people who were denied the privilege of enacting their own laws," and called upon the jury to "make such an example of the plaintiff, as might hereafter be a warning . . . not to dispute the validity of such laws, authenticated by the only authority which in his conception would give force to laws for the government of the colony. . . ." [48]

These inflammatory remarks consumed well over an hour.[49] Without taking time for deliberation, the jury retired, but returned almost immediately with a verdict awarding the plaintiff damages of one penny. In that moment Henry had established himself as a leader of the common people in a struggle against the old order. With the ending of the trial, they surged about him, wild with delight, and carried him on their shoulders out of the courtroom.[50]

[47] Quoted by William Wirt in his *Sketches of the Life and Character of Patrick Henry* (Philadelphia, 1817), p. 45.
[48] Henry, *Patrick Henry*, I, 42.
[49] *Ibid.*, 45–46.
[50] *Ibid.*

CHAPTER 5

Molasses, Rum, and American Prosperity

THE PROCLAMATION of 1763 issued by the Crown had endorsed in principle the Treaty of Easton (Pennsylvania) of 1758 negotiated with the Western Indians in the midst of the war. The royal proclamation, in line with it, reiterated the pledge of the English to respect the claims of the natives to lands west of the Appalachians and to refrain from disposing of them or settling in the area without their consent. The proclamation also provided for the establishment of the Provinces of Quebec, East Florida, and West Florida in North America and of the government of Grenada in the West Indies. The vast interior of North America up to the Mississippi River still remained to be brought under control. In the very year of the Proclamation the Indians, suspicious of British intentions, staged a great revolt. Even with the crushing of this revolt after a two-year campaign, it was deemed necessary to establish garrisons at strategic points to control both Indians and conquered French subjects. The search for funds for accomplishing this important purpose led directly to the Revenue Act of 1764, generally known as the Sugar Act.

The recent war—entered upon and waged primarily to maintain the territorial claims of the colonies—had proved to be the costliest conflict in which the British people had as yet engaged. Despite unprecedented wartime taxation, with the supply bills from 1756 to the end of 1766 reaching an annual average of some £14,500,000 or a total of over £145,000,000, the debt at the end of this decade was still over £133,000,000.[1] By 1755 the national debt had mounted to over £75,000,000—largely as the result of the earlier wars waged with France from the days of William III down to the Peace of Aix-la-Chapelle in 1748. During the course of the late war the ministry of the Duke of Newcastle and more particularly that of William Pitt, in order to induce the continental colonies to exert an all-out effort, had made large commitments with respect to the reimbursement of military expenses. To fulfill these promises Parliament made a series of appropriations between the years 1756 and 1763 totaling over £1,150,000, which was divided among the colonies upon the basis of their respective claims upon these funds.[2] Indeed, in the case of one of the colonies, Connecticut, the reimbursement policy was so generous that one may affirm that for every pound actually paid by the people of Connecticut in the way of taxes during the course of the war, the government of the mother country made a gift to the colony of an equal amount.[3]

With the conclusion of hostilities the people of Great Britain were expected to shoulder the national debt. In fact, no responsible statesman in power ever suggested, so far as existing evidence is available, that any part of it should be transferred to the colonies. Nevertheless, there was a feeling on the part of those both within and without the British ministry that, as far as meeting the extraordinary costs of maintining garrisons of professional troops at strategic points in North America was concerned, the colonials should assume their proper share. Pitt left office in 1761 and was succeeded by Lord Bute. The latter, after concluding peace with France and Spain in 1763, likewise stepped aside that same year in favor of George Grenville, Pitt's brother-in-law. Hence, it was the Grenville ministry that was obliged to face squarely the problem of financing the costs of the British garrisons in the New World.

Although it has been the custom of American historians, in par-

---

[1] *Annual Register, 1763,* p. 175; Harvey E. Fisk, *English Public Finance from the Revolution of 1688* (New York, 1920), pp. 93, 134, 138.

[2] L. H. Gipson, "Connecticut Taxation and Parliamentary Aid," *American Historical Review,* XXXVI, 731.

[3] *Ibid.,* 733.

ticular, to refer to Grenville in most uncomplimentary terms, it is probable that the Reverend Francis Thackeray's characterization of him as "one of the ablest men in Great Britain" of that period is not far from the truth.[4] What Pitt, who justly enjoyed so high a reputation in America, would have done had he been in power at this juncture is far from clear.[5] That he could possibly have avoided serious difficulties with the colonials had he maintained the policy of rigidly enforcing the trade and navigation laws, which he had inaugurated in the course of the war, is even less clear. That he would have receded from a policy he had adopted and pressed with vigor is highly unlikely. Moreover, it must be borne in mind that Pitt was not a financier and knew little of public finance. Nor can one point to any other man in public life better endowed with statesmanlike attributes than either Grenville or Pitt to deal with the American crisis that followed the termination of the war.

First of all, fiscal problems confronting the Grenville ministry were exigent. New sources of taxation, in light of the added burdens that victory had brought, simply had to be found. It had been determined by the Bute ministry in 1763 to lay not only a heavy duty of £8 a ton on French wines imported into Great Britain—a tax that would fall on the wealthy—but also an excise of 4s. on every hogshead of cider or perry produced at home, which was to be paid by the producers. Anticipating strong opposition to the latter measure—in view of the storm earlier aroused over Walpole's cider tax—a penalty of £25 had been provided for those who sought to produce these popular beverages at "unentered" places, that is, places not publicly designated for their production, and a penalty of £50 on every one guilty of any act opposing the collection of the excise.[6] In the words of the *Annual Register*, "taxes were full as

---

[4] *A History of the Right Honorable William Pitt, Earl of Chatham* (2 vols., London, 1827), II, 31. Thackeray goes on to say, respecting Grenville: "From his known abilities, experience, and integrity, scarcely any one appeared more proper to be entrusted with power" (*ibid.*).

[5] It will be noted that Lord Bute made an effort to place Pitt back into office in 1763, and George III was favorably disposed to the idea. Pitt, however, made such high demands, among these the removal from power of every leading man who had been concerned in making the peace with France and Spain, that the King could not in honor call him back. Hansard (ed.), *Parliamentary History of England* (36 vols., London, 1806–20), XV, 1321.

[6] 3 George III, c. 1 and 12, *Statutes at Large*, VII, 423, 433–435.

necessary at the conclusion, as during the continuance of the war," but "that necessity was not, to every person, so glaringly evident. . . . The advantages of the peace, though far more certain and solid, were less sudden and brilliant." [7] The news of the passing of the cider act was the signal for "tumults and riots" in the apple-growing counties of England, and many producers of cider threatened to cut down their orchards if the excise were collected.[8] Nevertheless, even additional sources of income were required in order to maintain the public service and credit. Among the supplies requested by Bute's successor, Grenville, in December, 1763, was an item of £372,774 for the support of the garrisons in the New World as well as at Minorca and Gibraltar, with most of this sum allocated to America.[9]

The question of adequate provision for the security of the British North American possessions, old and new, had been uppermost in the minds of the ministry since the coming of peace. Secretary at War Welbore Ellis as early as February 12, 1763, in writing to General Sir Jeffrey Amherst, commander in chief of the British forces in North America, had indicated that it was proposed that twenty battalions of troops should be retained for service in North America and had requested his recommendations as to their proper disposition.[10] In reply Amherst pointed out that two areas would require the greatest concentration of troops: one bordered the Mississippi; the other, Canada. At the same time he recommended that the major posts about the Great Lakes and in the interior should of necessity be guarded, as should Newfoundland, Cape Breton, St. John's Island (Prince Edward), Nova Scotia, Florida, and Mobile. In this connection he wrote:

> The Whole is an Immense Extent; And should His Majesty's Intentions be to Leave Four . . . Battalions in the Plantations . . . the Troops . . . can be but thinly Dispersed; so I believe it will be unavoidably necessary to Abandon all the Interior Forts and Posts of Communication. . . .[11]

---

[7] *Annual Register, 1763,* p. 33.

[8] W. Taylor and J. Pringle (eds.), *Correspondence of the Earl of Chatham* (4 vols., London, 1838–40), II, 253–254.

[9] *Parl. Hist.,* XV, 1419–1420.

[10] Amherst Papers, Packet 43 (Canad. Arch. Trans.).

[11] Amherst to Ellis, Apr. 26, 1763, Amherst Papers (Canad. Arch. trans.).

To help finance the cost of maintaining the forces needed for the security of North America, which, it was clear, could not be provided by colonial contingents, it was thought just and proper to place a part of the burden upon the colonies. Some money might be raised there under existing legislation. The Pitt war policy of rigid enforcement of the trade acts to prevent the American shipmasters trading with the enemy had borne fruit during the period of hostilities; but with peace established, illicit commerce had again flourished without restraint.[12] This not only involved the violation of the Molasses Act of 1733, with respect to duties on foreign products from the West Indies, but also the ignoring of the navigation code by direct trading with Holland and other countries, to the loss of much revenue.[13] Referring to this situation, the author of "Observations on the Trade and Revenue of North America," who offers a survey of American commerce from the close of the war until the end of 1766, declared that

it was a matter of Astonishment to observe what little care was taken to enforce the Laws. . . . The Breaches openly committed against the Acts of Trade, and the shameful prostitution of Office which prevailed in most of the Ports on the Continent could not escape the notice of

---

Under date of Aug., 1763, the following disposition was given of the troops then attached to Amherst's command: some five battalions were concentrated in the chief towns of Canada, nine companies were stationed in Nova Scotia, seven were at Fort Pitt at the forks of the Ohio and the same number in Florida and its dependencies, six were on Cape Breton Island and its neighbor St. John's, three were on the frontiers of South Carolina (the South Carolina Independent Companies), two were on Newfoundland, and a few troops were stationed at each of the lesser posts in upper New York and in the Great Lakes region (Plant. Gen., Series 323, Hist. Soc. of Pa., *Trans.*, vol. 19). The Indian uprising in the course of that year caused a shifting of troops.

[12] *Board of Trade Journal, 1759–1763* (London, 1935), pp. 359, 364; "Observations on the Trade and Revenue of North America," Livingston Papers, Richmond Collection, New York Historical Society.

That the additional funds needed to maintain the forces required to guard the critical areas in North America could have been secured by a reform of the fiscal system of Great Britain is the subject of a recent interesting study by Dr. V. L. Johnson entitled "Internal Financial Reform or External Taxation: Britain's Fiscal Choice, 1763", Amer. Philos. Soc., *Proceedings*, XCVIII, 31–37. As will be emphasized in the course of this volume, the British government even in taking such steps would not have relieved itself of the charge that the whole burden of defending North America was saddled on the people of Great Britain while those of North America were the chief beneficiaries of this protection.

[13] *Ibid.*

the most superficial Observer. . . . The Merchants . . . had commonly undertaken those Voyages which afforded the greatest prospect of gain, without any further Regard to their illegality than, that the Custom-House must be silenced, and, by what means was but too obvious.[14]

In view of the fact that most of the customs officers in America were apparently venal and those who sought to do their duty at the colonial ports were "harassed and persecuted," it seemed necessary to hit upon some device that would secure a degree of enforcement of the trade laws in peacetime America comparable with what Pitt had succeeded in bringing about during the later years of his war administration. The latter had used the Royal Navy as the chief instrument for breaking up these lawless activities. Parliament therefore was led to resort again to this device in 1762 in passing "An Act for the further Improvement of his Majesty's Revenue of Customs; and for the Encouragement of Officers making Seizures; and for the Prevention of the clandestine Running of Goods into any Part of his Majesty's Dominions." [15] Under the terms of this act American customs officers—most of whom had considered their posts as sinecures and were acting through deputies—were ordered to their posts. As an incentive to law enforcement, they were granted one half of all ships and cargo condemned as a result of their seizure, in place of the previous third. In addition, authority was given to the officers and crews of warships stationed in American waters to make seizures upon the same terms of reward as applied to condemnations by customs officers.

The extent to which goods were being smuggled into the colonies in the closing years of the war, in the face of Pitt's efforts to prevent trade with the enemy, is revealed by the official figures for the years

[14] *Ibid.*
[15] 3 George III, c. 22, par's 1 and 4, *Statutes at Large,* VII, 443–446. On Oct. 11, 1763, the Board of Trade directed a circular letter to the colonial governors that emphasized the necessity of making "the Suppression of the clandestine and prohibited Trade with foreign nations and the improvement of the Revenue the Constant and immediate objects of your care." In this connection the Lords Commissioners pointed out that as the result of connivance and fraud the customs duties were so inconsiderable in amount as not to be sufficient to defray a fourth part of the expense necessary for collecting them (*Archives of Maryland,* XXXII, 89; *Board of Trade Journal, 1759–1763,* pp. 389–390).

1760 and 1761 for imports in New England, New York, and Pennsylvania, for these colonies were the chief smuggling centers. In New England the legal imports, according to these figures, dropped from £599,644 to £334,168, in New York from £480,106 to £289,774, and in Pennsylvania from £707,998 to £204,064.[16] Some of this falling off could be laid to a decline in the need for war supplies. However, it is significant that those colonies that had never engaged in large-scale smuggling now substantially increased their imports from the mother country. Doubtless all the colonies, despite the official trade figures, shared in this pent-up demand for peacetime consumers' goods. This is indicated by exports to Georgia, South Carolina, Virginia, Maryland, Nova Scotia, and Canada. Exports to Canada rose from £51,629 in 1760 to £226,409 in 1761; the exports to Virginia and Maryland, the figures for which are combined, amounted to £80,000 above the value of those sent the preceding year; and those of South Carolina rose by £33,000.[17] Indeed, the Earl of Egremont, in writing to the governors in America on July 9, 1763, declared that the public revenue was greatly diminished as the result of fraudulent practices in the colonies, and that, for the purpose of enforcing the laws, His Majesty's ships stationed in the New World had been vested with enforcement powers by the act in question. The Secretary therefore called upon the governors to give their fullest support to rooting out

so iniquitous a Practice;—a Practice carried on in Contravention of many express and repeated Laws, tending not only to the Diminution and Impoverishment of the Publick Revenue, at a Time when this Nation is labouring under a heavy Debt incurred by the last war for the Protection of America; but also to expose every fair Trader to . . . even Danger of Ruin by his not being able to carry his Commodities to market on an equal footing with those who fraudulently evade the Payment of the just dues and Customs.[18]

He also signified that orders had been issued to commanders of forty-four vessels either already in American waters or about to sail

---

[16] "An Account of the Value of Exports from England to the North American Colonies from Xmas 1739 to Xmas 1761," Shelburne Papers, 3:22, in Clements Library.

[17] *Ibid.*

[18] Amherst Papers, 40 (Canad. Arch. trans.); Shelburne Papers, 53:1–7.

from England to use their utmost endeavors to stamp out the evil.[19]

However just and necessary it may have been in order to maintain the public credit to levy the cider impost in England and to enforce the trade laws in America, the apparent necessity of the government's course failed to discourage the growth of a highly articulate opposition both at home and in the New World. For, now that the war was over, it appeared that men wanted to be able "to relax and to forget public responsibilities in giving their attention to private advantage." Therefore, in the words of a writer in the *Annual Register* for 1763, "In these dispositions the people were ready to fall into very ill humours, upon any plan of supply which could be suggested." [20] Accordingly, the act levying an excise on cider was denounced by Englishmen as "iniquitous and oppressive" and the act to enforce the trade laws in the colonies castigated by the Americans, in view of their long-established commercial relations with the French West Indies, as a gross injustice. According to one account, when the news reached Boston of its enactment, this "caused a greater alarm in this country than the taking of Fort William Henry did in 1757." [21]

The Molasses Act of 1733 [22] had provided, among other things, that all molasses, rum, and sugar not produced in the British West Indies that was imported into the American colonies should carry a duty of 6d. per gallon for molasses, 9d. per gallon for rum, and 5s. per hundredweight for sugar. The law was designed to bring relief to the British sugar islands from a type of competition which, it was felt, was difficult to meet without proper protection. For not only were the planters on the French islands, on the one hand, heavily subsidized by the government at home to permit them to maintain their plantations in a flourishing condition for the production of sugar, but, on the other hand, they were prohibited—for the sake of protecting the brandy industry at home—from carrying their molasses or rum to the ports of France. Yet molasses was a necessary by-product in sugar production. In view of their successful effort to

[19] For the locations given to the ships under government orders, see "List of His Majesty's Ships, Stationed, and intended to be stationed at Newfoundland and in America" (*ibid.*).

[20] P. 33.

[21] *Letters of Governor Bernard, 1763–1768* (Boston, 1769), p. 9.

[22] 6 George II, c. 13, *Statutes at Large*, V, 616–619.

capture most of the European sugar market, the French planters were in a position to sell their molasses at cut-rate prices. In 1763, according to the author of "Observations on the Trade and Revenue of North America," the duty of 6*d.* a gallon on molasses "was little short of the Prime cost [of this commodity] in foreign Markets" (i.e., the French West Indies). He further maintained—in harmony not only with all contemporary American utterances but also with the contentions of writers in more recent times—that the duty "was confes'dly more than the Trade will bear." This argument deserves to be given careful analysis, for it was used to justify a deliberate course of lawlessness.

Assuming for the purpose of discussion that the price of foreign molasses in the West Indies was even twice the amount [23] indicated above, it is by no means evident that the duty of 6*d.* a gallon, if paid by *all* American importers, was in fact a ruinous duty. To begin with, in the eighteenth century, by the magic of Yankee ingenuity a gallon of molasses when distilled apparently produced about a gallon of rum.[24] Molasses was selling in 1760 at wholesale in Philadelphia at prices ranging from 2*s.* 4*d.* to 2*s.* 6*d.* Pennsylvania currency per gallon, New England rum for 3*s.* 6*d.*, and West India rum for 5*s.* 2*d.*[25] But "over the counter" retail prices for rum at inns or taverns in 1759, 1764, and 1765 in Maryland, for example, were 6*d.* a gill or at the rate of 16*s.* a gallon.[26] What the retail price for this commodity was on the African coast may be left to the imagination. At least it is clear that there was an enormous spread between wholesale and retail prices of rum. The whole history of the distilling industry in America down to the present day provides evidence of the ability of the industry to prosper while paying excises infinitely greater than that set by the Molasses Act.

[23] The price of this molasses is given at Boston in 1764 as 12*d.* sterling. A. C. Bates (ed.), *Fitch Papers,* Hartford, 1918–20, II, 263. This was supposed to cover its original purchase price, the cost of transportation, and the theoretical payment of the import duty of 6*d.*

[24] Witt Bowden, *Industrial History of the United States* (New York, 1930), p. 86.

[25] "Prices Current . . . in Philadelphia," *Pennsylvania Gazette,* Feb. 7, 1760.

[26] See the ledger of R. Chyne, Inn Keeper, Baltimore County, Maryland, in Church Historical Society Mss., Liber B.

For example, the Federal tax on whiskey [27] in 1949 amounted to $9 a gallon plus an additional state tax of $1.43. These taxes were passed on to the consumer apparently without great resistance, although some bootlegging is again in evidence.

Had the levy under the Molasses Act been as ruinous as asserted, there would have been, it is quite clear, no legal importation of foreign-produced molasses in 1760 and 1761. Yet, under the Pitt program of enforcement in the midst of war, at least 44,000 gallons of molasses were entered in American ports in 1760 and in 1761 over 47,000 gallons. The duties on these importations amounted to £1,170 and £1,189 respectively.[28] Thus one can hardly accept at face value the contentions of a brochure put out in December, 1763, by the Boston "Society for encouraging Trade and Commerce within the Province of Massachusetts Bay," representing the distilling interests. Designed to influence Parliament not to renew the act of 1733, then about to expire, it appeared under the title of "Statement of the Trade and Fisheries of Massachusetts." [29] The underlying thesis was that the duty of 6d. a gallon on molasses, were payment of it enforced,

would have the Effect of an absolute Prohibition on the Importation of molasses and Sugar from the foreign Islands; and consequently the same Effect on the Exportation of Fish, Lumber and other Commodities from hence to those Islands. . . . The Loss of the Trade to the foreign Islands on which a great Part of our other Trade depends must . . . entirely destroy the Fishery of this Province, and at Newfoundland likewise. . . . The Destruction of the Fishery will be very prejudicial to the Trade of Great Britain. . . .

Here is a picture of the province laid in virtual ruin should the provisions of the Molasses Act of 1733 be extended and enforced.

Once the agitation against the act had begun in Boston, it spread to other towns. Jared Ingersoll of New Haven, representing the distilling interests of Connecticut, memorialized the Assembly in behalf of his clients that that body should remonstrate against the act; [30]

---

[27] New York *Herald Tribune*, Oct. 9, 1949.

[28] "An Account of the duties collected on molasses under 6 George II," in G. L. Beer, *British Colonial Policy, 1754–1765* (New York, 1922), p. 116.

[29] This is printed in the *Fitch Papers*, II, 262–273.

[30] For this memorial, see *ibid.*, pp. 275–276. See also "Remarks on the Trade

and Benjamin Franklin, writing from Philadelphia on March 14, 1764, declared: "The rigorous Execution of the Sugar Act, occasions much Commotion among our Merchants in North America."[31] There was a general clamor for free intercourse with the foreign West Indies, and, if this could not be secured, it was asked that at least the import duty on foreign molasses be not over a penny a gallon.[32]

This agitation had its influence upon the ministers at home, at least with respect to the foreign-molasses duty. Charles Townshend, while President of the Board of Trade, proposed in the spring of 1763 to reduce the duty of 6*d*. to 2*d*. a gallon, and Grenville later expressed himself as agreeable to the idea. But, after all, the British West India planters also felt that their interests were affected and called for an even higher rate than would have satisfied Grenville.[33] As a result, when on April 5, 1764, Parliament finally passed the Sugar Act[34] that amended the Molasses Act of 1733, the duty on foreign-produced molasses imported into the colonies was placed at 3*d*., one half of the old duty—clearly a compromise between the demands of the colonial merchants, on the one hand, and of the sugar planters, on the other, but considered to be highly favorable

---

of the Colony," written in Jan., 1764, from New London, Connecticut (*ibid.*, 277–278), which follows the line of reasoning of the Boston statement.

[31] Benjamin Franklin to Richard Jackson, Mar. 14, 1764, Carl Van Doren (ed.), *Letters and Papers of Benjamin Franklin and Richard Jackson, 1753–1785* (Philadelphia, 1947), pp. 146–147.

[32] Massachusetts Historical Society, *Publications*, 1st s., VI, 193.

[33] *Ibid.*, p. 194.

[34] 4 George III, c. 15, *Statutes at Large*, VII, 457–466. On March 10, from the Committee of the Whole of the House of Commons, twenty resolutions were reported aimed specifically at raising a revenue in the colonies. These resolutions, upon hearings in the Committee on Ways and Means, were subjected to some amendment, and the fifteenth among them (the fourteenth according to the *Parl. Hist.*, XV, 1427), providing for stamp duties, was laid aside temporarily. On Mar. 22 the duty on foreign-produced molasses, the most controversial of the resolutions, was agreed to by the House, and the following day the rest of the import duties provided for by the resolutions were adopted with some changes favorable to the colonies. For example, the seventeenth and eighteenth resolutions, placing duties on foreign linens and East India goods ranging from 20 to 43 per cent, were changed to from 2½ per cent to 5 per cent (*Pennsylvania Gazette*, May 17 and 31 and June 7, 1764). By Apr. 5 the bill had passed in the House of Lords and had been signed by the King. The *Parl. Hist.*, curiously, leaves out the resolution for imposing heavy duties on foreign-produced sugar.

to the former group. As compensation to the planters, the duty in the act on foreign-produced sugar sent to the colonies was raised from 5s. to £1 7s. per hundredweight. With respect to rum, which had carried a 9d. duty, if of foreign origin, its importation into the colonies was now forbidden; finally, high duties were placed by the act on wines directly imported, and substantial duties imposed on coffee, indigo, and pimento, all of foreign growth, and also on East India and a few other foreign fabrics, such as linens and lawns.

While the act thus sought to balance the continental American merchant interest against that of the West India planters, its chief purpose, in line with the newly established policy of the ministry, was to secure a revenue in America to help defray the expense "of defending, protecting and securing the same." It was calculated that the income from this might amount to some £45,000.[35] The act not only aided the American distillers by lowering the duty on molasses, but they were now given, by the prohibition of the importation of foreign-made rum, a virtual monopoly of the market in the colonies and were also favored by the high duties placed on wines carried directly from Madeira to America. Southern producers of indigo, especially the people of South Carolina, were also protected from foreign competition; and the sugar planters of the British West Indies, by the high duty placed on foreign sugar, were given needed encouragement to expand their plantations, especially in Jamaica, where much fertile land was still lying idle. It therefore seemed at the time of its enactment to be a measure of wise planning, one which, while making provision for meeting at least a small portion of the expense of maintaining garrisons in the newly acquired areas of North America as well as in the western Indian country, would not seriously disturb the American colonial economy. In fact, Parliament showed some solicitude for the American economy by passing at the same session an act favoring American whalers and the importation into England of whale fins by colonials which remitted all duties except a small perpetual duty granted in the days of Charles II, known as the Old Subsidy.[36] This law has been credited with doubling the number of New England ships

[35] Beer, *Brit. Colon. Policy,* pp. 283-284.
[36] 4 George III, c. 29, *Statutes at Large,* VII, 481.

engaged in whaling.[37] Another act permitted the planters of South Carolina to send their rice—an enumerated commodity—to any part of America to the southward, subject only to the same duty paid for the privilege of exporting this commodity directly to places in Europe south of Cape Finisterre.[38] Finally, a third act provided a generous bounty for hemp and flax raised in the colonies and exported to the mother country.[39]

Whatever optimistic prospects the ministers might have had of the success of their endeavors to bring about an equitable sharing of the burden of defending North America through Parliamentary enactment, the news of the passage of the Sugar Act evoked an immediately unfavorable response in the colonies. Governor Hopkins, voicing the view of the Rhode Island distillers, declared:

> The duty of 3d. per gallon on foreign molasses is well known to every man . . . the least acquainted with it to be much higher than that article can possibly bear and therefore must operate as an absolute prohibition.[40]

This viewpoint was also upheld by Jared Ingersoll, who on July 6, 1764, wrote his friend Thomas Whately, one of the joint secretaries of the Treasury:

> I think Parliament have overshot their mark and you will not, in the event, have your Expectations in any measure answered from the Provisions of the late Act.

He then went on to say that there was not a single voyage undertaken to the French and Dutch West Indies "with the most Distant intention to pay the Dutys"; and that while "a Seizure will be made of perhaps one Vessel in a Hundred," the attempt under given conditions to end the practice of smuggling would be like "burning a Barn to roast an Egg." [41] A committee of the Massachusetts Bay

---

[37] D. Macpherson, *Annals of Commerce* . . . (4 vols., London, 1805), III, 567–568.

[38] 4 George III, c. 27, *Statutes at Large,* VII, 479–481.

[39] 4 George III, c. 26, *ibid.,* VII, 477–478. The bounty on hemp or undressed flax was £7 a ton.

[40] Quoted by A. M. Schlesinger, *The Colonial Merchants and the American Revolution* (New York, 1918), pp. 55–56.

[41] *Ingersoll Stamp Act Correspondence* (New Haven, 1766), p. 3.

House of Representatives, under the chairmanship of the redoubt-able James Otis, went further. It challenged this revenue measure—and any other with the same intent that Parliament might enact for the colonies—not on grounds of mere financial and economic in-expediency, but on the basis of rights under the British Constitution. In its communication to Governor Fitch of Connecticut of June 25, 1764, the committee declared that such

measures have a tendency to deprive the Colonies of some of their most essential Rights as British Subjects, and . . . particularly the Right of assessing their own Taxes.[42]

In injecting constitutional issues into a controversy that had hitherto been conducted on an economic plane, the colonists went far beyond the position they had taken when the drastic Molasses Act had been passed back in 1733. It is doubtful if they would have advanced these constitutional objections even a decade earlier. Indeed, that influential South Carolina rice planter, Andrew Rutledge, after seeking the advice of several merchants and "men of experience" in Charleston, openly advocated back in 1755 that, for the protection of the American frontiers, Parliament should lay import duties on the colonies sufficient to raise £100,000 for the support of four regiments.[43] What colonial would have proposed such a measure in 1764?

[42] *Fitch Papers,* II, 284.
[43] Andrew Rutledge to Attorney General Murray (soon to become Lord Mansfield), Jan. 10, 1755, B. M. Add. Mss. 32852, f. 142.

CHAPTER 6

Imperial Security and
Internal Taxation

ON MARCH 10, 1764, Thomas Whately, a Joint Secretary of the Treasury, presented to the House of Commons from the Committee of the Whole a series of resolutions providing for the raising of revenue in North America and the West Indies to aid in meeting the expense of defending these areas. The fifteenth resolution called for the levying of stamp duties.[1] Had it not been for the strong opposition not only of Americans in England without official standing, as well as the London agents of the colonies, but also of Grenville himself, who now favored postponement of the measure,[2]

[1] *Pennsylvania Gazette*, May 17, 1764. Apparently the entire Cabinet Council approved of the proposal for American taxation. See Dora M. Clark's "George Grenville as First Lord of The Treasury and Chancellor of The Exchequer," *Huntington Library Quarterly*, XIII, 389.

[2] The student is referred to the illuminating article by Professor Edmund S. Morgan entitled "George Grenville and the Postponement of the Stamp Act" in *William and Mary Quarterly*, July, 1950. This points out that Grenville's remarks, preliminary to the introduction of the resolution of March 10, were interpreted by some who heard him to mean that if the colonies would take the initiative and provide an American fund for the purpose of aiding in the defense and the policing of the new acquisitions and the trans-Appalachian area, Parliament would not be called upon to pass an American stamp bill. Morgan shows the influence of this view on later apologists for the government and suggests the hollowness of Grenville's alternative proposal. For an extended treatment of the Stamp Act crisis, the reader is referred to the thorough treatment of the subject in Edmund S. and Helen M. Morgan, *The Stamp Act Crisis* (Chapel Hill, 1953).

it is likely that this resolution would have been adopted and embodied in the Revenue Act of 1764. It is certain that by the beginning of the year 1764 Richard Jackson, a member of the House of Commons,[3] Grenville's secretary, and London agent for the colonies of Pennsylvania, Massachusetts Bay, and Connecticut, saw that this measure had been determined upon by those in authority. In writing to his friend Benjamin Franklin, he declared:

I have long since given up all hopes of preventing some Parliamentary Tax to be imposed on N America as well as the W Indies for the maintenance of the Troops kept there. . . .[4]

In view of the fact that the duties provided in the Sugar Act were not expected to bring into the royal exchequer more than a portion of the sum that it was felt should be raised in the New World for the above purpose, it is not surprising that the Treasury officers should have thought of a levy of internal duties in the form of a stamp tax. Such a tax had been in force in England ever since the year 1694.[5] In 1760 a total of £290,000 had been raised by this means in Great Britain, and this amount was increased in 1765 by raising of some of the duties.[6] Regardless of the arguments over its merits, the fact remains that to this day the stamp duty has served in Great Britain as one of the most acceptable ways of raising money.

The extension of stamp duties to America, as a means of securing a revenue for the support of the Empire, was urged as early as 1722 by Archibald Cummings, surveyor of customs at Boston,[7] and in 1742 by Sir William Keith, who had been deputy governor of Penn-

---

[3] One of the members of the House of Commons elected by Weymouth and Melcombe Regis.

[4] Jackson to Franklin, Jan. 26, 1764, in Carl Van Doren (ed.), *Letters and Papers of Benjamin Franklin and Richard Jackson, 1753–1785* (Philadelphia, 1947), p. 138.

[5] The first levy of stamp duties was 5 and 6 William and Mary, c. 21, *Statutes at Large,* III, 536–543. In all, twenty distinct acts had provided for stamp taxes in England down to and including 5 George III, c. 46, *ibid.,* VII, 547–556.

[6] For increases in the British stamp duties in 1765, as well as increases in other taxes, see the *Annual Register, 1765,* pp. 244–245, 248–249; see also Dowell, *A History of Taxation and Taxes* (London, 1884), III, 377, and likewise his *A History and Explanation of Stamp Duties* (London, 1873), p. 21.

[7] Edward Channing, *A History of the United States* (New York, 1912), III, 48.

sylvania;[8] in 1754 and 1757 the Newcastle administration had considered such a tax to help meet the financial problems presented by the colonies in the midst of war;[9] and in 1763, soon after Grenville took office, Henry McCulloh, a gentleman with a large interest in Carolina lands, who had acted also as supervisor of royal revenues and land grants in North Carolina but was then in England, suggested to the Treasury a series of stamp duties that he felt would produce in America alone, without regard to the West Indies, some £60,000 sterling per annum.[10] His recommendation doubtless carried weight in persuading the ministers to include in the revenue bill of 1764 a resolution to this end. When Grenville was led to withdraw it for fuller consideration and in order to gather more precise information from America, he was at the same time granted permission by the House of Commons to submit a bill providing for such duties at a later date should he see fit and in case the colonies did not offer a more acceptable revenue plan. It was at this juncture that an unnamed correspondent—possibly it was Richard Jackson, a great friend of the colonies—writing on March 24 from London to a correspondent in America, proposed that the colonies themselves request the tax:

All the Well-wishers to America are of Opinion that as the Tax in itself is an equitable one, and the least injurious that can be proposed, the several Assemblies should signify their Assent and Desire to that Tax, under the present Exigencies of the State, and the Necessity of the Case, by which they avoid every Appearance of an Infringement of their Liberty, and shew their Inclination to pay the Obedience to a British Parliament, which has the Power to make every Part of its Dominions submit to such Laws as they may think proper to enact; by this Means they will prevent a Precedent from internal Taxes being imposed without their Consent, which will inevitably be the Case next Session, if they withhold their Assent to the Stamp Tax.[11]

[8] "Sr Wm Keith's Proposal for laying a Duty on Stampt Papers in America, Dec. 17, 1742," Brit. Mus., Add. Ms. 33,028, fol. 376.

[9] Brit. Mus., Add. Ms. 35,910, fols. 160–163 and 165–166.

[10] W. J. Smith (ed.), *The Grenville Papers* (London, 1853), II, 374; James High, "Henry McCulloh: Progenitor of the Stamp Act," *North Carolina Historical Review*, Jan., 1952, also *ibid.*, July, 1952, for letters of Professors Sellers and High.

[11] *Pennsylvania Gazette*, June 7, 1764. It may be conjectured that the

Whether or not Richard Jackson wrote this letter, it is clear nonetheless that, while he was opposed to the idea of Parliament itself, without solicitation from America, placing stamp taxes upon the colonials,[12] he had, in the spring of 1764, proposed to Franklin that the colonies should apply to have such duties levied. In his reply the Philadelphian made it perfectly clear that this suggestion would not be favorably received. These are Franklin's words:

I note what you say of the Colonies applying for a Stamp Act. In my Opinion there is not only no Likelihood that they will generally agree in such an Application, but even that one Colony will propose it to the others. Tho' if a gross Sum were generally requir'd of all the Colonies, and they were left to settle the Mode of raising it at some general Congress, I think it not unlikely that instead of settling Quotas, they would fall on some such general Tax, as a Stamp Act, or an Excise on Rum, etc. or both;—because Quota's would be difficult to settle at first with Equality, and would, if they could be made equal at first, soon become unequal, and never would be satisfactory; whereas these kind of Taxes would nearly find their own Proportions.—And yet I think I could propose a better mode by far, both for us and for you, if we were together to talk it over. . . .[13]

Assuming that it were just and proper that the colonies should have some definite share of the total expense of maintaining the defenses of North America, both the Jackson proposal and that of Franklin offered constitutional ways out of a developing impasse. In one case recognition would have been given to the supreme authority of Parliament to levy taxes on America with the express consent of the colonial assemblies; in the other, Parliament would have recognized the right of the colonials to establish a general Congress with exclusive power to levy taxes upon all the inhabitants of the colonies

American who received the above letter was Franklin, although it is given a New York date line of June 4.

[12] Jackson to Franklin, Jan. 26, 1764, *Franklin-Jackson Letters,* p. 138.

[13] Franklin to Jackson, June 25, 1764, *ibid.,* p. 168. Part of the letter from Jackson to Franklin, it may be surmised, was the preceding quotation.

As to Franklin's own plan for raising an American revenue, this involved the creation by Parliament of a general American Loan Office, on the order of the profitable Pennsylvania Loan Office, that would issue and loan an American currency. Carl Van Doren (ed.), *Benjamin Franklin's Autobiographical Writings* (New York, 1945), pp. 155–157; V. W. Crane (ed.), *Benjamin Franklin's Letters to the Press, 1758–1775* (Chapel Hill, 1950), pp. 25–29.

whenever their general welfare seemed to demand such a step. The Jackson approach could have laid the foundation for an imperial Parliament; Franklin's, for the creation of an American federal system, comparable possibly to the present status of the Dominion of Canada. But either solution, carried out in a spirit of harmony, would have demanded exceptional perspicacity as well as the good faith of persons in public life on both sides of the Atlantic. Unfortunately, such perspicacity and such confidence were wanting. The people of the colonies, in fact, failed to see the necessity of acquiescing in the exercise of such powers either by Parliament or by an American congress. Nor is it likely that either the ministry or Parliament would have given a sympathetic reception to the Franklin proposal.

The question of American representation in Parliament—after the manner of the present representation of Algiers and French Guiana in the French Parliament—as a logical if dubious solution seems to have been discussed and seriously considered before the Stamp Act was passed in the spring of 1765.[14] But the ministry, it would appear, was discouraged from making any formal proposal

[14] W. T. Laprade, "The Stamp Act in British Politics," *American Historical Review*, XXXV, 746. London advices, Nov. 13, 1764: "It is certainly on the Carpet for the British plantations to have the privilege of representatives in the House of Commons in England; but we are told that they are not to be chose by the whole body of the people of our colonies, but by and from the members of the assemblies of the several provinces" (*Pennsylvania Gazette*, Feb. 28, 1765). Also London advices, April 1, 1765: "We hear, should the scheme for introducing American representatives in parliament be laid aside, such colony agents, during their residence here in a public character, will nevertheless be vested with certain privileges; among others, the liberty of franking letters, and their persons to be exempted from arrests for debts, in common with members of the house" (*ibid.,* June 6, 1765). See also *St. James's Chronicle,* Nov. 24–27 and Dec. 15–18, 1764, and the [London] *Evening Post,* Dec. 4–6, 1764.

Among the Chatham Papers is an undated "Scheme for the better uniting and cementing the mutual interest and peace of Great Britain and her Colonies by representation in the Parliament of Great Britain and Dominions thereto belonging." According to this plan Massachusetts Bay, Pennsylvania, and Virginia would each have as many as four members; Connecticut, New York, and Jamaica, three; Canada, the East and West Jerseys, Maryland, and South Carolina, two; and, finally, Nova Scotia, New Hampshire, Rhode Island, the lower counties on the Delaware, North Carolina, Georgia, East Florida, West Florida, Bahamas, Bermuda, Barbados, Antigua, St. Christopher, Nevis, and Granada, one each (*English Historical Review,* XXII, 756–758).

to that end. Certainly it received small encouragement from those in a position in England to speak the mind of America. In fact, Grenville could not find any evidence that the colonies had the least inclination toward such a representation and was made quite aware that there were "many Reasons why they should not desire it." Among the reasons that colonials were prepared to urge, and that apparently had been presented to him, were that, since members of Parliament received no pay, the expense of sending representatives would fall upon the colonies. Again, the influence of American representatives in Parliament could not possibly be dominant, for they realized that they could not hope to have a majority of the seats in the House of Commons. Finally, they were persuaded that the representatives would be confronted with many serious inconveniences in carrying on their activities in Parliament, both by reason of the fact that the latter would be widely separated from their constituencies and by their lack of familiarity with the English setting. Therefore, when later in the presence of a group of the most influential American London agents, including Richard Jackson, Jared Ingersoll of Connecticut, and Benjamin Franklin of Pennsylvania, Grenville set forth what he had been led to feel were the most important objections of the colonials to representation in Parliament, not a single agent disputed their validity.[15] That they were not mistaken as to the unwillingness of any of the colonies to assume this responsibility was later to be made quite clear as the result of the deliberations of the Stamp Act Congress. In its fourth declaration the Congress rejected this proposed solution in these words: "that the people of these colonies are not, and, from their local circumstances, cannot be represented in the House of Commons in Great Britain."

Other possibilities were considered, among them the plan for a so-called "American Fund" proposed formally by the ministry at

---

[15] Jared Ingersoll to Governor Fitch, March 6, 1766, *Ingersoll Stamp Act Correspondence,* pp. 25–28. For example, the Pennsylvania Assembly, in sending to Richard Jackson instructions in Sept., 1764, to oppose the passing of a stamp bill for America by Parliament, stressed the fact that the colonials "neither are or can be represented, under the present Circumstances" in that body (*Franklin-Jackson Letters,* p. 184); this was in line with the resolutions of such other colonies as South Carolina and Virginia. *South Carolina Gazette,* Dec. 17, 1764, and *Journal of the House of Burgesses of Virginia, 1761–1765,* p. vii.

the beginning of the late war. But only one colony, South Carolina, even in face of the great emergency, could be prevailed upon to contribute to it. Again, there was the system of requisitions upon the basis of quotas, whereby the ministers could, as had Newcastle and Pitt, call upon the colonial assemblies to provide aid in matters of general importance lying beyond the capacity or jurisdiction of a single colony. But this method had certain fatal defects, as Benjamin Franklin had already pointed out to his friend Jackson. In fact, during the course of the Great War for the Empire, despite the excellent record of Massachusetts Bay, Connecticut, and New York, most of the colonies only partially met their quotas, while some, such as prosperous Maryland, ignored all of the requisitions. Therefore, when Franklin at the conference with Grenville pleaded that the old method by the King's requisition should now be followed, he must have done so in his official capacity without reference to his personal views; for no one in America was in fact more clearly aware of the unfairness of this system in its actual operation than was Pennsylvania's London agent. Grenville then asked Franklin whether the colonials could "agree upon the several proportions Each Colony should raise" [16] in order to provide the equivalent for the forty or fifty thousand pounds that he hoped to secure by a stamp tax. But the agents were honestly unable to answer, nor was it possible for the government at home to assess the financial capabilities of the respective colonies. Grenville then pushed his advantage. "What then?" he asked. "Shall no Steps be taken and must we and America be two distinct Kingdoms, and that now immediately, or must America be Defended entirely by Us, and be themselves quite excused, or left to do just what they shall please to do? Some, perhaps, will be pleased to do something, and others Nothing?" In a prophetic mood he ventured the observation that perhaps "from the nature of our Situations, it will happen and must be Expected that

[16] *Ingersoll Stamp Act Corresp.*, pp. 25–28. Deputy Governor James Hamilton of Pennsylvania, writing to Lieutenant Governor de Lancey on June 2, 1754, at the beginning of the Great War for the Empire, expressed the conviction that the progress of the French in North America could never be effectively opposed—by reason of the attitude of the assemblies toward voting appropriations—until by an act of Parliament the colonies would be compelled to contribute without reference to the assemblies their respective quotas for the common service (*Pennsylvania Archives*, 4th ser., II, 284–287).

one Day we shall be two distinct Kingdoms," but he hastened to add that he was convinced that a separation would be mutually disadvantageous. To resolve the present difficulty, he urged that "mutual Confidence and mutual Uprightness of Intention take Place and no considerable Ills can follow." [17]

The London agents had been silenced by Grenville's logic and by the manifest fairness of the idea that Americans should assume some definite share of the expense involved in garrisoning the new acquisitions and the Indian country beyond the Appalachian Mountains. But the colonial assemblies—irrespective of their willingness or reluctance to make any contribution to these ends—chose to stand on what they considered to be their rights, whether prescriptive or constitutional. News of the proposed addition of a stamp act to the revised import duties aroused the liveliest resentment in colonial legislatures. South Carolina, Massachusetts, Virginia, Pennsylvania, Rhode Island, New York, and Connecticut framed petitions against the proposal. Among all the remonstrances against it that were sent to England, none is more deserving of attention than that sent by the Connecticut Assembly under title of *Reasons Why the British Colonies in America should not be charged with Internal Taxes by Authority of Parliament humbly offered for Consideration in Behalf of the Colony of Connecticut*.[18] The thesis embodied the idea that by "the Constitution, Government and Laws of Great Britain the English are a Free People." Therefore, it is the right of every Englishman

not to be subjected to Laws made without his Consent . . . lodged in the Hands of Representatives, by them elected and chosen for that Purpose. . . . For if the Privilege of not being taxed without their Consent, be taken from them, Liberty and Freedom are certainly gone with it.

While admitting that Parliament enjoyed a general authority, a supreme jurisdiction, over all his Majesty's subjects, the Assembly insisted that this body was also the guardian of their liberties and therefore "doth not extend its Taxations to such . . . as are not represented in that grand Legislature of the Nation." [19] For the

[17] *Ingersoll Stamp Act Corresp.*, pp. 25–28.
[18] This was printed at New Haven in 1764.
[19] Governor Fitch in writing to Richard Jackson on Dec. 7, 1764, made clear

people of the colonies "situate at a great Distance from their Mother Country . . . cannot participate in the general Legislature of the Nation. . . . Yet . . . it may not be justly said they have lost their Birth-Right by . . . their Removal into America." The argument was then advanced that the colony had honored requisitions made upon it in times of emergency and had supported itself at other times without aid from England. Before closing, the point was stressed that should it be judged necessary to make an addition to the charges on America, this should not be done in a way that would infringe on the constitutions of the colonies. 'This, it is conceived, might be effected by a Duty . . . on the Importation of Negroes, and on the Fur Trade, etc.," rather than by internal taxes.[20]

Here is presented that sharp distinction made between external customs duties, where constitutionality is conceded, and internal levies, denounced as inconsistent "with those Authorities and Privileges which the Colonies and the People in them legally enjoy. . . ." [21] This same distinction was likewise made in another remarkable paper, the author of which possessed full knowledge of American conditions. While not in the handwriting or following the orthography of Benjamin Franklin, the paper was certainly written in the spirit and style that characterize his compositions. In it the argument is developed that. if the colonies are considered to be

to him that the position taken by the Assembly in the *Reasons* "avoided all Pretence of objection against the Authority or Power of Parliament as the Supreme Legislature of all the King's Dominions, to Tax the Colonies and have therefore Endeavoured to Shew that the Exercise of Such Power in that Particular Instance or in like Cases will take away Part of our Antient Priviledges etc. . . . and in the whole have Endeavoured to Express our Sentiments With becoming Modesty Decency & Submission and we trust, as was intended, without offense." A. C. Bates (ed.), *Fitch Papers* (Hartford, 1918–20), II, 304.

[20] This pamphlet is reprinted in the *Conn. Col. Rec.*, XII, Appendix.

[21] The distinction between internal and external taxation was also voiced by the London agent Richard Jackson. Writing to Benjamin Franklin on Jan. 26, 1764, he declared: "I am most averse to an Internal Tax [on the colonies]. . . . Customs as well as Prohibitions on Trade have been at all Times, laid by England [on them] from the time of the long Parlt[.] I wish this to be the Rule of Conduct on this Occasion" (*Franklin-Jackson Letters*, pp. 138–139). Franklin in February indicated to Jackson that, if money must be raised in America to support the troops there, he would approve of import duties on such items as foreign molasses and wines, tea, East India goods, and Negroes (*ibid.*, p. 140).

constituent parts of the Empire, then not only stamp duties but every tax imposed on a resident of Great Britain "should be extended over the whole Empire."

And with this System and the consequences necessarily resulting from it the Americans would possibly be very well pleased. They would gladly (it may be) pay their share of the general Taxation as they would of course partake of all the Advantage which the residents of Great Brittain are entitled to. They would have a right of representation in the Brittish parliament according to their magnitude . . . but what they would consider as of much more consequence, they would upon the footing of general equity have a right of exporting their products Duty free and to the best Market they could find . . . they would likewise save all the Duties which are now imposed upon foreign or British commodities upon Exportation or Reexportation from Great Brittain to America.

Under this system, the writer insisted, the taxes collected in America would not in any way be the equivalent of the duties previously paid. It was finally argued that the extension of all taxes to the colonies would not only be too complicated but "so Absurd and Chimerical that nothing but the present attempt to Tax America internally can justify the bringing it into Supposition." [22]

Despite the arguments advanced by the opponents of internal taxes, work on a stamp bill was continued by the Treasury officials. The forms of the various legal instruments used in the colonies had previously been requested of the governors by the Secretary of State, and the request seems to have been honored. The purpose of this procedure was not only to obtain light upon American business methods but "to make the tax as little burdensome as possible." [23] Early in November, 1764, the bill had begun to assume form,[24] but

[22] Shelburne Papers, 85:71–77, Clements Library. The above statements are in perfect harmony with the broad implications of Franklin's advice to Richard Jackson, contained in his letter of May 1, 1765: "If you chuse to tax us, give us Members in your Legislature, and let us be one People" (*Franklin-Jackson Letters*, p. 157), as well as his views expressed on December 22, 1754, in writing to Governor Shirley respecting the taxation of the colonies by Parliament. John Bigelow (ed.), *Works of Benjamin Franklin* (10 vols., Philadelphia, 1887), II, 384–387.

[23] Thomas Whately to John Temple, Aug. 14, 1764, Mass. Hist. Soc., *Coll.*, 6th ser., IX, 23.

[24] London advices, Oct. 27, 1764, *Pennsylvania Gazette*, January 24, 1765.

was yet to have the specific stamp rates attached to it, and the inclusion of certain items was also still a matter of discussion.[25] In writing on November 5, 1764, to John Temple, Surveyor General of Customs for the Northern District of America, Thomas Whately of the Treasury attempted to clear up one misconception. He pointed out that the alarm in the colonies that they would be drained of their currency was groundless in view of the fact that the revenue to be raised in America was "to be applied to the support of the troops there, and consequently will not be sent hither in order to be sent back." [26]

The American stamp bill in its final form was much more favorable to the colonists than would have been the case had the stamp act then in force in Great Britain been extended to include them.[27] Indeed, from the point of view of Whately, chief architect of the bill, not only would there be no drainage of gold and silver from the colonies as a result of the payment of the stamp duties, but the sums that would have to be sent from England to defray most of the expense of American defense would help to ensure to the colonies a continuous and abundant supply of specie.[28] According to Whately's estimate, less than a third of this expense would be met by combined internal and external revenues raised in America.[29]

On February 7, 1765, the bill, in the form of fifty-five resolutions, was reported to the House of Commons from the Committee of the

[25] Whately to Temple, Nov. 5, 1764, Mass. Hist. Soc., *Coll.*, 6th ser., IX, 37.

[26] *Ibid.*, p. 38. On July 10, 1765 Thomas Whately of the Treasury wrote to the Stamp Commissioners that the entire proceeds of the American Stamp Act were to be paid to the Deputy Paymaster in America so that the sums arising might be applied to the subsistence of the troops there (P.R.O., Treasury Papers, 1. 439 fol. 94).

[27] Jared Ingersoll used his influence with Whately to have the stamp duties placed on certain instruments, such as those for marriage licenses, for the commissions of justices of the peace, and for notes-in-hand, dropped from the bill (*Ingersoll Stamp Act Corresp.*, p. 19). On land conveyances, according to Whately, the rates were much lower for small tracts of land than in England, as were other items, such as bonds for the payment of money, probates of wills, letters of administration, and commissions for office (Whately to Temple, Feb., 1765, Mass. Hist Soc., *Coll.*, 6th ser., IX, 49–51). For an analysis setting forth the differences between the British Stamp Act then in force and the American Stamp Act, see P.R.O., Treasury Papers, 1. 433 fol. 416.

[28] *Ibid.*

[29] *Ibid.*, p. 59.

Whole House.[30] It was on this occasion that certain members of the House spoke in opposition to the measure.[31] But aside from Alderman Beckford of London, who held large West Indies interests, no one at that time denied that Parliament had the authority to lay such taxes. Even Colonel Isaac Barré, most eloquent of those urging rejection, conceded that "Great Britain has an undoubted right," yet he cautioned that its authority "ought to be exercised with the same Tenderness as parents do theirs over their children, and not lay too heavy burthens upon them in infancy, least they prevent their growth or deform them." [32] It was on this occasion that, in reply to Charles Townshend's description of "the Americans as children of our own, planted by our care, nourished by our indulgence," he retorted:

Children planted by your care! No! your oppression planted them in America. . . . They nourished by your indulgence! They grew by your neglect of them. . . . They protected by your arms! They have nobly taken up arms in your defence . . . for the defence of a country whose . . . interior parts have yielded all its little savings to your enlargement. . . .[33]

But, despite this protest, the resolutions were approved by an overwhelming majority of some 250 to 50.[34] The submission to the House on the 15th of February of the bill embodying these resolutions prompted a flood of petitions against its passage. A petition from the West Indies was presented but withdrawn after objections

[30] These resolutions—apparently sent by Franklin in care of Captain Calef, who sailed for Boston—when printed in the *Pennsylvania Gazette* under date of Apr. 18, 1765, in six-point type, covered over a full page of this paper and indeed appeared as a very formidable document, to say the least.

[31] These were Beckford, Colonel Isaac Barré, Richard Jackson, and Sir William Meredith. Jared Ingersoll to Governor Fitch, Feb. 11, 1765, *Fitch Papers*, II, 321.

[32] Mass. Hist. Soc., *Coll.*, 6th ser., IX, 46–47.

[33] T. C. Hansard (ed.), *Parliamentary History of England* . . . (36 vols., London, 1806–20), XVI, 38–39. Although Horace Walpole (*Memoirs of the Reign of George III* [Philadelphia, 1846], I, 283) and John Adolphus (*History of England to 1783*, 4 vols. [London, 1840–45], I, 171) have questioned the authenticity of the Barré address, Jared Ingersoll listened to it from the visitors' gallery in the House of Commons and transmitted it to America (Ingersoll to Fitch, *Fitch Papers*, II, 323). Barré, a bitter opponent of Grenville and a friend of Pitt, later was given a lucrative office on the Irish Establishment where his eloquence was silenced for a time.

[34] *Ibid.* Walpole (*Memoirs*, I, 283) gave the vote as 245 to 49.

were raised. Then came one from Virginia denying the right of Parliament to tax the colonies. This petition was rejected by a very large majority and a Connecticut petition, though more moderate in tone than that from the West Indies, suffered the same fate. As to those from Massachusetts Bay and New York, neither petition was formally presented; the one, based on Otis's *Rights of the British Colonies*, took very high ground respecting the late Sugar Act as well as the issue of internal taxation, and the other "was conceived in terms so inflamatory" that Robert Charles, the New York London agent, could not prevail upon any member of the House to present it. Grenville, in fact, took his stand upon a general parliamentary rule (of long duration) that petitions against money bills could not be received.[35] The final vote at the third reading of the bill was 205 to 49; in the House of Lords it was adopted without a division; and on March 22, as the result of the indisposition of the King, it received the royal assent "by commission." [36]

The ministry anticipated that there might be some difficulty in enforcing the Stamp Act. Even in England it had been found by experience that cases of revenue evasion could not be left to jury trials in the localities where the violations occurred, and they were automatically transferred to London.[37] Accordingly, the act itself provided that cases involving its provisions might be tried at the option of the prosecutor in either a court of record, that is a com-

[35] Ingersoll to Fitch, Mar. 6, 1765, *Fitch Papers*, II, 333–335. General Conway at this stage of the debate joined with Alderman Beckford in denying the right of Parliament to tax the colonies. They were the only members of Parliament that at the time took this position (Walpole, *Memoirs*, I, 283). Professor E. S. Morgan, in his article "Thomas Hutchinson and the Stamp Act" (*New England Quarterly*, XXI, 462–466), indicates the likelihood that Conway leaned heavily upon a manuscript prepared by Lieutenant Governor Hutchinson against the passing of the Stamp Act which he sent to Richard Jackson the summer of 1764 and which Jackson presented to Conway. This interesting document outlining Hutchinson's position at the time is included in the article. *Ibid.*, pp. 480–492; also Morgan, *Stamp Act Crisis*, pp. 213–216.

[36] The act is 5 George III, c. 12; although not printed by Eyre and Strahan in their collection of statutes, it is given in Pickering's *Statutes at Large*, XXVI, 179–204; it is also to be found in the *Journals of the House of Burgesses of Virginia, 1761–1765*, pp. lix–lxiv. The last-named volume also contains the Address to the King, the Memorial to the House of Lords, and the Remonstrance to the House of Commons, all approved by the Virginia House of Burgesses on Dec. 18, 1764, and directed against the passing of a stamp act by Parliament (*ibid.*, pp. liv–lviii).

[37] Ingersoll to Fitch, Mar. 6, 1765, *Fitch Papers*, II, 335. Although W. E. H. Lecky, in his *History of England in the Eighteenth Century* (8 vols., London,

mon law court, or a court of vice-admiralty.[38] The effect of this provision was to enlarge still further the vice-admiralty jurisdiction in America. The earlier limited jurisdiction of the American vice-admiralty courts had been extended in 1696 to include all cases arising out of the comprehensive navigation statute of that year.[39] After this date it was further extended: in 1722, to embrace the unlawful destruction of the white-pine trees of New England;[40] in 1733, to include violations of the Molasses Act;[41] in 1764, to enforce the Sugar Act of that year;[42] and finally, in 1765, to implement the Stamp Act.

But this provision for trial of violators of the Stamp Act by itself would not ensure enforcement. Stamps must be printed and carried to America and a distributor for every one of the colonies appointed. To Grenville it seemed a matter of great importance that in each case the appointee should be a colonial of high standing in the colony where he would exercise his office. Such a person, he felt, would be better situated than one coming from Great Britain to determine where the act "pinches and will certainly let us know it, in which Case it shall be Eased."[43] He therefore proceeded with care and deliberation in the choice of the colonial distributors.[44]

In view of the willingness of colonists of standing to accept appointment as Stamp Distributors, it is apparent that the idea of the parliamentary taxation of the colonies might look quite different

---

1878–90), III, 328, affirmed that cases of revenue fraud could be tried in an admiralty court and thus without a jury, this does not seem to be true. See James Kent's *Commentaries* (ed. of 1891), I, 375–378, for authorities cited against this proposition.

[38] 5 George III, c. 12, pars. lvii and lviii.

[39] 7 and 8 William III, c. 22, *Statutes at Large,* III, 584–589.

[40] 8 George I, c. 12, par. iv, *ibid.,* V, 259.

[41] 6 George II, c. 13, *ibid.,* V, 616–619.

[42] 4 George III, c. 15, *ibid.,* VII, 457–466.

[43] *Ingersoll Stamp Act Corresp.,* p. 32.

[44] On April 3, 1765, warrants were issued to Andrew Oliver for Massachusetts Bay, Jared Ingersoll for Connecticut, Augustus Johnston for Rhode Island, George Meserve for New Hampshire, William Coxe for New Jersey, and John Hughes for Pennsylvania and the three lower counties on the Delaware, as Stamp Distributors. On May 1 warrants were signed for Robert Seaman for Grenada, Thomas Graham for East Florida, John Mackenzie for Montreal and Trois Rivières, Colin Drummond for Quebec, Jacob Blackwell for West Florida, James McEvers for New York, and, on the 27th, for George Mercer for Virginia. Then on June 13 came the warrants for Archibald Henchelwood for Nova Scotia, Zachariah Hood for Maryland, John Howell for Jamaica, William Tuckett for St. Christopher, and John Slater for Bermuda, and, two days later,

to a colonial of broad views who happened to be sojourning in London, and on intimate terms with men in high office, than it would to a colonist resident in America, far removed from these reassuring contacts and disturbed by the ominous reports coming from across the Atlantic.[45] Men of the stature of Jared Ingersoll, Connecticut's London agent, George Meserve of New Hampshire, and Colonel George Mercer of Virginia—the latter in England to protect the interests of the Ohio Company of Virginia—accepted appointments as Stamp Distributors for their colonies before returning home. As Ingersoll, a tried friend of his native Connecticut, declared later when under fire: "Upon my honor, I thought, I should be blamed if I did not accept the Appointment." [46] In fact, even Benjamin Franklin seems temporarily to have lost touch with the people of Pennsylvania. After his ardent supporter and friend, John Hughes,[47] had received the distributorship for Pennsylvania, apparently on his recommendation, we find him writing to the latter from London on August 9, with respect to the possibility of Stamp Act disturbances in America:

A firm Loyalty to the Crown and faithful Adherence to the Government of this Nation, which is the Safety as well as the Honour of the Colonies to be connected with, will always be the Wisest course for you and I to take, whatever may be the Madness of the Populace or their blind Leaders, who can only bring themselves and Country into Trouble, and draw on greater Burdens by Acts of rebellious Tendency.[48]

---

for William Whitefield for Barbados. On July 9 commissions were signed for Caleb Lloyd for South Carolina and William Houston for North Carolina, and on August 10 for George Angus for Georgia. Finally, on September 27 a warrant was issued to William Ottley, Jr., for all the Leeward Islands except St. Christopher. For these appointments see Treasury Papers, 1. 439 fols. 57 and 62, Library of Congress transcripts.

[45] See the author's *Jared Ingersoll: A Study of American Loyalism in Relation to British Colonial Government* (New Haven, 1920), pp. 136–137.

[46] *Ibid.*, p. 146.

[47] Both Franklin and Hughes were members of the Pennsylvania Antiproprietarial party in the Assembly and both were Philadelphians. When Franklin was attacked by the Proprietarial party after leaving for England, Hughes came strongly to his defense (*Pennsylvania Gazette,* Dec. 20 and 27, 1764).

[48] A. H. Smyth (ed.), *Writings of Benjamin Franklin* (10 vols., New York, 1907), IV, 392.

As the London agent of his province Franklin had done his duty in opposing the passage of the act. So had such other agents as Ingersoll, Jackson, Charles, and Garth. When called upon by Grenville to present some more equitable and less burdensome substitute for stamp duties, they failed to produce a practicable alternative. While they pleaded that the colonies were still in debt, under heavy taxation, and faced with a business recession with the ending of the boom war years, they could scarcely have been ignorant of the fact that the per capita public debt which the people of Great Britain were obliged to carry was immensely greater than that of the most heavily debt-burdened colony, and that British taxes must remain indefinitely at war levels, with little relief in sight. As the result of parliamentary reimbursement and other factors, colonial taxes had in fact already been greatly lightened and would be largely liquidated in the course of a very few years. Nor could these colonial agents have been unaware of the bad times prevalent in England; of the fact that in the year 1764 an estimated 40,000 people were languishing in jail for debt.[49] They must have known that the riots in western England over the imposition of the cider tax, piled upon other taxes the preceding year, had necessitated the calling out of troops; that some 50,000 silk-industry workers had descended upon London in May, 1765, to demand relief from cutthroat French competition and from the exorbitant prices of the necessities of life;[50] and that this protest demonstration was in turn followed by thousands of wool weavers from Norwich and elsewhere.[51] These conditions may well have persuaded the American agents of the equity of the Stamp Act. If they failed to see the storm that was to come, one may well understand the apparent shortsightedness of Grenville and his fellow ministers about the constitutional crisis they were precipitating.

[49] *Pennsylvania Gazette,* Nov. 22, 1764.

[50] *Pennsylvania Gazette,* Dec. 27, 1764, and Aug. 1, 1765. It would appear that with peace established between England and France, the industrialists of the latter country began dumping their manufactures in England with disastrous results to home industry, and that the demand for food products on the Continent was so great as to lead to vast exports of these from England, with the consequent raising of the prices of the necessaries of life to a point beyond the ability of many thousands of people to purchase them. These are characteristics of many postwar periods.

[51] *Pennsylvania Gazette,* Aug. 8, 1765.

CHAPTER 7

The Stamp Act Resisted

WHAT men in the past have believed to be true may well be as important to the historian as the actual truth. Keeping this in mind, we should examine the Stamp Act crisis, being careful to distinguish between the assumptions of fact which impelled people to act and the facts themselves.

Let us begin with the facts. As John Adams saw clearly, for over a century prior to 1764 the inhabitants of the colonies had been indirectly taxed by Parliament for the support of the Empire through the operation of the Navigation and Trade Laws. Writing as late as 1774, he conceded:

> Great Britain has confined all our trade to herself. We are willing she should, so far as it can be for the good of the Empire. . . . We are obliged to take from Great Britain commodities that we could purchase cheaper elsewhere. This difference is a tax upon us for the good of the Empire.[1]

Furthermore, the colonists had had their internal affairs regulated by many acts passed by Parliament after the latter had assumed the chief prerogative powers of the Crown in 1689. Nevertheless, this was the first time they had been called upon by Parliament to pay into the receipt of the British Exchequer money raised within the colonies without consent of their assemblies.[2] They were therefore

[1] C. F. Adams (ed.), *The Works of John Adams* . . . (10 vols., Boston, 1850–56), IV, 46.

[2] Virginians, however, were required by act of assembly in 1658 to pay into the Exchequer 2s. on every hogshead of tobacco before it could be exported,

justified in viewing the Stamp Tax as an innovation. Indeed, it had apparently been so regarded by the people of England when it was first levied in the mother country in 1694.

Beyond these facts there were certain assumptions of fact that are of even greater significance for an understanding of the issue that now arose. There was the assumption that no person within the British Empire could be taxed by any legislative body without his consent as expressed through his direct representative in it; that no exigency in the life of the Empire was therefore sufficient to justify Parliament in extending its authority to levy a direct tax upon the people of the colonies; and, finally, that to do so, no matter for what purpose of general welfare, was not only a violation of the constitution of the Empire but an act of tyranny.

Anyone who reads the newspapers or pamphlets that appeared in America during the course of the Stamp Act crisis is likely to wonder if he could possibly have escaped sharing in full measure the sharp resentment against the authors of the act had he been living in the New World at the time. In fact, the number of Americans who thought that the act represented a just and proper use of the power of Parliament was as few as the number of people in Great Britain who, taking all things into consideration, thought at the time of its passing that the measure was unjust or improper. Thus the Empire was suddenly faced with a sectional crisis as dangerous to its integrity as was the sectionalism that preceded the Civil War in America almost a century later. Both the American colonies in 1765 and the South before 1861 insisted that certain local or states' rights could not be impaired by a central authority and set forth these claims in impassioned tones.

The first real act of defiance to the claims of Parliament came from a group of up-country members of the Virginia House of Burgesses under the leadership of Patrick Henry. On May 29, 1765, Henry laid certain resolutions before the House. The four that were finally adopted, signed by its clerk and forwarded to England by Governor Fauquier, did not go beyond the assertion of rights embodied in several of the colonial memorials of the preceding year.[3]

---

and the people of the Leeward Islands and Barbados paid 4½ per cent ad valorem on all dead exports, as did those of the British Windward Islands after 1764. These levies were in each instance granted in perpetuity.

[3] "Great Britain, Privy Council, Papers and Letters relating to the . . .

Still they were forceful enough. Not only did they embody the notion that the people of Virginia possessed "all the Liberties, Privileges, Franchises, and Immunities that at any Time have been held, enjoyed, and possessed by the People of Great Britain" and that among these privileges was an exclusive right of taxation; but they also stated that any attempt to vest that power in any body other than the Virginia Assembly "has a Manifest Tendency to Destroy AMERICAN FREEDOM." Moreover, the two rejected resolutions, according to the *Maryland Gazette*, read as follows:

That his Majesty's Liege People, Inhabitants of this Colony, are not bound to yield Obedience to any Law or Ordinance whatsoever, designed to impose any Taxation upon them, other than the Laws or Ordinances of the General Assembly. . . .

That any person who shall, by Speaking or Writing, assert or maintain That any Person or Persons, other than the General Assembly of this Colony . . . have any Right or Authority to lay or impose any Tax whatever on the Inhabitants thereof, shall be Deemed, an *Enemy to his Majesty's Colony.*[4]

Their presentation led to a dramatic scene in the House. In charging that the Stamp Act was an act of tyranny, Henry was reported many years later to have exclaimed: "Tarquin and Caesar had each his Brutus, Charles the First his Cromwell, and George the Third——" At this point he was interrupted by the Speaker of the House, who declared that he had spoken "Treason!" After a pause Henry continued: "——may profit by their example! If *this* be treason, make the most of it."[5] Clearly, the Burgesses as a

---

Stamp Act," Huntington Library Mss., H.M. No. 1947, pp. 2–9; *Journals of the House of Burgesses of Virginia, 1761–1765*, p. 360.

[4] *Maryland Gazette*, July 4, 1765. The *Gazette* gives in all seven resolutions. For the most scholarly account of the debate on the resolutions in the House of Burgesses, see E. S. and H. M. Morgan, *The Stamp Act Crisis* (Chapel Hill, 1953), pp. 88–97.

[5] William Wirt, *Sketches of the Life and Character of Patrick Henry* (Philadelphia, 1817). An eyewitness account by a French traveler suggests that Henry apologized for the tone of his remarks (*American Historical Review*, XXV, 745). That the traditional account, as given above, of the scene in the House of Burgesses is fairly accurate is indicated by the fact that the journal of this traveler, under date of May 30, refers to "very strong Debates" there, in the midst of which Henry "in the heat of passion" declared that "Tarquin and Julus had their Brutus, Charles had his Cromwell . . . and was going to continue, when the speaker of the house rose and said, he . . . had spoke traison . . ." (*ibid.*).

body were not prepared to join any such defiance of both the King and the Parliament of Great Britain. Yet the resolutions they finally agreed to, stripped of Henry's inflammatory phrasing, were sufficient testimony of their firm opposition to the imposing of internal taxes on America by the mother country.

The importance of what seems to have been the Henry resolutions—as distinguished from the official Virginia Resolves—lies in the fact that they were erroneously accepted throughout the colonies as the actual ones adopted by the House of Burgesses. Their widespread publication inspired Americans everywhere to resist the enforcement of the act. Published first in the Newport *Mercury* on June 24 and copied by the Boston *Gazette* on July 2,[6] they, according to Governor Bernard of Massachusetts Bay, served as "an Alarm Bell" to the people of New England.[7] Before this event he had felt that the people of the colony would finally submit to the enforcement of the act without serious opposition, in spite of the fact that "Murmurs . . . were continually heard." In time, he was convinced, such murmurs would die away.[8] At the May session of the Assembly he had, in fact, addressed the members, reminding them that

in an Empire, extended and diversified as that of Great Britain, there must be a supreme legislature, to which all other powers must be subordinate. It is our happiness that our supreme legislature [Parliament] is the sanctuary of liberty and justice, and that the prince who presides over it, realizes the idea of a patriot king. Surely, then, we should submit our opinions to the determination of so august a body, and acquiesce, in a perfect confidence that the rights of the members of the British Empire will ever be safe in the hands of the conservators of the liberties of the whole.[9]

But this appeal fell upon deaf ears.

Even before the news of the Henry resolutions reached Boston, the House of Representatives of Massachusetts Bay on June 6 had

[6] W. W. Henry, *Patrick Henry, Life, Correspondence and Speeches* (3 vols., New York, 1891), I, 91.

[7] Bernard to the Board of Trade, Aug. 15, 1765, Huntington Library Mss., H.M. No. 1947, p. 35.

[8] *Ibid.*

[9] Thomas Hutchinson, *History of Massachusetts,* (ed. J. Hutchinson, London, 1828), pp. 117–118.

determined to consider not only "what dutiful, loyal and humble
Address may be proper to make to our Gracious Sovereign and his
Parliament in relation to the several Acts lately passed for levying
Duties and Taxes on the Colonies," but the desirability of a meeting of "committees" representing the popular branch of the assembly
in each of the continental colonies "to consult together on the
present Circumstances." [10] On June 8 a circular letter, framed in
unobjectionable terms, was agreed upon, which recommended a
gathering of such committees in New York the second Tuesday in
October. Thereupon the Speaker was ordered to sign and transmit
copies of it to the several Houses of Representatives, to bring about
"a General and united, loyal and humble representation of their
Condition to his Majesty and the Parliament, [and] to implore
Relief." [11]

When, however, the news of this plan for an American congress
reached the Lords Commissioners for Trade and Plantations late
in September, they viewed the popular movement as of a "dangerous Tendency" for the future of the Empire. Without delay they
proceeded on October 1 to frame a representation [12] covering both
the proposed congress and the Virginia Resolves, addressing it to the
King in Council. The latter thereupon referred the representation
to its own committee, the Lords of the Committee of Council for
Plantation Affairs, which reported on October 3. This report was
considered on October 18, when it was agreed "That this is a
Matter of the Utmost Importance to the Kingdom and Legislature
of Great Britain, and is of too high a Nature for the Determination
of Your Majesty in Your Privy Council, and is proper only for the
Consideration of Parliament. . . ." [13]

Aside from some rather inflammatory letters and articles appearing in the Boston *Gazette,* there were no demonstrations in Massachusetts Bay once the preliminary work of laying the foundations
of an American united front had been laid. When Jared Ingersoll,

[10] "Proceedings of the House of Representatives, June 6, 1765," Huntington
Library Mss., H.M. No. 1947, pp. 16–20.

[11] For this letter see *ibid.*

[12] See its representation of Oct. 1, 1765, to the King in Council, *ibid.,* pp.
23–24.

[13] J. Munro (ed.), *Acts of the Privy Council of England, Colonial Series*
(Hereford, 1911–12), IV, 732.

the Connecticut Stamp Distributor, landed at Boston on July 28, all was quiet.[14] But it was an ominous quiet just before the breaking of the storm.

Early on the morning of August 14 an effigy of Andrew Oliver, the provincial secretary and newly appointed Stamp Distributor for Massachusetts Bay, was seen hanging from a tree on High Street in Boston. When Governor Bernard ordered it taken down, the sheriff reported that his deputies were not able to do it "without Imminent Danger of their Lives." Summoning his Council, the Governor immediately raised the question of the best method to deal with the situation. Some members thought it should be ignored as a prank; others felt that it was already a most serious affair, "a preconcerted Business, in which the greatest part of the Town was Engaged," and that an attempt to act without any force to oppose to them would only inflame the people.

Since the Council was all but unanimous that nothing should be done, Bernard declared that this advice should be entered in the official record. To this the members were opposed, and it was finally agreed to order the sheriff to assemble all the peace officers of Boston. But by this time it was already quite dark. The crowd that had been gathering during the afternoon now went into action; carried the effigy past the Town House, where the Council was sitting; gave three cheers of defiance; and then directed its attention to a new brick building that Oliver was erecting "to let out for Shops," but which was reputed to be intended as the future "Stamp Office." Leveling this to the ground, the mob then proceeded to the Stamp Distributor's home, beheaded the effigy and broke the windows fronting on the street, and then passed on to nearby Fort Hill where it burnt the effigy in a huge bonfire. Returning to the Oliver home, the crowd broke down the doors and streamed through the house in search for the owner, who, luckily for him, had prudently left. When Chief Justice Hutchinson and the sheriff of Suffolk County thereupon sought to persuade the mob to disperse, they were greeted by a volley of stones. The colonel of the militia regiment thereupon was ordered to beat the alarm to summon his regiment, but he informed Bernard that this order

[14] Jared Ingersoll to Richard Jackson, Nov. 3, 1765, *Ingersoll Stamp Act Correspondence* (New Haven, 1765), pp. 50–51.

would be impossible to execute since no drummer would dare to obey it and, anyhow, all the regimental drummers were also probably among the rioters.[15]

The next morning the governor again called together the Council and recommended that steps be taken to protect not only the lives of Oliver and his family, but his property as well. In reply, the members conceded the impotence of the government to take proper action, but nevertheless agreed that a proclamation should be issued for discovering the chief offenders in the riot and that the justices of the peace and the selectmen of the town should be assembled and ordered to use every means within their power to keep the peace. These steps were taken, but with no effect. In the afternoon, with the end of the Council meeting, the Stamp Distributor was approached by a group of gentlemen who strongly advised him to resign his office. They warned him that unless he did so "his House would be immediately Destroyed and his Life in Continual Danger." Without protection or reasonable expectation that it would be forthcoming, Oliver now authorized the group to declare publicly that he would immediately apply for leave to resign his post and would not act in it until receiving further orders.[16] In reporting the disturbances, Bernard declared:

Every one agrees that this Riot had exceeded all others known here, both in the Vehemence of Action and Mischievousness of Intention and never had any Mob so many Abettors of Consequence as this is supposed to have had. . . .[17]

After the Sons of Liberty of Massachusetts Bay had led the way, those of other colonies went into action, in each instance employing much the same means for forcing the resignations of the Stamp Distributors. Following the lead of Boston, an effigy of the stamp master, with a "boot" over his shoulder—in derision of Lord Bute—and the devil peeping out of it holding a Grenville stamp, was frequently raised by the people, as at Norwich and New London. At Newport the anger of the people was directed not only against Augustus Johnston, who without his knowledge had been

[15] Bernard to the Board of Trade, Aug. 15, 1765, Huntington Library Mss., H.M. No. 1947, pp. 35–43.
[16] Bernard to the Board of Trade, Aug. 16, 1765, *ibid.*, pp. 42–50.
[17] *Ibid.*

appointed Rhode Island Stamp Distributor, but against Martin Howard, a lawyer, and a Dr. Moffatt, both of whom were men of wealth who had spoken and written in defense of the Stamp Act. They were not only hung in effigy, but after this ceremony "a prodigious multitude" proceeded to Howard's home and, before departing, left it a wreck; the Moffatt home was treated in the same manner after its cellars were emptied of "a large quantity of fine old wine." The only thing that saved the house where Augustus Johnston was living was the fact that he was not its owner. But the mob was still not satisfied and proceeded to the lodging place of the collector of customs, John Robinson. Fortunately for him, he had taken refuge on board the man-of-war *Cygnet* in the harbor.[18]

In face of the spread of resistance throughout the colonies, Johnston resigned his Rhode Island office on August 29. His resignation was followed by that of James McEvers of New York and William Coxe of New Jersey. Zachariah Hood of Maryland was so thoroughly intimidated by the violent actions of mobs at Annapolis and Baltimore that he fled from the province and sought refuge in Flushing, Long Island, where late in November he was located and compelled to resign by the New York Sons of Liberty. On September 10 George Meserve of New Hampshire, on his return from England, was forced to give up his post, and on the 19th Jared Ingersoll of Connecticut was obliged to follow suit; on October 5 John Hughes of Pennsylvania signed a declaration that he would not act; so did George Saxby, inspector, and Caleb Lloyd, distributor, in South Carolina on the 28th. On the 30th Colonel George Mercer, just arrived in Virginia from England with his stamp master's commission, was compelled to agree not to use it; on November 12, John Parnham, the deputy for George Angus, the distributor for Georgia, signed a declaration that satisfied the populace; and finally, on November 16, upon landing at Wilmington, Dr. William Houston, distributor for North Carolina, was forced to resign.[19] Nor was violence restricted to the continental

[18] *Pennsylvania Gazette,* Sept. 12, 1765; William Almy to Elisha Story, Newport, August 29, 1765, Massachusetts Historical Society, Proceedings, LV (1922), 234–237.

[19] W. L. Saunders, *et al.* (eds.), *The Colonial Records of North Carolina* (10 vols., Raleigh, 1886–90), VII, 143. See the *Pennsylvania Gazette* for the months of September, October, and November for vivid accounts of the

colonies. The people of New Providence in the Bahamas were so determined that the local distributor should give up his office that, according to a news item, they threatened to bury him alive; upon his refusal they forced him into a coffin and thereupon lowered it into a grave which they began to fill up before the official yielded.[20]

But the contagion had assumed epidemic proportions. In Boston the mob now turned its vengeance upon those who in previous years had been active in enforcing the trade laws. The issue of some four years' standing involving the writs of assistance was now also revived. In this connection, it was charged by one of the opposition against the government that when he was in London some two years earlier he saw certain depositions that had been sent over to London by officers of the Crown, according to which the "whole Body of [Boston] Merchants had been represented as Smugglers." [21] Soon a clamor arose among those engaged in trade and quickly "descended from the Top to the Bottom of the Town." On the 26th rumors swept through the town that there would be action that night. These rumors were amply substantiated.

Toward evening a bonfire was lighted on King Street in front of the Town House as a signal for the gathering of the mob. Soon a great crowd was massed about it, crying "Liberty and Property." According to Governor Bernard, this was "the Usual Notice of their Intention to plunder and pull down a house." [22] After being well fortified with strong drink,[23] the populace moved off to the home occupied by Charles Paxton, marshal of the court of vice-admiralty. The owner diverted them to a tavern, where he purchased a barrel of punch. Now doubly fortified, they made their way to the home of a Mr. Story, the register of the vice-admiralty court. Entering the dwelling, they laid their hands on all the records of the court and consigned them to the fire, and then proceeded to wreck the house

---

actions of the mobs leading to the resignations of the American stamp distributors.

[20] New Haven advices, Oct. 11, *Pennsylvania Gazette,* Oct. 31, 1765.

[21] Bernard to the Board of Trade, Aug. 31, 1765, Huntington Library Mss., H.M. No. 1947, pp. 72–90. Bernard denied that any such sweeping charge as the above had been made in the depositions.

[22] *Ibid.* For Josiah Quincy, Jr.'s, account of the riot in his diary, see Mass. Hist. Soc., *Proc.* IV, 47–51; see also Hutchinson's "Summary of the Disorders," Massachusetts Archives, 26: 180–184.

[23] Thomas Hutchinson, *Hist. of Mass.,* p. 124.

and its contents.[24] Another mob plundered and wrecked the elegant new home of Benjamin Hallowell, Comptroller of the Customs, and consumed his wine. Then came the great adventure of the evening. The two mobs, having joined forces, in blind, drunken fury under the leadership of the shoemaker Ebenezer Mackintosh, moved upon the mansion of Thomas Hutchinson, Lieutenant Governor and Chief Justice of the province. Hutchinson, who was at supper at the time, was warned that his life was in danger. Sending away his family, he determined not to leave, "conscious that he had not in the least deserved to be made a party in regard to the Stamp Act or the Custom House." [25] But his eldest daughter soon returned and refused to go without him. Whereupon he withdrew.

Built in the spirit of the English houses erected by Inigo Jones, the Hutchinson home was one of the finest examples of domestic architecture in North America; massive in construction, it was buttressed as well as adorned with Ionic pilasters and surmounted with a large cupola. Smashing the heavy doors with broadaxes, the rioters swept into the house. Everything that they could not carry off was systematically destroyed.[26] A great collection of manuscripts, many of a public nature relating to the history of Massachusetts Bay from the earliest period down to Hutchinson's own days, was burned. Determined to wreck the building after disposing of its contents, men mounted the roof. It took three hours to dislodge the cupola and it was daybreak before more than a portion of the roof was uncovered, so sound was the construction. The rising of the sun alone called a halt to the night's activities.[27]

[24] Bernard to Board of Trade, Aug. 31, 1765, Huntington Library Mss.

[25] *Ibid.* Hutchinson was never a friend of the Stamp Act. As has been made clear in the preceding chapter, he had written in 1764 a lengthy and vigorous protest against the passing of an American Stamp Act and had sent it to Richard Jackson in London. (This is appended to the article by Professor Morgan on "Thomas Hutchinson and the Stamp Act," *New England Quarterly,* XXI, 480–492.) When the earlier riot took place in Boston over the act, he was not, significantly, singled out for attack. But his connection with the enforcement of the trade laws is clear. While employing language of great tact in connection with the issue that arose in 1761 over the writs of assistance that came before him as Chief Justice, he, nevertheless, refused to declare them void and, by referring the issue to England, was to that extent responsible for the declaration of their legality in the colonies.

[26] Bernard to the Board of Trade, Aug. 31, 1765, Huntington Library Mss.

[27] Hutchinson, *Hist. of Mass.,* p. 125. For a recent critical account of the

At Castle William, Governor Bernard now hurriedly summoned a meeting of the Council at Cambridge, but was induced to hold it at the Boston Town House when assured that the affair of the preceding night "had given such a turn to the Town that all Gentlemen in the Place were ready to support the Government in Detecting and punishing the Actors in the last horrid Scene." [28] Not a single participant, however, was ever brought to account, in spite of the rewards which were offered. When a warrant was issued to apprehend Mackintosh as "a chief actor in destroying the lieutenant-governor's house," Sheriff Greenleaf, who executed it, was surrounded by leading merchants and others of "property and character" who assured him that if the man was not released not a citizen would appear at nighttime to help provide security to the town.[29] Some six or eight other people of less consequence were, it is true, committed; but before their trial a crowd entered the home of the jailer and compelled him to surrender the keys. Yet, there were many in Massachusetts Bay, outside official circles, who would doubtless have agreed with the sentiments penned by the Reverend Gideon Hawley in a letter to Hutchinson: "When thousands, who never saw your Honor, perhaps never heard of the great humanity, integrity, and goodness of your Character, have exprest a mixture of grief and indignation at your . . . very abusive treatment, from an ill-diverted, lawless rabble, it would be unpardonable in me not to shew my sorrow and resentment upon the occasion." [30]

When the Stamp Act Congress met in New York on October 7, the moderates were in the majority. Although Massachusetts Bay chose among its delegates James Otis—one who in his openly avowed writing was prepared to grant to Parliament unlimited power and who even expressed his dislike of the Henry resolutions, but who in his daily actions was an extremist—it also sent Oliver Partridge and Brigadier Timothy Ruggles, both strong conservatives. Rhode Island was represented by Metcalf Bowler, Associate Justice of the Superior Court, and Henry Ward, secretary of the colony. Connecticut sent Eliphalet Dyer, a governor's assistant;

---

riots, see E. S. and H. M. Morgan, *The Stamp Act Crisis* (Chapel Hill, 1953), chap. VIII.

[28] Bernard to the Board of Trade, Aug. 31, 1765, Huntington Library Mss.

[29] Hutchinson, *Hist. of Mass.*, pp. 125–126, 140.

[30] Hawley to Hutchinson, Oct. 22, 1765, Mass. Arch., 25:37.

William Samuel Johnson, a distinguished member of the Anglican Church; and Judge David Rowland—all with conservative leanings, although Dyer, hailing from radical Windham, was deeply involved in the Susquehanna Company activities. The unofficial New York delegates numbered John Cruger, the brothers Robert R. and Philip Livingston, William Bayard, and Leonard Lispenard. Those from New Jersey, all irregularly chosen, were Robert Ogden, Speaker of the Assembly and like Ruggles an extreme conservative, Hendrick Fisher, and Joseph Borden. Pennsylvania sent John Dickinson, already prominent in provincial politics and soon to gain an intercolonial reputation for his *Letters of a Farmer in Pennsylvania;* John Morton, later a justice of the provincial Supreme Court; and George Bryan, destined to occupy a similar post and to enjoy even higher political honors. From Delaware came Caesar Rodney and Thomas MacKean, both to achieve prominence in political life; [31] like the delegates of New York and New Jersey, they were without formal credentials. From Maryland came William Murdock, Edward Tilghman, and Thomas Ringgold. The South Carolina delegates were Thomas Lynch and Christopher Gadsden, both extreme radicals, along with John Rutledge, at the time perhaps more moderate than his colleagues. [32] No delegates appeared from the provinces of Quebec, Nova Scotia, New Hampshire, Virginia, North Carolina, Georgia, East Florida, or West Florida. In New Hampshire the influence of the Wentworth family was still potent [33] and in Virginia, North Carolina, and Georgia the assemblies had adjourned before the invitation to attend the Congress was received. [34] As for the newer colonies, conditions were unfavorable for such political activity.

The first act of the Congress, an extralegal body, was to organize.

[31] Jacob Kollock was also designated to attend by the majority of the members of the General Assembly, not then in session, but did not appear.

[32] For the list of delegates see the official minutes of the Congress published in *Niles' Weekly Register* (Baltimore, 1812), II, 337. These minutes were prepared by John Cotton, clerk of the Congress.

[33] See the proceedings of June 20, 1765, in the New Hampshire House of Representatives (*ibid.,* II, 355).

[34] Governor Fauquier of Virginia, in view of the notoriety of the Henry resolutions, dissolved the Assembly on June 1, 1765; then, by a series of prorogations, after the election of burgesses, prevented it from meeting until November 1, 1766 (*Journals of the House of Burgesses, 1761–1765,* p. 364; *ibid., 1766–1769,* pp. 5–9).

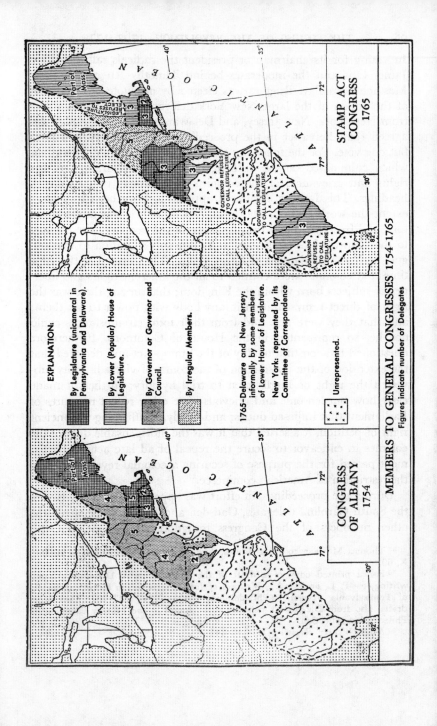

MEMBERS TO GENERAL CONGRESSES 1754–1765

Figures indicate number of Delegates

EXPLANATION:

By Legislature (unicameral in Pennsylvania and Delaware).

By Lower (Popular) House of legislature.

By Governor or Governor and Council.

By Irregular Members.

Unrepresented.

1765–Delaware and New Jersey: informally by some members of Lower House of legislature. New York: represented by its Committee of Correspondence.

CONGRESS OF ALBANY 1754

STAMP ACT CONGRESS 1765

In voting for its chairman or president the radicals rallied behind James Otis and the moderates behind Timothy Ruggles, both of Massachusetts Bay. Ruggles was elected by one vote, as the result of the action of the large New York delegation.[35] The committees from New York, New Jersey, and Delaware were seated, and it was agreed that thereafter in the proceedings each colony would have but one vote. For the following eleven days there were deliberations which culminated on the 19th in a series of "declarations of the rights and grievances of the colonists in America" under thirteen headings. This famous document appears to have been to a large extent the work of John Dickinson.[36] Although it was moderate in tone and freely admitted the allegiance of the people of the colonies to the Crown of Great Britain and "due subordination to that august body the parliament of Great Britain," it affirmed at the same time that colonials were entitled to all the inherent rights and liberties of subjects born within the Kingdom; that among these was the right of direct representation in any body with power to tax them; and that they were not, and from their local circumstances could not be, so represented in the House of Commons. It therefore questioned the constitutionality of the Stamp Act and declared that the extension of the jurisdiction of the courts of vice-admiralty subverted the right of Englishmen to trial by jury; further, it made clear how burdensome and grievous were other recent measures of Parliament that imposed duties; and finally, in affirming the ancient right of petition, it asserted that it was the indispensable duty of the colonies to endeavor to secure the repeal of all late acts of Parliament passed for the purpose of securing a colonial revenue and for the restriction of American commerce.[37]

During the proceedings an effort was apparently made by two of the South Carolina delegates, Gadsden and Lynch, to persuade the other members of the Congress to ignore Parliament, but this

[35] Thomas McKean to John Adams, Aug. 20, 1813, *Works of John Adams,* X, 60.

[36] For a printed copy of a draft of the declarations in Dickinson's handwriting, see P. L. Ford (ed.), *Writings of John Dickinson,* in Historical Society of Pennsylvania *Memoirs* (Philadelphia, 1895), XIV, 183–187. Two other drafts, also from Dickinson's pen, are to be found in the Library Company of Philadelphia collection.

[37] *Niles' Weekly Register,* II, 340–341.

failed.[38] It is, however, perhaps not without significance that Lynch should have been elected chairman of the committee for drawing up the address to the House of Commons, and Rutledge chairman of that for the address to the Lords. Robert R. Livingston, of New York, a great landholder and a bitter enemy of Lieutenant Governor Colden, headed the committee to frame the address to the King.[39] It will thus be noted that a subordinate role was assigned to the New England delegates in the actual proceedings of the Congress, although one of their members had been chosen to serve as presiding officer. Doubtless the violence that had characterized the opposition to the Stamp Act and Navigation Acts in both Massachusetts Bay and Rhode Island influenced the choice of the moderates. Although Otis was considered "the boldest and best speaker," he and other radicals were constantly held in check by those delegates, who in the words of McKean acted "as if engaged in a tratorous conspiracy." [40]

The addresses, framed by the committees after receiving "sundry amendments," and finally approved,[41] were all much more moderate

[38] J. C. Miller, *Origins of the American Revolution* (Boston, 1943), p. 138.

[39] The committees were composed of the following delegates: that for addressing the King, Robert R. Livingston, William Samuel Johnson, and William Murdock; that for addressing the Lords, John Rutledge, Edward Tilghman, and Philip Livingston; and that for addressing the House of Commons, Thomas Lynch, James Otis, and Thomas McKean (*Niles' Weekly Register*, II, 341).

[40] McKean to John Adams, Aug. 20, 1813, *Works of John Adams*, X, 60.

[41] It should be noted that the petitions to the King and to the House of Commons and the memorial to the House of Lords were addressed to them only by the freeholders of Massachusetts Bay, Rhode Island, New Jersey, Pennsylvania, Delaware, and Maryland—six out of the seventeen continental colonies, including Quebec, Nova Scotia, East Florida, and West Florida. Of the colonies represented by delegates that did not join in the addresses, those from Connecticut were instructed to form "no such junction with the other commissioners, as will subject you to the major vote of the commissioners present"; the New York delegates did not feel that they were authorized to sign for the General Assembly; and those of South Carolina were bound by instructions which read: "That the result of their consideration shall, at their return, be laid before the house [Commons House of Assembly] to be confirmed or not, as the house shall think proper" (*Niles' Weekly Register*, II, 338–340).

When it came to signing the petitions and the proceedings of the Congress by the officers of the Congress, only the clerk of the Congress, John Cotton, could be prevailed to affix his signature. President Ruggles, when called upon to do so by McKean of Delaware, refused to sign, signifying "it was against his *conscience.*" When McKean upbraided him, Brigadier Ruggles challenged him to a duel; but it never came off, since Ruggles, completely out of sympathy with in tone than the "declarations of rights and grievances." The latter were designed to rally all colonials behind the opposition to the Sugar and Stamp Acts; the addresses, on the other hand, were drawn up for the double purpose of attesting to the loyalty of Americans to the British constitution and asserting the need for relief as the result of the hardship caused by the recent legislation. While reference therein was made to the abridgement of the "invaluable rights and liberties" of the colonials, none of the addresses ventured to assert that the protested legislation was unconstitutional.[42] The petition to the House of Commons declared that the laws in question had deprived the colonials of "two privileges essential to freedom"—taxation by consent and trial by jury—but at the same time conceded that Americans "glory in being subjects of the best of Kings having been born under the most perfect form of government." [43] In fact, no one could have outdistanced the petitioners in their expression of loyalty to the government of Great Britain. They formally avowed:

That we esteem our connection with and dependence on Great Britain, as one of the greatest blessings, and apprehend the latter will be sufficiently secure, when it is considered that the inhabitants in the colonies have the most unbounded affection for his majesty's person, family and government, as well as for the mother country, and that their subordination to the parliament is universally acknowledged.[44]

the proceedings, left New York before dawn the next day (McKean to John Adams, Aug. 20, 1813, *Works of John Adams*, X, 60–61).

[42] The closest that any of the addresses came to asserting the unconstitutionality of the Stamp Act was in the petition to the King, in which the following statement is made: "The invaluable rights of taxing ourselves are not, we most humbly conceive, unconstitutional but confirmed by the Great Charter of English liberties" (*Niles' Weekly Register*, II, 342).

[43] *Ibid.*, p. 354.

[44] *Ibid.*

CHAPTER 8

Parliament's Strategic Retreat

DESPITE the admission by the Stamp Act Congress that the subordination of the people of the colonies to Parliament was "universally acknowledged,"[1] the termination of its proceedings was followed by no diminution whatsoever in the determination of the colonies to resist the authority of the British Government to levy American taxes. The presiding officer of the Congress, an arch-conservative, Brigadier Ruggles, was on his return home publicly censured by the House of Representatives for his refusal to endorse what he considered to be its radical proceedings.[2] Another conservative delegate, Speaker Ogden of the New Jersey Assembly, was not only burned in effigy in several New Jersey counties, but removed from his speakership and forced under fire to resign his seat in the Assembly.[3]

In fact, in all thirteen colonies, with the exception of Georgia, no man could any longer safely take issue with any position assumed by the popular party, now committed to preventing the distribution of stamps on November 1, 1765, when the Stamp Act was to go into effect. There is no question that the public was aroused. An anonymous American wrote to "a Gentleman in London":

[1] "Proceedings of the Stamp-Act Congress," *Niles' Weekly Register*, II, 354.

[2] For the reprimand of Ruggles by the Speaker of the House of Representatives, see the *Pennsylvania Gazette* for Feb. 27, 1766; for his defense, see *ibid.*, May 15, 1766.

[3] Thomas McKean to John Adams, Aug. 20, 1812, C. F. Adams, *The Works of John Adams* . . . (10 vols., Boston, 1850–56), X, 61; *Pennsylvania Gazette*, Dec. 5, 1765.

As soon as this shocking Act was known, it filled all British America . . . with Astonishment and Grief. . . . We saw that we, and our Posterity were sold for Slaves. . . . We considered the Act over and over . . . it was framed with the most deep laid inveterate Design for the entire Extirpation of Liberty in America . . . the meaning was dreadfully evident, and slavery, with all its terrible Train, fenced us in on every Side.[4]

As for the stamps, on September 23 fourteen boxes of them had arrived in Boston for use in Massachusetts Bay, New Hampshire, and Rhode Island. Without distributors to receive them, the boxes containing the stamps for Massachusetts Bay had been placed in Castle William, and the other boxes had been held in the harbor on board ship protected by two men-of-war. On October 5 the stamps for Pennsylvania, New Jersey, and Maryland had reached Philadelphia. All the ships in the harbor thereupon had flown their flags at half mast and the bells of the city had tolled throughout the day. Since there was no strong place for the reception of the stamps in the Quaker city, they had been transferred from the merchant ship that brought them to an armed sloop.[5] Then on October 22 the merchantman *Edward* had appeared in New York harbor with ten parcels of stamps for New York and Connecticut. With the news of their arrival there had immediately been posted throughout the city the following notice:

> Pro Patria
> The first Man that Either distrib-
> utes or makes use of Stampt Paper
> let him take care of his House,
> Person, & Effects
> Vox Populi
> We dare! [6]

With no one qualified by law to receive the consignment, most of the stamps here had also been temporarily transferred to the King's ships, and then, to ease the minds of the people, had been placed in the city hall in the custody of the municipal council.[7]

---

[4] *Pennsylvania Gazette,* Nov. 14, 1765.

[5] *Ibid.,* Oct. 10, 1765.

[6] E. B. O'Callaghan and B. Fernow (eds.), *Documents Relative to the Colonial History of the State of New York* (15 vols., Albany, 1853–87), VII, 770.

[7] *Ibid.,* p. 768.

November 1 was generally observed in America as a day of mourning. The bells tolled. In Boston, the sharp reaction of people of property to the riot of August 26 served to restrain the more lawless elements temporarily. However, the Sons of Liberty saw fit to assemble at the Liberty Tree. There they hung in effigy not only Grenville but a former Boston citizen, John Huske, who had removed to England, had become a member of Parliament, and was thought mistakenly to have proposed the American Stamp Act to Grenville. In the evening the effigies were bundled into a cart and, followed by thousands of people, were conveyed, first to the Town House where the Assembly was sitting, then to the gallows, and, after being suspended there, were cut down and destroyed.[8]

Only in New York City, in fact, was there any unusual display of violence on the day that the act legally went into force. In the evening several thousand people, carrying effigies of Lieutenant Governor Colden and the devil, marched up to the gate of Fort George. After challenging the garrison there, the crowd proceeded to break open Colden's coach house, took his carriage, and, after hanging the effigies, consigned them and the carriage to a great bonfire. Thence the mob streamed to the rented home of Major Thomas James of the Royal Artillery, who had not only been active in putting the fort in a condition to be defended, but had incautiously characterized the mob as a "Pack of Rascals" that he could drive out of the city with "four and twenty men." The Sons of Liberty forced their way into the house, stripping it of all its furnishings and the major's other personal possessions, all of which were used to rekindle the patriotic bonfire. The Major may well have owed his life to being safely behind the battlements of the fort at the time of the raid.[9]

In all the older continental colonies, even where violence did not take place, the radical elements, banded together under the name of Sons of Liberty,[10] assumed after November 1 *de facto* governing

[8] Thomas Hutchinson, *The History of the Province of Massachusetts Bay* . . . (London, 1828), pp. 135–136.

[9] Lieutenant Governor Colden to Secretary Conway, Nov. 5, 1765, *New York Colon. Doc.*, VII, 771; General Gage to the Earl of Granby, Nov. 6, 1765, C. E. Carter (ed.), *Correspondence of General Thomas Gage* (2 vols., New Haven, 1931–33), II, 311.

[10] The first group to rally under the name Sons of Liberty came into existence in Connecticut; this organization thereupon spread rapidly into other colonies.

authority. Although under the terms of the Stamp Act no court could be held, no ship leave port, or no newspaper appear without the use of stamps, nevertheless, during the last weeks of 1765 and the early months of 1766, a gradual nullification of the statute took place. As a result, courts here and there began to do business, ships began leaving their ports, and newspapers resumed publication—all without use of stamps. Yet remittances due to British merchants were withheld and a practical ban on trade relations between the mother country and the American colonies ensued.

What would be the answer of His Majesty's Government to this concerted resistance? When in July, 1765, the short-lived Grenville ministry was dismissed by the King, it was succeeded by one under the young and inexperienced Marquess of Rockingham.[11] The new ministry was composed of those who by and large had been in opposition to Grenville as Chancellor of the Exchequer and as leader of the House of Commons. Among them was General Henry Seymour Conway, outspoken opponent of Parliament's right to tax the colonies. This "lute string ministry, fit only for the summer," as Charles Townshend called it,[12] had the unpleasant as well as the unwelcome duty of upholding the dignity and the laws of the Empire in the face of the rising spirit of resistance in the New World to both the Sugar and Stamp Acts. In a very real sense it held the fate of the Empire in its hands. We have already considered the October deliberations of the Cabinet Council over the ominous news from America, and the consensus of opinion that these matters were "too

---

H. H. Trumbull, "Sons of Liberty in 1755," *The New Englander*, XXV, 308, 311; L. H. Gipson, *Jared Ingersoll: A Study of American Loyalism in Relation to British Colonial Government* (New Haven, 1920), pp. 156–157; Herbert Morais, "The Sons of Liberty in New York," in *The Era of the American Revolution*, ed. by R. B. Morris (New York, 1939), pp. 269–289.

[11] The Grenville dismissal had nothing to do with American affairs, but among other things involved a slight to the King's mother—in plans for a regency that would operate at any time that George was incapacitated as the result of illness—and a difference of opinion over appointments to office. *London Gazette*, July 10, 1765; *Annual Register, 1765*, pp. 42–45; Horace Walpole, *Memoirs of the Reign of George III* (4 vols., London, 1894), I, 335–342; W. S. Taylor and J. H. Pringle (eds.), *Correspondence of William Pitt* (4 vols., London, 1838–40), II, 315–317; Sir John Forescue (ed.), *Correspondence of King George the Third* . . . (6 vols., London, 1927–28), I, 162 ff.

[12] *Pitt Corresp.*, II, 315–317.

high" to be dealt with by the mere exercise of the powers of the Crown and must be referred to Parliament. One might have assumed that, with the meeting of Parliament on December 17, an effort would now be made by the ministry to submit to that body the official reports of the alarming reaction in America. However, the King's speech opening the session, as framed by the ministry, was a masterpiece of understatement. George III declared that

matters of importance have lately occurred in some of my colonies in America, which will demand the most serious attention of Parliament; and as further informations are daily expected from different parts of that country, of which I shall order the fullest accounts to be prepared for your consideration; I have thought fit to call you now together in order that opportunity may thereby be given to issue the necessary writs on the many vacancies that have happened in the House of Commons since the last session; so that the parliament may be full to proceed immediately, after the usual recess, on the consideration of such weighty matters as will then come before you.[13]

The reply to the address, as presented by Lord Cavendish in the House of Commons, was in much the same vein.[14] Although the press and all strangers were strictly barred from this session, and therefore the debates that then occurred in the House were not reported, it is clear from the correspondence of contemporaries that a sharp division took place in the House and that an attempt was made by Grenville, now leader of the opposition, to amend the Cavendish address so as to include the expression of

our just resentment and indignation at the outrageous tumults and insurrections which have been excited and carried on in North America, and at the resistance given by open and rebellious force to the execution of the laws in that part of his majesty's dominions. . . .[15]

He was, nevertheless, after an animated debate, led to withdraw the amendment since even such members as Charles Townshend, who spoke "with vehemence" in support of the Stamp Act, were not disposed to press at the time for any change in the address.[16]

[13] T. C. Hansard (ed.), *Parliamentary History of England* (36 vols., London, 1806–20), XVI, 83.
[14] *Ibid.*, p. 88.
[15] *Pitt Corresp.*, II, 351.
[16] George Cooke to Pitt, Dec. 17, 1765, *ibid.*, II, 350–352.

However, in the House of Lords, Phillip Yorke, Earl of Hardwicke, in moving an address of thanks to the King, took a more realistic view of the American crisis when he asserted that "the state of affairs in America . . . is indeed of the highest magnitude; if I had not heard that term so often misapplied, I should say the greatest in its extent and consequences, that ever came before parliament. . . ." [17] An effort was likewise made by the opposition among the peerage to alter this address along the lines of the Grenville amendment in the lower house, but it was not approved. In other words, most of the members of Parliament took the position that not until the fullest information had been secured on the actual situation in the colonies were they prepared to consider a course of action. As a result, the two houses soon adjourned until January 14 of the new year.

By the fall of 1765 it was apparent not only that Great Britain was faced with a political and constitutional crisis in the New World, but that her commercial interests were profoundly disturbed. In fact, so closely were these public and private interests joined in the public mind that it is impossible to separate them. A Bristol merchant reported in August: "The present Situation of the Colonies alarms every Person who has any Connection with them. . . . The Avenues of Trade are all shut up. . . . We have no Remittances, and are at our Witts End for Want of Money to fulfill our Engagement with our Tradesmen." [18] In the long run the growing commercial paralysis of trade between colonies and Great Britain was even more disadvantageous to the latter than the former. Anglo-American business was, in the main, done on credit. British North America, a rapidly developing area, was a heavy borrower. This debt balance was to tip the scales in favor of the colonials in their struggle to secure repeal of the Stamp Act. In the words of Horace Walpole:

But the weapon with which the Colonies armed themselves to most advantage, was the refusal of paying the debts they owed to our merchants at home, for goods and wares exported to the American provinces. These debts involved the merchants of London, Liverpool, Manchester, and other great trading towns, in a common cause with

[17] *Parl. Hist.*, XVI, 84.
[18] *Pennsylvania Gazette*, Oct. 24, 1765.

the Americans, who forswore all traffic with us, unless the obnoxious Stamp Act was repealed.[19]

These debts, amounting to some £4,000,000 sterling owing to British merchants on the part of colonials,[20] were now wielded as a club with telling force.

On December 6 the so-called Committee of Merchants of London, trading to North America through their chairman, the American-born Barlow Trecothick, addressed a memorial to the Mayor of London which pointed out that they not only faced the loss of their property in America but even the annihilation of the trade itself, and, in consequence thereof, called upon the city to petition Parliament to grant "every Ease and Advantage the North-Americans can with propriety desire. . . ." [21] In fact, early in the new year Parliament was inundated by petitions not only from the merchants of the leading commercial centers, such as London, Bristol, Liverpool, Manchester, Leeds, and Glasgow, but from most of the other trading towns and boroughs of Great Britain. These set forth their plight as well as that of many thousands of manufacturers, seamen, and others dependent upon them who were reported to be in dire distress as the result of the virtual stoppage of all commercial intercourse with the colonies.[22] These petitions ignored the constitutional issue and urged the modification, if not repeal, of the late acts relating to America in order to bring about a resumption of a trade that in the past had proved to be so mutually beneficial.[23]

[19] Walpole, *Memoirs*, I, 352.

[20] *Annual Register, 1766*, p. 36; *Parl. Hist.*, XVI, 205.

[21] *Pennsylvania Gazette*, Feb. 27, 1766. For a sketch of the career of Trecothick, see T. O. Jervey's "Barlow Trecothick," *South Carolina Historical Magazine*, XXII, 157–169.

[22] *Annual Register, 1766*, p. 35; F. J. Ericson, "The Contemporary British Opposition to the Stamp Act," Michigan Academy of Science, Arts and Letters, *Papers*, XXIX (1944), 489–505. A copy of the general letter (among the Rockingham papers), addressed by the London merchants "to the Outports & Manufacturing Towns" on December 6, 1765, to urge them to protest against the Stamp Act, has the following notation on the margin: "This letter concerted between the Marquess of R. and Mr. Trecothick" (Wentworth-Woodhouse Papers, R. 1, 310, Sheffield Reference Library). It would also appear that the agents of the Rockingham ministry were very active in persuading the towns to send up petitions against the Act, according to George Grenville (Grenville to Lord Botetourt, November 3, 1765, Grenville Letter Book, Huntington Library).

[23] See, for example, the petition of the merchants of London trading to

The ministry, less than lukewarm toward the Grenville legislation, was not unwilling to yield to these economic pressures at home. Nevertheless, it could hardly ignore the defiance of the government on the part of the colonials. Its position was, in truth, one of extraordinary delicacy. Were it to attempt to enforce the Stamp Act by the sword—a step which some of its members, such as Conway, had strenuously opposed and which Lord George Sackville (to become Lord Germain in 1770) had advocated—it risked uprisings in support of the colonials in many of the leading trading towns of England.[24] On the other hand, were it meekly to propose the repeal of the statute in the face of violence, such a course would, in the words of Horace Walpole, the friend of Conway, set "a precedent of the most fatal complexion." [25]

To chart a proper course for Parliament, many of the leading members of the ministry gathered during the Christmas recess at the London home of the Marquess of Rockingham.[26] It was there proposed that Parliament should first of all not only reaffirm its legislative power over America, but should provide that any one who by speaking or writing should impeach that authority would be guilty of high treason; then, with the supremacy of the government of the mother country thus asserted, a bill should be brought in to amend and explain the Stamp Act "so as to render the operation easy, and its provisions unexceptionable." Among the suggested amendments to the statute was one to provide that the duties specified in it could be paid in the local currency of the particular colony, instead of in sterling; another would limit trials for its violation to courts of record, thus excluding the jurisdiction of the courts of vice-admiralty; while a third would ease American merchants by either eliminating or greatly reducing the stamp duties on ship cockets and clearances.[27] There was, however, sharp disagreement

North America, *Parl. Hist.*, XVI, 133–135; see also Massachusetts Historical Society, *Proceedings*, LV, 215–223, for other documents.

[24] Walpole, *Memoirs*, pp. 352–353.

[25] *Ibid.*

[26] In addition to Rockingham, who was First Lord of the Treasury, there were General Conway, Secretary of State for the Southern Department; William Dowdswell, Chancellor of the Exchequer; the Earl of Egremont, First Lord of the Admiralty; Charles Yorke, Attorney General; and the Earl of Dartmouth, President of the Board of Trade.

[27] John Adolphus, *The History of England* (London, 1805), I, 197–198.

even within this small group of high officials on these specific measures, and an understanding was reached only on the general terms of the King's speech to be delivered as soon as Parliament had reconvened.

If the speech from the throne on December 17 seemed diffident, that of January 14 was even more evasive. Reference was made to the fact that "matters of importance had happened in America, which demand the most serious attention of Parliament," and stress was also placed on the orders that had been sent to the provincial governors and commanders of the troops to suppress riots and tumults. But no specific course of action was suggested. The whole problem was thrown into Parliament's lap.[28]

The debates that followed in the House of Commons and the House of Lords on the nature of the replies to be made to the speech from the throne were among the most crucial that took place in Parliament in the entire course of the eighteenth century. While William Pitt had not been present either at the time of the debate on the bill to extend stamp taxes in America in the spring of 1765, or at the session in December when the problem of enforcement of the act first came before Parliament, he felt impelled, in spite of illness, to take his place in the lower house at this juncture. Writing from Bath to a friend on January 9, he declared that "if I can crawl, or be carried, I will deliver my mind and heart upon *the state* of America." [29] As a result, the eyes of all were upon the Great Commoner unhappily afflicted in body—and in mind. While he in no way stood sponsor for the Rockingham ministry and was hypersensitive to any such intimation, he had within the same circle many great admirers and was himself in sympathy with the critical attitude of these friends of the Grenville legislation. He proceeded to excoriate the Stamp Act. While denying that Parliament had the right to tax the colonies, he asserted, with an ambiguity characteristic of so many British public men, "the authority of this kingdom over the colonies, to be sovereign and supreme, in every circumstance of government and legislation whatsoever." In replying to Grenville, who stressed the evil consequences that would surely

---

[28] *Parl. Hist.,* XVI, 91–93.
[29] Pitt to Thomas Nuthall, Jan. 9, 1766, *Corresp. of Pitt,* II, 362.

follow the repeal of the act, founded as it was, he insisted, on principles of justice and equity, Pitt retorted:

I have been charged with giving birth to sedition in America. . . .
I rejoice that America has resisted. Three millions of people, so dead
to all feelings of liberty, as voluntarily to submit to be slaves, would
have been fit instruments to make slaves of the rest. . . . If the gentleman does not understand the difference between internal and external
taxes, I cannot help it . . . the gentleman asks, when were the
colonies emancipated? But I desire to know, when were they made
slaves? . . . In a good cause, on a sound bottom, the force of this
country can crush America to atoms. . . . But on this ground, on the
Stamp Act, when so many here will think it a crying injustice, I am
one who will lift up my hands against it. . . . America, if she fell,
would fall like a strong man. She would embrace the pillars of the
state, and pull down the constitution with her. . . . Upon the whole,
I will beg leave to tell the House what is really my opinion. It is, that
the Stamp Act be repealed absolutely, totally, and immediately.[30]

Stirred by this tremendous blast and influenced by the presence
in the House of a powerful representation from the leading trading
towns, Parliament finally framed an address which was as mild in
tone as was the speech from the throne. Conway thereupon submitted to the consideration of that body the official papers describing the American riots and the breakdown of orderly procedures.
On January 28 Benjamin Franklin appeared under orders before
the Committee of the Whole House for the purpose of supplying
additional information respecting New World developments.

The "examination" of Franklin was in a sense a trump card held
by the ministry. For this consummate diplomat was provided with
an unparalleled opportunity to discredit the idea of levying stamp
duties upon the colonials. In the course of his lengthy testimony he
very significantly voiced the view that the distinction between internal and external taxation on the part of Parliament had been
fundamental in the eyes of the colonials. He, however, hastened to
declare most prophetically: "Many arguments have been lately
used here to shew them that there is no difference, and that if you
have no right to tax them internally, you have none to tax them
externally, or make any other law to bind them. At present they do

[30] For Pitt's complete address, see *Parl. Hist.*, XVI, 97–108.

not reason so, but in time they may possibly be convinced by these arguments." Franklin's analysis of the causes of the late war revealed how differently the colonials were now viewing that conflict from ten years earlier:

I know the last war is commonly spoke of here as entered into for the defence, or for the sake of the people of America. I think it is quite misunderstood. It began about the limits between Canada and Nova Scotia, about territories which the crown indeed laid claim, but were not claimed by any British colony. . . . We had therefore no particular concern or interest in the dispute. As to the Ohio, the contest there began about your right of trading in the Indian country, a right you had by the Treaty of Utrecht, which the French infringed . . . they took a fort which a company of your merchants, and their factors and correspondents, had erected there to secure that trade, Braddock was sent with an army to re-take that fort . . . and to protect your trade. It was not until after his defeat that the colonies were attacked. They were before in perfect peace with both French and Indians. . . .[31]

Other contemporary statements, destined to become embodied in the American national tradition, constituted an even more drastic reinterpretation of the causes of the war.[32]

After the American correspondence and the oral testimony of Franklin and others had been carefully considered, certain resolutions were proposed in both houses of Parliament. On February 3 Conway opened the debate in the Commons. He now supported the "right" of Parliament to tax the colonials, but questioned the "Justice, Equity and Expediency" of doing so; Blackstone contended that Parliament is "the Representative of the Nation and not of Individuals"; Burke pointed out that the "British Empire must be governed on a Plan of Freedom for it will be governed by no other"; and Grenville warned that the Navigation Act had been injected

[31] *Ibid.*, XVI, 154, 158–159.

[32] See, for example, an article that first appeared in the Boston *Gazette* and was reprinted in the *Pennsylvania Gazette* of January 9, 1766. The writer denied the validity of the view—a view expressed by all responsible British political leaders in 1755—that the chief purpose of the military efforts on land and sea was to protect the colonials from the encroachments of France upon them in North America. Instead, it insisted that selfish commercial interests of the mother country were the chief factors that led England to engage in war with France—a view still voiced by some writers.

into the issue in view of the contention embodied in the "Virginia Pamphlet" that this was as much a tax on Americans as the Stamp Tax.[33]

On the 10th of this month, four resolutions were presented to the House of Lords from its Committee of the Whole, designed to re-affirm the authority of Parliament over British North America and to deny the validity of the votes and resolutions of the assemblies that had called into question the constitutional dependence of the colonies upon the mother country. This led to the first full debate that has been recorded in that House on the Stamp Act issue. In presenting the resolutions, the Duke of Grafton declared that the first resolution, later to be embodied in the Declaratory Act, had been reported because the right of taxing America had been ques-tioned not only by the colonials, "but by persons here, some of whom were eminent, and possibly the highest in the line they Tread." Lord Camden, Chief Justice of the Court of Common Pleas, was one of the few members of Parliament that Grafton had in mind. Taking issue with this resolution, Camden in the course of his remarks made clear that there were many things that Parliament as the supreme body could not do. To him taxation and representa-tion were inseparable. This idea he expanded when the resolution in question appeared in the form of the Declaratory Bill. To him the Bill was

absolutely illegal, contrary to the fundamental laws of nature and con-trary to the fundamental laws of this constitution . . . [for] taxation and representation are inseparably united; God hath joined them, no British parliament can separate them . . . it is itself an eternal law of nature . . . there is not a blade of grass, which when taxed, was not taxed by the consent of the proprietor. . . . For these reasons, my lords, I can never give my assent to any bill for taxing the American colonies, while they remain unrepresented, for as to . . . virtual repre-sentation, it is so absurd, as not to deserve an answer; I therefore pass it over with contempt.

However, it did not follow, this eminent jurist added, that the colonies could claim "an independence on this country, or that they have a right to oppose acts of legislature in a rebellious manner, even though the legislature has no right to make such acts." [34]

If Lord Camden planted his reasoning upon divine and natural laws, the Lord High Chancellor, Northington; the Chief Justice of the King's Bench, Baron Mansfield; and Baron Lyttelton warned of the implications of a priori reasoning of this type. Lyttelton pointed out that such Americans as Otis denied the distinction between external and internal taxes and that "if this be admitted, the same reasoning extends to all acts of parliament. The only question before your lordships is, whether the American colonies are a part of the dominions of the crown of Great Britain? If not, the parliament has no jurisdiction, if they are, as many statutes have declared them to be, they must be proper objects of our legislature. . . ." [35] The Lord High Chancellor was also moved to answer Camden. "Upon doctrines . . . so new, so unattainable, and so unconstitutional, I cannot sit silent," he declared. "The noble lord lays it down that the Americans have an exclusive right to lay taxes on themselves, and thinks we are not to meddle with them. . . . My lords, I seek for the liberty and constitution of this kingdom no farther back than the Revolution [of 1688]: There I make my stand. And in the reign of King William an act was passed avowing the power of this legislature over the colonies." [36] Finally, Chief Justice Mansfield laid down two propositions which he felt would not be seriously questioned:

1st, that the British legislature, as to the power of making laws, represents the whole British Empire, and has authority to bind every part and every subject without the least distinction, whether such subjects have a right to vote or not, or whether the law binds places within the realm or without.

2nd, that the colonists, by the conditions on which they migrated, settled, and now exist, are more emphatically subjects of Great Britain than those within the realm; and that the British legislature have in every instance exercised their right of legislation over them without any dispute or question till the 14th of January last.

The Chief Justice then went on to say:

[34] *Parl. Hist.*, XVI, 177–181.
[35] *Ibid.*, pp. 166–167.
[36] *Ibid.*, pp. 170–171.

But there are many statutes laying taxes in America; I know no difference between laying internal and external taxes; but if such differences should be taken, are not the acts giving duties, customs, and erecting a post office, to be considered as laying an internal tax? . . . Before I conclude I will take the liberty of laying down one proposition viz:

When the supreme power abdicates, the government is dissolved.[37]

When the great debate came to an end early in March, there were few members of Parliament who were prepared to deny that the body had the right to levy taxes on the colonies. The Declaratory Bill, affirming that right and declaring utterly null and void all resolutions of the colonial assemblies to the contrary, passed the House of Commons without a division, so unanimous was the sentiment in favor of it; in the House of Lords, where a division was sought, only five peers could be found to vote against it, among them Lord Camden and the Earl of Shelburne. On March 18 it became a law.[38] As to the repeal of the Stamp Act, in view of the all but unanimous sentiment in favor of the *right* of taxation of the colonials by Parliament, the ground for this could be sought only in the *inexpediency* of the measure. Upon this ground the ministry was able to rally a large majority, prompted by two considerations: one was that to enforce the Act would involve the use of armed force against fellow countrymen; another, and equally powerful, was the fact that, if civil war did ensue, British mercantile and manufacturing interests, already heavily stricken by American non-intercourse, would be placed in an even more desperate plight.

Nevertheless, few bills have ever been more bitterly debated in the House of Lords than was the repeal bill. When on March 11 the vote was taken in that body to commit it, the resolution was carried by a majority of but thirty-four. Even then a group of those opposed, including Pitt's brother-in-law, Lord Temple, placed in the record a series of ten resolutions embodying their conviction that a repeal, in the words of Governor Bernard of Massachusetts, "would make the authority of Great Britain [in America] con-

[37] *Ibid.*, pp. 172–176.
[38] 6 George III, c. 12. The act is to be found in C. Eyre and A. Strahan (eds.), *The Statutes at Large* (10 vols., London, 1786), VII, 571.

temptible thereafter." As to the objections of the North American colonies, as embodied in their resolutions, "that they are not represented in the parliament of Great Britain," the protestors affirmed that were the validity of this argument granted it would also extend "to all other laws of what nature soever, which . . . parliament has enacted, or shall enact . . . and must (if admitted) set them absolutely free from any obedience to the power of the British legislature." They pointed out that the hardship of the Stamp Act could not be fairly urged since its estimated income, upon the basis of the schedules adopted, would be but some £60,000 a year, which, divided between at least 1,200,000 people, would mean but an average per capita tax of a shilling a year—or about one third of a day's earnings on the part of every American laborer and manufacturer. In this connection they quoted from a letter written by the commander in chief of the British forces in North America, General Gage, who expressed succinctly the view of the colonials:

That the question is not of the inexpediency of the Stamp Act, or of the inability of the colonies to pay the tax, but that it is unconstitutional, and contrary to their rights, supporting the independency of the provinces, and not subject to the legislative power of Great Britain.[39]

Despite such objections, however, the repeal bill passed both houses and received the King's signature on the same day that the Declaratory Act became law. The statute is brief and limits itself to stating that the continuance of the Stamp Act would be attended with "many Inconveniences, and may be productive of Consequences greatly detrimental to the Commercial Interests of these Kingdoms," and for that reason was made void.[40] The confusion and retreat of Parliament signalized in its enactment were little relieved by the unctuous phrases of the Declaratory Act. As for America, it was now on the march to free itself of outside control, a first step on the road to independence.

[39] *Parl. Hist.*, XVI, 181–188.
[40] The repeal act is listed as 6 George III, c. 11, *Statutes at Large*, VII, 571.

CHAPTER 9

Old and New Northern Colonies

BEFORE turning to the next phase of the American Revolutionary movement, it may be instructive to examine the various colonial establishments in the New World, to consider their special problems, financial stability, and competence to care for their more local needs and interests unaided by the mother country. For, despite economic and social differences, the thirteen colonies eventually did unite to resist Great Britain, while still other British colonies in the New World did not join them. A survey of their internal development may not only serve to throw light upon the extent to which they had attained political maturity by 1767, but also upon the reason why their paths diverged. The colonies fell into two categories. Some were by this date far removed from the status of infant plantations; others had hardly taken the first steps or learned the first lessons in self-government.

THE PROVINCE OF QUEBEC

From 1760, when the Marquis de Vaudreuil surrendered to General Amherst, down to 1763, Canada remained under British military rule. With the issuance of the Proclamation of 1763, along with a new commission and new instructions to General James Murray, who had acted as military governor, the so-called Province of Quebec was created.[1] The Proclamation held out the prospect of large-scale immigration into the province of English-speaking people, to be encouraged by the setting up of a general assembly, by the ex-

[1] A. L. Burt, *The Old Province of Quebec* (Minneapolis, 1933), pp. 74–101.

116

tension of the laws of England, and by generous grants of land. In other words, old French Canada was to be remodeled into a British colony.[2] But it was found that none of these objectives could be achieved. Few English-speaking people could be induced to settle in the midst of over 70,000 French-speaking inhabitants [3] whose mores were fundamentally different from those of the people of the old British colonies to the southward. In fact, such English-speaking people as had come with the army or arrived since 1763 were not interested in land cultivation but rather in merchandizing or tavern-keeping.[4] It soon became clear to both Murray and to his successor, Guy Carleton, that the Province of Quebec was not ripe for an English representative form of government, and that to attempt to establish it under existing conditions would have the effect of placing the entire population at the mercy of a handful of what was felt to be rapacious outsiders, who alone under the restrictions of English law, especially the Test Acts, could be elected to an assembly. Instead, efforts were concentrated on making the recently conquered people content with their lot.

While the old French taxes *"lots et vents"* and the *"cens et rentes"* were collected, as well as the "fifths" and "twelfths," these were so trivial in amount that Lieutenant Governor Carleton in the spring of 1767 declared in a letter to the Earl of Shelburne "that the expenses of this colony fall entirely on His Majesty's Treasury." [5] Not only was its tax burden light but its desire for a French Roman Catholic bishop was met by the return from France in that capacity of Jean Olivier Briand, the former Vicar-General, after election by the Quebec chapter and proper consecration. Courts of common pleas were also set up that determined cases agreeable to equity rather than according to the strict principles of English law; Ca-

[2] *Ibid.*, p. 82.

[3] The total Roman Catholic population of the province in 1766 was, according to Governor Murray, 76,275, including 7,400 Indians. Murray to Shelburne, Aug. 30, 1766, Shelburne Papers, 64:317–321, Clements Library.

[4] According to Governor Murray only nineteen Protestant families in 1766 were living on the land outside of Quebec and Montreal. Most of the rest of the Protestants, outside of the army, he reported, were either "Traders, mechanics and publicans," who resided in the towns and were of "mean education," or disbanded soldiers. As a lot, he thought them "the most immoral collection of men I ever knew" (*ibid.*).

[5] Shelburne Papers, 55:307–51.

nadians were permitted to act as advocates in court proceedings and were likewise admitted to the juries; and the people of the parishes were now permitted to elect bailiffs and sub-bailiffs, who performed the duties roughly of English constables. While these efforts to conciliate the French Canadians were being pushed forward, the governor, the British garrisons, and the British trading interests were involved in fierce disputes. The business group pressed for the fulfillment of the promise to establish an assembly to take over the duties of the nominated legislative council.

In the midst of these controversies, Murray was recalled in 1766 and Carleton took over the administration. Clearly, many of the steps that Murray had taken to improve conditions in the province for the great mass of the people were *ultra vires* and yet highly necessary. What would the government at home do to clarify the situation? Writing to Carleton on June 20, 1767, Shelburne, Secretary of State for the Southern Department, declared:

As the right Administration of Government is a matter of the greatest importance to that Province, the Improvement of its Civil Constitution is under the most serious and deliberate Consideration . . . of his Majesty's Privy Council. Every Light which can be procured on this Subject will be material . . . which can tend to elucidate how far it is practicable and expedient to blend the English with the French Laws in order to form such a System as shall at once be equitable and convenient both for His Majesty's Old and New Subjects in order to the whole being confirmed and finally established by Authority of Parliament.[6]

But work on a permanent constitution for the province was not to be hurried. In fact, it was not until 1774 that Parliament, in the midst of the American crisis, finally passed the Quebec Act.

THE PROVINCE OF NOVA SCOTIA

With the expulsion of the Acadians during the course of the late war, all portions of the Province of Nova Scotia had been opened for colonization. The response on the part of New Englanders, who knew of the fertility of the once flourishing Acadian farmlands, was prompt. Even before the peace of 1763, families from Massachusetts Bay, New Hampshire, Connecticut, and Rhode Island were making

[6] Shelburne Papers, 53:117–22.

their way into the province under the inducements of Governor Charles Lawrence's proclamation of 1759 offering lands on agreeable terms. Others followed. Many were husbandmen; some were interested in the fisheries; and a small minority, men of wealth, were mere land speculators.[7] Outside of the city of Halifax and the smaller communities established through the exertions of the British government along the eastern shore between 1749 and 1754 the province was in 1759 still largely depopulated. But by the end of 1763 it numbered close to 9,000;[8] by 1766 somewhat over 11,000[9] and by 1775 almost 20,000, three fourths of whom were New Englanders,[10] who introduced their townships and Congregational churches. Yet the New England men, numerous as they were by 1765, were impelled to acknowledge the binding power of the British connection and the authority of the provincial government— made up of the governor and Council, the Assembly, and the courts—centered at Halifax. Therefore, in spite of some hostility displayed here and there to the Stamp Act, it was enforced in Nova Scotia as well as in the province of Quebec.[11]

Nova Scotia was still a financial liability to the mother country, and from its beginnings as a British buffer province in 1749 had enjoyed a yearly parliamentary grant to meet most of the ordinary expenses of conducting the provincial government. In 1766 this grant amounted to £4,936 3s. 5d.[12] Funds for defraying extraordinary expenses, such as those incurred for the payment of members of the Assembly as well as for the encouragement of agriculture and the fisheries, for the making of roads and the establishment of new settlements, and for the care of unfortunates, were in theory to be raised by various import duties and license fees. These levies, however, did not meet the public expectations and, despite the sub-

[7] J. B. Brebner, *The Neutral Yankees of Nova Scotia* (New York, 1937), pp. 24–29.

[8] *Ibid.*, p. 64.

[9] The total number of inhabitants of Nova Scotia in 1766 was 11,272, including 1,500 Indians and 500 "Neutral French" or Acadians, according to figures submitted by President Benjamin Green of the Provincial Council to the Board of Trade in his letter of Aug. 24 (Shelburne Papers, 51:371).

[10] W. B. Kerr, "The Merchants of Nova Scotia and the American Revolution," *Canadian Historical Review*, XIII, 20.

[11] Brebner, *Neutral Yankees of Nova Scotia*, pp. 157–162.

[12] Governor William, Lord Campbell, to Shelburne, Apr. 4, 1767, Shelburne Papers, 55:182–192.

ventions from the mother country, the young colony was burdened with debt.[13]

In 1766 Newfoundland was still a great vacant island except for St. John's and the scattered fishing villages along the highly indented coast. Its government was also rudimentary. The governor, as in the past, was a naval officer who came to the island in a ship of war late in the spring and departed early in the fall to convoy to their destination the sack ships laden with fish. In addition, there were resident commissioners of oyer and terminer, as well as justices of the peace, and other minor officials; but the population of some 15,000 people was, according to a representation of the Board of Trade of April 29, 1765, to a great extent a law unto itself. The Lords Commissioners complained that too many of the people gave themselves up to debauchery and violence.[14] According to Captain Griffith Williams, not only had numbers of the inhabitants welcomed the French with open arms when the latter seized the island in 1762 in the midst of war, but they or others had appropriated most of the harbors and fishing conveniences belonging to the "bankers" who came each year from fishing towns of western England.[15] Admittedly, eighteenth-century Newfoundland was a lawless island, but the courage of its inhabitants matched their belligerence.

The chief wealth of the island was still based, as two hundred years earlier, upon the cod that swarmed its coasts and surrounding shallow banks as well as the shores of Labrador, its political dependency. The major problem which commanded the attention of Commodore Palliser, the governor of the island in 1766, was posed by the French who, now that peace had returned, crowded not only the islands of St. Pierre and Miquelon but also the coasts of northern Newfoundland, and sought likewise to appropriate the best of the cod fisheries off Labrador. In this latter enterprise, they were aided by New Englanders, who came that year in some three hundred ships to the Gulf of St. Lawrence, ostensibly to whale, but in fact to catch the Labrador cod in order to supply the waiting French vessels forbidden by treaty to approach the Labrador shores. The

[13] *Ibid.*
[14] *Papers Relating to Newfoundland* (London, 1793), p. 5.
[15] *Account of the Island of Newfoundland* (London, 1765), pp. 9–10.

New Englanders went so far, according to official reports, as to destroy the English fishing works located on these shores, to fire the woods, and to do "every kind of mischief." As a result, Palliser felt obliged to dispatch a ship of war in 1766 to warn them away from these shores and to send them back to their whaling.[16]

THE PROVINCE OF NEW HAMPSHIRE

While the Provinces of Quebec and Nova Scotia and the island of Newfoundland were financially dependent upon the mother country, the royal Province of New Hampshire—with a representative Assembly and a population in 1767 of somewhat over 50,000 people settled in 101 towns—was under ordinary peacetime conditions a self-sustaining colony.[17] In common with some other continental colonies, New Hampshire had received rather generous reimbursement from the British government for the extraordinary expenses incurred in the recent war. By shrewdly keeping much of this money in London on interest, the colony found itself in the fortunate position of being able to discharge all its war issues of bills of credit as these became due. As a result, Governor John Wentworth could report to the Earl of Shelburne early in 1768 that, by reason of ample funds still in England, the remaining obligations could be met. He thereupon added: "The Treasury having discharged all the Paper Bills, as provided for by Government will then be ballanc'd without either Debt against, or stock in Favor of the Province." [18]

What cod was to Newfoundland, the forests were to New Hampshire.[19] Wentworth, who had traversed much of this province, declared that it was "wonderfully cloathed with Forest Trees . . . Firs of many Sorts, Oaks . . . Beach, Ash, Maple, Walnut, Birch, Acacia, Cherry, Poplin, Hornbeam, growing to incredible Length & Diameter and good in Kind. . . . " [20] The lumber secured from

---

[16] Commodore Palliser to the Board of Trade, Oct. 21, 1766, Shelburne Papers, 51:253–265.

[17] Governor John Wentworth to the Earl of Shelburne, Mar. 25, 1768, Shelburne Papers, 85:164–179.

[18] *Ibid.*

[19] See R. G. Albion, *Forests and Sea Power . . . 1652–1862* (Cambridge, Mass., 1926), chap. VI; and L. H. Gipson, *The British Empire Before the American Revolution* (8 vols., Caldwell, Ida., and New York, 1936–54), III, chap. II.

[20] Shelburne Papers, 85:164–179.

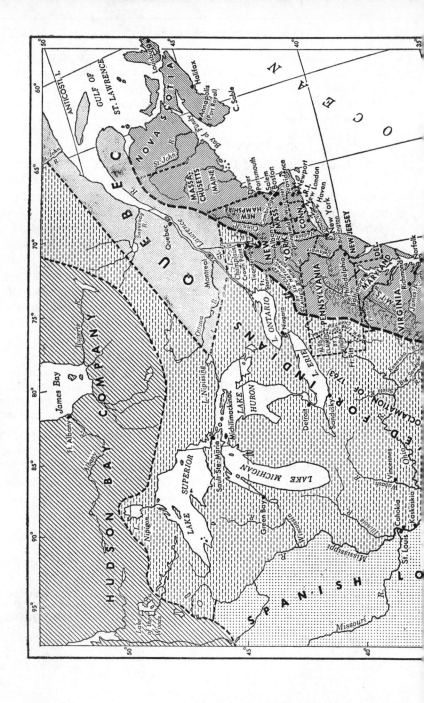

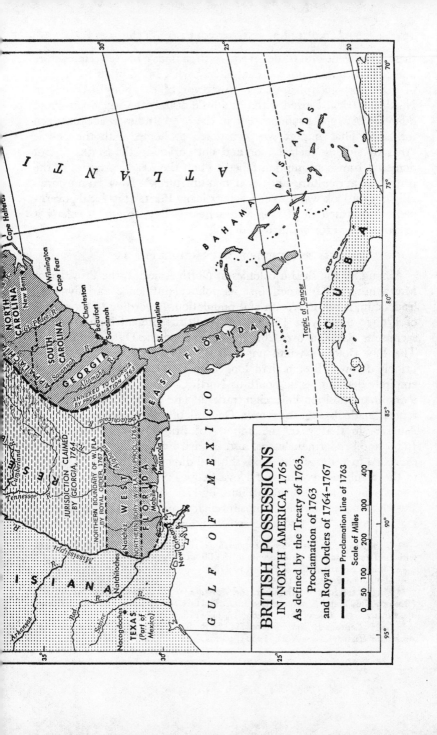

BRITISH POSSESSIONS
IN NORTH AMERICA, 1765

As defined by the Treaty of 1763,
Proclamation of 1763,
and Royal Orders of 1764–1767

– – – Proclamation Line of 1763

Scale of Miles

0   50 100   200   300   400

these trees went into trade. Wentworth, a native of New Hampshire and a man of exceptional character [21] who, in addition to his post of governor, occupied that of Surveyor of the King's Woods in North America, viewed with not a little dismay the fact that a great quantity of wood products sent to the West Indies was exchanged for rum. That import was consumed at home, with the people "thereby sinking their Labor and not enriching the State." [22] But domestic rum consumption failed to halt the steady progress of the people in agriculture and local manufactures.[23] New Hampshire's religious outlook was also characteristically Puritan; its local government conformed to that of Massachusetts Bay, to which colony it likewise looked for political leadership.

THE PROVINCE OF MASSACHUSETTS BAY

Among all the British colonies in North America, the Province of Massachusetts Bay stood first in political influence and dynamic leadership, if not in wealth and population. According to the census of 1765,[24] there were 184 towns within the present limits of Massachusetts Bay and over 200 if one included the District of Maine. The Bay Colony's white population totaled close to 250,000. Its principal town, Boston, had long been the heart of a commercial empire extending as far south as North Carolina. Once it had held a dominant position in foreign trade. As late as 1743, according to a report made by the Surveyor General of the Customs in North America in that year, the imports of British manufactures, East India goods, German linens, and Madeira wines into the province exceeded in value all the goods shipped directly from the Old World to the combined colonies of Nova Scotia, New York, New Jersey, Pennsylvania, and North Carolina. By 1766 the port of Philadelphia was challenging Boston's long supremacy, and New York was pressing forward.[25] The town, nevertheless, was still considered the most

[21] L. S. Mayo, in his *John Wentworth* (Cambridge, Mass., 1921), sets forth with understanding the chief events in the life of Wentworth.

[22] Albion, *Forests and Sea Power,* p. 175.

[23] Shelburne Papers, 85:164–179.

[24] This is set forth in detail in the *Abstract of the Census of Massachusetts* (Boston, 1860) and is summarized in A. B. Hart (ed.), *Commonwealth History of Massachusetts* (New York, 1928), II, 112–113.

[25] L. H. Gipson, *British Empire*, III, 9; R. B. Morris (ed.), *Encyclopedia of American History* (New York, 1953), p. 487.

important distributing center within the British Empire outside the mother country. By means of the prosperity that came to the province, following a temporary postwar depression, the people as the result of their industry and profitable trade found themselves by the beginning of 1770 not only freed of their war debts but in possession of a fund arising from the sale of provincial lands that obviated the need for taxes.[26] The progressive lightening of their public burdens is indicated by Governor Bernard's official report on the financial situation of Massachusetts Bay in the spring of 1767. This shows that it was possible for the Assembly to relieve the people of the excess taxes that had previously been levied to meet the provincial war debt.[27] The following year the governor was able to inform the Earl of Hillsborough that the debt of the colony, now amounting to but £75,000 sterling, could easily be liquidated in two years by continuing to pay the usual sum into a sinking fund as in former years.[28] By 1770, according to Lieutenant Governor Hutchinson, some £40,000 left as a provincial debt—beyond the liquidated war debt—could be met by a capitation tax that would not exceed 6s. a head.[29] But it did not seem politically expedient to take this step, if for no other reason than that the existence of any kind of a debt could be urged as one reason among others for opposing Parliamentary imposts.

Nevertheless, the province had never been in a more flourishing state. The fact that by 1768 bills of exchange on London actually stood at par, without the usual 2 per cent discount to pay charges, indicated that the balance of trade was now in favor of Massachusetts Bay.[30] Indeed, this colony was effectively capitalizing on its hard-money policy; for, alone of all the British continental colonies, it maintained a specie currency and each year, in the course of trade, drew from Spain, Portugal, the West Indies, and the other colonies such a quantity of gold and silver as to have "obtained the name of the silver money colony." [31] In fact, according to Bernard,

[26] Thomas Hutchinson, *The History of The Province of Massachusetts Bay* . . . (London, 1828), pp. 349–350.

[27] This report on public finance is contained in Bernard's letter to the Earl of Shelburne of Mar. 2, 1767 (Shelburne Papers, 55:154–165).

[28] Bernard to Hillsborough, July 16, 1768, *ibid.*, 85:201–204.

[29] Hutchinson, *Hist. of Mass.*, p. 350.

[30] Shelburne Papers, 85:201–204.

[31] Hutchinson, *Hist. of Mass.*, p. 350.

some businessmen in 1768 considered the flood of specie an embarrassment. "I have heard it averred by a Gentleman well acquainted with Money," he wrote Hillsborough, "that greater Inconveniences arose to the Trade here from abundance of Specie than from the want of it. . . . It is certain that there is no Appearance of the want of Money at present." [32]

THE COLONY OF RHODE ISLAND

The Colony of Rhode Island had also experimented with a paper currency in the course of the eighteenth century, but unlike Massachusetts had continued to favor this type of circulating medium. As a result of the gradual depreciation of its currency by the constant issuing of bills of credit without a policy of redemption, its money, which under the terms of Queen Anne's proclamation setting the value of colonial money should have had a value of at least 6s. to the Spanish milled dollar, had by 1762 sunk to a point that required 140s. to procure a dollar.[33] In 1766, as during the early decades of the eighteenth century, the agrarian elements of the population supported inflation and loans in bills of credit from the so-called "banks" set up from time to time by the Assembly for the distribution of this largess, and continued to oppose the repayment of the loans. With boundaries of the colony very restricted in nature, the population in 1755 was less than 40,000. By 1774 it had increased to some 60,000, all living in some twenty-eight towns, most of them small and rural in character, with the exception of Newport, Providence, and Portsmouth.[34]

The colony, founded in the seventeenth century as a libertarian religious refuge, retained its character, at least for Protestant dissenters if not for Catholics and non-Christians, and expanded its libertarian views to other fields. Many of its traders not only bore the character of smugglers, but during the late war had come under the strong indictment of General Loudoun for trading with the enemy; when it applied for reimbursement of expenses, some of its

[32] Shelburne Papers, 85:201–204.

[33] E. R. Potter and S. S. Rider, *Some Account of the Bills of Credit or Paper Money of Rhode Island* (Providence, 1880), p. 24.

[34] J. Bartlett (ed.), *Records of the Colony of Rhode Island and Providence Plantations in New England* (10 vols., Providence, 1856–65), VI, 522–523; S. G. Arnold, *History of the State of Rhode Island and Providence Plantations* (2 vols., New York, 1859–60), II, 197, 332–333.

accounts were also rejected by General Amherst because his auditors charged that they had been padded. Further, in 1764 unruly elements had compelled the commanding officer at Fort George on Goat Island to fire upon a revenue cutter, attempting to put a stop to smuggling, and had threatened to burn the vessel if the customs officer did not desist in his activities; [35] and the following year, in the midst of the Stamp Act crisis, another mob had terrorized supporters of the government and destroyed the homes of two of them. Altogether, a lawless but influential minority in the colony had given Rhode Island an unsavory reputation in official circles, one which was not improved by the secretiveness of its government. A report made to the Earl of Shelburne, apparently by Maurice Morgann in 1766, reflected the animus of this group toward the colony:

> Rhode Island is in consequence of its constitution and of the Confusion arising from their enormous and fraudulent Emission of Paper, a very licentious Colony, and they hold very little correspondence with any office [in England]. . . . They do not even transmit the Votes or Proceedings of the Assembly.[36]

Rhode Islanders, it is clear, were *sui generis* and did not easily fit into any pattern of effective British imperial control.

THE COLONY OF CONNECTICUT

Unlike Rhode Island, the Colony of Connecticut was not founded upon the principle of "soul liberty," but by Puritans from Massachusetts Bay who proceeded to establish the Congregational Church. While some other churches were permitted by law openly to function in the eighteenth century, the battle for religious toleration was not won prior to the early national period.

As a colony, Connecticut was largely rural. Of its seventy-six towns that were enumerated in the census of 1774,[37] only New London had any important direct trade relations with Great Britain. The inhabitants of the colony, almost 200,000 in number, were chiefly engaged in tilling the soil or supplying the multifarious needs

[35] J. Munro (ed.), *Acts of the Privy Council of England, Colonial Series* (Hereford, 1911–12), IV, 690–692.

[36] Shelburne Papers, 51:607.

[37] C. J. Hoadly (ed.), *Public Records of the Colony of Connecticut* (15 vols., Hartford, 1850–90), XIV, 483–496.

of those who did. Hemmed in by Rhode Island on the east, by Massachusetts Bay on the north, by New York on the west, and by the Atlantic and Long Island Sound on the south, the little colony supported a teeming population. Between the years 1756 and 1774, that population increased by over 67,000. With the better lands within the colony already under cultivation, by 1766 many families were forced to emigrate. Some moved up the Connecticut River beyond the bounds of Massachusetts Bay. Others moved west of lower New York into the northern part of Pennsylvania, to which, as members of the so-called Susquehanna Company, they laid claim upon the basis of the sea-to-sea grant in the royal patent of 1662, which conflicted directly with the royal patent for the same lands granted in 1681 to William Penn.

The record of the colony during the Great War for the Empire was excellent, taking all things into consideration, perhaps the best of the continental colonies. Connecticut had called in its old, depreciated bills of credit; requisitions of men were generally met, and sometimes greatly exceeded; there was no fuss over the quartering of troops, even when Massachusetts Bay was making this an issue; and later, when New York refused to make provision for troops, they were quietly quartered in Connecticut. For its cooperative behavior Connecticut was rewarded by a series of parliamentary grants between the years 1757 and 1763 that reimbursed the colony for its war efforts to the extent of almost a quarter of a million pounds sterling.[38] By 1769 the war indebtedness of the colony amounted to but £31,713 in the form of circulating bills of credit; moreover, there was a total of £45,369 back taxes on the assessment books that had not been collected because this money simply was not needed. These back taxes were more than enough to liquidate the war debt.[39] In fact, in spite of official complaints to England of "a large and heavy Debt," the colony's fiscal position was so sound that for a period of five years between 1764 and 1770 it was not necessary to levy any colony taxes [40] whatsoever—a situation that the government of the colony discreetly kept from the

[38] L. H. Gipson, "Connecticut Taxation and Parliamentary Aid Preceding the Revolutionary War," *American Historical Review*, XXXVI, 721–739.
[39] *Ibid.*
[40] *Ibid.*

ministry at home.[41] With the return of colony taxation in the seventies, the rate was so low that the per capita tax amounted to but 7*d*. 2*f*. sterling as against a per capita tax in England of at least 20*s*.[42]

THE PROVINCE OF NEW YORK

The form and spirit of the government of the Province of New York were aristocratic. Even the House of Representatives of the General Assembly was aristocratic in its composition. Unlike the Colony of Connecticut, where each qualified individual voted once and the seventy-six towns, great and small, were equally represented, New York, following the practice of England, permitted plural voting for those possessing freeholds in more than one county or city or manor.[43] To vote in colony elections one had to hold a freehold to the value of £40, as against the 40*s*. freehold valuation in Connecticut. Finally, the seats in the House of Representatives were so distributed and so limited in number that most of the members of that body—but 31 in 1774 as against 152 Connecticut deputies— were chiefly either the proprietors of great manors or merchant princes, or, if not, were closely identified with those who were. Thus, the governor, the Provincial Council, and the Legislative General Assembly constituted in a sense both an oligarchy and a plutocracy.

While greatly surpassing Connecticut in size, the province had fewer inhabitants.[44] This was due not only to the fact that the confirmed policies of the owners of manors did not appeal to the prospective immigrant, but that within the boundaries of the province were settled the fierce Six Nations that were held in precarious alliance. No other colony, in fact, had benefited as much as New York from the protection afforded by regular troops posted along its frontiers. Yet at the very time of the repeal of the Stamp Act, the Assembly saw fit to make an issue over the terms of the Quartering Act (called by the English the Mutiny Act) passed by Parlia-

[41] Massachusetts Historical Society, *Collections*, 5th s., IX, 333–334.

[42] *American Historical Review*, XXXVI, 721–739.

[43] A. E. McKinley, *The Suffrage Franchise in the Thirteen English Colonies in America* (Philadelphia 1905), pp. 215–216.

[44] E. B. O'Callaghan and B. Fernow (eds.), *Documents Relative to the Colonial History of the State of New York* (15 vols., Albany, 1853–87) VIII, 449.

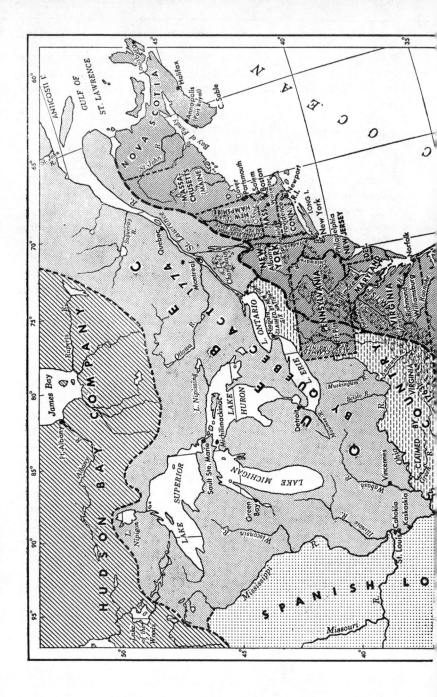

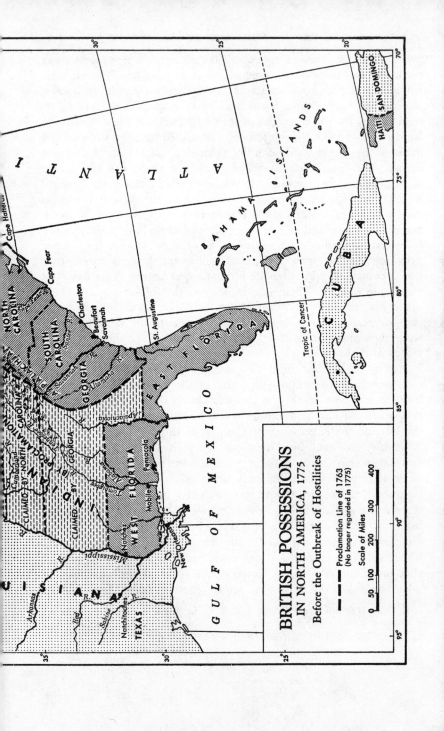

BRITISH POSSESSIONS
IN NORTH AMERICA, 1775
Before the Outbreak of Hostilities

— — — Proclamation line of 1763
(No longer regarded in 1775)

Scale of Miles

0   50 100   200   300   400

ment in 1765.[45] This statute provided that suitable provision should be made for troops marching through or quartered within any colony. In lieu of proper barracks, it was directed that dram houses, unoccupied houses, and barns and other outbuildings were to be made ready for the reception of troops by the local authorities, who were also to see that the soldiers were furnished with certain specified items such as firewood, candles, vinegar, salt, bedding, kitchen utensils, and limited quantities of small beer or cider at the charge of the colony in question. In December of that year, General Thomas Gage, the commander in chief of the British forces in North America, anticipating the arrival in New York of fresh troops from England to take the places of those long posted on the frontiers, applied to the governor, Sir Henry Moore, for proper provision for these new arrivals as well as for those already within the province. Moore presented the request to the Assembly, but nothing was done. Then, late in May of the following year, Gage made his second application. After some correspondence between the governor and the legislature, a bill was finally passed, which, while ignoring the Mutiny Act, made limited provision for the troops and also made clear that the Assembly expected to be reimbursed by the mother country for the expense entailed.[46]

The refusal to acknowledge the binding effect of the British statute upon New York—for this was clearly the issue at stake—did not stem from any opposition to the presence of British troops in the interior of the province on the part of those who controlled the Assembly. In fact, these men considered it a very fortunate circumstance that British regulars were at hand when in June a series of great riots over land tenantry broke out in Dutchess and Westchester counties and the rioters marched upon New York City threatening to burn it. They doubtless were also comforted by knowing that the regulars were available when called upon by the provincial government not only to suppress disorders in these counties, but in addition to put down those of an even more serious nature that broke out in Albany County as a result of the squatting on what was held to be New York lands by settlers from Massachusetts

[45] This law is listed as 5 George III, c. 33; its text is given in D. Pickering's *Statutes at Large*, XXVI, 305–318.

[46] J. Almon, *Prior Documents* (London, 1777), pp. 97–98.

Bay who would not pay quitrents and defied the authority of the New York magistrates.[47]

When the news arrived in England that the Assembly had refused to acknowledge Parliament's authority to pass the American Quartering Act, Pitt, now Earl of Chatham, was again at the head of the ministry. Although the statute involved the very principle of taxation without representation which he himself had upheld during the debates over the repeal of the Stamp Act, he was, nevertheless, determined that this law be enforced lest the whole system of American defense collapse.[48] Fortifying Pitt's resolve was the petition to the Commons framed by New York merchants late in 1766. This petition advocated free trade [49] and the virtual scrapping of the navigation and trade system. Always a firm supporter of the trade laws, Chatham was doubly persuaded that the time had come for the government to take a firm stand. The result was the passing by Parliament in June, 1767, of an act to suspend all legislative functions of the province until it had met fully the requirements of the Mutiny Act.[50]

Even before Parliament had taken this step, the New York Assembly had, however, come to realize that other colonial legislatures would not follow its lead. For example, the assemblies of Pennsylvania and Connecticut had quietly made the necessary quartering provisions for troops. Moreover, at this juncture, the colony had vital issues pending before the Privy Council in England, not least among them the boundary dispute with Massachusetts Bay. What it needed abroad was friends, not enemies. Nor could it plead financial distress, in view of Parliament's liberal reimbursement of its war expenses. To the contrary, General Gage informed the Earl of Shelburne early in 1767 that New York "is also happy in the State of its Finances, for I am credibly informed that every Farthing of

[47] *New York Colon. Doc.*, VII, 845–846, 867–868; C. E. Carter (ed.), *The Correspondence of General Thomas Gage* (2 vols., New Haven, 1931–33), I, 99, 102–103; Irving Mark, *Agrarian Conflicts in Colonial New York, 1711–1775* (New York, 1940).

[48] W. S. Taylor and J. H. Pringle, *Correspondence of William Pitt, Earl of Chatham* (4 vols., London, 1838–40), II, 188–189.

[49] For this petition see *Prior Documents*, pp. 163–167.

[50] This is 7 George III, c. 59, *Statutes at Large* (Eyre and Strahan), VIII, 52.

Debt will be paid off this year, and good revenues coming in." [51]
Despite protests by the radicals, the Assembly was forced to back
down, and a provincial bill for quartering troops in strict conformity
with the Mutiny Act was passed early in the summer of 1767.

THE PROVINCE OF NEW JERSEY

The Province of New Jersey was in a relatively sound economic
position during this period. Before the Great War for the Empire,
most Jerseyites did not know what it was to pay provincial taxes. [52]
During the war, it is true, personal and estate taxes were levied to
meet the extraordinary expenses of the government. [53] But the parliamentary reimbursement made it possible to do away with these
levies for some years. Nor was any provincial revenue raised in the
colony in 1766 even by means of excises, or on imports or exports. [54]
New Jersey owed its sound fiscal position to the strict control of
its issuance of bills of credit. Unlike such issues in Rhode Island,
the New Jersey loans had been fairly carefully collected when due,
along with 5 per cent interest. After the war, by using "a Surplusage
of money struck for His Majesty's service" during the war crisis, the
ordinary expense of the provincial government was met and the
public credit maintained, according to Governor Franklin. [55] It is
true that in 1769 the Assembly, feeling it to be high time to liquidate the remainder of its war debt, provided for the raising annually
of some £15,000 to that end. However, considering Jersey's estimated population in 1774 of 120,000, this meant an annual per
capita tax that could hardly have been more than 3s. [56] Back in
1742 the inhabitants of New Jersey were called "the most Easie and
happy people of any collony in North America." [57] With much
reason they could still be so characterized in 1767, although some

[51] *Gage Corresp.*, I, 118.

[52] D. L. Kemmerer, *Path to Freedom* . . . (Princeton, 1940), p. 237. Governor Belcher, writing to the Board of Trade on April 21, 1749, declared that
" 'tis 17 years since any Tax was raised on the people for the support of Government. . . . " (*New Jersey Archives*, 1st ser., VII, 246).

[53] Governor William Franklin to the Earl of Shelburne, Dec. 28, 1766, with
enclosure, *ibid.*, IX, 578–581.

[54] *Ibid.*

[55] *Ibid.*

[56] "Heads of Enquiry relative to New Jersey . . . and the Governor's Answers
thereto," 1774, *ibid.*, X, 447–448.

[57] Lewis Morris to Peter Collenson, May 24, 1742, *Papers of Governor Lewis
Morris* (New York, 1852), p. 147; Kemmerer, *Path to Freedom*, pp. 277–278,
281–283.

of them had, it is true, drifted into financial troubles after the easy-credit days of the war years.

The Province of Pennsylvania could boast of a population very conservatively estimated in 1775 at over 300,000.[58] Its inhabitants were about evenly divided between German- and English-speaking groups, and were split up in a multitude of religious groups. Since the beginning of the colony people were attracted to it by reason of the richness of its soil, the extent of its land available for settlement, and the "mildness" of its government. Boasting a great and flourishing seaport, a variety of products of the soil, iron furnaces and forges supplying both domestic and foreign markets, the province enjoyed considerable prosperity. While Connecticut settlers were squatting upon lands in northern Pennsylvania and Virginians were claiming the western part of the province beyond the mountains, such developments principally affected the interests of the Penn family rather than those of the average Pennsylvanian. After 1765 the bitter controversies with the Pennsylvania Proprietors had subsided and the dispute with the mother country seemed to many to be terminated with the repeal of the Stamp Act. Hence, when, in 1766, General Gage requested quarters for the Royal Highland Regiment, an appropriation of £4,000 was readily granted in accordance with the Mutiny Act.[59]

Indeed, in 1767 Pennsylvania enjoyed an almost total absence of public fiscal burdens. During the four-year period from 1760 to 1763 inclusive, no regular provincial taxes were levied since the reimbursement money that came from Great Britain was adequate to provide for all ordinary government charges.[60] In 1756 an excise on spirituous beverages, to run for ten years, had been imposed to sink £30,000 in bills of credit, but this had lapsed by 1767. In

[58] *Pennsylvania Archives* (ed. Samuel Hazard, Philadelphia, 1853), 1st s., IV, 597. There are difficulties facing the student who seeks accuracy in this matter of population. Deputy Governor Robert Hunter Morris in 1755 declared that the population was "upwards of three hundred thousand" (*ibid.*, 4th s., II, 372); see also various population estimates given by C. A. Herrick in his *White Servitude in Pennsylvania* (Philadelphia, 1926), pp. 177–180, and by E. B. Greene and V. D. Harrington in their *American Population Before the Federal Census of 1790* (New York, 1932), p. 115.

[59] Gage to Shelburne, Oct. 10, 1766, *Gage Corresp.*, I, 110.

[60] "The Establishment of Pennsylvania," 1767, Shelburne Papers, 56:188–219.

addition, a real estate and personal tax had been levied to liquidate the remainder of the war debt by 1772—also in the form of bills of credit—by raising £23,000 a year.[61] But this tax in fact amounted to an annual per capita levy of about 1s. 6d.

Not only were the inhabitants relieved of all *ordinary* charges of government during the years 1760–63 but, aside from a revived excise tax on liquors,[62] they also enjoyed such relief during the remainder of the period down to the Revolution. Moreover, the personal and estate taxes were eventually reduced to return annually but £15,000 for the liquidation of the remainder of the provincial debt. By 1775, such taxes represented a per capita levy of less than one shilling.[63] The explanation of this achievement is to be found in the issuing of bills of credit, strictly in terms of the statutes of Parliament of 1764 (4 George III, c. 34), limiting their use, and the loaning of these bills by the provincial Loan Office at 5 per cent to those desiring to improve their property [64]—a practice that New Jersey prudently followed. The profits from these loans, together with the proceeds of the excise on liquors, amounting in all to £8,000, were sufficient to defray both the ordinary and extraordinary needs of the government.[65]

Thus, with only trivial taxation burdens, with no militia to raise, equip, and pay, with no forts any longer to maintain, or other defensive measures to take in view of the protection afforded the back country by regular troops posted at Fort Pitt and supported by the mother country,[66] the people of Pennsylvania in 1767 might have justifiably been considered by Englishmen to be in an enviable position.

---

[61] *Ibid.*

[62] See *ibid.* and also "Answers to the Heads of Enquiry on the Condition of the Province, 1775," *Pennsylvania Archives,* IV, 598.

[63] *Ibid.,* pp. 598–599.

[64] For the Pennsylvania bills of credit acts from 1764 to 1775 see *Pennsylvania Statutes at Large,* VII, 101, 198, 205; VIII, 204, 284, 418. The student should be careful in studying these loan acts, all of which were to come under the scrutiny of the Board of Trade, not to take at their face value assertions in the preambles that a distressing load of debt was being carried by the people. The facts clearly refute the assertions.

[65] Except for the small tax to retire the remainder of the provincial debt. *Pennsylvania Archives,* IV, 598–599.

[66] *Ibid.,* pp. 599–600.

CHAPTER 10

Old and New Southern Colonies

IN THE year 1767 the Province of Maryland, a proprietary of Frederick, Lord Baltimore, may be regarded as typifying in most respects the economy of the South, with two exceptions. Small rather than large plantations were the rule [1] and the white population, estimated at about 115,000 in 1761, outnumbered the blacks by over two to one.[2] The population figures point to the dependence of the tobacco planters on white indentured labor as well as upon slavery. Such white labor was supplied in substantial part by transported British convicts. These were purchased by the planters at the rate of about a thousand a year between 1750 and 1775, generally for field work as a substitute for slave labor.[3] Because such traffic in whites was, for the most part, highly profitable and sustained the plantation economy, it was continued despite widespread criticism and the imposition by the Maryland legislature of a comparatively heavy duty on long-term indentured servants.[4]

[1] C. P. Gould, *The Land System in Maryland, 1720–1765* (Baltimore, 1913), pp. 65–68, 70–80.

[2] W. H. Browne (ed.), *Archives of Maryland* (64 vols., Baltimore, 1883–1947), XXXII, 25.

[3] R. B. Morris, *Government and Labor in Early America* (New York, 1946), pp. 323–337.

[4] L. H. Gipson, *The British Empire Before the American Revolution* (8 vols., Caldwell, Ida., and New York, 1936–54), II, 95–96; M. P. Andrews, *History of Maryland, Province and State* (New York, 1929), pp. 215–216; Morris, *Government and Labor*, pp. 334–336.

Unlike its neighbors Virginia and Pennsylvania, Maryland played a rather ignoble role in the Great War for the Empire. In fact, the General Assembly took the view that the war was secondary to the settlement of its quarrel with the Proprietor over questions of the disposition of fees and fines. However, with the conclusion of the war, the colony took a strong stand against the fiscal measures adopted by the British Parliament and found a champion in its brilliant young lawyer, Daniel Dulany, whose *Considerations on the Propriety of imposing taxes in the British Colonies* was one of the most provocative pamphlets issued on behalf of the colonies during the Stamp Act controversy.

Yet the people of Maryland could not conscientiously urge that they were heavily burdened to support their own government. In fact, upon the basis of a detailed report sent by Deputy Governor Sharpe to the Earl of Shelburne on May 14, 1767, all levies for the support of the provincial government—in contrast to those for the support of the clergy, the schools, and other county and parish charges—amounted to less than £5,500, an annual per capita tax of about a shilling.[5] The provincial debt of 135,000 Spanish dollars was not a matter of much concern since by 1767 Maryland was not only free of any war debt, which it never had incurred in the first place, but had invested in Bank of England stock, "over and above what has been drawn out to sink [all] the Bills of Credit." This sum, taken together with the specie lying in the provincial Loan

---

[5] Of the above sum, £1,100 on the average—raised by a perpetual duty of 14d. sterling per ton on all vessels trading to Maryland and not belonging to its inhabitants—was granted in 1661 to the Lord Proprietor; a duty of 1s. per hogshead on all tobacco exported was by another perpetual law of 1704 appropriated to the support of the governor, which brought in each year some £1,291 9s.; he also received, by another indefinite act of that year, all money secured by a duty of 3d. sterling per ton on all vessels trading to the province not built by or owned entirely by its inhabitants, which average £228 15s. 9d.; finally, he was entitled to exact a fee of 12s. for each marriage license issued within the province, which added about £341 4s. to his remuneration. The other items of expense on the provincial establishment—as distinguished from the county and parish establishments—were grants of 140 pounds of tobacco per day of actual service to the eight judges of the Supreme Court, as well as to the fifty-eight members of the lower house of the General Assembly, and 150 pounds of tobacco to the twelve members of the Council, which totaled some £2,388 4s. 3d. (Shelburne Papers, 55:351-426; Clements Library). In this connection it may be noted that the direct tax on tithables in tobacco to support the provincial government only amounted to an average per capita tax of about 5d.

Office, was adequate, in Governor Sharpe's opinion, to free the people of any public indebtedness, provided the Assembly issued a new supply of bills of credit supported by this fund to circulate for a period of ten years.[6] With no inclination to worry over problems or costs of defense, Marylanders had come to rely entirely upon measures taken by the mother country for the general security of the Empire without tangible contribution on their own part.

THE PROVINCE OF VIRGINIA

In 1767 Virginia boasted the largest population of any colony in the British Empire, with perhaps some 400,000 people dwelling within its fifty-four counties. As in Maryland, the whites outnumbered blacks by about two to one.[7] While most of the planters of the tidewater were established modestly enough on small plantations worked by themselves, assisted possibly by one or two slaves or indentured whites, there were, in contrast, scattered throughout this region the lordly estates of those who had much in common with the landed gentry and nobility of the mother country and whose dependents might be numbered in the hundreds.

Nowhere else in North America did the aristocracy exhibit greater ostentation and luxury. Nowhere else were the consequences of extravagant living and a readiness to pledge the future to meet present desires more evident than in Virginia. As a rule, British merchants were willing to extend liberal, long-term credit to those who would agree to remit to them the annual crop of tobacco in part payment at least of their accumulated indebtedness, and the planters had accustomed themselves to these business arrangements. Meanwhile the low price of tobacco, the process of soil exhaustion, and the chronic indebtedness of the planters were relentlessly undermining the position of the planter aristocracy. In short, plantation economics was potentially an explosive force in the political life of the province.

Equally explosive was the situation facing hundreds, if not thousands, of frontier families, who had been settling or resettling beyond the line of the royal Proclamation of 1763 previous to and

[6] Sharpe to Cecelius Calvert, Dec. 21, 1765, *Maryland Archives*, XIV, 250–254; see also *ibid.*, pp. 254–255, 352.

[7] For various estimates of the population of Virginia for the years 1763, 1764, and 1770, see Greene and Harrington, *American Population*, p. 141.

even after that date. For a time they were harassed by British officers at Fort Pitt who were under orders to keep the whites from squatting and hunting within the Indian reserve. Such orders were deemed necessary to conciliate the natives. But the troubled atmosphere was destined to clear in the West once such Indian groups as the Six Nations and the Cherokee agreed to sign away much valuable land. This they did by the treaties of Fort Stanwix, Hard Labor, and Lochaber.

However, not even the news of the repeal of the Stamp Act served to restore the inhabitants of the Old Dominion to a happy frame of mind. Writing to the Broad of Trade in the fall of 1766, Governor Francis Fauquier warned that "the Blood of the people is soured by their private Distresses" and that "party feuds will run high" with the meeting of the General Assembly.[8] When that body assembled on November 6, he, nevertheless, sought to calm them in declaring:

> Your Grievances have been redressed, the Act you thought oppressive repealed, and every Indulgence in Commerce which you could with Reason expect, or even desire, been granted you.[9]

In reply, the House of Burgesses on November 13, in presenting their address, acknowledged "the tender Regard shown by his Majesty to the Rights and Liberties of his People in his . . . gracious Assent to the Repeal of that oppressive Act," declared themselves ever ready to defend the Crown against all enemies, and, finally, expressed a wish that "the grateful Harmony of an indulgent Parent and dutiful children may constantly subsist between us." [10]

Running throughout their address was, however, a spirit of distrust along with a scarcely veiled threat that the union of the colonies and the mother country might in the future be imperiled should Parliament once again violate colonial rights. Fauquier, in reporting to his superiors in London, felt compelled to call it "a very extraordinary one in every Light," and asserted that it "shews great weakness and want of Judgment, but much Heat in the

[8] Fauquier to the Board of Trade, Oct. 8, 1766, P.R.O., C.O. 5:1331, pp. 341–342.

[9] J. P. Kennedy (ed.), *Journals of the House of Burgesses of Virginia, 1766–1769* (Richmond, 1906), p. 12.

[10] *Ibid.*, p. 23.

Composers. . . ." [11] Nor did the convening of the Assembly in the spring of 1767 serve to clear the political horizon. The public business was reported by the governor to have been carried on with "great Heat both on account of private Dissentions and Public Divisions" with "young, hotheaded, inexperienced Members" not only arrayed against "the cool, old Members of great steadiness and moderation," but now firmly in control of the House of Burgesses.[12]

While recognizing the full extent of the Assembly's discontent, we should bear in mind that Virginians carried much lighter public burdens than did Englishmen at that time. The salaries of provincial officials, including the income of the governor, were paid out of a fund raised by a perpetual export tax of 2s. on every hogshead of tobacco, together with a tax of 1s. 3d. per ton on all vessels trading to the colony, a tax of 6d. for every passenger who was brought in them, and the fines and forfeitures levied by the courts. After meeting all of these charges, there remained in the establishment fund, according to a report made by Richard Corbin in the spring of 1767, a surplus of £1,578 7s. 4d. Should this fund at any time not prove adequate to meet the provincial expenses, it was customary to draw upon the so-called right money, that is, the 5s. paid on each fifty acres of crown land at the time the purchaser secured a patent for it.[13] To meet other ordinary contingent charges, such as the cost of holding the General Assembly, of compensating the owners of slaves executed for capital offenses, and of supporting William and Mary College, a duty of 4d. per gallon was levied on all imported rum or wines as well, and another of 5 per cent on the value of each slave imported for sale.[14] In addition, there were fees for special services which were paid to public officials. For example, the governor was paid a fee for signing land patents (the so-called pistole fee), for marriage and innkeepers' licenses, for passes for

[11] P.R.O., C.O. 5:1345, pp. 314–315; T. P. Abernethy, *Western Lands and the American Revolution* (New York, 1937), pp. 149–154.

[12] Fauquier to Shelburne, Apr. 27, 1767, Shelburne Papers, 52:59. It may be noted that Fauquier, while representing the agitated nature of the session, stated that the members of the House were prudent enough to have nothing of this appear in their journal.

[13] "Account of the funds which are paid into the Receiver General with the salaries annually paid out of the produce thereof," Shelburne Papers, 55:270–307.

[14] *Ibid.*

ships, and for use of the great seal in authenticating papers; other fees were paid to the secretary of the province, to the collectors of the customs, to the admiralty office, and to the attorney general. Such fees seem to have been comparable to those paid in the other colonies, although on a lesser scale than those paid for like services in England.[15]

As regards the public debt, Virginia had issued between the years 1757 and 1763 a total of £412,962 10s. in so-called treasury notes for supporting the war—an amount equal to about £1 10s. per capita. During the same years taxes were levied to redeem these notes and to provide a surplus of £11,452 4s. 7d.[16] However, instead of destroying the treasury notes when they were called in, John Robinson, both the treasurer of the colony and Speaker of the House of Burgesses, in violation of law, reissued some £100,000 of them on loan to friends, accepting their personal paper as security. Robinson died in the spring of 1766, but for over a year he had been under a cloud.[17] To liquidate the resultant deficiency in the treasury, certain temporary taxes were levied, which were estimated in 1767 by Thomas Nelson, deputy secretary, as adequate to free the colony of all indebtedness within two years.[18] It is therefore clear that the province's indebtedness lay entirely at the door of its treasurer.

THE PROVINGE OF NORTH CAROLINA

In the year 1767 the Province of North Carolina was the scene

---

[15] *Ibid.*

[16] *Journals of the House of Burgesses, 1766–1769,* p. xi.

[17] *Ibid.,* p. xviii. An exhaustive treatment of the Robinson affair is found in D. J. Mays, *Edmund Pendleton* (Cambridge, Mass., 1952), I, 174–223, 358–385.

[18] Shelburne Papers, 55:288. The fund, to the end of clearing the colony of debt, was raised by a temporary land tax of 2s. on every hundred acres, a poll tax on all tithables of 4s., a duty of 5 per cent on the value of all slaves imported for sale, a tax of 2s. 6d. on all general court writs and another of 1s. 3d. on all other writs, a tax of 5s. per wheel for every carriage, and, finally, a tax of 2s. per hogshead on all tobacco exported (*ibid.*). For a report on public finances in Virginia in 1774, see "Answers to the Heads of Inquiry," enclosed in Lord Dunmore's letter of March 18 of that year (C.O. 5:1352, pp. 9–29). This report would indicate that none of these special taxes were then collected, but that the provincial government was supported almost entirely by its quitrents and its export duty on tobacco, which, in the words of the Board of Trade in 1767, "form an ample and sufficient fund for the payment of the civil establishments of this colony" (P.R.O., C.O. 5:67, p. 585).

of exceptional growth and, one might add, of exceptional internal disorders and mismanagement. Governor William Tryon reported to the Board of Trade in 1766 that the colony was settling faster than any other on the continent. A great migration from the North was pouring through North Carolina. Some settlers pushed on to the lower South; others, after viewing the lower country, returned to settle the "western and back countries" of North Carolina.[19] The population of the colony was not far short of 200,000.[20] In other words, the population had doubled in the twenty years before 1754, when it was estimated at 77,000; it then doubled again in the next decade.[21]

The inhabitants of the interior were described by Robert Jones, the attorney general of the province, as bold and intrepid in the art of war as well as hospitable to strangers, and as dirty, impertinent, and vain.[22] In this region Presbyterianism was entrenched[23] among those known familiarly as the Scotch-Irish. In the main eschewing slavery, the back-country settlers lived as ranchers and farmers and in word and deed were rugged individualists. In contrast to them was the entrenched planter aristocracy of the tidewater area affiliated with the Church of England.

Seeds of sectional discontent were nurtured in North Carolina. Before agreement was reached between Pennsylvania and Maryland as to the southern limits of the former province, hundreds of families moved into the northern parts of the disputed lands and, once established there, refused to recognize the authority of the Penn family; when the boundary was agreed upon, rather than take up the lands on terms offered by the proprietors, they moved southward along the Valley Road through Virginia and into North Carolina.

[19] W. L. Saunders (ed.), *The Colonial Records of North Carolina* (10 vols., Raleigh, 1886–90), VII, 248.

[20] *Ibid.*, VII, 145–146. For a description of plantation life in the Cape Fear region and a map of the leading plantations, see James Sprunt, *Chronicles of the Cape Fear Region, 1660–1916* (Raleigh, 1916), pp. 55–61.

[21] *N.C. Colon. Rec.*, V, 320. The editor of the *Records*, W. L. Saunders, took the position that there were nearly 100,000 people in the colony in 1754 (*ibid.*, Preface, p. xxxix).

[22] Robert Jones to Edmund Fanning, July 25, 1765, *ibid.*, VII, 101; see also Carl Bridenbaugh's lively description of the North Carolina frontier in chap. III of his *Myths and Realities: Societies of the Colonial South* (Baton Rouge, 1952).

[23] Tryon to the Society for the Propagation of the Gospel, July 31, 1765, *N.C. Colon. Rec.*, VII, 102; see also *ibid.*, V, Preface, xl.

Many of them settled without warrant in Mecklenburg County upon lands that had previously been in dispute—in this case between North Carolina and South Carolina—and thereupon proceeded to make improvements. But this area, earlier granted by royal patent to Henry McCulloh and Associates as part of a vast tract, had also been surveyed; with the running of a boundary line, it had become clear that it fell within North Carolina. The squatters refused to accept the relatively moderate terms offered to them early in 1765 by agents of the Associates.[24] When attempts were made to provide individual surveys of the holdings, they proceeded to band together and to commit acts of violence. This was a prelude to the Stamp Act rioting later in that same year, and again in 1766—rioting fomented in the eastern parts of the province by the Sons of Liberty. These disorders were to be succeeded in the newer counties by the much more violent action of the Regulators. Not only was the western population motivated by self-interest; the same motive, in less justifiable form, seems to have prompted the actions of the local officials appointed by the General Assembly, including the treasurers and sheriffs. In 1767 Governor Tryon wrote Shelburne:

The Treasurers have hitherto shewed so much Lenity toward the Sheriffs that upon a Medium the Sheriffs have embezzled more than one half of the public money ordered to be raised and collected by them. It is computed that the Sheriffs' Arrears to the publick amount to £40,000 Proclamation Money not five Thousand of which will probably ever come into the Treasury, as in many instances the Sheriffs & their Securities are either insolvent or retreated out of the Province. . . . By not seeing the Sheriffs in Arrear they [the Treasurers] obtain a considerable Interest among the Connections of those delinquent Sheriffs, which generally secures them a Re-election to their Office when expired.[25]

A combination of malfeasance in office and faulty administrative procedures reduced the public finances to a disorderly condition. An issue of paper money authorized in 1761 to support the war effort amounted to £20,000. Under the terms of the act, the paper was to be retired by an annual 2s. poll tax on all taxables, to begin in 1764 and to continue until the whole was called in and burnt.

[24] For the terms offered, see *ibid.*, VII, 19–20.
[25] Shelburne Papers, 52:139–140.

1. GEORGE III as a young King (circa 1763)

Engraved from the portrait by Allan Ramsay in the City Library, Guildhall, London (The New York Public Library)

2. WILLIAM PITT, EARL OF CHATHAM

Engraved by J. Chapman (The New York Public Library)

3. THE EARL OF SHELBURNE

(The New York Public Library)

4. LORD ROCKINGHAM

Steel engraving in *The Political Register*, October, 1771

5. WILLIAM, EARL OF DARTMOUTH

From an original picture by Gainsborough (The New York Public Library)

6. FRANCIS BERNARD, governor of
Massachusetts, 1760-1769

Engraving from the Copley painting

7. THOMAS HUTCHINSON, governor of
Massachusetts, 1769-1774

Photograph of a painting by Copley

8. LORD NORTH, First Lord Commissioner
of the Treasury

Engraving from a portrait by Dance (The
New York Public Library)

9. THE RT. HON. GEORGE GRENVILLE

Engraving from a painting by William
Hoare (Historical Society of Pennsylvania)

10. The Governor Hutchinson town house in Boston as reconstructed after 1765

11. Landing of the British troops at Boston on September 30, 1768. This engraving, published in 1868, follows the Paul Revere engraving of 1770.

12. SAMUEL ADAMS

Engraved for Samuel G. Drake's *The History and Antiquities of . . . Boston,* from a portrait by John Singleton Copley (The New York Public Library)

13. PATRICK HENRY

Engraved from a painting by J. B. Longacre (The New York Public Library)

14. JOHN ADAMS

Engraved from a painting by Copley (The New York Public Library)

15. JAMES OTIS

Engraved from a painting by J. Blackburn, 1755 (The New York Public Library)

16. "The Repeal or the Funeral Procession of Miss Americ-Stamp," a cartoon printed anonymously in England March 18, 1766. Leading the procession is the author of the Anti Sejanus papers, followed by Lords Mansfield and Norton; Grenville carries the Stamp Act coffin; behind him is Bute, followed by Bedford and Temple, the latter weeping; then comes Lord Halifax with Sandwich talking to him; finally Bishops Warburton and Johnson march together.

17. "The Deplorable State of America or SC—H Government," printed in London. March 22, 1765. Britannia, seated, offers Pandora's Box (The S——p Act) to America, an Indian. The latter appeals to the Goddess Minerva, who advises against taking the box. In front of America Liberty lies dying, and directly to the left Mercury, the God of Trade, is about to depart. In the background winds blow against the Liberty tree, and the sun in the shape of a boot (play on the word Bute) is bribed by the King of France to continue creating new disturbances.

18. A view of New York from the northwest, about 1772. Printed in the *Atlantic Neptune,* published by the British Admiralty.

19. A plan of New York as of 1767, by Bernard Ratzen. Engraved by T. Kitchin and published in London, January 12, 1776.

20. "The Bloody Massacre perpetrated in King's Street Boston on March 5th, 1770, by a party of the 29th Regt . . ." "Engrav'd, Printed & Sold by Paul Revere, Boston, 1770." Republished in Boston, March 5, 1832.

21. BENJAMIN FRANKLIN

By David Rent Etter, after Martin, in Independence Hall, Philadelphia

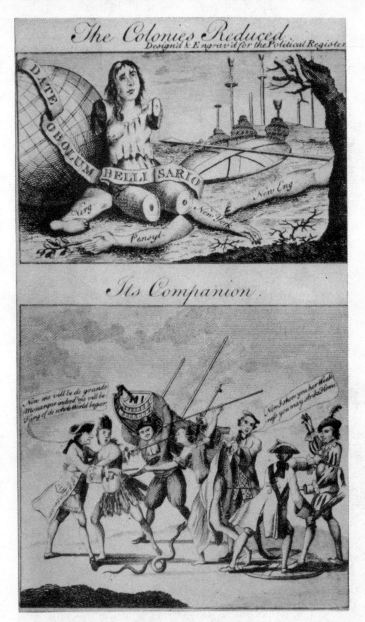

22. "The Colonies Reduced" and "Its Companion," from the *Political Register,* December, 1768. The latter shows America rushing for protection into the arms of France to save herself from Britannia, who in turn is being stabbed by Bute and also uncovered by him to receive a sword thrust from Spain.

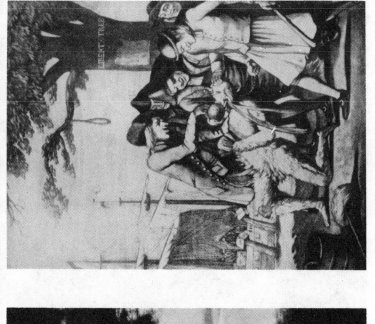

23. JOHN DICKINSON, author of the famous "Letters from a Farmer in Pennsylvania" which helped to arouse violent opposition to the Townshend Revenue Acts. Portrait in the Historical Society of Pennsylvania.

24. "The Bostonian's Paying the Excise-man, or Tarring & Feathering," probably the work of Philip Dawe, a pupil of Hogarth, issued in London on October 31, 1774.

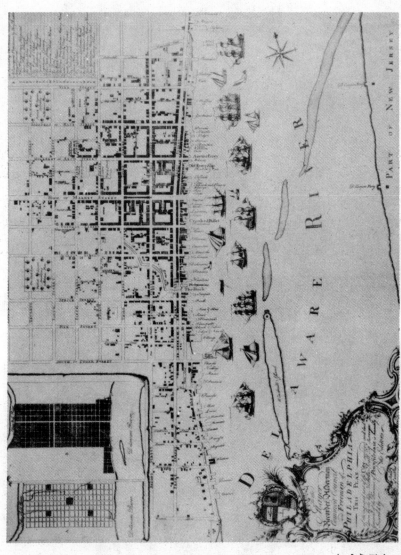

25. A plan of Philadelphia about the year 1761, probably engraved by James Turner, and issued in Philadelphia, November 1, 1762.

26. "The Balance Master," engraved for *The Political Register*, November, 1768, shows Britannia weighted down with the national debt while Grafton seeks to strike a balance between contending groups. Below is Lord Barrington between two devils.

27. "The Hydra," engraved for *The Political Register*, March, 1770, with heads of Bute, Mansfield, and Grafton, is shown attacking prostrate Britannia while Chatham with his crutch and Lord Rockingham and Lord Temple with the swords of truth are assailing the "Hydra." Even the heavens give aid.

28. "A Society of Patriotic Ladies at Edenton in North Carolina," probably the work of Philip Dawe, London, March 25, 1775, shows the ladies of Edenton agreeing to give up drinking tea until the tax is repealed.

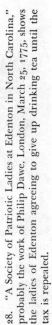

29. "The Alternative of Williams-Burg," probably the work of Philip Dawe, London, February 16, 1775, portrays the choice offered to Virginians reluctant to sign the Association of 1774. The tar and feathers are hanging from the gallows.

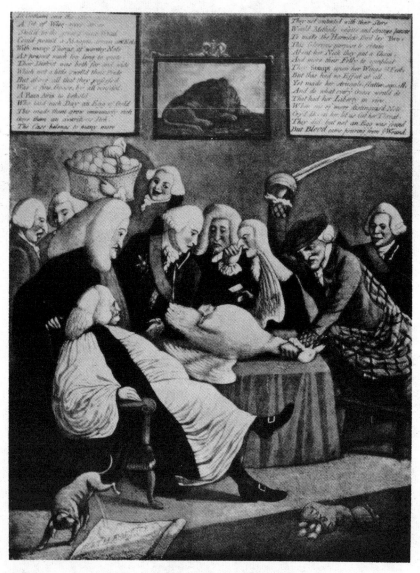

30. "The Wise Men of Gotham and their Goose," issued in London, February 16, 1776, suggests that the British Government is destroying the goose (America) that lays the golden eggs.

Earlier issues from 1754 to that date, amounting in all to £93,156, together with an issue of bills in 1748 amounting to £21,350, were supposed to have been liquidated by 1767 as the result of the imposition of poll taxes of either £1 or £2 and import duties on liquors.[26] But the taxes levied for sinking this indebtedness—the latter in the form of circulating medium—were either never collected when due or embezzled by the sheriffs. In fact, the bills-of-credit issues of 1748 and 1754, amounting to £21,350 and £40,000 respectively, were in large part still outstanding as late as in 1771, when debenture notes totaling £60,000 were issued to replace them.[27] A poll tax of 8d. was also enacted for the years 1767 and 1768, along with an import duty of 2d. per gallon on liquors for those years, to repay £5,000 appropriated from the school and glebe funds for building the governor's official residence at New Bern; but it is by no means clear that these levies were ever put into effect.

In short, the only provincial burdens actually shouldered by the people of North Carolina in 1767 were—aside from the obligation of sinking the bills of credit, which they were reluctant to do by reason of their need of a money medium—certain modest appropriations for supporting the offices of the chief justice, the attorney general, and the associate judge of Salisbury District in the West; for supporting a captain and ten men at Fort Johnson, for the running of the Cherokee boundary line, and for bestowing gifts on the Indians; and, finally, for granting a bounty on hemp and flax. In all, these amounted to but £1,829 sterling. To this total must be added a small duty on exported hides to pay for the bounties on

[26] Coralie Parker, *The History of Taxation in North Carolina . . . 1663–1776* (New York, 1928), pp. 119–120, 123; W. K. Boyd, "A Table of North Carolina Taxes, 1748–1770," *North Carolina Historical Review,* III, 475–476); "An Estimate of Monies emitted & paid . . . from the year 1748 to the year 1766," Shelburne Papers, 56:154–157. This estimate, of course, does not take into account the "debenture notes," later issued in 1771, to the amount of £60,000, to be redeemed by an annual poll tax of 2s. and to run for ten years, for calling in and sinking all the earlier issues of paper money.

[27] Parker, *Taxation in N.C.,* pp. 122–123; C. L. Raper, *North Carolina: A Study in English Colonial Government* (New York, 1904), pp. 200–203, 240. The student of colonial public finance should be cautioned that there is as much difference between the theoretical levying of taxes and their actual collection in North Carolina during the sixties of the eighteenth century as there is with respect to this in Connecticut during the same period.

hemp and flax.[28] By 1772 the only public levies, even theoretically due for collection, were a poll tax of 4s. and the import duty of 4d. per gallon on spirits to sink the remainder of the bills of credit, which the Assembly voted should not be collected thereafter.[29] With a per capita tax of only a shilling, North Carolinians could scarcely make out a valid case for excessive taxation by the eve of the Revolution.

THE PROVINCE OF SOUTH CAROLINA

If in the year 1767 North Carolina presented the appearance of a rather raw, pioneering region, outside of the Cape Fear River district, in contrast, the Province of South Carolina revealed to the visitor an entrenched, highly cultivated, and opulent planter aristocracy concentrated largely in the tidewater and the fertile lands adjoining it. In this area was located Charleston, the capital, cultural center and chief seaport of the province, a metropolis which at least in wealth and social amenities vied with the finest towns in the northern provinces. The city could count perhaps some 10,000 inhabitants [30] made up of merchants, rice and indigo planters, public officials, and the multitude of those who depended upon them for a livelihood, whether free or bound to service. Farther inland, beyond the area of the fresh-water cypress swamps, more elevated lands had been cleared on which were to be found maize and some wheat and other farm crops adapted to that climate; and still farther inland lay the region of the pine barrens extending into South Carolina from North Carolina and beyond, where men found a livelihood by exploiting the products of the red pine—its

[28] Shelburne Papers, 56:159–162; for levies for local purposes, see Parker, *Taxation in N.C.*, chap. VI.

[29] Shelburne Papers, 56:159–162; Raper, *North Carolina*, p. 203. Miss Parker leaves the impression (*Taxation in N.C.*, p. 120) that the poll tax continued to be levied until 1775 to sink the debenture notes. The salaries of the governor and other provincial officers were paid out of fees fixed by the Assembly and from the royal quitrents. As to the wages of members of the Council and the Assembly—amounting to 7s. 6 d. per diem during the sitting of the General Assembly, plus traveling expenses—these were apparently paid out of the sinking fund.

[30] For various estimates of the size of Charleston during this period, see E. L. Whitney, *Government of the Colony of South Carolina* (Baltimore, 1895), p. 119. For an account of the social life of the city, see Bridenbaugh, *Myths and Realities,* chap. II.

pitch, tar, turpentine, and resin—which, it was asserted, "administer more to the necessities and comforts of mankind than any other trees whatever." [31] Beyond the pine barrens was the country of the "pens," where cattle fattened and multiplied in the lush canebrakes and meadows lying about the sources of the numerous rivers of the province. Finally, still farther westward from the pens, there stretched the Indian country where South Carolina traders at the conclusion of the Cherokee Indian war once again congregated in the villages and bargained for dressed or undressed deerskins, still, as formerly, an important article of export.[32]

Under the old headright system that was still in force in South Carolina, the new settlers could obtain a hundred acres of land and fifty more for each dependent, free of quitrent payments for the first ten years.[33] In addition, they received so-called bounty money for the purchase of farm utensils and livestock, and, if diligent in improving their freeholds, "commonly left their children in easy circumstances." [34] In fact, one may question whether there were many parts of the world where the owners of lands could by frugality and industry succeed in doubling their capital "every three or four years," as the historian Ramsay affirmed was the case in South Carolina during the period of royal control of the province, which extended from 1720 to the outbreak of the Revolutionary War.[35]

Slavery seemed to be a cornerstone of this prosperity which rested on rice and indigo production. Whereas the number of taxable slaves in North Carolina—out of an estimated total population of 200,000—was placed at somewhat less than 13,000 in 1766, in South Carolina the number of Negroes was estimated in that year to be 95,000 as against some 40,000 whites.[36]

The tidewater, as the area of greatest wealth, dominated the political life of the province. Therein dwelt the governor, the

[31] David Ramsay, *The History of South Carolina* . . . (2 vols., Charleston, 1809), II, 284–285; 341.

[32] *Ibid.*, 284; Whitney, *Govt. of S. C.*, pp. 56–58; Gipson, *British Empire*, II, 166–167.

[33] Lord Charles Greville Montagu, governor of South Carolina, to the Earl of Shelburne, May 12, 1767, Shelburne Papers, 52:177–178.

[34] Ramsay, *Hist. of S.C.*, I, 114–116.

[35] *Ibid.*, p. 114.

[36] Whitney, *Govt. of S.C.*, p. 117.

Council, and other crown officials; there the courts of law convened for the trial of all civil as well as criminal cases, outside of trivial civil cases settled by the local justices; and therein, or in close proximity to it, dwelt a majority of the members of the Commons House of Assembly. This last condition was the result of the unequal distribution of representation among the parishes, which sent to the Assembly as many as four members or as few as one.[37]

Underrepresentation and the absence of courts bred discontent in the back regions. For, with the close of the Great War for the Empire, the settlers along the frontier had become the prey of swarms of horse and cattle thieves and other ruffians. A law passed in 1762 to grapple with this evil [38] had been ineffectual, as the thieves even upon being apprehended might have to be carried some two hundred miles for incarceration to stand trial at Charleston; moreover, some of the local justices of the peace seemed unwilling to exert themselves. Nor was still another law passed in 1767 any more effective in stamping out lawlessness.[39] Out of this intolerable situation grew a voluntary association in 1764 which, after the manner of the vigilance committees of the Far West a century later, began to take the law into its own hands and to mete out summary justice. Faced with this anarchic situation in the back country, Lord Charles Greville Montagu,[40] who became governor of South Carolina in 1766, clothed a man named Scovil with the powers of a high commissioner and dispatched him to the region to suppress the so-called Regulation, as it was called. But this was to no avail. By the fall of 1767 Montagu was obliged to write to Shelburne that some fifteen hundred men had agreed to support one another "in defiance of the Civil Magistrates and against the Laws

---

[37] For the official returns for the year 1773 from the various parishes, see John Drayton, *Memoirs of the American Revolution* (2 vols., Charleston, 1821), II, 46–47.

[38] J. F. Grimké (comp.), *The Public Laws of South Carolina, 1682–1790* (Charleston, 1793), p. xlix.

[39] Bridenbaugh, *Myths and Realities,* Ch. III.

[40] The governor of South Carolina was a younger son of the Duke of Manchester of the Montagu family. The confusion in the spelling of the name is cleared up by the fact, as evidenced in royal instructions sent to him in 1770, that he was addressed as "Charles Greville Montagu, Esquire, commonly called Lord Charles Greville Montague" (Drayton, *Memoirs,* I, 92–93).

of the Country." [41] Fortunately, with the extension of law courts into the back country, much of the ominous unrest disappeared after 1769.

The hostility the frontiersmen manifested toward the government of the province in 1767 does not appear to have been extended to the government of Great Britain. Once the Stamp Act was repealed, the frontiersmen looked to the home government for relief from these sectional difficulties. When the Commons House of Assembly was requested that same year to make provision under the terms of the Quartering Act for the King's troops, it refused to follow the lead of New York and, instead, "complied with every Requisition" to that end. [42]

As regards taxation grievances, it should be pointed out that, in spite of large appropriations for defense during the late war and in connection with the Cherokee Indian war that followed, the burden of taxation was far from oppressive and in some years was scarcely felt. For example, the levying of taxes to cover the expenditures of government from January 1, 1762, to December 31, 1763, which should have taken place in 1764, was further postponed in January, 1765; likewise, the levying of taxes to cover the expenditures of 1764, which should have taken place in 1765, was postponed in March, 1766. Apparently, from 1766 to 1769 appropriations were regularly made and taxes thereupon collected for the support of government; but from 1769 to 1777 no additional provincial taxes were collected other than port duties which were in no way onerous. [43] In 1770, £70,000 (equal to £10,000 sterling) was issued in

[41] Montagu to Shelburne, Oct. 8, 1767, Shelburne Papers, 52:188–189; *Pennsylvania Chronicle,* Oct. 3, 1768.

[42] Montagu to Shelburne, Aug. 14, 1767, Shelburne Papers, 52:183. It is true that in September, 1764, a committee of the Commons House of Assembly in addressing the provincial London agent, Charles Garth, laid stress on the need of additional paper money, with the circulating medium of the province amounting to but £106,500 currency or £15,214 sterling. R. W. Gibbs (ed.), *Documentary History of the American Revolution . . . 1764–1776* (New York, 1855), p. 7. In 1769 the old bills of credit were called in and exchanged for new bills; then the following year the currency was expanded by issuing £70,000 additional in paper, which brought the local volume of currency up to £176,500, where it continued until the outbreak of the American Revolution.

[43] *Public Laws of S.C.,* pp. l–lvi; Whitney, *Govt. of S.C.,* pp. 99–109. Whitney's figures leave the impression that no appropriations were made and no taxes raised in 1767 and 1768. However, the act of May 28, 1767 (No. 1077),

paper money, with the regular provision made for its redemption, in order to provide funds for the construction of courthouses and jails in the back regions to implement a reorganization of the judiciary prompted by the Regulation. But this issue was apparently not redeemed and served only to expand the currency to the benefit of all. Doubtless a good many South Carolinians, in the midst of that desolation that came with the Revolution, may have recalled with a certain nostalgia this period of great prosperity, when with "no tythes and very trifling taxes to pay [each person] reaped almost the whole fruits of his industry." [44]

THE PROVINCE OF GEORGIA

Founded as a trusteeship in 1732 for debtors of good character, the Colony of Georgia at the end of twenty years was turned over to the Crown to take its place among the royal provinces. Under the Trustees, the colony had at first progressed and at one time could count as many as 4,000 white inhabitants; but the number dwindled until in 1742 it was but 500—not only as the result of the War of Jenkins's Ear, but by reason of the restrictions placed upon it with respect to landholding and the prohibitions against slavery and rum. Under the royal regime the colony once again increased in population. Despite the Great War for the Empire, the white population by 1760 numbered 6,000 and their slaves exceeded 3,500. Six years later the white inhabitants had increased to 9,900 and their slaves to 7,800.[45]

---

provided for the granting and raising of £85,950 in the depreciated currency of the province, and in April, 1768, an act was passed for granting and raising the sum of £105,773 in the same currency (*Public Laws of S.C.*, pp. li, liii). It well may be that the money was never actually collected, as was true in Connecticut during the same years, where provision was made for taxes which, however, were not collected since the money was not needed for the support of government.

[44] Ramsay, *Hist. of S.C.*, I, 114. Dr. Ramsay, it may be noted, speaks with the most intimate personal knowledge of conditions both before the Revolutionary War and after its outbreak, since he was one of thirty prominent South Carolinians deported from Charleston by Lord Cornwallis in the midst of hostilities (*ibid.*, I, 371). In dealing with the period of Montagu's administration, Mrs. St. Julien Ravenel in her *Charleston* quotes (New York, 1906, p. 165) the Surveyor General William Gerard de Brahm as to the impressive building construction then under way and the lavish scale of entertaining then in vogue.

[45] Governor James Wright to the Earl of Shelburne, Shelburne Papers, 52: 199–201.

The growth of the once impoverished colony is also disclosed by other figures. In 1760, the people exported 3,400 barrels of rice and in 1765 over 10,000; in 1761, 42 vessels were adequate to carry on their commerce, but in 1765 it required 153 vessels of even greater burden. Not only were Georgians producing rice after the manner of the South Carolinians but also indigo, corn, and peas; they now had quantities of cattle, mules, horses, and hogs; they also made from their pine trees pitch, tar, and turpentine, shingles, barrel staves, and all types of lumber.[46] Their imports by 1766 had reached in value the very respectable figure of over £136,000 including manufactures from Great Britain, West India products, slaves from Africa, and commodities from the northern colonies; these were balanced by exports to the value of over £84,000, and by bills of exchange and gold and silver secured in the West India trade.[47] By the spring of 1767 over 500,000 acres of land lying within the province had been distributed—without reference to almost 90,000 acres of lands south of the Altamaha River hastily granted by the government of South Carolina in 1763 when in that same year the southern bounds of Georgia were extended to the St. Mary's.[48] With the headright system of granting lands and with the old restrictions on land alienation long since removed, by 1767 a planter aristocracy patterned after that of South Carolina had come into existence.[49]

Nevertheless, in spite of the many evidences of growth and prosperity, Georgia was still largely supported by an annual parliamentary grant, which in 1767 amounted to almost £4,000 sterling and which never dropped below £3,000 during the remainder of the colonial period;[50] in addition, until 1766 a sum amounting to

[46] Ibid.

[47] "A General State of the Trade from October 1765 to October 1766, Shelburne Papers, 52:207; P. S. Flippin, "Royal Government in Georgia," Georgia Historical Quarterly, IX, 224.

[48] Governor Wright to Shelburne, May 15, 1767, Shelburne Papers, 52:233–237. South Carolina had previously claimed all the land between the Altamaha and the Gulf of Mexico under its charter of 1665.

[49] For example, in 1769 Joseph Gibbons, a member of the Council, made a will giving to one son 1,500 acres of land, to another somewhat over that amount, to a third 1,000 acres, to a fourth over 2,700 acres, to a daughter 700 acres, to two other daughters each 1,000 acres, to a fourth daughter 500 acres, and to his wife he left "all the Town lot in Savannah with the Garden and Farm lot" (Georgia Wills, Book A, pp. 304–311, State Library).

[50] See the Annual Register, 1767, p. 219; ibid., 1773, p. 227; and ibid., 1775, p. 244.

£4,072 had been appropriated in England for the pay and subsistence of two troops of rangers which, with the establishment of
peace with the Cherokee, no longer seemed necessary for the protection of the inhabitants.[51] In contrast to these substantial sums, the
Assembly of Georgia granted that same year (1767) a mere £1,843
for the use and support of the government.[52] In addition, it imposed
a "small impost" on shipping to keep the lighthouse at the entrance
of the Savannah River in repair; a duty on deerskins, if exported
to any place other than Great Britain (for building a fort at the
entrance of the river); and a "small duty" on goods coming from
the northern colonies (for building a fort at Augusta and repairing
the one at Frederica).[53]

Despite the substantial aid the British Government extended to
what it still regarded as an infant foundation, the people of Georgia
carried the weight of imperial responsibility lightly. This attitude
was reflected in their stand on implementing the Mutiny Act.
Although the rangers had been disbanded in the province, a small
detachment of regulars was assigned by General Gage to frontier
duty and to garrisoning the fort at the entrance of the Savannah.
When Captain Phillips early in 1767 applied for necessaries for his
troops in accordance with the Mutiny Act, Governor Wright immediately requested the Assembly to make such provision. In reply the
Commons House of Assembly declared that

they humbly conceive that their complying with the requisition contained in your Excellencys message, would be a Violation of the Trust

[51] Wright to Shelburne, May 15, 1767, Shelburne Papers, 55:263-270.

[52] *Ibid.* It is by no means certain that even this modest sum was actually
raised. For the act passed in 1773 to issue £4,299 in certificates has the following preamble: "Whereas no tax act has been passed since May 10, 1770 [when
£3,355 9s. was voted for that year], which makes it necessary to raise a very
considerable sum, and whereas the tax laid several years before, was not duly
collected, by reason whereof there is a great deficiency," etc. *Georgia Historical
Quarterly,* IX, 211. The following sums of money were granted by the Assembly for the support of government: in 1763, £1,934 9s.; in 1764, £2,117
13s.; in 1765, £1,599 7s.; in 1766, £1,925 6s.; in 1767, £1,843 11s.; in 1768,
1,768 and £3,046 16s., the latter grant on Dec. 23, 1768, for the support of
government in 1769; in 1770, £3,355 9s.; and finally, in 1773, £5,171 15s.
A.D. Candler (ed.), *The Colonial Records . . . of Georgia* (17 vols., Atlanta,
1904-13), XIV, 63, 123, 242-243, 355, 456, 561, 639; XV, 175, 514-515. The
extent to which these sums were collected is not, however, clear.

[53] Wright to Shelburne, May 15, 1767, Shelburne Papers, 55:263-270.

reposed in them by their Constituents and providing a precedent they by no means think themselves justifiable in introducing.[54]

This legislative independence was manifest in other areas as well. When two bills for ferries passed the Commons House and were amended by the Council at the desire of the governor in order to conform to the requirement of the law passed by Parliament during the reign of Queen Anne [55] that postmen with official mail should be carried without being detained unnecessarily and without charge, the amendments were rejected. In writing to the Earl of Shelburne, the governor affirmed: "The true and avowed Reason (tho' not declared on the Conference) was that they would not seem to adopt or submit to an act of Parliament." [56] That he did not thereupon dissolve the Commons House of Assembly and order new elections was due to the boast of some of the leaders of the opposition that, should he do so, in the next Assembly there would be "none but what *they call Sons of Liberty*—that is," as he explained to Shelburne, "such as are disposed to strike at the Sovereignty of Great Britain." Yet, despite this intransigence, the Commons House of Assembly in an address to the King as late as 1774 declared:

Although your Majesty's Province of Georgia is at present in a florishing and desirable state of prosperity, although every year brings with it a very considerable augmentation of Wealth and success, we are yet very far from being able to Act against so numerous and dangerous an Enemy as the Indians without your Majesty's gracious support . . . therefore, allow us to solicit your Majesty for . . . protection and Assistance. . . .[57]

THE PROVINCE OF EAST FLORIDA

The Province of East Florida was in 1767 theoretically under a civil government, but actually run as a military colony, with St. Augustine and Fort St. Marks garrisoned by seven companies of Whitmore's (the 9th) regiment. The governor, Major General

---

[54] *Ga. Colon. Rec.*, XIV, 441. In the fall of the year the Assembly was led to make provision under the terms of the Mutiny Act for the soldiers after a letter from Shelburne with significant implications was laid before the Commons House of Assembly (*ibid.*, XIV, 479–480, 483–484).

[55] 9 Anne, c. 10, Sec. 29, *Statutes at Large*, IV, 425.

[56] Wright to Shelburne, Apr. 6, 1767, Shelburne Papers, 52:215–231.

[57] *Ga. Colon. Rec.*, XV, 543.

James Grant, who had fought the Cherokee under Montgomery, was immersed in plans to attract settlers to the colony. With the departure of the Spaniards upon the making of peace, East Florida, save for soldiers and the Indians, had been left virtually uninhabited. By the summer of 1767 sixty so-called mandamus and local grants of land totaling 120,000 acres had been made, among others to members of the English nobility and gentry and to a group of South Carolina planters. But most of this acreage had been too recently acquired to be put to cultivation.[58] Hence, despite Grant's efforts to promote settlement,[59] the white settlers numbered in 1767 a mere 120, chiefly concentrated in and about St. Augustine, and the slaves, 260.[60]

Although provision had been made in the governor's commission and instructions for the setting up of a representative Assembly, the colony was obviously not ready for one. Nor had any taxes been levied within East Florida by 1767. In short, the burden of maintaining this colony fell entirely upon the British treasury, from which £4,750 was drawn in 1767 for its civil establishment without reference to the support of its garrisons.[61]

Hopes had been entertained that many Bermudians would be attracted to the new province, and plans were laid to settle them on

[58] Grant to Shelburne, July 16, 1767, Shelburne Papers, 52:311–312, 55:421–433. For mandamus grants made between 1764 and 1767, see J. Munro (ed.), *Acts of the Privy Council of England, Colonial Series* (Hereford, 1911–12), IV, Appendix V, pp. 813–815; for Mandamus grants from 1767 to 1774, see *ibid.*, V, Appendix V, pp. 590–593. For a careful study of land grants both mandamus and local, see C. L. Mowatt's *East Florida as a British Province 1763–1784* (Berkeley, 1943), chap. V. Between the years 1764 and 1775, over 1,600,000 acres of land were granted, either locally by the Governor's Council or by British orders in council (*ibid.*, p. 62).

[59] For a portion of a proclamation issued by Grant setting forth the merits of East Florida, see J. G. Forbes, *Sketches, Historical and Topographical of the Floridas* . . . (New York, 1821), Appendix, pp. 186–187. The date of this proclamation is, however, given by Forbes as 1763, the year before Grant received the commission as governor which, on May 1, 1764, was ordered to be delivered to him (Board of Trade, *Journal, 1764 to 1767* (London, 1936), p. 46).

[60] Shelburne Papers, 55:427–433.

[61] *Annual Register, 1767,* p. 218. Not until the year 1781 was a representative assembly called, during the last phase of the Revolutionary War. Mowat (*East Florida,* p. 125) presents the reasons for calling an assembly at this critical period.

a bluff overlooking St. Marys River.[62] When the project failed, the enterprising Dr. Andrew Turnbull, one of the settlers, promoted a plan to import into the province as indentured servants several hundred Greeks from Smyrna within the Turkish Empire, in order to grow silk, grapes, and cotton. With Grant's full support, he went to England early in 1767 to promote his project. As a result, the home government, to encourage the planting of the colony, was led to offer a bounty of 40s. for every Greek up to five hundred who should be brought into the province.[63] Through great expenditures, Turnbull and his associate, Sir William Duncan, finally succeeded in that year in importing some fifteen hundred Greeks, Italians, and Minorcans, who were settled at New Smyrna, some sixty miles south of St. Augustine. There they were set to clearing the land and raising indigo, sugar cane, and other products. However, their hardships and misery caused them to revolt in 1768. Some seven years after the military had restored order among them, the provincial government was finally led to come to their protection and assistance. Freed from their indentures, they were thereupon peaceably and permanently settled on land in the northern part of St. Augustine.[64]

THE PROVINCE OF WEST FLORIDA

The British Province of West Florida consisted of that part of old Spanish Florida beyond the Chattahoochee and Apalachicola Rivers and most of the Province of Louisiana to the south of the 31st parallel of north latitude east of the Mississippi. Its western boundary was Lakes Pontchartrain and Maurepas and the Mississippi River. It included old Spanish Pensacola and the French towns of Mobile and Biloxi. Although the Spaniards seemed to have left Pensacola en masse following news of the signing of the treaty of cession, the French were induced to remain, as they had in Canada and Louisiana. As a result, even in 1767 the area about Mobile Bay was largely a French settlement and so remained throughout the

[62] Grant to Shelburne, Aug. 5 and Nov. 27, 1766, Shelburne Papers, 52:267, 289–290; see Mowat (*East Florida,* pp. 57–72) for other plans or suggestions for settling the province.

[63] Shelburne to Grant, May 14, 1767, Shelburne Papers, 53:231.

[64] R. B. Morris, *Government and Labor in Early America* (New York, 1946), pp. 178–181; Mowatt, *East Florida,* pp. 71–72; W. W. Dewhurst, *The History of St. Augustine, Florida* (New York, 1881), pp. 113–121.

history of the colony.[65] It is therefore clear that during the early years of the province, if not throughout its entire history, a majority of the white inhabitants were French-speaking.[66]

In 1764 Governor George Johnstone's commission was altered under the Great Seal so as to extend the northern boundary of the province northward from the 31st degree to a line running eastward from the mouth of the Yazoo to the Apalachicola River. This alteration brought in the former French town of Natchez and the vastly fertile lands about it. But although English garrisons were established at Natchez and at Manchac on the Iberville, few if any Englishmen settled in the western part of the province beyond Mobile. Nevertheless, the English had their eyes on the lands bordering the Mississippi. By the beginning of 1767 a total of twenty-eight mandamus grants had been issued, chiefly to army officers, of amounts ranging from as much as 20,000 acres to as little as 2,500.[67]

Although neither Quebec nor East Florida—in spite of the promises made in the Proclamation of 1763—elected a representative assembly before the outbreak of the Revolutionary War, Governor Johnstone was led to issue a call for one in West Florida in August, 1766. The franchise was broadly extended to persons who were heads of families and who occupied houses,[68] but it is not clear that the French-speaking householders were accorded the right to vote.

[65] Cecil Johnson, *British West Florida, 1763-1783* (New Haven, 1943), pp. 150-151.

[66] In 1766 the population of West Florida was estimated as between 1,800 and 2,000 (*ibid.,* p. 44); in 1774, exclusive of the Indians, at 4,900, 1,200 of whom were slaves (*ibid.,* p. 155). In 1766, according to one who prepared a "Survey of West Florida in 1768," there were in the District of Mobile, which included the area up to Lake Pontchartrain, some 140 houses and plantations; about 300 men able to bear arms; 200 white women and children; 360 Negro men, women, and children; and 8,000 head of cattle. The writer of this survey estimated that the population in the Pensacola District to the east could not be more numerous than that in the District of Mobile, if as numerous. This document is printed in Isabel M. Calder's *Colonial Captivities, Marches, and Journeys* (New York, 1935), pp. 228-235.

[67] *Acts of the Privy Council,* IV, Appendix V, pp. 813-815. Some seventeen additional grants were made from 1767 to the end of the life of the province (*ibid.,* V, Appendix V, pp. 393-394); see also C. N. Howard's "Colonial Natchez: the Early British Phase," *Journal of Mississippi History,* VII, 156-170.

[68] Cecil Johnson, *British West Florida,* p. 84; C. N. Howard, *British Development of West Florida,* p. 44. Howard does not think the franchise extended to French Catholics (*ibid.,* p. 29).

They were, of course, disqualified from holding public office. As for the work of the legislature, it made provision for some port dues and other levies, but practically the entire cost of maintaining both the civil and military establishment of the province fell upon the mother country, which in 1767 set aside £4,800 sterling for this purpose.[69] Although the colony was thus almost utterly dependent upon the government at home for support, Lieutenant Governor Montfort Browne was, nevertheless, obliged to complain to the Earl of Shelburne the following June that the Assembly was "protracting the Business of the Province . . . to enjoy the enormous salary they had voted themselves. . . ." [70] Furthermore, at its very first session the Assembly proceeded to adopt a strong memorial to the Board of Trade pointing out the need for substantial additional aids from Britain for the building of fortifications, churches, jails, and a hospital; for subsidizing the trade in slaves and deerskins and the growing of indigo, rice, and silk; and for supporting the poor of the colony. In all, these requests added up to some £68,000 in a four-year period. In addition, annual appropriation of some £11,600 was requested for maintaining a body of rangers to supplement the force of regulars stationed in the province as protection against powerful Indian tribes, especially the Choctaw and the Upper Creeks.[71]

The key to British policy in West Florida was the maintenance of friendly relations with the natives. Nevertheless, the Indians, especially the Creeks, committed a series of depredations upon the settlers apparently in reprisal for the behavior of the traders. Governor Johnstone thereupon determined to disregard his instructions and to make war upon the Upper Creeks.[72] When the Earl of Shelburne received the news of this plan, he was horrified and proceeded to secure permission from the King to recall the governor. Early in February, 1767, he was ordered to turn over the conduct of affairs in West Florida to Lieutenant Governor Montfort Browne.[73] A period of relative tranquility ensued.

[69] *Annual Register, 1767*, p. 218.

[70] Browne to Shelburne, June 29, 1767, Shelburne Papers, 52:365.

[71] "Representation of the Council and Assembly of West Florida, November 22, 1766," Shelburne Papers, 52:341–343.

[72] Johnstone to Colonel Taylor, Oct. 4, 1766, Shelburne Papers, 52:300–301; J. R. Alden, *John Stuart and the Southern Colonial Frontier* (Ann Arbor, 1944), pp. 224–226.

[73] Shelburne to Johnstone, Feb. 19, 1767, Shelburne Papers, 53:243–245.

BERMUDA AND THE BRITISH WEST INDIES

In turning from the mainland of North America to Bermuda, the Bahamas, and the British possessions in the Caribbean area in 1767, it should be noted that everywhere, outside of some of the new acquisitions that came with the treaty of peace of 1763, representative government was established and everywhere the assemblies were busy promoting popular local objectives. In Bermuda the influence of the northern continental colonies was very much in evidence, especially that of New York, and governor and assembly, as Lieutenant Governor George Bruere reported in 1766, were constantly embroiled in "Heats and animosities. . . . " [74] The following year Bruere clashed with the General Assembly over the issue of provisioning the garrison at St. George, the capital, under the terms of the Mutiny Act of 1765. Upon the repeated refusal of the Assembly to do so until His Majesty had confirmed a bill it had passed, Bruere felt impelled to dissolve it and order new elections.[75]

The Bahamas made slow progress in the eighteenth century and depended largely for support upon the mother country. William Shirley, for many years governor of Massachusetts Bay, was occupying the same office in these islands in 1767 and displayed his previously demonstrated ability to work harmoniously with his assembly. Thus, when early in the year the latter framed an address to Parliament praying that the island of New Providence should be made a free port to encourage trade with Cuba, he strongly supported the plea.[76] Despite the cloud under which Shirley had returned to England from New England in the midst of the Great War for the Empire, he was now held in high regard in Britain. When the time for his retirement had come, the Crown therefore granted him half pay for life as colonel and the government of the Bahamas was entrusted to his son.[77]

In Jamaica, the Assembly had by 1766 gone through a bitter contest over parliamentary privilege with the governor, William Henry Lyttelton. For a time no legislation was enacted and no

---

[74] Bruere to Shelburne, July 20, 1766, Shelburne Papers, 52:533.

[75] Bruere to Shelburne, Nov. 15, 1767, *ibid.*, 52:562–563. For two studies that throw much light on political unrest in Bermuda, see W. B. Kerr's *Bermuda and the American Revolution: 1760–1783* (Princeton, 1935) and H. C. Wilkinson's *Bermuda in the Old Empire* (London, 1950), chap. XII.

[76] Shirley to Shelburne, Jan. 24, 1767, Shelburne Papers, 52:492–494.

[77] Shelburne to Shirley, Nov. 14, 1767, *ibid.*, 54:155–156.

appropriations were made. When the Privy Council finally reviewed the controversy, it sustained the Assembly and recalled the governor.[78] Thereupon the Assembly, in an address to Lieutenant Governor Elletson, expressed its gratitude while at the same time it complained of many injuries suffered as the result of Lyttelton's "violent, rapacious and unconstitutional conduct" with respect to the fees of officers and other "extortions by the late Governor . . . so notoriously discouraging to trade." [79] However, in July, in another address to Elletson, the House of Assembly returned to the fray. Its members insisted that they as a body held the same "Rank in the System of their constitution as the House of Commons does in that of their Mother Country," and therefore possessed the powers to commit even royal officials and the right to frame money bills without amendment by the Governor's Council.[80]

Located on the eastern rim of the Lesser Antilles, Barbados had suffered a series of blows that hastened its decline from a once flourishing colony. A great conflagration in 1767 gutted Bridgetown, the capital and only seaport of the island. Never again would it shine in its former impressiveness as a West India center of wealth and culture.[81] Unlike most of the other British colonies, Barbados was not expanding. In fact, by 1767 the number of deaths actually exceeded the number of births.[82] Upon the shoulders of the planters there rested not only heavy taxation for local needs, but the payment to the Crown of the $4\frac{1}{2}$ per cent in specie on all "dead" commodities exported from the island, a levy which was considered to amount to a tax of 10 per cent on the profits drawn from the sugar fields.[83]

What was true of Barbados was also true of the British Leeward sugar islands: St. Christopher, Antigua, Nevis, and Montserrat, faced as they were by competition from the more fertile French

[78] *Acts of the Privy Council,* IV, 704–713. For a scholarly discussion of the issues involved in Lyttelton's dispute with the Assembly, see Mary P. Clarke's *Parliamentary Privilege in the American Colonies* (New Haven, 1943), pp. 252–257.

[79] Address of the Jamaica Assembly, June 1766, Shelburne Papers, 52:388–389.

[80] Address of the Jamaica Assembly, July 1766, *ibid.,* 52:389–392.

[81] President Rouse to Shelburne, June 10, 1767, *ibid.,* 52:483–485.

[82] *Ibid.*

[83] L. H. Gipson, *British Empire,* II, 256–257.

West Indies.[84] Aside from Jamaica, these West India islands colonized by the English in the seventeenth century had by 1767 seen
their best days.[85] On the other hand, Jamaica, having just been
made a so-called free port, was to enjoy its era of greatest prosperity,
an era which lasted until the abolition of slavery within the empire
in 1833, when it joined the rest of the British Caribbean Sea possessions as an island of impoverished planters.[86]

Of the Windward Islands, Dominica, lying between the French
islands of Guadeloupe and Martinique, along with St. Vincent,
Grenada, and Tobago, all to the southward, became a part of the
British Empire by the treaty of peace of 1763. They had, with the
exception of Tobago, previously been colonized to a greater or less
extent by the French.[87] After 1763 the problem was to attract British
planters and to establish a civil government for them. In 1766
Robert Melville served as acting governor of the four islands, with
headquarters in Grenada. He was supposed to have the assistance
of a General Council made up of residents from all the British
Windwards and of a lieutenant governor in each of the other three
islands, and it was also expected that a General Assembly made up
of those elected by the inhabitants of the four islands would be
established;[88] but neither Council nor Assembly could be set up.
Nevertheless, in October, 1766, he summoned an assembly for
Grenada and the Grenadines;[89] he was also able to write home the
following year that the wish of the people of St. Vincent for a
separate assembly had been granted.[90] With respect to Dominica,
far to the north of Grenada, its government in 1766 was, to say the
least, very rudimentary, although the island in that year had been
made a free port along with Jamaica.[91] In January, 1767, its
merchants, traders, and other inhabitants joined in a petition to the
King, representing that no courts of criminal justice had as yet been

[84] *Ibid.*, pp. 308–311.
[85] L. J. Ragatz, *The Fall of the Planter Class in the British Caribbean, 1763–
1833* (New York, 1928).
[86] *Ibid.*, pp. 138–139.
[87] L. H. Gipson, *British Empire*, V, 207–230.
[88] Egremont to the Board of Trade, July 14, 1763, Shelburne Papers, 64:
521–522.
[89] Melville to Shelburne, Jan. 15, 1767, *ibid.*, 52:444–448.
[90] Melville to Shelburne, May 23, 1767, *ibid.*, 52:454–455.
[91] 6 George III, c. 49, *Statutes at Large*, VII, 613–618.

set up and that it was impracticable to resort to Grenada to secure justice. Accordingly, they asked for their own governor, courts of law, and assembly.[92] Tobago got off to a slow start despite the inducements set forth in a royal proclamation issued in 1764 for the planting of the new British Windward Islands.[93] Even as late as 1767 few planters were yet settled thereon. Yet in all of the new acquisitions the institutions of representative government were introduced as soon as the inhabitants were ready to receive them.[94] In fact, most of those who settled the Windward Islands had come from the older British West India possessions and were accustomed to self-government.[95]

To summarize the main problems faced by the British colonies in the New World on the eve of the Revolution, it should be recognized first of all that most of the older colonies furnished impressive evidence of political and economic maturity as well as financial stability. The newer establishments, both on the continent and in the West Indies, offered ample proof of the determination of the home government that they should conform as rapidly as possible to the well-established pattern of British colonial representative government. Everywhere one found a disposition of colonials to set forth their local political rights in vigorous fashion, to stress their privileges if not their duties as Englishmen. Almost everywhere in British North America in 1767 the public financial burdens were lighter than those shouldered by the people in Great Britain. Finally, this survey of internal problems and issues in the colonies highlights the enormous complexity of the problems of imperial administration.

[92] Shelburne Papers, 52:467–468.

[93] For this see *American Antiquarian Society, Transactions,* XII, 218–224; for the sale of Crown lands in Tobago from 1765 to 1771, see Ragatz, *Fall of the Planter Class,* p. 116.

[94] Hume Wrong, *Government of the West Indies* (Oxford, 1923), pp. 46, 155.

[95] For economic conditions on these islands, see Ragatz, *Fall of the Planter Class,* pp. 114, 119–120.

CHAPTER 11

A Trial at External Taxation

THE GROWTH of the movement for complete American colonial autonomy between 1761 and 1775 was gradual but cumulative in its effects. Just as the English Parliament and English popular leaders in the course of the seventeenth century undermined the royal prerogative by their constant assertion of privileges and immunities based upon their own conception of the ancient constitution, so now, from 1761 onward, the colonial assemblies and popular colonial leaders, by appealing to what they considered to be their ancient English constitutional rights, were destined ultimately to free themselves from the system of imperial controls which the mother country during the preceding century had evolved for the orderly and effective administration of the colonies. Both parliamentary movements were alike, too, in their recognition of changed conditions that made the old order obsolete. In other words, the people of England at the close of the seventeenth century had a different set of aspirations from those held by their ancestors at the close of the War of the Roses. Similarly, the American colonials lived in an entirely different world from that of their forbears who settled the first colonies. In each case, finally, the constitutional crises were marked by periods of indecision, temporizing, and concession.

The news of the repeal of the Stamp Act was greeted with spontaneously joyful demonstrations on the part of all groups in the colonies. This enthusiasm was in no way dimmed by the fact that Parliament had taken care to pass the Declaratory Act, settling—so far as was possible within the legal framework of the constitution of the Empire—the question of the *right* of that body to levy taxes upon all who were subjects of the Crown of Great Britain. For the latter statute, in the words of Lieutenant Governor Thomas Hutchinson of Massachusetts Bay, "was considered as mere naked form." [1] Indeed, to colonial leaders of the opposition to the Stamp Act, its final repeal was a clear vindication of the soundness of the methods that they had employed to defeat its operation.[2] Flushed with success, the popular leaders in Massachusetts Bay now moved to get effective control of the provincial government.

By the terms of the charter granted under the Great Seal by William and Mary in 1691,[3] the members of the Council, which served in the double capacity of an upper chamber of the Great and General Court of Assembly and of a council for the royal governor, were not appointed by the King, as was the case in all the colonies that conformed strictly to the royal-colony pattern, but were annually elected by the Assembly itself. Were there to be eliminated from the Council all those who had during the recent crisis supported the home government, however timidly, it was clear that the royal governor could be effectively isolated.

This step was now determined upon less than a fortnight after the news of the repeal had been received. As a preliminary step, the House of Representatives proceeded on May 28, 1766, with its organization by electing James Otis as Speaker and Samuel Adams as clerk, thus choosing as its chief officers the two most dangerous opponents of Governor Bernard and of the system of controls that he as well as his predecessors had been commissioned to maintain. But Bernard possessed the power of negativing the choice of speaker [4] and proceeded, without hesitation, to reject Otis.[5] As a

---

[1] Thomas Hutchinson, *The History of the Province of Massachusetts Bay* . . . (London, 1828), p. 147.

[2] *Ibid.*

[3] *Acts and Resolves . . . of the Province of the Massachusetts Bay* . . . (21 vols., Boston, 1869–1922), I, 1–20.

[4] In 1725 the Crown issued an explanatory charter upholding the right of the governor to negative the choice of a speaker by the House of Representatives. J. Munro (ed.), *Acts of the Privy Council of England, Colonial Series* (Hereford, 1911–12), III, 94–95, 103.

[5] C. F. Adams (ed.), *The Works of John Adams* . . . (10 vols., Boston, 1850–56), II, 195.

result, Thomas Cushing was selected and, although a follower of Otis and Adams, was permitted by the governor to assume the chair. With the House now organized, the business of electing the members of the Council was taken up that same afternoon. In the voting, supporters of Bernard were rejected, including the lieutenant governor, the provincial secretary, and the attorney general; in their places were chosen others who could be counted on to obstruct the governor in any policy not approved by the House of Representatives. John Adams recorded the achievements of that day in his diary in these words: "Thus the triumph of Otis and his party are complete." [6]

But Bernard proceeded to negative the choice of six of the twenty-eight newly elected members of the Council who were *persona non grata* to him, including Colonel Otis, the father of James Otis. He also denounced the action of the House as an attack upon government for the deliberate purpose of depriving him of men "whose only crime was fidelity to the crown." [7] But since he could not force the Assembly to carry out his wishes, he had to

[6] *Ibid.*, II, 195-196. It may be pointed out that the elimination of Lieutenant Governor Hutchinson from the Council was an especially severe blow to Bernard, who leaned much on him for advice. It would moreover appear that he had a right *ex officio* to a vote in the Council and did not require election under the terms of the charter. This at least was the construction placed by the Board of Trade on the charter when it was being considered by that body before it passed the Great Seal. Its minute of August 20, 1691, on this matter reads as follows: "The lieutenant or deputy governor, during residence of the governor within the colony, to have first place in the council, and, at all times, to have a vote there, and in the assembly, as [one of] the assistants" (Hutchinson, *Hist. of Prov. of Mass.*, p. 174). However, when Bernard later sought to have Hutchinson present in the Council, although not voting, this brought a strong protest from the House. As a result, Hutchinson wrote a letter to the governor declaring that he would absent himself thereafter from the Council (his letter is printed in the *Pennsylvania Gazette*, Mar. 19, 1767). This step virtually conceded the right of the House of Representatives to act as the interpreter of the constitution of the province.

[7] Hutchinson, *Hist. of Prov. of Mass.*, pp. 149-150; W. V. Wells, *The Life and Public Services of Samuel Adams* (3 vols., Boston, 1865), I, 121-123. Adams wrote the reply of the House to Bernard and embodied in it what might have been considered by the governor rather disingenuous language. The following is an excerpt of the reply: "Had your Excellency been pleased in season to have favored us with a list [of councilors], and positive orders whom to choose, we should in your principles have been without excuse. But even the most abject slaves are not to be blamed for disobeying their master's will and pleasure, when it is wholly unknown to them" (*ibid.*, I, 124).

reconcile himself to the fact that henceforth the Council would cease acting as a buffer between governor and representatives.[8]

Shortly after this second triumph of the radical group, the governor received a circular letter from Secretary of State Conway dated March 31, enclosing a resolution of the House of Commons that called upon the colonies to make proper compensation to those who had suffered from the Stamp Act riots. On June 7 Bernard, appearing before the Assembly to carry out this order, declared that "the Justice and Humanity of this Requisition is so forceable that it cannot be controverted. The Authority [that is, the resolution of the House of Commons and the Conway letter] with which it is introduced, should preclude all Disputation about Comply^g with it." [9] The House of Representatives was quick to take exception to the use of the word "requisition," employed so frequently during the late war to cover a variety of requests made upon the colonies by the government, and asserted:

If the Authority with which it [the requisition] is introduced should preclude all Disputation about Comply^g with it we should be glad to know what Freedom we have in the Case.[10]

While the House declared itself ready, if possible, to bring the perpetrators of the riots "to exemplary Justice and if it be in their Power, to a pecuniary Restitution of all Damages," it had come by June 25 to take the position that for the province itself to make up these losses to the sufferers would not be "an Act of Justice but rather of Generosity." Moreover, the representatives indicated a

[8] *Ibid.,* I, 122. The Council, although now purged of six members considered by Bernard to be the most hostile to his work as governor, addressed him in terms that, according to Hutchinson, went even farther than the House in vindicating the recent elections to that body (Hutchinson, *Hist. of Prov. of Mass.,* p. 154). In fact, the Board, now under the leadership of James Bowdoin, when it came to the issues that subsequently arose in the controversy between Parliament and the colonies, in almost every instance united with the House in opposition to the governor and the lieutenant governor (*ibid.,* p. 156; see also F. G. Walett, "The Massachusetts Council, 1766 to 1774 . . ." *William and Mary Quarterly,* 3rd ser., VI, 605–627, and his "James Bowdoin . . ." Bostonian Society, *Proceedings,* 1950, pp. 28–29).

[9] In Bernard's letter to Conway, July 19, 1766, Shelburne Papers, 58:1–47, Clements Library. Conway's letter is printed in E. B. O'Callaghan and B. Fernow (eds.), *Documents Relative to the Colonial History of the State of New York* (15 vols., Albany, 1853–87), VII, 823–824.

[10] Shelburne Papers, 58:1–47.

doubt whether they had authority to make their constituents charge-able for damage committed in Boston.[11] On the 27th the House asked the governor whether the detection of persons responsible for the "Mischiefs" would be necessary to entitle those whose property had been destroyed to receive compensation. To the representatives it seemed to be the intention of King and Parliament "that a Veil should be cast over the late Disturbances, provided it be covered by a dutiful Behaviour for the future." Be that as it may, the House took the position that the whole matter should be referred to the towns and thereupon to the next assembly. Accordingly, it asked to be permitted to adjourn since, in its opinion, it had done everything at present that "our most gracious Sovereign and his Parliament can reasonably expect of us."[12]

The issue of compensation for the destruction of property in Boston in 1765 has a very direct bearing upon a similar issue which arose in 1773 over the destruction of the chests of tea. In each case the British Government insisted upon compensation being made to the owners of the property destroyed. In the early crisis, however, there was general acceptance in the province of the principle that compensation was justly due, even to those who had become per-sonally obnoxious to the Sons of Liberty. In fact, the only question in the minds of the more responsible people was this: Who was to make the compensation? But this acceptance was still somewhat theoretical. To attempt to bring the chief promoters of the riots of 1765 to justice and to force them to pay was apparently never seriously considered by the provincial leaders. Indeed, no man in the Assembly, no judge, no other officer of the peace, or no grand jury would have dared to have taken part had such an effort been made in 1766.[13] If, then, the responsibility were to be shouldered,

[11] The argument ran as follows: "If the Indemnification is to be considered an Act of Justice it ought to come from the Town of Boston; if it is to be paid by the Province at large it will be an Act of Generosity to the Town of Boston from whom it is in justice due. The people throughout the country expect it shall be paid by Boston only" (Shelburne Papers, 58:1–47).

[12] Ibid.

[13] It is true that the House of Representatives, in reply to the Governor's message of June 27, informed Bernard that it had appointed a committee to sit during the adjournment to make an inquiry into the riots of the preceding year and to discover the persons concerned therein (Boston Evening Post, July 14, 1766).

it would have to be either by Boston or by the entire colony, although John Adams's lawyer friend, Robert Treat Paine, was of the opinion, significantly, that "the continent ought to have paid the damage." [14]

During the recess of the Assembly the towns gave the issue their consideration. Although there was general opposition in Boston and in the towns of Plymouth County to the payment of any compensation, most of the towns within the province favored payment, but by Boston alone.[15] Boston's bitter opposition to accepting sole responsibility might have led to a stalemate had not Dennys De Berdt, the Massachusetts Bay agent in London, written most tactfully in August and again in September, stressing the unfavorable impression that refusal to make compensation would have upon the friends of the colonials in England.[16] Moreover, news that Pitt—the man who had, according to private letters, called the Stamp Act "the most impolitic, arbitrary, oppressive, and unconstitutional Act that ever was passed"[17]—had organized a new ministry, prompted the Boston leaders to avoid embarrassing his administration. Finally, the New York Assembly had set an example by agreeing to provide compensation to the chief sufferers from the Stamp Act riot in New York City.[18]

These developments contributed to an abrupt reversal of the attitude of the Boston popular leaders. The town meeting was now led to instruct its deputies in the Assembly to use their endeavors to have compensation paid out of the funds of the province.[19] The result was a temporary impasse between those who felt that Boston alone should pay and those who favored appropriating the money

[14] Adams, *Works of John Adams*, II, 204.

[15] *Ibid.*; see also Bernard to Shelburne, Nov. 14, 1766, Shelburne Papers, 58:21–23.

[16] De Berdt's letters are printed in the *Massachusetts Gazette*, Nov. 13, 1766.

[17] Adams, *Works of John Adams*, II, 190–191; Boston *Gazette*, Oct. 27, 1766.

[18] The only person who failed to be compensated for his losses was Lieutenant Governor Cadwallader Colden, whose carriage was taken from his coach house by the mob and burnt. To Major Thomas James, who was responsible for the defense of Fort George and whose house was sacked by the mob, compensation was granted in June by a very close vote. Colden to Conway, June 24, 1766, *New York Colon. Doc.*, VII, 832–834.

[19] Shelburne Papers, 58:1–47.

from the provincial treasury.[20] However, this stalemate was resolved by Joseph Hawley, a leading radical lawyer of Northampton, who thenceforward was closely associated with Otis and Samuel Adams. Hawley now proposed that compensation be paid only on condition that a general amnesty be granted to all involved. Defying the Declaratory Act, he declared: "The Parliament of Great Britain has no right to legislate for Us." Otis then rose from his seat and thanked him.[21] Under his guidance the House eventually framed a bill entitled "An Act for granting compensation to the sufferers, and of free and general pardon, indemnity and oblivion in the late times," which was passed early in December. It not only assumed the authority to grant compensation to the Stamp Act sufferers, but also the unprecedented power, hitherto reserved to the Crown alone, to grant pardons. In this regard the bill was revolutionary in nature.[22]

Realizing that the statute was one of "extraordinary nature and importance," the Lords Commissioners upon its receipt referred it to the Attorney General and Solicitor General for their opinion, and thereupon sent a representation to the Privy Council.[23] Then on May 13, 1767, the latter body, after due consideration, disallowed the law.[24] The following day both the House of Lords and the House of Commons requested the ministers to lay before them not only a copy of the act in question but all papers bearing upon it.[25] There the matter rested. Before the news of disallowance reached Massachusetts Bay, compensation had been granted to Hutchinson and to the other victims of the riots. As for the organizers of the rioting, while no specific pardon could be granted them, the act of oblivion,

[20] Hutchinson to Shelburne, Nov. 15, 1766, Shelburne Papers, 51:495–496.

[21] W. V. Wells, *The Life and Public Service of Samuel Adams* (3 vols., Cambridge, Mass., 1866) II, 127.

[22] Among the Shelburne Papers are two having to do with the pardoning power of the Crown. One is entitled "An Account of several Acts of Grace" (*ibid.,* 58:223–224) and the other "Original Question as to the King's Prerogative of Pardoning" (*ibid.,* 58:227–257). The latter enumerates instances of pardon by the Crown of American subjects and includes pardons granted in 1676 on the occasion of Bacon's Rebellion, in 1690 in connection with Leisler's Rebellion, in 1711 to rioters in St. Christopher, and in 1747 to rioters in New Jersey.

[23] *Board of Trade Journal, 1764–1767,* pp. 375, 380–381.

[24] *Acts of the Privy Council, Col. Ser.,* V, 87.

[25] *Ibid.* See also the *Board of Trade Journal, 1764–1767,* p. 388.

although disallowed, continued to be recognized as effectively protecting their persons. They appeared in public with a feeling of perfect security, "even such as had been rescued out of prison." [26] In other words, while the Privy Council nullified the provincial law, the Massachusetts Bay radicals in turn just as effectively nullified that body's disallowance.

With the prospect of obtaining an American fund for defraying some of the expense of defending North America virtually blasted, the Rockingham ministry after the repeal of the American stamp tax was obliged to look to other sources of income. The earlier tax of 1761 on houses, windows, and lights in Great Britain [27] was expanded to include the humblest dwelling, which previously had been exempt, with rates now graduated from a minimum of 3s. in England and 1s. in Scotland to 2s. on each window of every house in Great Britain containing twenty-five or more windows or lights. [28] Further, additional duties were placed on imported spirits, [29] the fund for sinking the public debt was drawn upon, [30] and a public lottery was authorized. [31] Thus, while public burdens in America were rapidly lightening, those in Great Britain were markedly increasing. In taking these steps the ministry showed an embarrassing reluctance to offer explanations, [32] except to defend its failure to fulfill the promise made to the British taxpayers that the land tax should be reduced from the high war level of 4s. on the pound. [33]

Lacking the confidence both of the King and of those who looked to Pitt for leadership, the Rockingham ministry was doomed. Thus, soon after Parliament was prorogued on June 6, a series of resignations took place; and, with the way now prepared, Pitt once again, though a stricken man, agreed to form a ministry supported by the

[26] Hutchinson, *Hist. of Prov. of Mass.*, p. 160.

[27] 2 George III, c. 8, *Statutes at Large*, VII, 367–368.

[28] 6 George, c. 38, *ibid.*, VII, 598–601. This act remained in force until 1784, when it was made vastly more comprehensive and even much higher rates were provided (24 George III, Sess. 2, c. 38).

[29] 6 George III, c. 47, *ibid.*, VII, 610–611.

[30] 6 George III, c. 41, *ibid.*, VII, 604.

[31] 6 George III, c. 39, *ibid.*, VII, 601.

[32] The Bishop of Carlisle to George Grenville, May 29, 1766, W. J. Smith (ed.), *The Grenville Papers* (4 vols., London, 1852–53), III, 242.

[33] T. C. Hansard (ed.), *Parliamentary History of England* . . . (36 vols., London, 1806–20), XVI, 227.

Duke of Grafton as First Lord of the Treasury and the Earl of Shelburne and General Conway as Secretaries of State. But the man once hailed as the Great Commoner now quit the House of Commons to take a seat among the peers of the realm as the Earl of Chatham, and chose for his ministerial post that of Lord Privy Seal, from which, in the words of his brother-in-law and political opponent, George Grenville, he could *"guide everything* in a sinecure office and be *responsible for nothing."* [34] Yet in avoiding responsibility he actually did little to direct the government and his difficulties were increased, not only by illness, but by loss of both popularity and prestige. [35]

Upon the reassembling of Parliament in November, the country was confronted with a crisis. Popular unrest in England was widespread. Bread riots were common occurrences. [36] Thomas Whately, who had served in the Treasury under Grenville, attributed this rioting "in a great measure . . . to the multiplicity of taxes." [37] However, an effort to amend the reply to the King's address of the 11th to take cognizance of this serious situation was defeated by the supporters of Chatham, who were inclined to view events in a more optimistic light. [38] But all was not well and, so long as the huge land tax remained, farmers were compelled to sell their wheat at ex-

[34] *Grenville Papers,* III, 298.

[35] London advices printed in the *Pennsylvania Gazette* of Oct. 30, 1766, state: "The papers are full of the most severe and cutting reflections upon the late great commoner, who seems now entirely to have lost his popularity. . . ."

[36] From London, under date of Sept. 20, the following item appeared in the *Pennsylvania Gazette* of Nov. 27, 1766: "Grievous are the complaints of the poor in every part of the Kingdom on account of the extravagant price of provisions of all sorts. Every post brings fresh accounts of tumults, occasioned principally by the high price of bread." On September 30 it was stated that "there is nothing but Riots and Insurrections over the whole Country, on Account of the high Price of Provisions, in particular Corn" (*ibid.,* Dec. 11, 1766). In this connection rioters seized wheat in storage and burned down flour mills.

[37] Whately to Grenville, Oct. 20, 1766, *Grenville Papers,* III, 335.

[38] These amendments to the reply framed by the opposition were defeated one after the other in the House of Commons. The third read as follows: "To assure his Majesty, that we will apply ourselves with diligence, to diminish the public expense, and to lessen the most burthensome taxes, from which the present distresses of his Majesty's subjects in Great Britain, have in great measure arisen; and in consequence of which, if a timely and affective remedy be not applied, there is too much reason to fear that these distresses will not only continue, but increase" (*Parl. Hist.,* XVI, 243).

orbitant prices. The government sought to bring down the price of this commodity by imposing a temporary embargo on its export, but to financial experts this means of relief seemed but a temporary expedient. The true remedy, they felt, was the diminution of the public debt and the reduction of the land tax.[39]

Unhappily, Chatham was not a financier nor temperamentally suited to dealing with domestic problems. What was needed was a statesman-financier of outstanding ability and sanity of mind whose ideas would command the respect of Parliament. The only man in the Cabinet who seemed at all to measure up to these demands, according to Secretary of State Conway, who later was to deliver in the House of Commons a panegyric on his talents,[40] was the Chancellor of the Exchequer, Charles Townshend, a name that has become synonymous with reckless statesmanship. Responsible both for presenting the annual budget and assuming leadership of the Cabinet, Townshend appeared before the House of Commons on February 25, 1767, and proposed the continuation of the land tax at the war rate of 4s. on the pound. This proposal was vigorously opposed by William Dowdeswell, his predecessor in office, as well as by George Grenville, both of whom demanded that it be reduced to 3s. Their motion to that effect was supported by a majority of the House.[41] Despite his defeat, Townshend chose to retain his post and accommodated himself to the stand of the majority. Since the shilling reduction in the land tax amounted to some £500,000, Townshend was forced to look elsewhere for revenue. The imposts on malt, rum, cider, and perry (pear cider) that were about to expire were therefore continued;[42] additional import duties were

[39] *Grenville Papers,* III, 336.

[40] *History, Debates and Proceedings of Both Houses of Parliament of Great Britain from the Year 1743 to the Year 1774* (London, 1792), IV, 474. For the characterization of Townshend by John Adolphus, which is in harmony with the opinion of General Conway, see his *History of England* (London, 1805), I, 304–305. Pitt, in inviting Townshend into the Cabinet, wrote to him laconically: "Sir, you are of too great a magnitude not to be in a responsible place: I intend to propose you to the King to-morrow for Chancellor of the Exchequer," thus, as Horace Walpole points out, elevating him to a post that paid £2,700 in place of a post as paymaster in which he was paid £7,000. *Memoirs of the Reign of George the Third* (4 vols., London, 1894), I, 416.

[41] Grenville's diary, *Grenville Papers,* IV, 211; *History, Debates and Proceedings of Parliament, 1743–1774* (London, 1792), IV, 474.

[42] 7 George III, c. 6, *Statutes at Large,* VIII, 2.

imposed not only on straw hats and the materials from which they were made but also on lawns, canvas, and linen; [43] again, as in the preceding years, the sinking fund was drawn upon and a lottery likewise authorized to cover the necessary expenditures of that year, estimated in excess of £8,500,000.[44]

But still additional revenue was needed. Could the British taxpayer be called upon to do more? If not, where could economies be made without surrendering the public interest? Should all efforts to retire the national debt be given up?

That there was strong popular opposition to any increase in taxes in 1767 has been made quite clear. It is equally clear that much of this resentment stemmed from the conviction that the colonials were not bearing their fair share of the burden of empire. The distinguished Connecticut lawyer, William Samuel Johnson, writing from London in March, declared:

> Great pains have been taken to irritate the people of England against America, especially the freeholders, and to persuade them that they are to pay infinite taxes and we [the colonials] none; they are to be burdened that we may be eased; and, in a word, that the interests of Britain are to be sacrificed to those of America.[45]

It is apparent that the ministry felt that this charge of favoritism by the government toward the colonials had to be met squarely. That Americans made a substantial contribution under the operation of the navigation system was recognized. Yet past experience had shown that this system was a two-way road which, even under a fair degree of enforcement, had permitted not only the people at home but those in the colonies to prosper. That the latter were now prospering and comparatively free of taxes seemed to be clear by all evidence obtainable in 1767. It was equally clear that the agencies for the enforcement of the system, together with the Sugar Act of 1764, were no longer effective.

Accordingly, Townshend sought in the spring of that year to solve the complex problem by proposing new colonial import duties in addition to those provided for in the Sugar Act. He had early in

[43] 7 George III, c. 20 and 28, *ibid.*, VIII, 5 and 11.
[44] *Parl. Hist.*, XVI, 369–373.
[45] Johnson to Jonathan Trumbull, Mar. 14, 1767, Massachusetts Historical Society, *Collections*, 5th ser., IX, 486–487.

February referred to the distinction that Franklin had made in the committee of the House in 1766 between internal and external taxations by Parliament. Declared Townshend in the Commons: "I do not know any distinction between internal and external taxes; it is a distinction without a difference, it is perfect nonsense; if we have a right to impose one, we have the other." Then, looking toward the colonial agents seated in the gallery, he continued: "I speak this aloud, that all you who are in the galleries may hear me." [46] On May 13 he declared, according to William Samuel Johnson, that while he himself could find no difference between the two kinds of levies, "yet since Americans were pleased to make that distinction he was willing to indulge them and chose for that reason to confine himself to regulations of Trade, by which a sufficient revenue might be raised in America." [47]

As a result, on June 2 there emerged from the Committee of the Whole House a series of resolutions providing that duties be collected on imports to America of all glass, paper, paint, and tea. In the debate that arose George Grenville, convinced that this measure did not go far enough and that the Empire was facing a great crisis,

[46] Johnson to Governor Pitkin, Feb. 12, 1767, "Trumbull Papers," Mass. Hist. Soc., *Coll.*, 5th ser., IX, 215–216; see also Thomas Whately to John Temple, Feb. 25 and May 2, "Temple Papers," Mass. Hist. Soc., *Coll.*, 6th ser., IX, 79, 83.

That there was a clear distinction drawn between internal taxes and external duties in the minds of most colonials from the date of the passing of the Molasses Act of 1733 down to 1766 is confirmed not only by the statement made by Franklin, when he appeared for his examination before the House of Commons (*Parl. Hist.*, XVI, 158–159), but by Thomas Hutchinson. The latter, writing in protest to his friend Ebenezer Silliman, one of the governor's assistants in Connecticut, declared: "Your distinction between duties upon trade and internal taxes agrees with the opinion of most People here [that is, in Massachusetts Bay]" (*New England Quarterly*, XXI, 476). The Connecticut Assembly, in fact, in its very able pamphlet, *Reasons Why the British Colonies in America should not be charged with Internal Taxes* (Hartford, 1764), proposed as a substitute for a stamp tax, in case it was found necessary for Parliament to raise funds in the New World, duties on the importation of slaves and on the export of furs (*Public Records of the Colony of Connecticut*, 15 vols., Hartford, 1850–90, XII, Appendix, 670). The contrary position—that the colonists did not accept the distinction between external and internal taxes —is argued by Edmund S. and Helen M. Morgan, *The Stamp Act Crisis* (Chapel Hill, 1953).

[47] Johnson to Pitkin, May 16, 1767, "Trumbull Papers," Mass. Hist. Soc., *Coll.*, 5th ser., IX, 229.

pressed for the enactment of a law whereby every colonial who held office or a seat in an assembly should be compelled to make a declaration, in harmony with the Declaratory Act of 1766, acknowledging the sovereignty of Great Britain and the right of Parliament to legislate for and place taxes upon America. But this proposal was sweepingly rejected by the House, anxious that no further seeds of future discord with colonies be sown.[48] Nevertheless, despite this desire for harmony, the speeches in the House of Commons were colored by the facts that New York had refused to obey the Mutiny Act and Massachusetts had sought by law to usurp the powers of the King by granting pardons to the Stamp Act rioters. What was especially remarkable about the debates that preceded the enactment of the Townshend revenue bill was that no voices whatsoever were raised in opposition to its enactment on the ground that it was unfair to the colonials, and that those who spoke against it took the position that it was not drastic enough.

The Townshend revenue act,[49] which became law on July 2, did not go very far toward raising an American fund by the duties imposed on the designated articles.[50] In fact, at the time the bill was introduced it was estimated that it would produce at best but between £35,000 and £40,000 annual revenue,[51] or not even one tenth of the amount of revenue lost in reducing the land tax in Great Britain by one shilling. Yet it was a gesture to reassure the people at home that at least an effort was being made in the direction of calling upon the colonials to make a more definite contribution to the costs of supporting the Empire beyond the old Navigation and Trade Acts and the more recent Sugar Act.

The American fund to be raised by the Townshend Act was, according to the enacting clause, to be devoted to

[48] *Ibid.*, 231–233.

[49] 7 George III, c. 46, *Statutes at Large,* VIII, 38–42.

[50] On plate and other fine glass the duty was 4s. 8d. per hundredweight; on common green glass it was 1s. 2d.; on red and white lead and painters' colors it was 2s.; on paper, depending upon the quality, it varied from 12s. to as little as 3d. on the ream; finally, on tea it was 3d. a pound.

[51] Walpole, *Memoirs,* II, 26. In fact, the act produced much less than was hoped. The gross receipt on *all* import duties in America, including those arising from the Sugar Act, during the period from September 8, 1767, to January 5, 1771, was but a total of £124,758. 17s. 3d. Public Record Office, Treasury Papers, 1. 514, fol. 226.

defraying the Charge of the Administration of Justice, and the Support of Civil Government, in such Provinces where it shall be found necessary; and toward further defraying the Expences of defending, protecting, and securing the said Dominions. . . .[52]

More particularly, the fund was to be used not only for the American defense program but also to support the governors and judges in those colonies where assemblies wielded their power to withhold salaries as a club over royal officials. How far the powers conferred by the statute would be used throughout America was to be determined thereafter by the conduct of the colonies themselves. Nevertheless, it would appear that there was no intention on the part of the ministry to have it apply to the two self-governing charter colonies of Connecticut and Rhode Island,[53] despite the fact that its first application was to be made in the neighboring royal colony of Massachusetts Bay, where defiance of the royal authority had assumed the most serious aspect.

But the Revenue Act of 1767 did not stand alone. To aid in the enforcement of the Townshend Act as well as the navigation and trade laws and the Sugar Act, a bill, which had been in contemplation for some time, was passed at the same session of Parliament [54] setting up in America a board of customs commissioners to take over the powers hitherto exercised by the customs commissioners in England established under Charles II for the "better securing of the Plantation Trade." [55] Under the terms of the new law all American customs officials were placed under the authority of this board, the members of which were appointed under the Great Seal and had their headquarters at Boston. Furthermore, the new system for trade enforcement was rounded out the following year by the creation, likewise under the Great Seal, of four American vice-admiralty districts, in each of which a judge and other officials were to be appointed with power not only to hear appeals from the local colonial vice-admiralty courts but also to have original jurisdic-

[52] Charles Eyre and Andrew Strahan (eds.), *Statutes at Large* (10 vols., London, 1786), VIII, 38.
[53] Johnson to Pitkin, July 13, 1767, "Trumbull Papers," Mass. Hist. Soc., *Coll.*, 5th ser. IX, 249.
[54] 7 George III, c. 41, *Statutes at Large,* VIII, 24–25.
[55] 25 Charles II, c. 7, *ibid.*, III, 357–359.

tion.[56] After some delay, these courts were set up at Halifax, Boston, Philadelphia, and Charleston. Thus, finally, it seemed that instrumentalities had been created that would make enforcement of the trade and revenue acts almost as effective in the colonies as it was in the mother country.[57]

[56] By reason of the laxity of the local vice-admiralty courts in the colonies in enforcing the trade laws, a vice-admiralty court for all America was created in 1764 and established at Halifax (*Acts of the Privy Council, Col. Ser.,* IV, 663–664). The powers of this court were only concurrent with those of the other courts; moreover, by reason of its location, it proved to be inconvenient of access. As a result, the Treasury Board sought in 1765 to transfer it to Boston and to create two other courts, one sitting at Philadelphia and the other at Charleston (*ibid.*). Nothing, however, was done until Parliament in 1768 passed an act "for the more easy and effectual Recovery of the Penalties and Forfeitures inflicted by the Acts of Parliament relating to the Trade or Revenues of the British Colonies" (8 George III, c. 22, *Statutes at Large,* VIII, 60–61). The law implied that new vice-admiralty jurisdictions would be created by the Crown. Soon after its enactment, the Privy Council determined to set up four courts, instead of three, as at first contemplated, with powers now enlarged to hear cases in the first instance and to determine finally appeals from the local vice-admiralty courts (*Acts of the Privy Council, Col. Ser.,* V, 151–153).

[57] C. M. Andrews, *The Colonial Period of American History* (New Haven, 1938), IV, 271. For the new frictions created by the American customs commissioners at Boston, see O. M. Dickerson, *The Navigation Acts and the American Revolution* (Philadelphia, 1951), pp. 208–265.

CHAPTER 12

Again America Resists

WITH the creation of the four vice-admiralty district courts for North America, the British administrative system for the continental colonies was now complete. The superstructure of this system rested squarely upon the conception that sovereignty within the Empire was not in the King or in the lords or in the commoners, as distinct entities, but rather in all three acting jointly in Parliament assembled. In other words, it was the King's High Court of Parliament that alone possessed final authority not only over all matters relating to the realm but also over the British dominions beyond the realm. This constitutional position drastically altered the older view that obtained during the first half of the seventeenth century that the King could act without interference from his Parliament in regulating the affairs of the colonies beyond the realm.

The first great blow at the unrestrained exercise of the royal prerogative with respect to the overseas possessions had come with the Great Rebellion and the interregnum. During this period, business relating to the colonies was supervised by a committee of Parliament, and Parliament itself passed the Navigation Act of 1651. With the Restoration, Parliament no longer accepted the passive role of the years before 1643, but henceforth actively participated in colonial affairs. As former Governor Thomas Pownall, in his *Administration of the Colonies,* expressed it:

Upon the restoration of the monarchy . . . the constitutions of the colonies received their great alteration: the King participated the sovereignity of the colonies with the parliament.[1]

Nevertheless, the King, without interference from this body, continued to exercise his royal prerogative in the establishment of additional colonies, which thereupon came within the legislative scope of parliament.

Until the Revolution of 1688 and the repudiation of James, the statutes of the realm that most directly affected the colonies related exclusively to matters of trade and its regulation. However, under William and Mary and their successors this legislation was immensely broadened. The comprehensive navigation statute of 1696 (7 and 8 William III, c. 7, § 9) declared that all colonial laws repugnant to it, "or to any other law hereafter to be made in this kingdom, as far as such law shall relate to, and mention the said Plantations, are illegal, null and void to all intents and purposes whatsoever." Statutes, moreover, were subsequently passed relating to many things having to do with the internal colonial economy, such as naturalization, coinage, the paper currency, banking, preservation of the white-pine timber, and the manufacturing of wool, beaver hats, iron, and steel. As to the relationship of Parliament to the Great Seal after the Revolution, it is clear that at first King William was determined to exercise the old royal prerogative as freely as had Charles II after the Restoration. He issued to Massachusetts Bay its charter of 1691 and brought into existence the Board of Trade in 1696, both under this seal. Persuaded that he still possessed the right without interference from Parliament to issue letters patent granting charters to overseas companies, as had his predecessors, he sought to follow such a course in connection with the reorganization of the East India Company. But in face of the unyielding opposition of Parliament, the King was forced in 1698 to scrap his own plan and accept Parliament's, which accordingly was embodied in the new charter. The constitutional importance of the struggle lay in the fact that never again did any English monarch attempt to use the seal in derogation of the rights now claimed by Parliament as the sole custodian of the great prerogatives of the

[1] Thomas Pownall, *The Administration of the Colonies* (4th ed., London, 1768), p. 125.

Crown.[2] The statute against piracy passed in 1700 (11 and 12 William III, c. 7, § 15) significantly declared that if any governor or person in authority in a colony should refuse obedience to the act, such refusal would operate as a forfeiture of all charters granted for "the government or propriety" of such plantation. The creation later of colonial establishments—Georgia in 1732 and Nova Scotia in 1749—while carried out, it is true, by authorization under the Great Seal, was really a parliamentary enterprise and directly subsidized by appropriations made for that purpose. Final proof that the Great Seal was but an instrumentality of Parliament, to be used or not according to circumstances, came with the alteration in 1774 by statute, and not by orders in council, of the letters patent granted by the King to Massachusetts Bay in 1691.[3]

This concentration of authority in Parliament, as the result of the evolution of the British constitution, was what Pownall called in 1768 "the Empire of King, Lords, and Commons, collectively taken, as having the whole supream power in them. . . ."[4] In other words, in the eighteenth century and thereafter the British constitution rested upon the fundamental principle of the sovereignty of Parliament—of the King, the House of Lords, and the House of Commons.

Not only did Parliament legislate on a variety of subjects having to do with the colonies but it interested itself also in the strengthening of colonial administration, most notably in enlarging the powers of the vice-admiralty courts set up in America in 1697 to include powers not exercised by admiralty courts in Great Britain.[5] As a

[2] For the development of this point by the author, see *Canadian Historical Review*, XXIII, 39–41.

[3] 14 George III, c. 45, *Pickering, Statutes at Large*, XXX, 381–390. In 1725, in connection with a dispute between the governor and Assembly of Massachusetts Bay, the Privy Council issued an explanatory charter (*Acts and Resolves of the Province of Massachusetts Bay* (Boston, 1869), I, 21–23). However, this body, realizing the inadequacy of its powers to enforce its own decisions, accepted the recommendation of its Committee for Appeals that, should the explanatory charter not be accepted by the colony, "it may be proper for the Consideration of the Legislature [Parliament] what further Provision may be necessary to support and preserve Your Majesty's Just authority in this Province and prevent such presumptuous Invasion for the future." J. Munro (ed.), *Acts of the Privy Council of England, Colonial Series* (Hereford, 1911–12), III, 104.

[4] Pownall, *Administration of the Colonies*, p. 119.

[5] The gradual extension of the vice-admiralty jurisdiction by acts of Parlia-

result, not only were violators of trade acts subject to trial in such courts without juries, but also violators of other statutes, including those protecting the American white-pine timber.[6] The explanation of this broad extension of vice-admiralty authority at the expense of the common law courts in America is readily found. Jury trials were found in practice to be unsuited to the enforcement of the laws of trade. In effect, this imposed some limitation upon rights that Americans might claim as Englishmen. Moreover, to make sure that imperial policy would be carried out in the colonies, not only were important colonial officials—most of the governors, most colonial councilors, all the fiscal and customs officers, all vice-admiralty judges and others—appointed to their offices by the home government, but also most colonial laws were required to be submitted to the Privy Council, which asserted the power of disallowance, and, finally, the Privy Council exercised the right of review in cases coming before colonial courts. Thus we have the British imperial system of the eighteenth century, based upon the idea of the subordination of all other powers within the Empire to the sovereign authority of Parliament and of the Crown agencies acting for it, such as the Privy Council that now expressed its will.

The system had its great merits and in the past had operated in the main without severe restrictions on colonial liberties. However, in the period of more than a century during which this system was evolving, the colonies were growing in population, in wealth, in political experience, and their inhabitants were becoming less and less British in their political and cultural outlook and more and more peculiarly American. This growing American nationalism clashed with the increasing centralization of the British Empire.[7] The chief instrumentality of colonial resistance was the assembly, and at the very time that imperial authority was being centralized in Parlia-

---

ment in matters relating to the colonies is outlined in a lengthy document which Thomas Whately sent to Charles Yorke on February 16, 1765. It is among the Hardwicke Papers in the British Museum (Add. Mss., No. 35911). This shows that even before the setting up in 1697 of American vice-admiralty courts, provision was made for the use of the admiralty jurisdiction "for the Recovery of Forefeitures or Penalities for offenses Committed in the Plantations."

[6] The student is referred to C. M. Andrews, *The Colonial Period of American History* (New Haven, 1938), IV, chap. 8, for a broad and learned discussion of the history of vice-admiralty jurisdiction in America from 1697 to 1768.

[7] For an elaboration of this point, see *ibid.*, IV, 419–428.

ment, there took place a remarkable development within the colonial assemblies of conceptions of parliamentary privilege, destined, with the developing constitutional crisis, to flower by 1774 into the assertion of complete local legislative autonomy.[8]

In September, 1767, the news reached America of the passing of the Townshend laws, and early in October the text of the Revenue Act appeared in the newspapers. Later that month a Boston town meeting, with James Otis in the chair, adopted resolutions drawn up by a committee which avowedly called upon the people to extricate themselves from their financial embarrassments by manufacturing for themselves a long list of articles, including wearing apparel and furnishings, coaches, anchors, cordage, loaf sugar, malt liquors, cheeses, watches, and jewelry. A request for a meeting of the General Assembly was also voted.[9] A roll for the signatures of those who would agree to rid the province of the need for importing these articles "by the disuse of foreign superfluities" was thereupon placed in the hands of the town clerk and the public was called upon to sign it. This nonconsumption movement was promoted by those who were opposed to the sort of violence that had characterized resistance to the enforcement of the Stamp Act, and in harmony with this idea the selectmen of the town called upon the inhabitants to avoid mobs and riotous assemblies. Back of it all, nevertheless, was a determined opposition to paying the new duties. Otis, in a measured understatement of the situation, declared to the public on November 28 in the columns of the Boston *Gazette:*

The TAX! the TAX! is undoubtedly at present the apparent matter of grievance; and this I think a great one: But redress is to be fought in a legal and constitutional way.[10]

The most impressive and elaborate attack upon the Townshend legislation, however, came not from Otis and his radical associates in Boston, but from the mild, cultivated John Dickinson in his

[8] For a study of the growth of the idea that the colonial assemblies were really local parliaments, see Professor Mary P. Clarke's *Parliamentary Privilege in the American Colonies* (New Haven, 1943).

[9] The proceedings of the Boston town meeting of October 28 are printed in the Boston *Gazette* of Nov. 22, 1767.

[10] Otis's appeal to the public appeared in other colonial newspapers, such as the *Pennsylvania Gazette* for Dec. 10, 1767.

famous *Letters from a Farmer in Pennsylvania to the Inhabitants of the British Colonies,* the first of which appeared in the December 2, 1767, issue of the *Pennsylvania Chronicle and Universal Advertiser* and the twelfth and last in that of February 15 of the following year.[11] While admitting the right of Parliament not only to regulate but even to suppress commerce and industry in the colonies, the author denied its authority to levy internal or external taxes and affirmed in one letter that it was heaven itself that "hath made us free."[12] In referring to Great Britain in another letter, Dickinson wrote:

Moderation has been the rule of her conduct. But now, a generous humane people, that so often has protected the liberty of strangers is inflamed to tear a privilege from her own children, which if executed, must, in their opinion, sink them into slaves: *And for what?* For a pernicious power, not necessary to her . . . but horridly dreadful and detestable to them.[13]

As to the argument that the people of Great Britain were sinking under an immense debt in large part contracted in defending the colonies, he asserted that in reality the colonies gave Great Britain hearty assistance in the late war, *"undertaken solely for her own benefit,"* and that the territories acquired as the result of it were "greatly injurious to these colonies" and the latter therefore owed her nothing.[14] Nevertheless, while he called upon Americans to take care of their rights and not to sacrifice *"a single iota"* of their privileges, he was opposed to their use of violence and counseled them to conduct their affairs at the present juncture *"peaceably—prudently—firmly—jointly."*[15]

The Dickinson position in 1768 denying the legality not only of internal taxes but of port duties levied by Parliament was far more

[11] These letters were reprinted in most of the colonial newspapers as they appeared and then gathered together and published in pamphlet form not only in Philadelphia, but in New York, Boston, Williamsburg, London, and Amsterdam. The letters are available in P. L. Ford (ed.), *The Writings of John Dickinson* (Philadelphia, 1895), I, 277–406.

[12] *Ibid.,* p. 322.

[13] *Ibid.,* pp. 341–343.

[14] In order to give logical development to Dickinson's argument, these quotations have been transposed (*ibid.,* pp. 360–363).

[15] *Ibid.,* p. 405.

extreme on paper than the view expressed by Benjamin Franklin before the Committee of the Whole of the House of Commons in 1766 with reference to port duties. This is what Franklin had to say on the subject in answer to the following question put to him in the course of his "Examination":

You say the colonies have always submitted to external taxes, and object to the right of parliament only in laying internal taxes; now can you shew, that there is any kind of difference between the two taxes to the Colony on which they are laid?

To which Franklin replied:

I think the difference is very great. An external tax is a duty laid on commodities imported . . . and, when it is offered for sale, makes a part of the price. If the people do not like it at that price, they refuse it; they are not obliged to pay it. But an internal tax is forced upon the people without their consent, if not laid by their own representatives.

Later in the course of the questioning he indicated why he differentiated between port duties and internal taxes, pointing out that

the sea is yours; you maintain, by your fleets, the safety of navigation in it, and keep it clear of pirates; you may have therefore a natural and equitable right to some toil or duty on merchandizes carried through that part of your dominions, towards defraying the expense you are at in ships to maintain the safety of that carriage.[16]

The *Letters from a Farmer* represented a repudiation of an untenable or, at least, unpracticable distinction in taxation and indicated that Franklin was not abreast of American opinion. To William Knox, who had acted as a Crown official in Georgia and later as the London agent for that colony and East Florida, and who in 1769 published in London his *The Controversy between Great Britain and her Colonies Reviewed*, Dickinson's distinction between the regulation and even suppression of colonial trade and industry and their taxation was "of all absurdities, the most ridiculous that ever was contended for." In taking this position Knox, to illustrate the inconsistency, contrasted the duties on molasses levied

[16] A. H. Smyth, *The Writings of Benjamin Franklin* (10 vols., New York, 1907), IV, 424 and 431.

upon the basis of the statute of 1733 with those levied upon the basis of the revision of this act in 1764:

The right of Parliament to charge foreign molasses with a duty of six-pence was unquestionable; but, for parliament to *reduce* the six-pence to three-pence, is a violent usurpation of unconstitutional authority, and an infringement of the rights and privileges of the people of the Colonies. . . . But (says Mr. Dickinson) the heavy tax would have operated as a prohibition, which is a *regulation of trade;* the light tax is intended *to be paid* and laid for the *purpose of revenue.*[17]

Dickinson, Knox argued, conceded the greater right of Parliament through regulation to choke and even to destroy American commerce and industry by extending at will the principles embodied in the Molasses Act of 1733 and the Iron Act of 1750, but denied the lesser right of reducing prohibitive regulatory imposts for the purpose of securing a revenue. Whatever defects the *Letters from a Farmer* possess from the viewpoint of eighteenth-century British, or even twentieth-century American, constitutional law, they quickly became the political Bible of Americans until early in 1776 when Thomas Paine's *Common Sense,* calling for a declaration of independence, supplanted them as a new evangel. Numerous reprints crystallized the opposition to the Townshend Acts.

To Governor Bernard of Massachusetts Bay the only way out of the oncoming impasse was the extension to the colonies of representation in Parliament—and this he strongly recommended to the home government. Nonetheless, he conceded that by and large Americans did not desire it. At the same time he urged that by this means every objection to levies by Parliament on the colonies would be met.[18] To support the administration and silence the radicals,

[17] William Knox, *The Controversy between Great Britain and her Colonies Reviewed* (London, 1769), pp. 35–37.

[18] Bernard to Lord Barrington, Jan. 28, 1768, E. Channing and A. C. Coolidge (eds.), *The Barrington-Bernard Correspondence . . . 1760–1770* (Cambridge, Mass., 1912), pp. 133–139. In this letter, the governor accused a certain leader of the opposition, presumably Otis, with propounding, as a part of the political strategy of the radicals, the thesis "that the Power of parliament over the Colonies was absolute, with this Exception, that they ought not to tax them untill they allowed them Representatives"; this position, Bernard affirmed, was for the purpose of making "an American Representation

Brigadier Ruggles called upon the Massachusetts House of Representatives in December to choose members to Parliament and to
send them to England to claim their seats,[19] an action the farthest
possible removed from the sentiments of this body and, of course,
without proper legal basis.

It is therefore not surprising that the House, while proceeding to
set forth with firmness its objections to the recent legislation of
Parliament, rejected with equal firmness the idea of parliamentary
representation.[20] In a petition to the King and in numerous letters
to officials in London, it voiced its deep apprehension as to the
unhappy fate in store for the colonies should their rights and privileges as Englishmen be denied.[21] Then, after some little hesitation
about taking the step,[22] on February 11, 1768, it addressed the
famous "Circular Letter" drawn up by Samuel Adams to the other
colonial assemblies denouncing the Townshend Acts as violating the
principle of no taxation without representation. This summarily disposed of the notion that representation in Parliament would satisfy
the colonies by declaring, "this House think that a taxation of their
constituents, even without their consent, grievous as it is, would be
preferable to any representation that could be admitted for them
there." The House went still further, and attacked the constitution-

---

necessary by the Objections they [the colonials] made to all Acts of parliament
for Want of Representatives," while at the same time opposing in practice such
representation.

[19] *Ibid.*

[20] "We are assured, that while the House have been setting forth the un-
speakable Grievance of Subjects being taxed unrepresented, the greatest Care
has been taken to shew, that an equal Representation of this Province in the
British Parliament is utterly impossible." Boston advices, Feb. 15, *Pennsylvania
Gazette*, Mar. 3, 1768.

[21] The petition to the King and the letters to De Berdt, Shelburne, Rockingham, Camden, Chatham, Conway, and the Commissioners of the Treasury are
printed in John Almon's *A Collection of Interesting Authentic Papers . . .
1764–1775* (London, 1777), pp. 167–191. This collection carries the general
pagination title of *Prior Documents*.

[22] On January 21, 1768, the proposal was first made to the House that a
circular letter be sent to the other assemblies; this was then defeated. However,
on February 4, the proposal was then brought forward and passed by a large
majority and the first vote was ordered to be erased (*ibid.*, p. 208). Bernard,
writing to Lord Barrington on February 20, stressed the fact that during the
early part of the session the friends of the administration, "to keep the factious
Party in awe," prevailed on the first vote by two to one against a circular
letter, but ultimately lost ground (*Barrington-Bernard Corresp.*, pp. 145–146).

ality of the proposals of the government to provide, through the Crown, salaries for governors and other civil offices, as well as the dangerous implications of the Mutiny Act. In conclusion, while soliciting proposals for united action, the Circular Letter took pains to deny that there was any disposition in the colonies to seek independence of the mother country.[23]

The Circular Letter evoked in the Earl of Hillsborough, Secretary of State for the Colonies, an immediate reaction. He felt that it tended to create in America "unwarrantable combinations" and "to excite an unjustifiable opposition to the constitutional authority of Parliament." Therefore, after consulting the King, he proceeded without delay to instruct the governor to call upon the House of Representatives in his Majesty's name, not only to rescind the resolution that was the basis for this letter, but also to repudiate the latter under penalty of immediate dissolution and reference to Parliament of the whole issue to the end "that such provisions as shall be found necessary may be made, to prevent for the future a conduct of so extraordinary and unconstitutional a nature." [24]

Bernard proceeded to carry out his instruction on June 21, although at first he held back the latter part of the Secretary's letter until the House demanded it. Then on June 28, instead of conforming to the Earl of Hillsborough's request, the House by overwhelming vote agreed to send home a detailed defense of its conduct. In this communication it pointed out the impropriety of the King's request as one for which there was no precedent in the relations of the Kings of England with the House of Commons since the time of the Revolution. Such a request, it contended, could only have been the result of an attempt to instill in his Majesty "a jealousy of his faithful subjects," which was "a crime of the most malignant nature." The letter ended with a request that the Secretary should therefore represent to the King that all the actions of the House which had been the basis of complaint were those "of affectionate and loyal subjects." [25] Thereupon, with the signing of the letter by the speaker, a motion to rescind was voted down, only seventeen

---

[23] The Circular Letter is printed in the *Prior Documents*, pp. 191–193.
[24] For Hillsborough's letter dated April 22, 1768, see *ibid.*, 203–205.
[25] For the letter to Hillsborough of June 30, see *ibid.*, pp. 206–210.

voting affirmatively.[26] So informed, Bernard, in conformity with his orders, dissolved the House two days later.

Meantime, the Circular Letter had been endorsed by New Hampshire, Virginia, Maryland, Connecticut, Rhode Island, Georgia, and South Carolina,[27] either by their respective assemblies or by the Speaker where the Assembly was not sitting. Their defiant stand attested to the leadership in the movement of resistance which the Massachusetts Bay House of Representatives had now assumed.[28]

The nonconsumption movement started by Boston in October, 1767, and supported by other towns had its chief impact in New England.[29] Dickinson in his *Letters* now called for a revival of nonimportation agreements, such as had been so effective in the opposition to the stamp tax. In view of the doubtful pressure of nonconsumption upon the merchants and manufacturers of England, Boston importers now took the lead in March, 1768, in reviving American nonimportation.[30] In April, New York agreed to this plan, provided that Boston and Philadelphia would go along. Although the former was already committed, there was hesitation in the Quaker City. As a result, New York did not finally act until August, by which date it seemed that Philadelphia would move into line.[31] The merchants of the latter city had difficulty making up

[26] *Ibid.*, pp. 210–215. The names of those who voted to rescind the resolution were given to the press together with their towns and counties so that "in the Annals of America . . . the Names of Seventeen will be handed down with Infamy to the latest Posterity" (*Pennsylvania Gazette*, July 14, 1768). The Boston *Chronicle*, John Mein's conservative organ, does not print these names nor does the Boston *Gazette*, but the latter denounced these men in violent terms in its issue of July 4, 1768.

[27] For these see *ibid.*, July 7 and 21 and August 25, 1768; also *Prior Documents*, pp. 213–222.

[28] Hillsborough on April 21 sent a circular letter to all the governors—except those of the provinces of East Florida and Quebec, which were without legislatures—calling upon them to use their efforts to prevent their assemblies from supporting the Massachusetts Bay position. For copies of this letter, see *ibid.*, p. 220, and *Pennsylvania Colonial Records* (12 vols., Harrisburg, 1852), IX, 546–547. The letters to the governors of Connecticut and Rhode Island varied somewhat from the other letters (Shelburne Papers, 85:182–183).

[29] A. M. Schlesinger, *The Colonial Merchants and the American Revolution, 1763–1776* (New York, 1918), pp. 106–112.

[30] Thomas Cushing to Dennys De Berdt, Apr. 18, 1768, Mass. Hist. Soc., *Coll.*, 4th ser., IV, 350–351.

[31] Virginia D. Harrington, *The New York Merchant on the Eve of the Revolution* (New York, 1935), p. 335.

their minds. Letters in both the *Pennsylvania Chronicle* and *Pennsylvania Gazette* revealed a divided opinion. Writing under the *nom de plume* of "A Chester County Farmer," Joseph Galloway intimated that the merchants of the city had "discovered some secret Intentions in the New-England Scheme, that would be very disadvantageous to the Trade of this Province." [32] He in turn was answered by Charles Thomson [33] and by Dickinson, the latter posing as "A Gentleman in Virginia." [34] In fact, it was not until almost a year after the Boston merchants had agreed on nonimportation, and in face of the most stinging denunciations of the Philadelphia merchants for their lack of cooperation in this movement, that the latter—doubtless influenced by the failure of a petition to the King drawn up by the Pennsylvania Assembly and signed on September 22, 1768, by the Speaker of the House and directed against the Townshend Acts [35]—were led to support the plan already adopted by the two other great American seaports. [36]

By the time that the Massachusetts Bay Circular Letter had been sent out, the American customs commissioners in Boston realized that they were faced by a hopeless task in endeavoring to enforce not only the revenue acts but the trade regulations as well. In a letter directed to the Commissioners of the Treasury and signed on February 12, 1768, they declared that, although smuggling had reached great proportions in New England during the last two and a half years, but six seizures had been made and of these only one had been prosecuted with success. Of the remaining five, one ship had been rescued at Falmouth, Maine, and another at Newbury (Newburyport) on the Merrimac, in both of which instances the local customs officers were resisted by mobs; a third, at New London in Connecticut, had been carried off clandestinely while the case was under prosecution, and the last two were released in Rhode Island by acquittal "through the Combination and Influence of the People." The situation was succinctly stated in these words:

[32] *Pennsylvania Gazette,* June 16, 1768.

[33] *Ibid.,* July 21, 1768.

[34] *Writings of John Dickinson,* I, 439–445.

[35] For this petition, see C. F. Hoban (ed.), *Pennsylvania Archives* (Harrisburg, 1935), 8th ser., VII, 6271–6273; see also R. I. Brunhouse's "The Effect of the Townshend Acts in Pennsylvania," *Pennsylvania Magazine of History and Biography,* LIV, 355–373.

[36] Schlesinger, *Colonial Merchants,* pp. 125–130.

Our Officers were resisted and defeated in almost every Attempt to do their duty when the Right of Parliament to lay external duties was acknowledged. Now that the Right of Parliament to lay any taxes whatsoever on the Colonies is denied, we have every reason to expect that we shall find it totally impracticable to enforce the Execution of the Revenue Laws until the Hand of Government is strengthened. At present not a ship of war in the Province, nor a company of soldiers nearer than New York, which is two hundred and fifty Miles distant from this Place.[37]

In fact, the Commissioners complained that they were the object of continual personal affronts.[38] Doubtless the arbitrary and venal behavior of some of the customs officials contributed to the low esteem of the service in America.[39]

By the spring of 1768 Governor Bernard was convinced that Massachusetts Bay was on the verge of an insurrection, with the radicals threatening "that no Pensioner of Great Britain, no, not one that recieves [sic] a Stipend from thence shall live in this Province. . . ." [40] News of these alarming developments persuaded the ministry that troops were needed in the province to assist the magistrates in upholding law and order. Accordingly, on June 8 the Earl of Hillsborough wrote Major General Thomas Gage, commander in chief of the British forces in North America, then at New York, ordering him to dispatch at least one regiment of troops to Boston.[41] In anticipation of a request from Bernard, Gage had already made preparations to move troops from Halifax to Boston. But Bernard had made it clear to the General that he could take no such step without the recommendation of his Council, which he felt he could not possibly obtain.[42]

[37] Shelburne Papers, 85:188–190.
[38] Bernard to Lord Barrington, May 9, 1768, *Barrington-Bernard Corresp.*, pp. 156–159.
[39] For a discussion of "customs racketeering" in this period, see O. M. Dickerson, *The Navigation Acts and the American Revolution* (Philadelphia, 1951), pp. 208–265.
[40] *Barrington-Bernard Corresp.*, pp. 156–159.
[41] C. E. Carter (ed.), *The Correspondence of General Thomas Gage* (2 vols., New Haven, 1931–33), II, 68–69.
[42] Bernard to Barrington, July 20, 1768, *Barrington-Bernard Corresp.*, p. 167. It may be noted that on July 7 the Governor's Council agreed upon a petition to the King against the levying of duties provided for in the Townshend revenue law. *Bowdoin and Temple Papers*, Mass. Hist. Soc., *Coll.*, 6th ser., IX, 93–99.

By the summer of 1768 a state of virtual anarchy apparently existed in Boston, the assertions of the radical leaders to the contrary notwithstanding. Early in June the *Romney,* a fifty-gun ship, had appeared in the harbor and on the 10th its crew seized John Hancock's ship *Liberty* for alleged violation of the trade acts.[43] Three days later the American customs commissioners, in face of the fury of the mob, took refuge on board the *Romney.*[44] When news of this breakdown of authority reached England, two regiments of troops from the British Isles (the 64th and 65th) were ordered to Boston.[45] In addition, General Gage notified Governor Bernard on September 12 that he was dispatching to Boston two other regiments from Halifax (the 14th and the 29th), under command of Lieutenant Colonel Dalrymple, and that these could soon be expected.[46] These troops, in fact, appeared on transports on the 29th; and, had the more violent elements had their way, hostilities would have soon begun, for plans were laid by the Sons of Liberty, according to Hutchinson, to rouse the country by lighting a beacon on Beacon Hill.[47] Although these plans were dropped at the last moment, a so-called convention of delegates of the towns of the province was assembled at the call of the Boston selectmen. Bernard refused its petition as emanating from an illegal body, and forced it

[43] Earlier in April, an effort was made to search Hancock's *Lydia,* on which the customs officers thought there was reason to believe dutiable articles had been brought from London. But the tidewaiter was so terrified by the reception he received that he gave up the attempt. Then, early in May, the *Liberty* appeared, loaded, it was charged, with Madeira wine. An effort likewise was made to inspect the hold of the vessel for undeclared articles, but the tidewaiter, Thomas Kirk, was forced below deck and kept there for some hours while the work of removal, as he asserted, went on. Upon the basis of Kirk's testimony on June 10, the vessel was seized the same day and carried away under the guns of the *Romney.* W. T. Baxter, *The House of Hancock* (Cambridge, Mass., 1945), pp. 260–266; Herbert S. Allen, *John Hancock, Patriot in Purple* (New York, 1948), pp. 105–108.

[44] Bernard to Barrington, June 18, 1768, *Barrington-Bernard Corresp.,* p. 160; "A Memorial in behalf of the Inhabitants of Boston," *Prior Documents,* p. 222.

[45] Hillsborough to Gage, July 30, 1768, *Gage Corresp.,* II, 72–73; Hillsborough to Bernard, July 30, 1768, Shelburne Papers, 85:206–211.

[46] *Bowdoin and Temple Papers,* pp. 100–111.

[47] Thomas Hutchinson to Thomas Whately, Oct. 8, 1768, Massachusetts Archives, 25:281–282.

to disband.[48] Hence, when the troops landed on October 1, outwardly all was calm. Despite the strong verbal protests not only of the selectmen of Boston but even of the Governor's Council, the soldiers were finally billeted in houses that Gage, now on the scene, managed to rent.[49]

The people were deeply suspicious of the presence of British regiments. For alarming reports had been circulated by the radical leaders that the regulars had been ordered to the province with three purposes in mind: to disarm the inhabitants, to place the colony under martial law, and, finally, to apprehend "a number of gentlemen, who have exerted themselves in the cause of their country," who after being seized would be sent to Great Britain for trial.[50] But to Gage the sending of troops to maintain order had come only as the result of the "Treasonable and desperate Resolves" of the Boston leaders, who had "delivered their Sentiments in a Manner not to be Misunderstood, and in the Stile of a ruling and Sovereign Nation, who acknowledges no Dependence." [51] In fact, it is clear from available evidence that the ministry had nothing more in mind than the restoration of the orderly processes of government in the distracted province. That this was at least partially achieved soon after the soldiers had settled into quarters was affirmed by Gage, who, writing to Hillsborough from Boston early in November, was able to report that once again there was "the Appearance of Peace and Quiet in this Place." [52]

Nevertheless, the British ministry, thoroughly aroused about the seriousness of the American crisis, particularly in Massachusetts, decided to place before the House of Lords for consideration at its

[48] For the circular letter of September 14 of the Boston selectmen and the petition of some seventy delegates from towns of the province, see the Boston *Chronicle*, Sept. 19, 1768; see also J. C. Miller, "The Massachusetts Convention, 1768," *New England Quarterly*, VII, 445–474.

[49] Bernard to Hillsborough, Nov. 1 and 5, 1768, *Letters to the Right Honorable Earl of Hillsborough from Governor Bernard and General Gage* (Boston, 1769), pp. 3–10; *Gage Corresp.*, I, 202–205. It should be pointed out that the Boston town authorities and the Governor's Council insisted that under the terms of the quartering act the barracks at Castle William must be used. But Gage, supported by Bernard, insisted that troops at such a distance from the town would not serve the purpose for which they were sent.

[50] Boston *Gazette*, Sept. 26, 1768.

[51] Gage to Hillsborough, Sept. 26, 1768, *Gage Corresp.*, I, 195–196.

[52] *Ibid.*, p. 206.

December session a body of papers containing, among other things, the votes, resolutions, and proceedings of the House of Representatives of that colony and copies of Boston newspapers.[53] The examination of material, incendiary on its face, prompted the passage of a series of resolutions and an address to the King to which the House of Commons was asked to give its assent. The resolutions, eight in number, were concerned with the denial of the authority of Parliament on the part of the inhabitants of the colony, with the efforts of the towns of that province to hold an illegal convention, and with the disorders in Boston. The address to the King backed his efforts to uphold the constitution of the Empire in the Bay Colony and urged him to direct the Massachusetts governor to secure the fullest information touching "all treasons, or misprision of treason" committed within the province during the past year, and to appoint a special commission to judge the evidence of these offenses under the provisions of the treason statute (35 Hen. VIII) for bringing the accused to England for trial.[54]

Little opposition developed in the House of Lords. Even Lord High Chancellor Camden sat silent. But in the House of Commons, before final endorsement of the resolutions and the address, a great debate took place, with former Governor Thomas Pownall of Massachusetts Bay, Edmund Burke, Colonel Barré, and even Mr. George Grenville, among others, speaking eloquently against these measures. The address to the King was the object of such sharp animadversions that Grey Cooper, Secretary of the Treasury, speaking for the government, was impelled to assure the House "that it was not meant to put the act (of Henry VIII) in execution, but only to shew to America what government could do if pushed to it." [55] On February 8 the resolutions finally passed the House by a vote of 159 to 65. In answer to the address the King declared that he would not fail to give the orders that Parliament had recommended "as the most effective method of bringing the authors of the late unhappy disorders in that province to condign punish-

---

[53] A number of the papers laid before Parliament were published in the *Annual Register, 1768*, pp. 235–255.

[54] The resolutions and address are to be found in *Parl. Hist.*, XVI, 476–480.

[55] *Ibid.*, XVI, 507. For a fairly lengthy account of the debate, see *ibid.*, XVI, 480–510, and also William Samuel Johnson to Governor Pitkin, Feb. 9, 1769, Mass. Hist. Soc., *Coll.*, 5th ser., IX, 312–331.

ment." [56] But for the next six years these remarks remained a mere threat hanging over the colony. Rumor persisted for a time, however, that James Otis, Samuel Adams, and Thomas Cushing were to be apprehended, carried to London, tried, and hung.[57]

The ministry was, in fact, faced by a hard dilemma. The Townshend duties, imposed to alleviate burdens of the British taxpayer, had by the spring of 1769, according to a remarkable communication in the January 17, 1769, issue of the London *Public Advertiser,* which was reprinted in the *Pennsylvania Gazette* and other American newspapers, brought in no more than £3,500; while the business loss to the British public from the American nonimportation and nonconsumption agreements was put at the staggering figure of £7,250,000. The author of this letter, which appeared under a pseudonym, was probably none other than Benjamin Franklin.[58] The letter concluded with a warning that continuation of this revenue policy would surely lead to a revolt of "the whole fifteen colonies" containing 3 million inhabitants; that it would take an army of 25,000 men supported by a fleet at least ten years to subdue them and at a cost of not less than £100,000,000, not to speak of the loss of life on both sides and the aftermath of hatred that would follow the conclusion of the war. By the time this letter appeared, most men in public life were persuaded that to attempt to collect such duties in face of colonial opposition was economically unsound and politically unwise. On the other hand, there was an equally strong conviction that the government could not give way without bringing about a disruption of the Empire.

It is easy for the student of today to point the direction that the government should have taken for meeting the perplexing prob-

[56] *Parl. Hist.,* XVI, 510–511.

[57] See the *Pennsylvania Gazette* of Mar. 9 and 30 and Apr. 13, 1769.

[58] *Ibid.,* Apr. 13, 1769. In this issue of the *Pennsylvania Gazette* in the Lehigh University Library, there is written in ink opposite the printed signature the words "B Franklin" in Franklin's characteristic hand. Whether this was actually signed by Franklin is a matter in dispute, although Professor V. W. Crane of the University of Michigan has sufficient proof over and beyond it that the article was from his pen (Bibliographical Society of America, *Papers,* XXVIII, Pt. I, p. 24 n.). This interesting article is one of over 140 contributions that Franklin made to the press under his *nom de plume.* V. W. Crane (ed.), *Benjamin Franklin's Letters to the Press, 1758–1775* (Chapel Hill, 1950).

lem—especially with the example of the British Commonwealth of Nations before him.[59] But who of all the British statesmen of the eighteenth century would have ventured for one moment to have advocated such a revolutionary departure? Or who among them even believed in the desirability of seeking such a solution of the impasse? Did Chatham or Burke or Shelburne or Barré or Thomas Pownall, or even Camden, among those known as the "friends of America"?

For all practical purposes, the ministry at the moment was without a head. The Earl of Chatham, neither physically nor mentally fit to face the tremendous responsibilities resting on the administration after taking office in August, 1766, had gradually faded from the picture before resigning his post of Lord Privy Seal in October, 1758; the Duke of Grafton, well meaning but mediocre, and the titular head of the government, possessed little authority among his associates. Lord Camden, the Lord High Chancellor, who in 1766 had spoken in strong opposition to the right of Parliament to levy taxes on the people of America, was now silent during the debates on American affairs in the House of Lords, and was in such bitter opposition both to a majority of the ministers and to the majority in Parliament as to be quite lacking in influence. In fact, the following year he was forced out of office.

Indeed, the only individual who at the moment enjoyed both the respect of Parliament and the esteem of the public was the Chancellor of the Exchequer, later the Earl of Guilford, better known as Lord North.[60] This fact, combined with North's characteristic good temper and quiet humor, and his assiduous application to his duties,

[59] The idea of the establishment of a British federal system in the eighteenth century has been most fully developed by the late Randolph Greenfield Adams in his provocative *The Political Ideas of the American Revolution: Britannic-American Contributions to the Problem of Imperial Organization, 1765 to 1775* (Durham, N. C., 1922). In 1770 a comprehensive scheme of federal union was, in fact, embodied in a pamphlet published as *Considerations on the Expediency of admitting Representatives from the American Colonies into the British House of Commons* (London, 1770), which sought to distribute power between Parliament and the colonial Assemblies. Josiah Tucker, however, in his *The True Interest of Great Britain set forth in Regard to the Colonies* (see R. L. Schuyler's *Josiah Tucker* (New York, 1931), pp. 343-355), shows how futile any project of federal union was after 1763.

[60] On September 4, 1767 Charles Townshend died and North was thereupon made Chancellor of the Exchequer.

seemed to have induced those influential in governmental circles to look to him as the one man most likely to give the nation the sort of leadership in public affairs then so sorely needed. He certainly could not be expected to preside passively over an unobstructed dissolution of the Empire. Accordingly, after Grafton's resignation in January, 1770, of his post as First Lord of the Treasury, North assumed this office in March and with it the direction of the administration. His principal efforts were directed toward two ends: the maintenance of the authority of Parliament throughout the Empire, and the endeavor to avoid giving the colonists any legitimate ground for claiming that they were being oppressed. Looking back on the year 1770 from our vantage point, we may well ask whether it was within the capacity of any British leader of the eighteenth century to accomplish this extraordinary feat of statesmanship in view of the sweeping advance in America of a revolutionary ideology and a new spirit of nationalism.

CHAPTER 13

The Failure of Imperial Regulation

IN THE debate in the House of Commons early in 1769 on the proposal to bring to England for trial those leaders in Massachusetts Bay accused of stirring up insurrections against the authority of the mother country, Edmund Burke declared:

> Why are the provisions of the statute of Henry the Eighth to be put in force against the Americans? Because you cannot trust a jury of that country. Sir, that word must carry horror to every feeling mind. If you have not a party among two millions of people, you must either change your plan of government, or renounce your colonies for ever.[1]

Burke was correct in asserting that no jury could be found in North America that would convict a man of treason or misprision of treason for leading the people to resist laws passed in Great Britain that were unpopular in the New World. He was also correct in insisting that there must be a change in the plan of governing the colonies. The established methods had manifestly failed. But the crux was to find a new, workable plan. The inability of British statesmen to arrive at some formula that would be equally satisfactory to an effective majority both of the members of Parliament and of the members of the colonial assemblies was, in fact, to spell the doom of the old British Empire.

All hope of securing a revenue from America by any process of internal and external taxation had disappeared by the close of 1768.

[1] Sir H. Cavendish (ed.), *Debates in the House of Commons during the Thirteenth Parliament of Great Britain, 1768–1771* (2 vols., London, 1841–43), I, 191–225.

This was confirmed when Hillsborough on May 13 of the new year directed a circular letter to the American governors. He strongly insisted that "no measure ought to be taken which can in any way derogate from the legislative authority of Great Britain over the colonies," but at the same time he revealed that not only had the administration no intention of proposing any further taxes on America, but that it also was now ready to recommend that the duties upon glass, paper, and paints be dropped as "contrary to the true principles of commerce." [2] In fact, only by a vote of one did the majority of the Cabinet Council of May 1 agree to the retention of the tea tax, and that tax was retained simply for the purpose of vindicating the principles laid down in the Declaratory Act of 1766.[3]

Sound reason lay behind this decision to eliminate the duties: the trade to America during the past year had fallen off to the extent of £700,000 in value as the result of the nonconsumption and nonimportation agreements.[4] Such a step might well fall short of placating those in Parliament who were reported as convinced "that America will not be satisfied with anything less than the repeal of all acts of Parliament relating to the Colonies, even that of Navigation. . . ." [5] Chatham, who advocated the repeal of all the Townshend duties, warned the Lords in the spring of 1770 that if Americans carry "their notions of freedom too far, as I fear they do—if they will not be subject to the laws of this country—especially if they would disengage themselves from the laws of trade and navigation, of which I see too many symptons . . . they have not a more determined opposer than they will find in me." [6] Accordingly, when on March 5 Parliament was called upon to repeal all the late duties except that on tea, North urged that this remaining duty be retained

---

[2] For this letter and other interesting documents bearing upon it furnished by the Duke of Grafton, see Horace Walpole's *Memoirs of the Reign of King George the Third* (2 vols., London, 1894), II, Appendix, pp. 368–373. Hillsborough's letter was, unfortunately, not written in the terms agreed upon by the ministers and was particularly lacking in frankness. As a result, it was severely censured by both Grafton and Camden (*ibid.*).

[3] *Ibid.*, p. 372.

[4] William Samuel Johnson to Jonathan Trumbull, Mar. 6, 1770, Massachusetts Historical Society, *Collections*, 5th ser., IX, 424.

[5] William Samuel Johnson to Jonathan Trumbull, Feb. 3, 1770, *ibid.*, p. 406.

[6] *Ibid.*, p. 425.

"as a mark of the supremacy of Parliament, and an efficient declaration of their right to govern the colonies." [7] Although no voice was raised against the amendment of the Townshend act, many members of the House of Commons thougth it best also to drop the tea duty— on the ground of its insignificance and its likely encouragement of smuggling.[8] But in the act, as finally approved by Parliament, the tea duty was retained, along with the preamble of the earlier act, which assumed the right of Parliament to levy such a duty.[9]

Little did even those in Parliament who were the sturdiest supporters of what they thought was the American point of view realize how great a revolution had already taken place in the political thinking of colonials. To Benjamin Franklin, not only was the retention of the tea duty "with that obnoxious Preamble" viewed as a deep grievance, but the keeping of armed troops in Boston in time of peace without the consent of the Assembly was a further infringement of colonial rights. It is clear that he had already reached the conclusion that the colonies were really separate states with sovereign rights even in their relations to Great Britain. He now affirmed that

while we continue so many distinct and separate states, our having the same Head, or Sovereign, the King, will not justify such an Invasion of the Separate Right of each State to be consulted on the Establishment of whatever Force is Proposed to be kept within its Limits, and to give or refuse its Consent, as shall appear most for the Public Good of that State.

Moreover, he insisted that at the very beginning the colonies "were constituted distinct States, and intended to be as such," and that "the Parliament here has usurp'd an Authority of making laws for them, which before it had not." [10] This conception of the colonies

---

[7] *Ibid.*, p. 421.

[8] The vote to drop the tea duty also was defeated 142 to 244. *Ibid.*, p. 423.

[9] 10 George III, c. 17, *Statutes at Large,* VIII, 108.

[10] Franklin to Samuel Cooper, June 8, 1770, A. H. Smyth (ed.), *The Writings of Benjamin Franklin* (10 vols., New York, 1907), V, 259–260. As early as the year 1766 we find Franklin making a private notation on a document upholding the Stamp Act in which he denied that colonials were subjects of the British state; instead, he affirmed that "we are different states, subject to the King." V. W. Crane, *Benjamin Franklin, Englishman and American* (Baltimore, 1936), p. 124. In 1767 he took the next step in indicating to his friend Lord Kames that the colonies, as the result of the peculiar manner of their origin,

as states, free from the authority of Parliament to legislate for them, may be contrasted with Franklin's earlier point of view back in 1754. In his "Short Hints toward a Scheme for Uniting the Northern Colonies," drawn up in that year, he had taken the position that Parliament—not the Crown—alone possessed a power capable of altering the constitutions of the dependent colonies. Therefore he had embodied in it a recommendation that after the plan therein outlined had been "well considered corrected and improved by the commissioners at Albany," it should "be sent home, and an act of Parliament obtained for establishing it" [11]—thus circumventing probable constitutional objections on the part of the colonies by imposing through statutory procedure a union upon them that would possess the power, without consulting the assemblies, to levy excises and port duties on all the inhabitants embraced within it.[12]

Doubtless the views Franklin expressed in 1770 about the constitutional status of the colonies were still far in advance of most Americans. Nevertheless, his very radicalism recommended him as the logical man to care for the interests of Massachusetts Bay in England and to be entrusted by the Assembly with the London Agency. Indeed, it is clear that most of the radicals in that particular body were not far behind him in their thinking. On July 1, 1769, in a series of ringing resolves, the House had unanimously declared:

That this House do concur in and adhere to . . . that essential Principle, that no man can be taxed, or bound in Conscience to obey any Law, to which he has not given his Consent in Person, or by his Representative.[13]

"seem so many separate little states. . . ." Jared Sparks (ed.), *Works of Benjamin Franklin* (7 vols., Boston, 1836–40), VII, 332–333. For an excellent analysis of this point, see Max Savelle, *Seeds of Liberty* (New York, 1948), pp. 338–342. Burke, in the Stamp Act repeal debates, declared in referring to the colonies: "They were mere Corporations, Fishermen, and Furriers (in the beginning), they are now commonwealths" (*American Historical Review*, XVII, 571), thus expressing a more accurate view of colonial political evolution than did Franklin.

[11] Smyth, *Writings of Benjamin Franklin*, III, 199.

[12] L. H. Gipson, *The British Empire Before the American Revolution* (8 vols., Caldwell, Ida., and New York, 1936–54), V, 126.

[13] For this and other resolves as originally framed, see the Boston *Gazette* of July 3, 1769; see also Thomas Hutchinson, *The History of The Province of Massachusetts Bay* . . . (London, 1828), pp. 240–241.

But this defiant stand was watered down on sober second thought, and the resolution was changed to read:

That the sole right of imposing taxes on the inhabitants of this his majesty's colony of the Massachusetts Bay, is now and ever hath been vested in the house of representatives . . . with the consent of the council, and of his majesty the king of Great Britain, or his governor for the time being.[14]

Nevertheless, it was the original resolve rather than the milder substitute that was given wide currency in America,[15] just as the original resolves of Patrick Henry in 1765 had been given the widest circulation, even though the two most extreme were in fact deleted by the House of Burgesses.

While in all the thirteen colonies men were reaching out for a new order of things, Massachusetts Bay had been and was to remain the dynamic center of the revolution. It is therefore important to follow events in that province with some care.

Before the Massachusetts resolve of July 1, 1769, had found its way into the print, General Gage, confident that order had been restored, had decided to withdraw two of the four regiments stationed in Boston. Both regiments (the 64th and the 65th) had, in fact, been ordered to return to Halifax—one had already sailed and the other was in the process of embarking on the transports. Gage was even contemplating removing the two remaining regiments (the 14th and 29th).[16] Then on July 3 the unamended resolves appeared in the press and rumor spread that circular letters had been sent from Boston to every assembly on the continent to obtain their concurrence.[17] In view of the revival of the controversy, Gage decided to leave one regiment in the town and place the other in Castle William; but since the Assembly refused to make the necessary

---

[14] Boston *Gazette,* July 10, 1769, and Hutchinson, *History,* Appendix, p. 498. Many of the other nineteen resolves, it may be added, were greatly toned down, as can be noted in contrasting those printed in the *Gazette* of July 3 with those presented there on the 10th. For Hutchinson's comment on this, see *Hist. of Prov. of Mass.,* pp. 498–502.

[15] The *Pennsylvania Gazette,* while printing the original resolves, did not see fit to publish the revision of them.

[16] Gage to Hillsborough, July 22, 1769, C. E. Carter (ed.), *The Correspondence of General Thomas Gage* (2 vols., New Haven, 1931–33), I 229.

[17] Hutchinson, *History,* pp. 241–242.

repairs there or furnish supplies in accord with the Mutiny Act, the plan was temporarily put aside.[18] Early in August Governor Bernard, after a stormy session of the Assembly, left for England never to return. Lieutenant Governor Hutchinson now took over the administration. His position could hardly have been more difficult; for he was bound by his oath of office "to support an authority to which the body of the people refused to submit. . . ." Later, in surveying the years of his tenure of the offices of lieutenant governor and governor, Hutchinson in his *History* observed:

At first, indeed, the supreme authority (of Parliament) seemed to be admitted, the cases of taxes only excepted; but the exceptions gradually extended from one case to another, until it included all cases whatsoever. A profession of "subordination," however, still remained; it was a word without any precise meaning to it.[19]

In short, by the beginning of 1770 effective regular government in Massachusetts Bay was virtually at an end. Defiant assemblies had supplanted the legal administration, particularly as regards enforcement of the nonimportation agreement. Violators were proscribed by name.[20] To Judge Israel Williams of Hatfield, this was the crisis. "The Sword is drawn," he declared, "I am as much for liberty, for supporting the rights of the Colonys and for taking every prudent reasonable measure to maintain and defend them as any of my Countrymen. But I differ widely from the generality, as to what they are, wherein they have been invaded, and also as to the methods of redress." [21]

But if Gage had thought that the continued presence of the soldiery would have a quieting effect on the town of Boston, he was to be swiftly disabused. In the early part of 1770 several minor clashes broke out between the townsmen and the soldiers. Then on March 5 occurred the so-called Boston Massacre. This tragic incident resulted when a guard dispatched to the customhouse to protect the sentry there from abuse was goaded into firing upon a hostile crowd. As a result, five people were killed and others

[18] *Gage Corresp.*, I, 229, 232.
[19] Hutchinson, *Hist. of Prov. of Mass.*, p. 256.
[20] *Ibid.*, pp. 266–268.
[21] Massachusetts Archives, 25:352–353.

wounded.[22] The indignation of the Bostonians quickly communicated itself to the inhabitants of nearby towns, who were prepared to use force to drive the two regiments out of the town. Since such a step might well have entailed heavy loss of life and property, the popular leaders prudently held the people in check, while at the same time demanding that the guard that had opened fire should be surrendered to the civil authorities to stand trial for murder and that all the troops should be withdrawn from Boston. To these demands Hutchinson and Lieutenant Colonel Dalrymple were impelled reluctantly to submit.[23]

The consequent removal of the troops to Castle William constituted a great victory for the liberty party in Boston. John Adams, reflecting in after years upon the incident of March 5, declared: "On that night the foundation of American independence was laid." [24] The temper of the inhabitants during this period can be judged from the instructions that were given on May 15 by the

[22] J. C. Miller, *Sam Adams, Pioneer of Propaganda* (Boston, 1936), p. 186. For Hutchinson's account of this affair, in his letter to Sir Francis Bernard of March 12, 1770, see the Mass. Archives, 25:380-382; for the account sent to the Earl of Shelburne in behalf of the town and framed on March 23, 1770, by James Bowdoin, Samuel Pemberton, and Joseph Warren, see the Shelburne Papers, 88:1-2, Clements Library. The Boston *Gazette* of March 12, appearing in mourning with an extended account of the fray, placed the blame fully on the soldiers of the 29th Regiment, who before it took place, it was asserted, "were parading the Streets with drawn Cutlasses and Bayonets, abusing and wounding Numbers of the Inhabitants" with the idea of bringing on an encounter. Major Thomas Moncrieff has left us his version of the incident under date of April 16, 1770, which claimed that the rioting was preconcerted by the mob. Amherst Papers, Packet 48, Can. Arch. transcripts. Clashes between Boston ropewalk journeymen and British redcoats arising from labor friction immediately preceded the Boston Massacre and, according to R. B. Morris, *Government and Labor in Early America* (New York, 1946), pp. 190-192, were closely connected with the tragic events of March 5.

[23] Hutchinson, *Hist. of Prov. of Mass.,* pp. 271-278. The trial of the soldiers by the court was, in spite of fears to the contrary, a fair one. Robert Auchmuty, John Adams, and Josiah Quincy were retained for Preston and the other defendants. All the accused were finally acquitted of the charges of murder; two of the common soldiers were convicted of manslaughter and were thereupon released after submitting to having their thumbs burnt upon pleading benefit of clergy. C. F. Adams, *The Works of John Adams . . .* (10 vols., Boston, 1850-56), I, 90-114; II, 230-232, 317; J. R. Alden, *General Gage in America . . .* (Baton Rouge, 1948), p. 183: Wade Millis, "A Monument to the American Sense of Justice," *Michigan Law Review,* XXV, 143-168; and Catherine D. Bowen, *John Adams and the American Revolution* (Boston, 1950), chap. XX.

[24] Adams, *Works of John Adams,* VIII, 384.

town meeting to their representatives in the General Assembly. Reference is made in these to "a deep-laid and desperate plan of imperial despotism . . . for the extinction of all civil liberty" in America; in them was also embodied a protest "against the pretended right or power of . . . any exterior authority on earth, to determine, limit, or ascertain all or any of our constitutional or chartered, natural or civil, political or sacred, rights, liberties, privileges, or immunities," and in particular "the unwarrantable practice of ministerial instructions" to the governors of the province was singled out for attack.[25] To the earlier denial by the Boston town meeting of the power of Parliament to bind the colony by statute was now added the even more revolutionary rejection of the binding power of the King and his ministers to instruct the governor. In these assumptions Hutchinson could only see "designs of particular persons to bring about a revolution, and to attain to independency. . . . " [26] He also recorded in his *History* some of the techniques of propaganda so effectively employed at this juncture by Samuel Adams and his associates. In place of the old terms "court house" or "Town house," "state house" was now substituted; "his majesty's commons" was employed to designate "the house of representatives of Massachusetts Bay"; in place of "the debates of the assembly," the expression "parliamentary debates" was used; instead of "the province laws," we now find "the laws of the land"; in lieu of "the acts of parliament," it was now "the acts of the British parliament; and, finally, for the "charter" was significantly substituted the word "compact." [27]

But while the education of the public for complete autonomy, if not independence, was thus proceeding in Massachusetts Bay, news arrived late in April, 1770, of the repeal of all the Townshend duties but that on tea. This news evoked the question as to whether nonimportation should continue. Already some Boston merchants, in anticipation of total repeal of all duties provided for in the statute of 1767, had ordered goods from England. But at a town meeting held in Faneuil Hall shortly after the news of the partial repeal had

---

[25] For these resolutions, see the Boston *Gazette*, May 21, 1770.

[26] Hutchinson, *Hist. of Prov. of Mass.*, p. 290.

[27] *Ibid.*, p. 413. The word "original contract" was also employed in place of the word "charter," as expressed, for example, by a writer in the Boston *Gazette* of May 21, 1770.

arrived, the inhabitants went on record, expressing "their unalter-
able Resolution to support the non-importation Agreement against
all Opposition of Tyrants and their Minions."[28] As a result, some
of the goods were returned to England on a ship leased for that
purpose.[29] Then on May 24, in reply to a letter from a committee
of Philadelphia merchants inquiring whether nonimportation should
continue, it was again unanimously voted that there should be no
relaxation until a total repeal of the duties took place.[30] Further, on
the 28th, upon receiving information that traders at Newport were
importing both English and East India goods, it was voted to break
off all commercial relations with that town.[31] Two days later a
gathering of people in New York drafted similar resolutions.[32] Early
in June the Philadelphia merchants agreed "almost unanimously"
to stand by nonimportation.[33] At the same time a group of Newport
merchants determined to take steps against those who had violated
the agreement. It therefore seemed that nonimportation would
stand, since most colonies aside from Rhode Island, New Hampshire, and Georgia appeared to be fairly hearty in maintaining it.[34]

But deep cleavages soon appeared. A letter from a London merchant to a New York correspondent affirmed that Bostonians had
secretly imported prohibited goods to the volume of £150,000
sterling.[35] The committee of New York merchants, repudiating the
action of the artisans taken on May 30, now abandoned hope of
repeal of the tea duty and early in June called for a congress of
merchants of the commercial colonies to meet at Norwalk, Connecticut, on the 18th to "adopt one general solid System for the
benefit of the Whole, that no one Colony may be liable to the
Censure or Reproaches of another. . . ."[36] But this congress did
not materialize. As the result of various polls instituted in New York
City to ascertain the attitude of the inhabitants, the merchants of

[28] Boston *Gazette,* Apr. 30, 1770.

[29] *Ibid.*

[30] For these see *ibid.,* May 28, and *Pennsylvania Gazette,* June 7, 1770.

[31] Boston *Gazette,* May 28, 1770.

[32] *Pennsylvania Gazette,* June 7, 1770.

[33] *Ibid.*

[34] Boston *Gazette,* June 11, 1770; A. M. Schlesinger, *The Colonial Merchants
and the American Revolution, 1763–1776* (New York, 1918), pp. 197–217.

[35] *Pennsylvania Gazette,* June 14, 1770.

[36] Schlesinger, *Colonial Merchants,* p. 221.

that town decided during the first days of July to resume importations from England, and the regular packet about to sail was delayed in order to permit the merchants to fill out their orders.[37]

On September 20 matters came to a head in Philadelphia. At a meeting of subscribers to the agreement, the merchants who favored importation aside from tea carried the day, but their intention to resume trade relations was ineffectively denounced at a mass meeting of inhabitants called on the 27th, where demands were made that the continuation of the agreement be kept in force.[38] Boston could no longer hold out, and on October 15 her merchants agreed to follow the lead of Philadelphia.[39] With the defection of the merchants of the three great ports, nonimportation was doomed in America. By July 1771, with the repeal of the Association in Virginia, it became a thing of the past.[40]

This temporary check to the radical movement coincided with an upsurge of colonial prosperity. Massachusetts Bay, for example, was not only now free of all debt but had a surplus in the treasury, and its substantial income from the sale of public lands made it unnecessary to levy provincial taxes.[41] This prosperity was widespread.

The one area of discontent was North Carolina; here the grievances could not be attributed to the action of the mother country, but were local in origin. Along with other colonies, North Carolina's western counties were inadequately represented in her General Assembly. In fact, governmental power rested largely in the hands of the well-to-do in the tidewater and Piedmont regions. This class monopolized the local offices as well as the bar. The newcomers— people who had poured down from the north by way of the great Valley Road of Virginia: Ulster Scots, Germans, Welsh, and English—were strong individualists, opposed to governmental red tape, and overready to take the law into their own hands. They had

[37] For a bitter criticism of the proponents of nonimportation penned by "Philo-Veritas," see *Pennsylvania Gazette,* July 12, 26, 1770; E. B. O'Callaghan and B. Fernow, *Documents Relative to the Colonial History of the State of New York* (15 vols., Albany, 1853–87), VIII, 220–221.

[38] *Pennsylvania Gazette,* Sept. 27 and Oct. 4.

[39] Boston *Gazette,* Oct. 15, 1770.

[40] Schlesinger, *Colonial Merchants,* pp. 233–236.

[41] Hutchinson, *Hist. of Prov. of Mass.,* pp. 345–350.

numerous grounds for grievance. They claimed to be discriminated against in taxation; they denounced the chicanery of the sheriffs, the exorbitant fees charged both by the clerks of the courts, on the one hand, and by the lawyers they were obliged to hire to defend them in suits, on the other. In vain had Governor Tryon issued in 1766 a proclamation against "Exorbitant Fees." [42] The practice continued unabated,[43] as did seizure and sale of property for non-payment of taxes or in case of unsatisfied court judgments.[44]

Out of this discontent within the Piedmont arose the movement of the so-called Regulators. After petitions [45] to the governor and Assembly and to the Superior Court from the inhabitants of Anson, Rowan, Orange, and other counties had failed and no relief seemed in sight, the Regulators were prepared for action. In their own defense they asserted:

Our only crime with which they [their oppressors in the counties] can charge us is vertue in the very highest degree, namely, to risque our all to save our Country from Rapine and Slavery in our detecting of practices which the Law itself allows to be worse than open Robbery.[46]

The next step was violence. The court at Hillsboro was invaded and overawed by a mob, men were beaten and forced to flee, and the orderly processes of government in some of the counties of the back country came to an end. In December, 1770, the Assembly met in the midst of alarming rumors that the Regulators were planning to march on New Bern to overawe the government, if not to burn the town. Deeply apprehensive, the Assembly passed an act for suppressing riots which provided that all who avoided a court summons for sixty days were to be considered outlaws and might be killed with impunity. It should be noted in passing that this act was later declared by Richard Jackson, the legal adviser to the Board of Trade, to be "altogether unfit for any part of the British Empire." [47] Tryon

---

[42] W. L. Saunders *et al.* (eds.), *The Colonial Records of North Carolina* (10 vols., Raleigh, 1886–90), VII, 230–231.

[43] *Ibid.,* VII, 773–782; VIII, 638.

[44] J. S. Bassett, "The Regulators of North Carolina," American Historical Association, *Reports* (1894), pp. 150–155.

[45] *N.C. Colon. Rec.,* VIII, xiv–xviii, 75–80, 231–234.

[46] *Ibid.,* p. 234.

[47] *Ibid.,* IX, 249. The Board of Trade recommended that the Privy Council

thereupon ordered the arrest of the leaders of the Hillsboro riots and, to implement this order, called out the militia in the spring of 1771.

Detachments were raised from among elements hostile to the Regulators, not only in the tidewater counties of New Hanover, Onslow, Carteret, Craven, and Beaufort, but also from Dobbs,[48] Johnston, and even from Orange, Anson, Mecklenburg, and Rowan counties. On May 16 this army of about one thousand, led personally by Tryon, confronted some two thousand Regulators near the Alamance River. Devoid of commanding officers, the latter broke and fled. Nine of their number had been killed, a good many wounded, and a few taken prisoner. One of the prisoners, a man named Few, who had been outlawed, was executed on the spot, and six more under outlawry were hung at Hillsboro.[49] The remainder of the Regulators were offered pardon by taking the oath of allegiance. By July 4 some six thousand had taken advantage of the amnesty.[50]

Thus the Regulator movement ended in blood and terror. Many of the settlers thereupon deserted their homes to find new ones in what is now Tennessee;[51] others remained, bearing a deep resentment, not against the government of Great Britain, but against their own. Accordingly, when the very same men of the East who had commanded the troops against the Regulators in 1771 appeared in 1775 in arms against the King, those who had so recently taken an oath of allegiance to him became Loyalists. The issue was joined at the battle of Moore's Creek Bridge early in 1776, when Highlanders and Regulators fought side by side against the Patriots.[52]

But to return to the developing imperial crisis. The period from

---

repeal it (*ibid.*, IX, 285). As the law ran for only one year, the Council contented itself with an instruction that should another law be passed for quelling riots it should not embody this objectionable feature which was "irreconcileable to the Principles of the Constitution" (*ibid.*, IX, 286).

[48] Dobbs County came into existence in 1750 and in 1791 was abolished; the territory that it covered now embraces Lenoir and Greene counties.

[49] "From a gentleman of North Carolina to a friend in New Jersey," July 24, *Pennsylvania Journal*, Oct. 8, 1771.

[50] *N. C. Colon. Rec.*, IX, 9.

[51] *Ibid.*, VIII, 655.

[52] Bassett, "The Regulators of North Carolina," *Amer. Hist. Assoc. Rep.* (1894), pp. 209–210; *N.C. Colon. Rec.*, X, xiv.

the failure of nonimportation down to the year 1773 was characterized by a fair degree of tranquility, yet the spirit of resistance was
by no means dead. Late in 1771 a revenue vessel that had seized a
boat entering the lower Delaware loaded with undeclared wine and
tea was boarded by men with blackened faces; after overpowering
the crew of the ship and cutting its rigging and sails to pieces, the
attackers carried off the seized boat with its contents. Nor did a
proclamation issued by Governor Penn offering a reward of £200
for information leading to the arrest of those involved induce anyone to inform against them.[53]

The following year a far more inflammatory incident occurred
in Narragansett Bay in Rhode Island waters, one involving another
revenue vessel, the *Gaspee,* commanded by Lieutenant Dudingston.
Dudingston's overzealous efforts to eliminate violations of the trade
laws from that great smuggling center had earned him the enmity
of the traders and merchants.[54] While moving up the Bay on June
9, his own ship ran fast aground not many miles from Providence.
That night a number of men boarded the vessel and burned it after
wounding its commander by gunfire and overpowering its crew.[55]
Three years earlier the revenue sloop *Liberty* had been boarded
when docked and, after being turned adrift, had been burnt by
Newport people upon its stranding off Goat Island.[56] But the
Gaspee affair constituted not only wanton destruction of property,
but a deliberate affront to the King's officer and his men. As such,
it could not be ignored. A royal proclamation was accordingly issued
offering a large reward for information leading to the conviction of
the culprits, and a royal commission—consisting of the governor of

[53] *Pennsylvania Journal,* Dec. 12, 1771.

[54] The accusation on the part of the people of Rhode Island that Dudingston
had acted illegally in sending a vessel with property seized in Rhode Island
waters to Boston to be condemned by the district court of vice-admiralty sets
forth no specific impropriety. This court, designed to cover just such con-
tingencies, was set up by letters patent under the Great Seal in 1768, with both
original and appellate jurisdiction for all of New England (see Order in Council
of July 6, 1768, P.R.O., C.O. 324).

[55] The principal documents relating to this are printed in the Bartlett
*Records of the Colony of Rhode Island and Providence Plantations in New
England* (10 vols., Providence, 1856-65), VII, 55-192. See also James B.
Hedges, *The Browns of Providence Plantations: Colonial Years* (Cambridge,
Mass., 1952), I, 208-213.

[56] *R. I. Colon. Rec.,* VII, 59.

the colony; the chief justices of Massachusetts Bay, New York, and New Jersey; and the judge of the court of vice-admiralty for the New England district—was convened to probe the incident. But though the guilty parties were Providence men of great prominence who had acted openly in organizing the expedition and who had boarded the ship without disguise, they were so well shielded both by their fellow citizens and by the government of the colony that no evidence could be obtained against them.

The extent to which the growing crisis between the mother country and the continental colonies was welding the liberty forces all along the Atlantic seaboard into a united front, despite the failure of nonimportation, is highlighted by a series of resolutions adopted by the Virginia House of Burgesses on March 12, 1773, during the progress of the inquiry of the royal commission into the *Gaspee* incident. Thomas Jefferson, referring to a preliminary gathering of a small group, including Patrick Henry, Richard Henry Lee, and himself, to consider some plan of action, stated:

> We were all sensible that the most urgent of all measures [was] that of coming to an understanding with all the other colonies, to consider the British claims as a common cause of all, and to produce a unity of action. . . .[57]

The resolutions adopted by the House challenged the legality of the Rhode Island court of inquiry, and in particular its powers "to transmit persons accused of offenses committed in *America* to places beyond the seas to be tried." In addition, they demanded the appointment by the House of a

> Committee of Correspondence . . . whose business it shall be to obtain the most early and authentic intelligence of all such acts and resolutions of the British Parliament or proceedings of Administration, as may relate to or effect [*sic*] the British colonies in *America,* and to keep up and maintain a correspondence and communication with our sister colonies, respecting these important considerations. . . .[58]

[57] P. L. Ford (ed.), "Autobiography," *Writings of Jefferson* (10 vols., New York, 1892–99), I, 7–9. Dumas Malone, *Jefferson, The Virginian* (Boston, 1948), pp. 170–171; E. D. Collins, "Committees of Correspondence of the American Revolution," Am. Hist. Assn., *Ann. Rep., 1901,* I, 250–252.

[58] J. P. Kennedy (ed.), *Journals of the House of Burgesses, 1773–1776* (4 vols., Williamsburg, 1905–7), pp. 39, 41–43.

A committee of eleven was thereupon appointed, which sent copies of these resolutions to the speakers of the other colonial assemblies. Almost all replied.[59] Speaker Metcalf Bowler of the Rhode Island House of Deputies declared "that a firm Union of the Colonies is absolutely necessary for the Preservation of their ancient, legal and constitutional Rights"; while Speaker Thomas Cushing of the Massachusetts Bay House of Representatives endorsed the proposal to revive the intercolonial committees of correspondence, and affirmed that

those who have aimed to enslave us . . . have ever been united in their Councils and their Conduct. . . . The Object which the Conspirators against our Rights seem late to have had much in View, has been either to lull the Colonies into a State of Profound Sleep and Security, which is forever the Forerunner of Slavery; or to forment Divisions among them.[60]

With the appointment by the various colonies of committees of correspondence for the purpose of promoting intercolonial solidarity, a revolutionary American political union was in the making. Though relatively inactive for a time, its organization helped prepare the way for the gathering in Philadelphia the following year of the revolutionary Continental Congress, likewise initiated by Virginians, that was to assume the constitutional authority of delimiting the right of government of Great Britain (termed in its resolves a "foreign power") to interfere in American affairs.

But to return once more to developments in Massachusetts. The news of the repeal of most of the Townshend duties failed to end violence in Boston. General Gage was obliged to report:

They are going on in the usual way at Boston, one of the [American Customs] Commissioners, and some of the inferior officers have been attacked, a Tide-waiter not long ago was tarred, rolled in Feathers and in that Condition carted through the streets—these Proceedings have drove the whole Board of Customs once more to the Castle. . . .[61]

For a time disorders lessened, largely because royal officials were

[59] The Assembly of New Jersey made no reply.
[60] *Journals of the House of Burgesses,* pp. 48, 50.
[61] Gage to Amherst, July 7, 1770, Amherst Papers, Packet 48, Can. Arch. transcripts.

completely ineffective in enforcing the acts of Parliament. Hoping to strengthen the hands of Hutchinson and the other crown officials, and acting in accord with the preamble of the Townshend revenue act, which remained unrepealed, the ministry now decided to settle upon them salaries out of the royal exchequer.

This news of the intention of the home government to assure the governor his salary led the House of Representatives in July, 1772, to denounce the step "as a dangerous innovation" that "exposes the province to a despotic administration of government." [62] As to the payment by the Crown of the judges of the Superior Court, the Boston town meeting on October 30 declared in a petition to Hutchinson that "the most distant thought of its taking effect fills their Minds with Dread and Horror." [63] A committee of twenty-one persons was thereupon appointed by the town to state the rights of the colonists and of Massachusetts Bay in particular. Its report, according to the governor, embodied principles that "would be sufficient to justify the colonies in revolting, and forming an independent state; and such instances were given of the infringement of their rights by Parliamentary authority as . . . could justify an exception to the authority in all cases whatsoever. . . ." [64]

The Boston town meeting report was sent by Sam Adams and his supporters to every town in the province and every member of the House of Representatives for their endorsement, and transmitted to all the colonial assemblies for their concurrence. In fact, before the gathering of the Assembly, almost one third of the towns had approved it, and some in most inflammatory language. [65]

In view of this development, Hutchinson seized the opportunity at the next meeting of the Assembly to expound his views of the constitution of the Empire. His address of January 6, 1773, represents perhaps his greatest effort to reconcile his fellow countrymen to the British concept of that constitution. He began by stating that

[62] The report of the committee of the House of Representatives, which was approved in July, 1772, is printed by Hutchinson (*Hist. of Prov. of Mass.*, Appendix, pp. 545–546); Hutchinson's reply to it is also given (*ibid.*, pp. 546–551). The Boston town meeting declared on October 28, 1772, that the people view the above step on the part of the ministry "as tending rapidly to compleat the System of their slavery . . ." (Boston *Gazette*, Nov. 2, 1772).

[63] *Pennsylvania Gazette*, Nov. 11, 1772.

[64] Hutchinson, *Hist of Prov. of Mass.*, pp. 364–369.

[65] See the Boston *Gazette* for Dec. 14, 21, and 28, 1772, and Jan. 7, 1773.

"so much of the spirit of Liberty breaths through all Parts of the English Constitution that although from the nature of government there must be one supreme authority over the whole, yet the Constitution will admit of subordinate Powers with legislative and executive, greater or less according to local and other circumstances." He then affirmed that under this constitution "for more than one hundred years the Laws both of the supreme and subordinate authority were, in general, duly executed. . . . At length the constitution has been called in question and the authority of the Parliament of Great Britain to make and establish Laws for the Inhabitants of this Province has been, by many, denied. . . ." Thereupon he solemnly declared, with the Massachusetts Bay crisis particularly in mind:

I know no line that can be drawn between the supreme authority of Parliament and the total independence of the Colonies. It is impossible that there should be two independent Legislatures in one and the same state, for although there may be but one head, the King, yet two legislative bodies will make two Governments as distinct as the Kingdoms of England and Scotland before the Union.[66]

This address was answered by the two houses. The Council, while denying any move for independence, stressed the fact that Parlia-

[66] Boston *Gazette,* Jan. 11, 1773. Among the Hutchinson papers are undated notes that indicate that the governor took great care in formulating his ideas before he framed his address (Mass. Archives, 25:433–436). When his speech finally appeared in print in England, the Secretary of State for the Colonies expressed doubts as to whether he should have gone so fully into this delicate subject (Hutchinson, *Hist. of Prov. of Mass.,* p. 385). With reference to the power of Parliament to legislate for America, Franklin in the spring of 1768 had written to his son, Governor Franklin: "The more I have thought and read on the subject, the more I find myself confirmed in opinion, that no middle doctrine can be well maintained, I mean not clearly with intelligible arguments. Something might be made of either of the extremes: that Parliament has a power to make *all laws* for us, or that it has a power to make *no laws* for us; and I think the arguments for the latter more numerous and weighty, than those for the former. Supposing that doctrine established, the colonies would then be so many separate states, only subject to the same King as England and Scotland were before the Union" (Jared Sparks, *Works of Franklin,* (10 vols., Boston, 1836–42), VII, 391–392). Thus Hutchinson and Franklin, while disagreeing on the question whether Parliament could exercise sovereign authority over the colonies, were agreed that two legislatures could not each exercise supreme power within a single state. For a broad discussion of the problem of adjusting theory to practice within the old British Empire, students should consult R. G. Adams, *Political Ideas of the American Revolution* (Durham, N.C., 1922).

ment had but a limited authority; otherwise those under it were but "slaves." [67] The reply of the House of Representatives, which was given its finished form by John Adams [68] and is one of the most important of all the revolutionary papers, admitted freely that "it is difficult, if possible, to draw a Line of Distinction between the universal Authority of Parliament over the colonies (as laid down in the Declaratory Act), and no authority at all." Accepting Hutchinson's argument that no line can be drawn between the supreme Authority of Parliament and the total independence of the colonies, it proceeded to argue:

If there be no such Line, the Consequence is, Either that the Colonies are Vassals of the Parliament, or, that they are totally independent. As it cannot be supposed to have been the Intentions of the Parties in the Compact, that we should be reduced to a State of Vassalage, the Conclusion is, that it was their Sense, that we were thus independent.

Support for posing the crucial question was found in Franklin's compact theory of the Empire: "May we not then further conclude, that it was their (that is the parties to the compact) Sense that the Colonies were by their Charters made distinct States from the Mother Country?" Indeed, whether, in fact, a line could possibly be drawn between "the Supreme Authority of Parliament, and the total Independence of the Colonies" posed a question, the answer to which, it was stated, was so "arduous an undertaking and a matter of such importance to all the colonies" that no decision on this point could be made "without their Consent in Congress." In affirming, finally, an allegiance to the King, the point was stressed that "should the People of this Province be left to the free and full

[67] Hutchinson, *Hist. of Prov. of Mass.*, pp. 372–374.

[68] According to Hutchinson, it was Sam Adams and Joseph Hawley who were the chief authors of the reply, assisted by John Adams (*ibid.*, p. 374). According to the diary of John Adams (*Works*, II, pp. 310–314), the latter, in going over the preliminary report, which was "full of popular talk, and of those democratical principles which have done so much mischief in this country," got these expunged and "furnished the committee with the law authorities, and the legal and constitutional reasonings that are to be seen on the part of the House in that controversy." If one is to assume the correctness of Adams's statement, the original draft of the report, apparently written by Dr. Joseph Warren, must indeed have been a very radical document based upon the doctrine of natural rights.

Exercise of all Liberties and Immunities granted to them by Charter there would be no Danger of an Independence [of] the Crown." [69] But in making this concession, the premise at the same time seemed to be implicit throughout the address that the colonies themselves were the final judges of those liberties and immunities that they claimed to enjoy. Nowhere was it even faintly suggested that the constitutional issues which had now arisen should be referred for a final decision to those instrumentalities in the mother country that had rendered constitutional decisions for over a century before the beginning of the American crisis, but instead it was maintained that these issues could only be settled by a device unknown to the constitution, a truly revolutionary device—a congress of the colonies.

[69] This reply was printed in the *Pennsylvania Gazette* of Feb. 10, 1773, which omitted the governor's address. On the fundamental problem presented between the years 1763 and 1774 of reconciling centralized imperial control with colonial home rule, see A. M. Schlesinger's "The American Revolution Reconsidered," *Political Science Quarterly*, XXXIV, 61–78.

CHAPTER 14

The Colonies Announce Their
Autonomous Status

THERE may still be some who labor under the impression that the American revolutionary movement was caused simply, or at least largely, by the deeds or misdeeds of particular men such as Sam Adams, John Hancock, Arthur Lee, Richard Henry Lee, or Patrick Henry, on the one hand, and George III, Lord North, George Grenville, Governor Hutchinson, or Lord Dunmore, on the other. To accept this interpretation would be to ignore the mass of available evidence of the growth of nationalism and a sense of self-sufficiency in the colonies after 1763. Perhaps no single factor was more responsible for this development than was the acquisition of Canada. As Thomas Hutchinson saw it in 1773:

Before the peace I thought nothing so much to be desired as the cession of Canada. I am now convinced that if it had remained to the French none of the spirit of opposition to the mother country would have yet appeared and I think the effects of it [that is, the acquisition of Canada] worse than all we have to fear from French and Indians.[1]

Indeed, who with the facts before him would venture to argue soberly that had the French succeeded in winning the war and enclosing the British colonials within the area to the east of the Appalachian barriers and south of the waters flowing into the St.

[1] Hutchinson to Dartmouth, Dec. 14, 1773, Massachusetts Archives, 27:586–588.

Lawrence, there would have arisen any violent and sustained opposition to an act of Parliament that with good reason sought to strengthen the North American defenses of the Empire by some method of securing a fund from the colonies as an aid to that end? But the war ended otherwise. The peace therefore ushered in an era in the history of North America utterly unlike any that had preceded it. Indeed, British colonials faced in a sense a new world and inevitably adjusted their ideas to conform to a new set of values.

It is clear that all political communities in a free society—in contrast to a police state—are in the final analysis bound together by self-interest. Therefore, only where this self-interest promotes a sense of solidarity among the members can there be real stability. That the old British Empire up to 1760 exhibited, as a free society, such a remarkable degree of stability can be attributed to the fact that most of those living within it were convinced that the benefits derived from membership far surpassed the disadvantages. That the colonials were fully aware of the disadvantages of having to submit to orders in council, to governors' instructions, and to an impressive body of regulations laid down by Parliament between the years 1660 and 1760 cannot be questioned. Nevertheless, it cannot be doubted that they appreciated the fact that, in spite of their subordination to the government of Great Britain, they alone among colonial people were permitted so extensive a degree of self-government; and that for more than a century their security had rested largely upon the readiness of the mother country to defend them.

However, the elimination of France from North America and of Spain from Florida radically altered the basis of the relationship of the colonies to the mother country. After 1760, revenue and regulatory measures of Parliament that under earlier conditions might have been accepted with some equanimity were now deemed intolerable. The history of the period from 1760 to 1775 is really the history of the transformation of the attitude of the great body of colonials from one of acquiescence in the traditional order of things to a demand for a new order. This undoubtedly came with the growing conviction on their part that the disadvantages of continuing in a subordinate position within the Empire as colonials outweighed the advantages of that status. To what extent responsible leaders prior to 1775 aimed at outright independence from Great Britain cannot be easily ascertained; but it is perfectly clear that the radical leadership sought to end that status of colonial subordination by securing a larger measure of local autonomy than the government of the mother country was prepared to grant.

Incidents such as the publication in the spring of 1773 by the Massachusetts Bay House of Representatives of letters written in 1768 and sent by Hutchinson to a private friend in London, and by others holding positions under the Crown in the province, must be passed over as having only an indirect bearing upon the larger issue.[2] They contained little that was new, but served the purposes of the liberty group in keeping its agitation alive.[3]

But Parliament itself, by a law enacted in May, 1773, assumed responsibility for greatly intensifying the revolutionary movement. This so-called Tea Act permitted not only the drawback of duties paid on all tea above 10,000,000 pounds held by the East India Company in its warehouses before being exported to the colonies, but also the direct exportation of this excess amount of tea to America by the Company itself under special license—should it see fit to undertake this.[4] At the time there were some 17,000,000 pounds of tea on hand and a good deal of it had been there for seven years.[5] The Company, by reason of extraordinary expenses involved in the support of troops in India required to establish political control and order in Bengal, Bihar, and Orissa, and to put down the powerful Maratha confederacy, had found itself in deep

[2] These were printed by Edes and Gill under title of *Copy of Letters sent to Great Britain, by his Excellency Thomas Hutchinson, the Hon. Andrew Oliver, and several other Persons, born and educated among us* (Boston, 1773).

[3] Franklin in London secured the letters by means that are not clear and sent them to Boston, not for publication, but for the private inspection of the popular leaders. For his part in this episode he was summoned before the Lords of the Committee for Plantation Affairs of the Privy Council, very harshly treated by Solicitor General Alexander Wedderburne, and then dismissed from his office of Deputy Postmaster General in North America. Franklin to Thomas Cushing, Feb. 15, 1774, A. H. Smyth (ed.), *The Writings of Benjamin Franklin* (10 vols., New York, 1907), VI, 182–193; *Pennsylvania Gazette*, Apr. 20, 1774; Carl Van Doren, *Benjamin Franklin* (New York, 1938), pp. 440–478.

[4] 13 George III, c. 44, *Statutes at Large*, VIII, 228–230.

[5] London advices, *Pennsylvania Gazette*, Sept. 8, 1773.

financial difficulty.[6] To save it from bankruptcy, Parliament loaned it £1,400,000.[7] Along with the Tea Act went an India regulating act, which submitted the affairs of the Company to a greater degree of supervision on the part of the Crown.[8] The Company hoped that the sale of its tea in America under favorable terms to consumers might help to right its affairs. At the same time Parliament took the opportunity to reassert its supreme authority within the Empire.

The first news of the Tea Act caused little stir in America.[9] Not until the East India Company had determined to become the chief exporter of its tea to the colonies, and to set up warehouses in Boston, New York, and Philadelphia for the sale of this article, were the American importers alarmed. Raising the cry of monopoly, they now made common cause with Sons of Liberty groups who had continued to agitate against the payment of the tea duties.[10] For it should be understood that even at Boston tea had for years been received from London in rather large quantities and duties had been paid upon it, although this was not apparently a matter of general public knowledge until the facts were published in the papers in November, 1773.[11] Indeed, it was apparently overlooked in view

[6] I. C. Hansard (ed.), *Parliamentary History of England* . . . (36 vols., London, 1806–20), XVII, 885.

[7] *Ibid.*, 908–931. V. A. Smith, *The Oxford History of India* (Oxford, 1923), pp. 518–519; *The Cambridge History of the British Empire,* IV, H. H. Dodwell (ed.), *British India, 1497–1858* (New York, 1929), p. 188.

[8] *Ibid.*, 188–191; *Parl. Hist.*, XVII, 887–917. The act for regulating the affairs of the East India Company is 13 George III, c. 63, *Statutes at Large,* VIII, 248–257.

[9] *Pennsylvania Gazette,* July 14, 1773.

[10] According to London advices printed in the *Pennsylvania Gazette* of Sept. 29, six hundred chests of tea would be sent by the Company to Boston, New York, and Philadelphia respectively, where there would be four public sales of it each year. The fear of an American tea monopoly certainly exercised a great influence in bringing the mercantile elements into the radical camp. In the words of Major General Haldimand, writing to the Earl of Dartmouth from New York on December 28, 1773: "I conceive that the Fear of an Introduction of a Monopoly in this Country has induced the mercantile part of the Inhabitants to be very industrious in opposing this Step of the Honorable East India Company under the Sanction of Parliament, and added Strength to a Spirit of Independence already too prevalent." Shelburne Papers, 88:3–9, Clements Library.

[11] In 1769 duty was paid on over 329 chests of tea; in 1770, on more than 153 chests; in 1771, on over 709 chests; in 1772, on over 323 chests; and in 1773, up to October 23, on over 349 chests. *Pennsylvania Gazette,* Nov. 17,

of the vast quantities of cheap Bohea tea brought from Holland and smuggled into the colonies, especially into those south of New England. But with the low price that could now be set on legal high-quality tea, all those who had prospered by evading the customs would be adversely affected.

New York was the first seaport to set the pattern of American resistance. On October 15, a little over a month after the text of the Tea Act appeared in a New York paper, the merchants drafted a letter expressing their thanks to those New York ship captains who had refused to load their ships, while docked at London, with the East India Company tea for the "insidious purpose of levying the Duty in America." [12] The following day the Philadelphia merchants resolved that whoever would directly or indirectly countenance the efforts of the Company to import tea to America for the purpose of helping to enforce "this Ministerial Plan . . . is an Enemy to his Country." [13] A committee was also appointed to wait upon the consignees of the tea to be shipped to Philadelphia and to secure their resignations. This was done. On October 21 the Massachusetts Bay intercolonial Committee of Correspondence called on all the colonies to prevent the East India Company tea from landing in America; on the 25th the Boston *Gazette* reprinted a threatening Philadelphia handbill addressed "to the Commissioners appointed by the East India Company for the sale of tea in America"; [14] and then on November 3 a mass meeting was held at the Boston Liberty Tree to secure the resignation of the Boston consignees. Previously, similar action had been taken at Philadelphia; New York followed on December 1 and Charleston the next day. When the Boston meeting failed to achieve its objectives, a meeting was called for the 5th. But the consignees—Thomas and Elisha Hutchinson, Benjamin Faneuil, Richard Clark and Sons, and Joshua Winslow—were determined not to quit, and were forced to seek refuge at Castle William.

In spite of some difficulties, the East India Company succeeded in placing its tea on four ships loaded with other supplies and bound

---

1773. For many years Hutchinson, among others, had been an importer of tea; later his sons took over the business. "Hutchinson Correspondence," Mass. Arch., 25:98–9; 26:157, *passim*.

[12] *Pennsylvania Gazette*, Oct. 27, 1773.

[13] *Ibid.*, Oct. 20, 1773.

[14] Massachusetts Historical Society, *Proceedings*, 1st ser., XIII, 162.

for Boston; ships likewise destined for New York, Philadelphia, and Charleston also received allotments. In all, some seventeen hundred chests were shipped. Only at Charleston was the tea permitted to be landed—and then after heated debate. It was consigned to a public warehouse, where it was destined to remain for three years, ultimately to be disposed of for the support of the new state of South Carolina.[15]

When the first of the four Boston ships, the *Dartmouth*, arrived on November 27, it was compelled by Sam Adams's "Mohawks" to moor at the docks, as were the other two ships that arrived soon after.[16] In attempting to uphold the authority of the royal government, Hutchinson found himself virtually isolated. Even support from the military at Castle William and from the commanders of the British warships in the outer harbor was ineffective. Arrayed against him now were not only the Governor's Council and members of the House of Representatives, most of the people of Boston and the neighboring towns, but also the liberty elements in the other northern colonies, which through the committees of correspondence organized public opinion to oppose the landing of the tea. To the governor the issue was simple: Should mob rule supplant the legal government in Massachusetts Bay? To the popular leaders the issue was equally simple: Should American rights and liberty be weakly sacrificed to the manifest determination of the British ministers to establish the principle of the supremacy of Parliamentary statutes throughout the Empire? Once the issue at stake was clear, neither side would give way, nor under the circumstances could easily give way. After a series of great mass meetings had failed to break the impasse, a band of men disguised as Indians and protected by a great cordon of the populace boarded the three ships the night of December 16, broke open the tea chests, and threw the contents into the bay.[17]

[15] F. S. Drake (ed.), *Tea Leaves: a Collection of Letters and Documents relating to the Shipment of Tea to the American Colonies in the Year 1773 by the East India Company* (Boston, 1884), pp. 339-342.

[16] The fourth ship by reason of a storm did not succeed in reaching Boston with its consignment of tea until long after the three other ships had appeared, and the tea that had not been previously landed on the Cape Cod coast, as an emergency measure, was received at Castle William.

[17] Mass. Hist. Soc., *Proc.*, 1st ser., XIII, 170-173; *Tea Leaves*, pp. xvi—cxlii, 245-364.

This open defiance of the British Government was aggravated by the fact that there was no longer in Massachusetts Bay a conservative group sufficiently influential to insist that financial amends be made to the East India Company for the destruction of its property. Even the Council had unanimously approved an address to the governor on November 29 denouncing the Tea Act as introducing "monopolies and tending to bring on them [the colonials] the extensive evils there arising." But the Council's greatest objection to the law was that it was "manifestly intended . . . more effectually to secure the payment of the Duty upon Tea . . . which Act in its operation deprives the Colonies of the . . . exclusive Right of Taxing themselves . . . which they hold to be [such] an essential one, that it cannot be taken away, or given up without their being degraded, or degrading themselves below the character of men." Moreover, the Council recognized the plan to apply the money to be raised under the act for the support of civil government and the administration of justice in the colonies as constituting in operation a "diminution" of "charter Rights." [18]

The news of the destruction of the tea at Boston spread along the Atlantic seaboard like wildfire—and so did the spirit of resistance. Governor Tryon, who had previously felt that the tea could be landed at New York despite opposition, now wrote to the Earl of Dartmouth that this could only be accomplished "under the Protection of the Point of the Bayonet and Muzzle of the Cannon, and even then I do not see how the Sales or Consumption could be effected." [19] When on December 25 the ship *Polly* reached the Delaware with 697 chests of tea, a crowd of some 8,000 was on hand and Captain Ayres was readily persuaded to return to England immediately with his cargo. [20] When in April of the following year the ship *London* arrived at New York with a private consignment of tea, which the captain sought to conceal, a mob boarded the vessel and destroyed the tea; whereupon the bells of the churches rang out

[18] "Proceedings of the Council," Nov. 29, 1773, Gage Papers, American Series, vol. 119, Clements Library.

[19] Tryon to Dartmouth, Jan. 3, 1774, *Letters and Papers of Cadwallader Colden*, New York Historical Society, *Collections* (9 vols., New York, 1917–23, 1934–35), VII, 200.

[20] For the principal documents relating to this episode, see the *Pennsylvania Magazine of History and Biography*, XV, 385–393.

for joy. But another tea ship, the storm-tossed *Nancy,* was permitted to return to England with its freight after repairs on it had been made.[21] Nor were these demonstrations confined to the great ports.[22] The boycott of tea was universal throughout America.

Some writers have seen fit to argue that had not the Tea Act of 1773 been passed, the people of the colonies would have become reconciled to the constitutional views of the British ministry and Parliament. For proof they point to the period of comparative quiet which followed the repeal of most of the Townshend duties. But it should be understood that the position of the popular Atlantic sea-board leaders had not altered and that peace had come in no small part as the result of the evasion of the tea duties by widespread smuggling. The colonies, in other words, had not retreated an inch on the constitutional issue of the supremacy of Parliament. Nowhere was that issue more acute than in Massachusetts Bay. Before the news of the passing of the Tea Act had arrived, the Assembly on June 15, 1773, in a series of resolves and a petition that were forwarded to Franklin, had called upon the King to remove from office the governor and the secretary on the ground that they were guilty of plotting to "overthrow the constitution of the province." [23] While in England, Franklin, as the agent of the colony, could state to Dartmouth that "the Assembly have declared their desire only to be put in the situation they were in before the Stamp Act." [24] In Massachusetts, Franklin's view that the Bay Colony was and always had been a "separate," distinct state was rapidly gaining acceptance. Early in 1774, Franklin, in a communication to the Speaker of the House of Representatives, significantly described his activities in London on behalf of the Massachusetts Bay legislature as intended "to lessen the breach between two states of the same empire . . . by showing that the injuries complained of by one of them did not proceed from the other, but from traitors among themselves." [25] As Franklin saw it, the attempt of Hutchinson and other supporters of

---

[21] *Pennsylvania Gazette,* Apr. 27, 1774.

[22] Some contemporary writers had noted the protest of fifty people from Plymouth over the proceedings at Boston, but this was disposed of by a writer signing himself "an Old Colonist" (*ibid.,* Jan. 12, 1774).

[23] Smyth, *Writings of Franklin,* VI, 276–280.

[24] *Ibid.,* p. 281.

[25] *Ibid.,* p. 190.

the Crown to uphold the Parliament against the Assembly was
nothing short of treason.

Had the ministry, when on March 4, 1774, it had the King
summon Parliament to consider the disturbances in America, fully
realized the gravity of the crisis that now confronted the British
Empire and the nature of the forces that were arrayed in America
against the mother country, it is hard to believe that it would have
acted as it did. Franklin perceived far more clearly than did the
King and Lord North the realities of the situation. He recognized
the fact that the old continental colonies, in actuality if not in
theory, had become states within the Empire and would no longer
be treated as immature political dependencies. Previously the British
Government had sought rule by consent. Now the concept of rule
by consent was to give way to rule by coercion. But the new formula
was first to be applied not against *all* the colonies but rather against
one—the chief center of resistance.

When may coercion be applied by a state to restrain subordinate
units or groups within it? Was President Lincoln justified in calling
upon Congress to permit him to save the Federal Union by the use
of force against the southern secessionists who insisted that the
Union was only a conditional pact between fully sovereign states?
Were the King and Lord North justified under existing circumstances in asking Parliament to take drastic action to curb the in-
subordination of the radical elements in Massachusetts Bay in order
to save the old British Empire from disintegration? In each instance
subordinate units defied the central government, demanding that
the latter must accept their own interpretations of what was constitutional on the one hand and unconstitutional on the other. In each
instance subordinate units set themselves up as ultimate judges of
the constitutionality of particular measures, and in each case their
stand challenged the concept of national unity. In the face of this
challenge George III and North, whether wisely or not, did not
hesitate to act—any more than did Lincoln.

The new policy of coercion was embodied in a series of proposed
laws. On March 18 there was presented to Parliament the Boston
Port Bill, closing that port to commerce until compensation for the
loss of its tea had been granted by the inhabitants of the town to the
East India Company, and transferring the customhouse temporarily

to Marblehead in the port of Salem. After long debate, in which Charles James Fox, Dowdeswell, Burke, Rose Fuller, and former Governor Johnstone of West Florida attacked the bill as discriminating against Boston and as designed to drive Americans into a confederation, it finally passed its third reading on the 25th without a division; on the 30th, it was approved by the House of Lords, also without division; and on the following day it received the royal assent.[26]

This was followed on April 15 by a bill regulating the government of Massachusetts Bay, whereby the provincial Council was made appointive, as in other royal colonies, rather than elective; further, the governor was now clothed with exclusive power to appoint and dismiss all inferior officers of the law, including inferior judges and the sheriffs; the town meetings were also severely restricted; finally, the method of appointing juries was altered. Again there was a full debate, with Sir George Savile, Colonel Barré, Stephen and Charles James Fox, General Conway, and Burke leading a strong opposition in the House of Commons. But the bill passed its second reading by 239 votes to 64 and its third reading by "a prodigious majority." In the House of Lords there were also determined efforts to defeat the measure by a small group, but without avail; and after some amendments, in which the House of Commons concurred, it received the royal approval on May 20.[27]

While this measure was still being debated in the lower house, a third bill was presented on April 15 which had as its purpose the protection of the persons of those officers who, in attempting to execute the laws in Massachusetts Bay, might otherwise be brought before the local courts and convicted. It provided that such persons, if accused of capital offenses in the performance of their official duties, might be tried in some other colony or in Great Britain at the discretion of the governor. To Colonel Barré the bill was big with evil consequences, and there were others who opposed it; but it finally passed the Commons on May 6 by a vote of 127 to 24, and after

[26] 14 George III, c. 19, Pickering, *Statutes at Large,* XXX, 336–341; Peter Force (ed.), *American Archives* (Washington, 1837), 4th ser., I, 5–66; *Parl. Hist.* XVII, 1159–1192.
[27] 14 George III, c. 45, Pickering, *Statutes at Large,* XXX, 381–390. *Amer. Arch.,* 4th ser., I, 66–105; *Parl. Hist.,* XVII, 1192–1199, 1277–1289, 1300–1316.

being approved by the House of Lords was signed by the King on the same day, as was the preceding bill.[28]

Furthermore, at the time that the bill concerned with the administration of justice was introduced into the House of Commons, a bill "for the better providing suitable quarters" for troops that might be stationed in any part of America was likewise proposed. This bill was intended to end the kind of disputes that had arisen in Massachusetts Bay over whether troops in a colony must be assigned to barracks if their presence away from them was needed. For it stated that they might be quartered by order of the governor in uninhabited houses, outhouses, barns, or other buildings that were more suitably located than barracks for the particular purpose in mind. It passed the lower house without a division or debate on May 4 and was sent to the House of Lords. Only there did it meet opposition when Chatham spoke for leniency in the treatment of the colonials and seized the occasion to condemn the Boston Port Act in the strongest terms. On June 2 it received the royal assent by the Lords Commissioners.[29]

While debate on these coercive measures was in progress, Rose Fuller, who opposed them all, declared on April 15 that he intended to propose the repeal of the Tea Act, and on the 19th he so moved. This touched off a lively debate in which Edmund Burke, speaking in favor of the motion, put forth one of his greatest efforts in behalf of conciliation. With a solemnity fitting the occasion, he reviewed the history of the relations of the mother country and the colonies since the repeal of the Stamp Act. Fox and Barré spoke to the same point. But on a vote of the House a motion to repeal was rejected late that night by 182 to 49.[30] The arguments in favor of repeal were based upon the assumption that there was at stake not a question of the whole system of control of the Empire by Parliament but simply the issue of taxation of the colonies by that body, and that the retention of the trivial tea duty would bring on rebellion. Those who spoke against repeal indicated their conviction that were this

[28] 4 George III, c. 39, Pickering, *Statutes at Large,* XXX, 367–371. *Amer. Arch.,* 4th ser., I, 111–129; *Parl. Hist.,* XVII, 1199–1210, 1274–1277, 1289–1297.

[29] 14 George III, c. 54, Pickering, *Statutes at Large,* XXX, 410. *Amer. Arch.,* 4th ser., I, 165–170; *Parl. Hist.,* XVII, 1351–1356.

[30] *Amer. Arch.,* 4th s., I, 133–165; *Parl. Hist.,* XVII, 1210–1273.

step to be taken, it would indicate such weakness on the part of the mother country that Britain would never again be able to control the colonies.

One final measure affecting the colonies must now be considered—a bill for the government of the Province of Quebec. This measure, long in maturing, originated in the House of Lords on May 2. On the 17th it passed its third reading and was then sent down to the House of Commons, where it was fully debated until June 13 and, after amendments, was returned to the House of Lords. Being there approved, it was signed by the King on the 22nd.[31] Under the terms of the act the Province of Quebec, created in 1763, was extended to include those French-speaking settlements in the valley of the Ohio and in the Illinois country which under the terms of the Proclamation of 1763 had been left without any provision for a civil government; further, in recognition of the overwhelmingly Roman Catholic, French-speaking character of the province, the old French civil law was retained with some modifications, along with the English criminal law and criminal procedure. In view of the fact that the *habitants* had only recently been enemies in arms, were unaccustomed to assuming political responsibilities, and could not qualify for seats in any lawmaking assembly under the English Test Act, an appointed legislative council of some twenty-two persons was set up with power to make laws. To guarantee Roman Catholics membership in that body, the Test Act in this instance was waived in favor of the oath of allegiance. Finally, the legality of the Roman Catholic religion within the province was not only recognized, but the right of the Church to continue to collect tithes was upheld. Much of the law of 1774 confirmed the actual practice of the provisional government set up in 1763. The extension of its authority into the Ohio Valley and Illinois country to include the French communities in those areas was, it should be made clear, restricted by one important qualification. It was specifically declared "that nothing herein contained, relative to the Boundary of the province of Quebec, shall in anywise affect the Boundaries of any other Colony." [32] This would seem to indicate

[31] 14 George III, c. 83, *Statutes at Large,* VIII, 405–407.

[32] Section II of the act. Lord North stated in the debate that the bill was not intended to affect the just rights of any of the colonies (*Amer. Arch.,* 4th ser.,

that insofar as boundaries were concerned, the act was provisional in nature.

While the Quebec Act was attacked during its passage both in the Commons, by John Dunning, Barré, Fox, Thomas Townshend, and Burke, and in the Lords, by Chatham, as a "cruel, oppressive, and odious measure," [33] it has been the mature judgment of most of those who have studied its operation under the peculiar conditions then existing in Canada and in the Illinois country that it represented an honest and humane effort at a critical period in the history of North America to deal with a very difficult, pressing, and complicated problem.[34] But its timing, so far as America was concerned, was most maladroit. New fuel was now added to the colonies' resentment against the mother country. In the Suffolk County Resolves, drawn up at Dedham, Massachusetts Bay, on September 6, it was voted:

> That the late act of Parliament for establishing the Roman Catholic religion and the French laws in that extensive country now called Canada, is dangerous to an extreme degree to the protestant religion and to the civil rights and liberties of all America.[35]

The Coercive Acts made open rebellion in America inevitable. Burke, Fox, Chatham, Barré, and others of the opposition not only warned of it but played their part in encouraging the colonials to resist what they themselves denounced in Parliament as tyrannical

---

I, 185; *Parl. Hist.* XVII, 1358–1407). The determination of these rights looked to the future.

[33] *Ibid.,* XVII, 1402.

[34] The student is referred to A. L. Burt's *The Old Province of Quebec* (Toronto, 1933), chap. IX, for an unusually sympathetic discussion of the Quebec Act; see also R. Coupland, *The Quebec Act: A Study in Statesmanship* (Oxford, 1925), and his *The American Revolution and the British Empire* (London, 1930), chap. VII, and Appendix; Louise P. Kellogg's "A Footnote to the Quebec Act" (*Canadian Historical Review,* XIII, 147–156), which stresses the fear of deportation of the French in the Illinois country from 1763 to the passage of the Quebec Act; and A. Berriedal Keith's somewhat critical review of the Coupland book in the *English Historical Review* for Jan., 1926, pp. 137–139.

[35] *Amer. Arch.,* 4th ser., I, 777–778. For a study of the anti-Catholic feeling that swept the colonies with the passage of the Quebec Act, see F. J. Zwierlein's "End of No-Popery in the Continental Congress," *Thought,* XI, 357–377, and Father Charles Metzger's *The Quebec Act, a Primary Cause of the American Revolution* (New York, 1936).

laws. Moreover, the colonial newspapers now featured articles by English writers, many of them reprinted from English newspapers, that went even farther in upbraiding the ministry for a course of conduct that was branded as nothing less than criminal. Everywhere along the Atlantic seaboard the liberty groups made the cause of Boston and Massachusetts Bay their own; everywhere these groups proceeded with military preparations. County and provincial conventions were summoned and resolutions almost without number were adopted. Young Thomas Jefferson, in his revolutionary natural-rights pamphlet, *A Summary view of the rights of British America*—designed as a draft of instructions to the Virginia delegates to the Continental Congress—denounced *all* regulations of Parliament, even the seventeenth-century trade and navigation system, as acts "of arbitrary power . . . over these States." [36] As early as June 17 the Massachusetts Bay House of Representatives, in order to mobilize American public opinion, had called for a general meeting of the intercolonial committees of correspondence in Philadelphia or elsewhere, as might seem suitable.[37] On September 5 delegates from all the older colonies except Georgia finally assembled in the Quaker City and engaged in prolonged deliberations.

The Continental Congress, as this revolutionary convention was called, contained men of somewhat conservative views such as Joseph Galloway of Pennsylvania, moderates such as James Duane and John Jay of New York, and extreme radicals such as Sam Adams of Massachusetts Bay and Patrick Henry and Richard Henry Lee of Virginia. No one of the delegates, not even Galloway, could visualize a restoration of the old Empire. In fact, on September 28 it was Galloway who introduced a truly revolutionary Plan of Union that was designed to embrace the thirteen older colonies. This plan called for the setting up of a distinct American government with a legislative council, made up of representatives chosen by the respective assemblies, and a President General to be appointed by the King. This government, although it was to be inferior to that of Great Britain, was, nevertheless, to have authority to

---

[36] *Amer. Arch.*, 4th ser., I, 690–699. For critical editions of *A Summary View*, see that published by Professor T. P. Abernethy in *Scholars' Facsimiles & Reprints* (New York, 1943) and especially that in J. P. Boyd *et al.* (eds.), *The Papers of Thomas Jefferson, 1760–1776* (Princeton, 1950), I, 121–137.

[37] *Amer. Arch.*, 4th ser., I, 421.

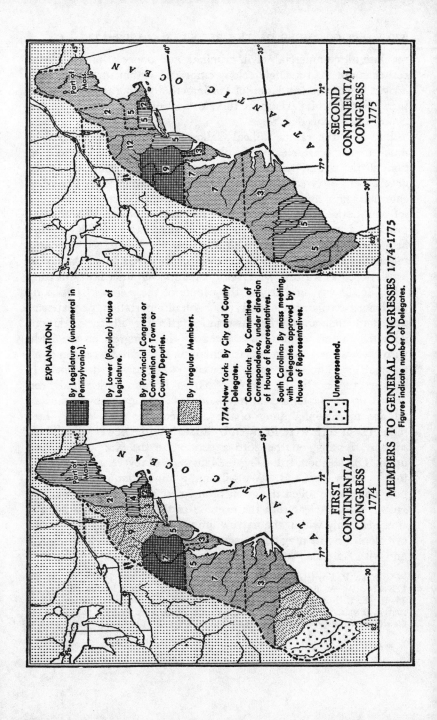

EXPLANATION:

By Legislature (unicameral in Pennsylvania).

By Lower (Popular) House of Legislature.

By Provincial Congress or Convention of Town or County Deputies.

By Irregular Members.

1774—New York: By City and County Delegates.

Connecticut: By Committee of Correspondence, under direction of House of Representatives.

South Carolina: By mass meeting, with Delegates approved by House of Representatives.

Unrepresented.

FIRST CONTINENTAL CONGRESS 1774

SECOND CONTINENTAL CONGRESS 1775

MEMBERS TO GENERAL CONGRESSES 1774-1775
Figures indicate number of Delegates.

regulate all commercial, civil, criminal, and police affairs that concerned more than a single colony embraced within the union, with
a right to veto all legislation of Parliament affecting the colonies. In
turn the right of Parliament to veto laws of the American Grand
Council was conceded.[38]

But even the rather radical Galloway proposal was rejected as
much too conservative, and in place of it on October 14 a declaration of rights and resolves was adopted. While conceding to the
government of Great Britain the authority to regulate the bona fide
external commerce of the colonies, this declaration at the same time
referred to the British Government as a "foreign power." The ancient
practice of appointment of provincial councilors by the King during
his pleasure was, consistent with this view, denounced as "unconstitutional, dangerous and destructive to the freedom of American
legislation," as was the Declaratory Act and all other laws affecting
"the life, liberty, property of the people of the colonies" passed by
the British Parliament since 1763.[39] A nonimportation, nonexporta-
tion, and nonconsumption Association affecting all trade relations
with the mother country was voted by the Congress on the 20th,
with the warning that it was to remain in force until a redress of all
colonial grievances had been secured. The following day not only
was an address to the people of Great Britain, which had been
drawn up on September 5, now adopted after amendment, but an
address to the inhabitants of the older colonies was voted. These
measures in turn were followed by appeals to the newer colonies for
support. Finally, on the 26th a petition to the King was agreed
upon. The petition, still using the language of reverence and loyalty
to his person, declared: "We wish not a diminution of the prerogative, nor do we solicit the grant of any new right in our favour." [40]
However, it is clear that the exercise of the royal prerogative was
conceded only within the narrow limits consistent with the reservoir
of colonial rights previously asserted in the declaration and resolves
and with America's own interpretation of them.

[38] Julian P. Boyd, *Anglo-American Union* (Philadelphia, 1941), pp. 32–39,
112–114; W. A. Brown, *Empire or Independence* (Baton Rouge, 1941), pp.
14–19; E. C. Burnett, *Letters of Members of the Continental Congress* (Washington, 8 vols., 1921–36), I, 51–54, passim; W. C. Ford (ed.), *Journals of the
Continental Congress* (34 vols., Washington, 1904–37), I, 43–52.
[39] *Ibid.*, pp. 63–74.
[40] *Ibid.*, pp. 75–121.

Thus the Continental Congress before finally adjourning had served notice on Parliament that the people of America no longer considered themselves bound by any of its laws, outside of its purely commercial regulations, and on the King that the exercise of his prerogatives must be consistent with American ideas about the nature of their liberties, on the one hand, and the limitations of his authority, on the other.

With the establishment of the Association in all the older colonies, the period of free discussion and indecision now came to an end in America.[41] Coercion in one form or another was now freely employed against both the ardent loyalists minority and the great body of moderates. However, the war that commenced the following year was to the revolutionist John Adams not really a "revolutionary" war at all. In reflecting later upon the events that followed the Peace of Paris of 1763, he affirmed that

the revolution was complete, in the minds of the people, and the Union of the colonies, before the war commenced in the skirmishes of Concord and Lexington on the 19th of April, 1775.[42]

In other words, if John Adams's position be accepted as correct—and the weight of evidence supports it—the American Revolution, in essence, is not to be found in any single formal pronouncement or overt act on the part of the colonials, but rather in the gradual evolution of their constitutional ideas and program.[43] This revolutionary movement began at the close of the Great War for the Empire and was virtually consummated in all essentials in the work of the Continental Congress in 1774. Independence of the British Empire was, however, not demanded during this period by the American patriots, except possibly by a few extreme radicals such

[41] That the Association was the first real act of separation of the colonies from the mother country is the conclusion of Henry Leffmann in his article "The Real Declaration of Independence: A Study of Colonial History under a Modern Theory, "*Pa. Mag. of Hist. and Biog.,* XLVII, 281–297.

[42] C. F. Adams (ed.), *The Works of John Adams . . .* (10 vols., Boston, 1850–56), X, 197.

[43] The reader is referred to C. F. Mullett's *Fundamental Law and the American Revolution 1760–1776* (New York, 1933), R. G. Adams's *Political Ideas of the American Revolution . . . 1765–1775* (Durham, N.C., 1922), and Clinton J. Rossiter's *Seedtime of the Republic* (New York, 1953), the last, the most exhaustive account extant of the political ideas and ideals of the American colonials.

as Sam Adams; rather, they were led increasingly to insist upon an autonomous position for the colonies within the Empire, such as would give them perfect freedom in all internal, and most external, matters. When this quest was discovered to be unattainable, they then took the perfectly logical and irrevocable step in 1776 and declared their independence of the Crown, as they, for all practical purposes, had previously done of Parliament. By this time George III rather than Parliament represented the human embodiment of all the discords that had arisen within the Empire since 1763.[44]

The people of the new British continental colonies and of the old British islands of the North Atlantic and the Caribbean Sea were not prepared to repudiate their allegiance to the King and join the older continental colonies in the work of creating a New World independent power based upon American revolutionary principles. Indeed, despite their various grievances against the British government, most of the inhabitants of these outlying and insular possessions were convinced that they had more to lose than to gain in embracing such principles, and therefore reconciled themselves without too much difficulty to a continued dependence upon the mother country for their protection and general welfare.[45]

A final word in summary. The rupture of the old British Empire, it may be affirmed, did not come about as the result of the actions of wicked men—neither of the King or Lord North, on the one hand, nor of American radicals, on the other—freely as this was charged on both sides of the Atlantic by those whose minds were inflamed. It had its source fundamentally in the fact that America now embodied a mature and powerful English-speaking community with a mind of its own and a future that it considered peculiarly its own. British statesmen as a group were responsible for the breach, to the extent of their failure to realize that the old system of imperial

[44] As to the attitude of the people of Great Britain toward the revolutionary movement in the colonies, see Dora M. Clark's comprehensive study, *British Opinion and the American Revolution* (New Haven, 1930).

[45] It is true that the Assembly of Jamaica, in support of the continental colonials, in 1774 memorialized the Crown, beseeching the King to act as the intermediary to reconcile his English and American subjects (*Amer. Arch.*, 4th ser., I, 1072–1074). Bermuda also, while refusing to defy the mother country, sought to remain on good terms with the rebellious colonials. H. C. Wilkinson, *Bermuda in the Old Empire* (London, 1950), chap. XIII, and W. B. Kerr, *Bermuda and the American Revolution* (Princeton, 1936).

control was no longer applicable to a society so highly cultivated, so extended, and so numerous. American radicals as a group were responsible for it to the extent of their failure in turn to realize that their own violent words and acts were provocative of coercion rather than conciliation. However, the coercive steps of the British Government served perfectly the purpose of those who sought to overturn the outmoded system of imperial relationships in favor of a new system. Among the extremely particularistic American people along the Atlantic seaboard, these measures generated a degree of emotional fervor in favor of unity of action that men previously had thought to be quite impossible; a unity, in fact, that was sufficiently effective to achieve the goal of complete political independence through the ordeal of war and, equally important, to lay the foundations for a great nation.

In bringing this volume to a conclusion, certain general reflections may now be made upon the crisis that developed within the Old British Empire between the years 1761 and 1775. First of all, one must accept the fact that the American patriots, on the one hand, and most of the people of Great Britain, on the other, were deeply convinced of the essential rightness of the respective positions they took on the issues that arose to separate them. Further, it is clear that a minority in America was as ardently sympathetic with the claims of the government of the mother country to exercise effective authority, including the right at least to levy external taxes throughout the Empire, as was a minority in Great Britain in supporting the American position denying this authority.

Again, one is faced with the anomaly that in our own day the fundamental positions taken by Great Britain and America in the year 1775 are reversed. For Great Britain in the twentieth century repudiated its earlier position that sovereignty was indivisible within the Empire by conceding that its self-governing units were distinct nationalities with complete freedom, should they so choose, to sever all political connections with the parent state. The United States, on its part, as a result of the outcome of the Civil War, has just as fully repudiated the Revolutionary War idea that each state is a sovereign entity within the federal system, in favor of the unitary concept of sovereignty as resting in the whole American nation—carrying with it the utter denial that the government of a particular state, despite its reserved powers, can determine the constitutionality of acts of Congress and as a consequence decide whether or not these acts shall be enforced within its borders or secede from the Union. Finally, on the issue of taxation without representation, the earlier American position has likewise been disregarded. With the erection of the District of Columbia, the establishment of territories, and the acquisition of overseas possessions, the federal government, sustained in its powers by the Supreme Court in the Insular Cases, assumes the right to tax people who are not and may never be represented in Congress. Such is the anomaly implicit in that historical evolution along diverse paths that took place within these two great divisions of the English-speaking world.

Bibliography

I. BIBLIOGRAPHICAL AIDS

The most important single aid to the student is the *Bibliography of British History: The Eighteenth Century, 1714–1789* (ed. Stanley Pargellis and D. J. Medley, Oxford, 1951).

Although published in 1888 Justin Winsor's *Narrative and Critical History of America,* vol. VI, is still an indispensable bibliographical aid to those interested in various phases of the history of the British American colonies for the period covering the years 1763–75. They will also derive very great help from the section entitled "Bibliography" in *The Cambridge History of the British Empire, Volume I, The Old Empire from its Beginnings to 1783* (ed. J. Holland Rose, A. P. Newton, and E. A. Benians, Cambridge, Eng., 1929), and from the "Critical Essay on Authorities," which constitutes chap. XVII of Evarts Boutell Greene's *The Revolutionary Generation* (New York, 1943); both of these works include materials that have appeared in print since the publication of Winsor's monumental work. The bibliographical essay at the end of George Elliott Howard's *Preliminaries of the Revolution* (New York, 1905) is still valuable. While in many respects outdated, A. P. C. Griffin's *Bibliography of American Historical Societies* (Annual Report of the American Historical Association, 1905) and A. R. Hasse's "Materials for a Bibliography of the Public Archives of the Thirteen Original Colonies" (in the Annual Report of A.H.A., 1906) can be consulted with profit. Of first importance are the annual *Writings on American History* (New York, New Haven and Washington), prepared largely by Miss Grace Gardner Griffin and published continuously from 1918 to 1938 as a part of the *Annual Report* of the A.H.A.; likewise, as part of the Report for 1914 there is the *General Index to Papers and Annual Reports of the American Historical Association, 1884–1914* (comp. by D. M. Matheson, Washington, 1918), and the Report for 1944 contains a *Guide to the American Historical Review, 1895–1945* (Washington, 1945). Mention must be made of other works, such as Charles Evans's *American Bibliography. A Chronological Dictionary of All Books, Pamphlets and Periodical Publications Printed in the United States of America from the Genesis of Printing in 1639 Down to and Including the Year 1820* (12 vols., (New York, 1941–42); *Bibliotheca Americana. A Dictionary of Books Relating to America from Its Discovery to the Present Time,* comp. by Joseph Sabin, Wilberforce Eames, and R. W. G. Vail (29 vols., New York, 1868–1936); *A Catalog of Books Represented by the Library of Congress Printed Cards Issued to July 31, 1942* (167 vols., Ann Arbor, 1942–46), and the *Supplement. Cards Issued August 1, 1942–December 31, 1947* (42 vols., Ann Arbor, 1948); *The British Museum. Catalogue of Printed Books, 1881–1900* (58 vols., Ann Arbor, 1946); E. G. Swem's *Virginia Historical Index* (2 vols., Roanoke, 1934–1936); and *A Guide to the Reference Collections of the New York Public Library* (comp. Karl Brown, New York, 1941).

Since the present volume is based to a considerable extent on manuscript sources, a word must be said about the principal printed guides to these. The most useful are Grace Gardner Griffin, *A Guide to Manuscripts Relating to American History in British Depositories Reproduced for the Division of Manuscripts of the Library of Congress* (Washington, 1946), C. M. Andrews, *Guide to Materials for American History to 1783, in the Public Record Office of Great Britain* (2 vols., Washington, 1912–1914), C. M. Andrews and F. G. Davenport, *Guide to the Manuscript Materials for the History of the United States to 1783, in the British Museum, in Minor London Archives, and in the Libraries of Oxford and Cambridge* (Washington, 1908), *A Guide to Items Relating to American History in the Reports of the English Historical Manuscript Commission and their Appendices,* published as a part of the A.H.A. *Report* for 1898 (Washington, 1899), *Guide to the Manuscript Collections in the William L. Clements Library* (comp. by W. E. Ewing and others, Ann Arbor, 1952), *Huntington Library. American Manuscript Collections* (comp. Norma B. Cuthbert, San Marino, Calif., 1941), Alice E. Smith's *Guide to the Manuscripts of the Wisconsin Historical Society* (Madison, 1944), *Guide to the Manuscript Collections of the Historical Society of Pennsylvania* (Philadelphia, 1949), *Newberry Library. A Checklist of Manuscripts in the Edward E. Ayer Collections* (comp. Ruth L. Butler, Chicago, 1937), E. B. Greene and R. B. Morris, *A Guide to the Principal Sources of Early American History in the City of New York . . .* (new ed., New York, 1953), and *Handbook of the Publications and Photostats, 1792–1933, of the Massachusetts Historical Society* (Boston, 1934). In this connection there should likewise be mentioned, the *Calendar of the Papers of Benjamin Franklin in the Library of the American Philosophical Society,* including "A Calendar of the Papers of Benjamin Franklin in the Library of the University of Pennsylvania" (ed. I. M. Hays, 5 vols., Philadelphia, 1908); *List of Benjamin Franklin Papers in the Library of Congress* (ed. W. C. Ford, Washington, 1905); *Manuscript Collections of the New York Public Library* (New York, 1901).

II. PRINTED DOCUMENTS

Great Britain

Among the more important of these are the following: *Statutes at Large* (Charles Eyre and Andrew Strahan, 10 vols., London, 1786); *Parliamentary History of England* . . . (T. C. Hansard, London, 1813), vols. XV–XVIII; *The Debates and Proceedings of the British House of Commons* . . . *1743–1774* (comp. J. Almon *et al.*, 11 vols., London, 1766–75); *Parliamentary Papers* . . . (J. Debrett, London, 1797), vols. II and III; *Debates of the House of Commons* . . . *1768–1771* (comp. Sir H. Cavendish, 2 vols., London, 1841–43); *Debates on the Declaratory Act and the Repeal of the Stamp Act, 1766* (contrib. C. H. Hull and H. W. V. Temperley, New York, 1912); *Debates in the House of Commons in the Year 1774, on the Bill for Making More Effectual Provision for the Government of the Province of Quebec* . . . (London, 1839); *Protests of the Lords* (ed. J. E. T. Rogers, 3 vols., Oxford, 1875); *Journals of the House of Commons* (London, 1763–1775), vols. XXIX–XXXVI; *Journals of the House of Lords* (comp. T. Brodie, London, 1817), vols. XXX–XXXIV; *Acts of the Privy Council of England, Colonial Series* (ed. J. Munro, Hereford, 1911–12), vols. IV–V; *Journal of the Commissioners for Trade and Plantations* (14 vols., London, 1920–37); *Calendar of Home Office Papers, 1760–1775* (3 vols., London, 1878–99); *Opinions of Eminent Lawyers on Various Points of English Jurisprudence, Chiefly Concerning the Colonies, Fisheries, and Commerce, of Great Britain* (comp. G. Chalmers, 2 vols., London, 1814); *Report of the Lords Committee, Appointed to Enquire into the Several Proceedings in the Colony of Massachusetts Bay* (London, 1774); *The Examination of Joseph Galloway by a Committee of the House of Commons* (ed. Thomas Balch, Philadelphia, 1855); and *The Annual Register* for the years 1761–75. Reference also should be made to the following compilations: *Statutes, Cases and Documents to Illustrate English Constitutional History, 1660–1832* (ed. C. G. Robertson, London, 1913); *Sources and Documents Illustrating the American Revolution* (ed. S. E. Morison, Oxford, 1923); and *The Debate on the American Revolution, 1761–1783* (ed. Max Beloff, London, 1949).

The Thirteen Colonies

New England. It would be well to survey this material by starting with the most northern of the New England colonies, New Hampshire, and then proceeding southward. Two collections of materials relating to New Hampshire are useful for our period: [*The New Hampshire*] *Provincial Papers* . . . *Documents and Records Relative to the Province of New Hampshire, 1623–1800* (ed. N. Bouton *et al.*, 31 vols., Concord, 1867–1907); and *New Hamp-*

shire. Acts and Laws of His Majesty's Province in New England, with Sundry Acts of Parliament 1696–1771 (Portsmouth, 1771). For Massachusetts the following are important: *Journals of the Honourable House of Representatives of the Massachusetts Bay* (Boston, 1723–1778); *Acts and Resolves, Public and Private of the Province of the Massachusetts Bay, [1692–1764]* (21 vols., Boston, 1869–1922); *The Charters and General Laws of the Colony and Province of Massachusetts Bay* (Boston, 1814); *Speeches of the Governors from 1765 to 1775; and the Answers of the House of Representatives . . . with Their Resolutions* (ed. A. Bradford, Boston, 1818); *Reports of Cases Argued and Adjudged in the Superior Court of Judicature of the Province of Massachusetts Bay, between 1761 and 1772* (comp. Josiah Quincy, Jr., Boston, 1865); *Documents Relating to the Last Meetings of the Massachusetts Royal Council 1774–1776,* Col. Soc. Mass. Pub. (ed. Albert Matthews, Boston, 1937), vol. XXXII; *Journals of Each Provincial Congress of Massachusetts in 1774 and 1775 . . . and Other Documents* (ed. Wm. Lincoln, Boston, 1838); and *Reports of the Record Commissioners of the City of Boston* (39 vols., Boston, 1876–1909). For Rhode Island students are obliged to rely upon the rather unsatisfactory *Records of the Colony of Rhode Island and Providence Plantations in New England, [1636–1792]* (10 vols., Providence, 1856–1865); and for Connecticut there are the *Public Records of the Colony of Connecticut, [1636–1776]* (15 vols., Hartford, 1850–1890); and *Acts and Laws of His Majesty's Colony of Connecticut in New England* (ed. of 1769 with supplement to 1779, New London, 1780).

The Middle Colonies. For New York there are the following important collections: *Documents Relative to the Colonial History of the State of New York* (ed. E. B. O'Callaghan and B. Fernow, 15 vols., Albany, 1853–87); *Documentary History of the State of New York* (ed. E. B. O'Callaghan, 4 vols., Albany, 1851); *Journal . . . of the General Assembly . . . of New York, 1691–[1765]* (2 vols., New York, 1764–66); *Journal . . . of the General Assembly . . . of New York, 1766–1776* (New York, 1820); *Journal of the Legislative Council of the Colony of New York . . . 1691–[1775]* (2 vols., Albany, 1861); and the *Annals of Albany, 1609–1858* (ed. J. Munsell, 10 vols., Albany, 1850–59). As for provincial New Jersey, the *Archives of the State of New Jersey, First Series, Documents Relating to the Colonial History, 1631–1800* (36 vols., Newark, etc., 1880–1941), are important and particularly vols. XVII and XVIII, containing the *Journal of the Governor and Council, 1756–1775;* there are two compilations of the provincial laws: *Acts of the General Assembly of the Province of New-Jersey, 1702–1776* (ed. S. Allinson, Burlington, 1776), and *Laws of the State of New Jersey, 1703–1799* (New Brunswick, 1800); finally, there are the *Minutes of the Provincial Congress and the Council of Safety of the State of New Jersey, [1775–1776]* (Trenton, 1879). For Pennsylvania: *Votes and Proceedings of the House of Represen-*

tatives of the Province of Pennsylvania (6 vols., Philadelphia, 1752–1776);
the *Pennsylvania Archives, First Series* (ed. S. Hazard *et al.,* 12 vols., Philadelphia and Harrisburg, 1852–99); *Pennsylvania Archives, Eighth Series* (ed.
C. F. Hoban, 8 vols., Harrisburg, 1935, particularly vols. VI, VII, and VIII
for the Assembly votes for the years 1757–76; the *Minutes of the Provincial
Council of Pennsylvania, 1763–1775,* which constitute vols. IX and X of the
Pennsylvania Colonial Records (12 vols., Harrisburg, 1852); *Reports of Cases
in the Courts of Pennsylvania . . . 1754–1806* (comp. A. J. Dallas, Philadelphia, 1790), vol. I; *Laws of the Commonwealth of Pennsylvania, 1700–1790*
(comp. A. J. Dallas, 2 vols., Philadelphia, 1793–97); *Statutes at Large of
Pennsylvania from 1682 to 1801* (comp. J. T. Mitchell and H. Flanders, 15
vols., Harrisburg, 1896–1911)—vol. I, which is the volume for the seventeenth century, was never published; and *Pennsylvania Archives, Fourth Series,*
vol. III, *Papers of the Governors, 1759–1785* (Harrisburg, 1900). Finally, for
Delaware, there are the *Laws of the State of Delaware, 1700–1797* (ed. G.
Read, 2 vols., Newcastle, 1797).

The South. Beginning with Maryland, the following may be used: *Proceedings of the Council, 1761–1770,* which constitutes vol. XXXII of the
Archives of Maryland (ed. W. H. Browne, Baltimore, 1912); *Maryland Reports* for the years 1658–1799 (comp. T. Harris and John McHenry, 4 vols.,
New York, 1809–18); *Proceedings of the Conventions of . . . Maryland . . .
1774, 1775 & 1776* (Annapolis, 1836); *Laws of Maryland at Large,* [1637–
1763] (comp. Thomas Bacon, Annapolis, 1765); and *Laws of Maryland Made
Since 1763* (Annapolis, 1787). For Virginia, the *Journals of the House of
Burgesses,* covering the years 1761–76 (ed. J. P. Kennedy, 4 vols., Williams-
burg, 1905–07); the *Legislative Journals of the Council of Colonial Virginia*
(ed. H. R. McIlwaine, 3 vols., Richmond, 1919); *Reports of Cases Determined in the General Court of Virginia, 1730–1740, 1768–1772* (comp. T.
Jefferson, Charlottesville, 1829); *Acts of Assembly, Now in Force, in the
Colony of Virginia, 1661–1768* (Williamsburg, 1769); *Collection of All Such
Public Acts of the General Assembly, and Ordinances of the Conventions of
Virginia Passed Since the Year 1768, as Are Now in Force* (Richmond, 1785);
and *The Statutes-at-Large, Being a Collection of All the Laws of Virginia,*
[1619–1792] (comp. W. W. Hening, 13 vols., Philadelphia and New York,
1810–23). As for North Carolina, there are *The Colonial Records of North
Carolina,* [1662–1776] (ed. W. L. Saunders *et al.,* 10 vols., *Raleigh,*
1886–90); and *Collection of the Statutes of the Parliament of England in
Force in the State of North Carolina* (comp. F. X. Martin, New Bern, 1792).
For South Carolina there are three works, the *Documentary History of the
Revolution . . . Chiefly in South Carolina . . . 1764–1776* (comp. R. W.
Gibbs, New York, 1855), *Public Laws of the State of South Carolina,* [1694–
1790] (comp. J. F. Grimké, Philadelphia, 1790), and *. . . Proceedings of the*

High Court of Vice-Admiralty . . . (Charleson, 1769). For Georgia there are *The Colonial Records . . . of Georgia* (ed. A. D. Candler, 17 vols., Atlanta, 1904–13) and *Acts Passed by the General Assembly of the Colony of Georgia, 1755–1774* (ed. C. C. Jones, Wormsloe, 1881). Finally, there are the documents on East Florida embodied in *The Loyalists in East Florida, 1774–1785* (ed. W. H. Siebert, 2 vols., Fla. Hist. Soc., *Pub.*, 1929).

Canada

The following collections of documentary material will be of value to those interested in the history of the British North American colonies covering the period from 1763–75: *Canadian Constitutional Development Shown by Selected Speeches and Despatches* (comp. H. E. Egerton and W. P. Grant, London, 1907); *Documents Relating to the Constitutional History of Canada, 1759–1791* (ed. Adam Shortt and A. G. Doughty, Ottawa, 1907); and *Selections from the Public Documents of the Province of Nova Scotia* (comp. T. B. Akins, Halifax, 1869). Mention should also be made of William Kingsford's *History of Canada, 1608–1841* (10 vols., London and Toronto, 1887–98) for many documents of importance.

Other Collections

Among other collections that will be found to be particularly useful are the so-called *Prior Documents* published by John Almon under title *A Collection of Interesting, Authentic Papers, Relative to the Dispute between Great Britain and America; Shewing the . . . Progress of that Misunderstanding, from 1764 to 1775* (London, 1777); *The Remembrancer, or Impartial Repository of Public Events for the year MDCLXXV* (London, 1775), also published by Almon; the *American Archives: Fourth Series . . . 1774–1776* (ed. Peter Force, 6 vols., Washington, 1837–46); the *Journals of the Continental Congress, 1774–1789* (ed. W. C. Ford, Washington, 1904), vol. I; *Select Charters and Other Documents Illustrative of American History, 1606–1775* (ed. William MacDonald, New York and London, 1906); *Diary of the American Revolution from Newspapers and Original Documents* (comp. Frank Moore, New York, 1860), vol. 1; *Principles and Acts of the Revolution in America* (comp. H. Niles, Baltimore, 1822, and New York, 1876).

III. COLLECTIONS OF WRITINGS

The Writings of Officials and Others in Public Life in Great Britain

The activities of King George III, the Earl of Bute, and Lord North are fairly well covered for the years in question by The *Correspondence of King George the Third from 1760 to December 1783* . . . (ed. Sir John Fortescue, 6 vols., London, 1927–28), Vol. I of which should only be used in connection with L. B. Namier's *Additions and Corrections to Sir John Fortescue's Edition of the Correspondence of King George The Third* (Manchester, 1937); *the Letters from George III to Lord Bute, 1756–1766* (ed. R. Sedgwick, New York, 1939); the *Correspondence of . . . George III with Lord North, 1768–1783* (ed. W. B. Donne, 2 vols., London, 1867); and *George III and the American Revolution: The Beginnings* (ed. F. A. Mumby, Boston, 1923), which is really a source book with a strong anti-Tory bias. For William Pitt, Earl of Chatham, there are two collections of letters: *Correspondence of William Pitt, when Secretary of State, with Colonial Governors and Military and Naval Commissioners in America* (ed. Gertrude S. Kimball, 2 vols., New York, 1906), of chief value for the period 1757–61; and *Correspondence of William Pitt, Earl of Chatham* (ed. W. S. Taylor and J. H. Pringle, 4 vols., London, 1838–40). For George Grenville and Richard, Earl Temple, his brother, *The Grenville Papers* (ed. W. J. Smith, 4 vols., London, 1852–53) are available; for Rockingham one should consult the *Memoirs of the Marquis of Rockingham* (ed. Earl of Albemarle, 2 vols., London, 1852). For his supporter, Edmund Burke, numerous editions of his works have been published, among these the *Works of Edmund Burke* (9 vols., Boston, 1839); the *Correspondence of . . . Edmund Burke* (ed. Earl Fitzwilliam and Sir R. Bourke, 4 vols., London, 1844), the latter very incomplete; and the *Works of . . . Edmund Burke* (ed. J. C. Nimmo, 12 vols., London, 1899). Then there are for the period also the *Memorials and Correspondence of C. J. Fox* (ed. Lord John Russell, 4 vols., London, 1853–57); the *Correspondence of John, 4th Duke of Bedford* (ed. Lord John Russell, 3 vols., London, 1842–46); the writings of Horace Walpole, among which are the *Memoirs of the Reign of King George the Third* (ed. Sir Denis Le Marchant, 2 vols., Philadelphia, 1845, and G. F. Russell Barker, 4 vols., London, 1894), and the *Yale Edition of Horace Walpole's Correspondence* (ed. W. S. Lewis, New Haven, 1937–51); the *Journal of the Reign of King George the Third, from the Year 1771 to 1783* (ed. Dr. Doran, 2 vols., London, 1859); *Josiah Tucker. A Selection from His Economic and Political Writings* (ed. R. L. Schuyler, New York, 1931); The *Autobiography* of the Duke of Grafton (ed. Sir W. R. Anson, London, 1898); and *Correspondence of . . . John Wilkes . . .* (ed. John Almon, 5 vols., London, 1804–5).

The Writings of British Officials and Others Connected with American Public Service

One of the most important collections of published documents relating to the American service during the years covered by this volume is *The Correspondence of General Thomas Gage* (ed. C. E. Carter, 2 vols., New Haven, 1931–33). Also for this period, Thomas Hutchinson's *The History of the Province of Massachusetts Bay, from the Year 1750 to June 1774 . . .* (London, 1828, the latest edition edited by L. S. Mayo, Cambridge, Mass., in 1936), *Additions to Thomas Hutchinson's History of Massachusetts Bay* (ed. Catherine B. Mayo, Worcester, Mass., 1949), and the *Diary and Letters of His Excellency Thomas Hutchinson, Esq.* (ed. P. O. Hutchinson, 2 vols., Boston, 1884–86) are of great value, as are the *Barrington-Bernard Correspondence . . . 1760–1770* (Cambridge, Mass., 1912); the *Bowdoin and Temple Papers* (Mass. Hist. Soc., *Coll.*, 6th s., IX, Boston, 1897); *Jasper Mauduit, Agent in London for the Province of the Massachusetts Bay, 1762–1765* (Mass. Hist. Soc., *Coll.*, vol. LXXIV, Boston, 1918), which includes many important letters to and from Mauduit; *The Correspondence of the Colonial Governors of Rhode Island, 1723–1775* (ed. Gertrude S. Kimball, 2 vols., Boston, 1903); the *Fitch Papers. Correspondence and Documents during Thomas Fitch's Governorship of the Colony of Connecticut, 1754–1766* (ed. Albert Bates, Conn. Hist. Soc., *Coll.*, vols. XVII and XVIII, Hartford, 1918–20); *The Pitkin Papers . . . 1766–1769* (ed. Albert Bates, Conn. Hist. Soc., *Coll.*, vol. XIX, Hartford, 1921); the *Jared Ingersoll Papers* (ed. F. B. Dexter, New Haven Colony Hist. Soc., *Papers,* vol. IX, New Haven, 1918); and the *Trumbull Papers* (Mass. Hist. Soc., *Coll.*, 5th ser., vol. IX, Boston, 1885), which contain (pp. 211–490) "Letters of William Samuel Johnson to the Governors of Connecticut." There are also available *The Letters and Papers of Cadwallader Colden* (New York Hist. Soc., *Coll.*, 11 vols., New York, 1877–78, 1918–24, 1935, 1937); *The Papers of Sir William Johnson* (ed. James Sullivan, A. C. Flick, M. W. Hamilton, and A. B. Corey, 10 vols., Albany, 1921–51); vol. II of the *Papers of Henry Bouquet* (ed. S. K. Stevens, D. H. Kent, and Autumn L. Leonard, Harrisburg, 1951); the *Correspondence of Governor Sharpe of Maryland* (ed. W. H. Browne, *Arch. of Md.*, Baltimore, 1895), vol. III; the "Letters of Charles Garth," *Md. Hist. Mag.*, V; the "Correspondence of Charles Garth, Agent of the Colony of South Carolina" (ed. J. W. Barnwell and T. L. Jervey), in the *S.C. Hist. and Geneal. Mag.*, XXX–XXXIII (1929–32); and "Letters from Governor Sir James Wright to the Earl of Dartmouth and Lord George Germain . . ." Ga. Hist. Soc., *Coll.*, VII.

The Writings of Nonofficial American Leaders

Among the most useful of the collected works of Americans not already listed in the preceding sections are *The Works of John Adams . . .* (ed. C. F. Adams, 10 vols., Boston, 1850–56); *The Writings of Samuel Adams* (ed. H. A. Cushing, 4 vols., New York, 1904–08); *Some Political Writings of James Otis* (ed. C. F. Mullett, Columbia, Mo., 1929); *Memoir of the Life of Josiah Quincy, Junior, 1744–1775* (3rd ed., Boston, 1875), vol. III; *The [Silas] Deane Papers, Vol. I, 1774–1777,* New York Hist. Soc., *Coll.* (New York, 1887); the *Works of Alexander Hamilton* (ed. H. C. Lodge, 12 vols., New York, 1904); *The Writings of Benjamin Franklin* (ed. A. H. Smyth, 10 vols., New York, 1907), which supersedes in most respects the earlier editions by Jared Sparks (pub. between 1836 and 1840) and by John Bigelow (pub. in 1887); *Letters and Papers of Benjamin Franklin and Richard Jackson, 1753–1785* (ed. C. Van Doren, Philadelphia, 1947); V. W. Crane, "Certain Writings of Benjamin Franklin on the British Empire and the American Colonies," Biblio. Soc. of Amer., *Papers,* XXVIII (1934) 1–27; and (*Benjamin Franklin's*) *Letters to the Press* (col. and ed. V. W. Crane, Chapel Hill, 1950). Other important collections are *The Writings of Thomas Paine* (ed. M. D. Conway, 4 vols., New York, 1894–96); *The [Charles] Thomson Papers, 1765–1816,* New York Hist. Soc., *Coll.* for 1878 (New York, 1879); James Wilson's *Works* (ed. Bird Wilson, 3 vols., Philadelphia, 1804, rev. 1896); *Selected Political Essays of James Wilson* (ed. R. G. Adams, New York, 1930); *The Writings of John Dickinson* (ed. P. L. Ford, Philadelphia, 1895); *Letters to and from Caesar Rodney, 1756–1784* . . . (ed. G. H. Ryden, Philadelphia, 1933); *The Writings of Thomas Jefferson* (ed. P. L. Ford, 10 vols., New York, 1892–99); *The Papers of Thomas Jefferson, Volume I, 1760–1776* (ed. J. P. Boyd, Princeton, 1950); W. W. Henry's *Patrick Henry; Life, Correspondence and Speeches* (3 vols., New York, 1891); *The Letters of Richard Henry Lee* . . . (ed. J. C. Ballagh, 2 vols., New York, 1911–14); Arthur Lee's correspondence is in vol. I of *The Revolutionary Diplomatic Correspondence of the United States* . . . (ed. Francis Wharton, Washington, 1889); *Letters of William Lee* . . . *1766–1783* (ed. W. C. Ford, 3 vols., Brooklyn, 1891); *Writings of James Madison* (ed. Gaillard Hunt, 9 vols., New York, 1900–1910); *The Diaries of George Washington, 1748–1799* (ed. J. C. Fitzpatrick, 4 vols., Boston, 1925); and *The Writings of George Washington* . . . (ed. J. C. Fitzpatrick, 39 vols., Washington, 1931–44), which supersedes the earlier editions by Jared Sparks (pub. 1837) and by W. C. Ford (pub. 1889–93); "Correspondence of Henry Laurens" (ed. J. W. Barnwell and Mabel L. Webber), *S.C. Hist. Mag.,* XVIII (1927)–XXXI (1930), with "Letters from Hon. Henry Laurens to His Son John, 1773–1776," *ibid.,* III (1902)–V (1904), and "Letters from John Laurens to His Father . . . 1774–1776," *ibid.,* V (1904); and, finally, *Letters of Members of the Continental Congress* (ed. E. C. Burnett, Washington, 1921), vol. I.

IV. CONTEMPORARY ACCOUNTS OF EVENTS AND OTHER CONTEMPORARY WORKS *

Published in England
Abingdon, Earl of, *Thoughts on the Letter of Edmund Burke* (London, 1776).

* In addition to the collected works of individuals just listed, there is in existence an exceedingly important body of writings that sets forth the temper of people both in England and in America.

Adams, John, "History of the Dispute with America . . ." in Almon's *Remembrancer* (London, 1775), I.

Address of the People of Great Britain to the Inhabitants of America, The (London, 1775).

Allen, William, *The American Crisis; a letter addressed . . . to Earl Gower . . . on the present alarming disturbances in the colonies . . . And an idea is offered towards a complete plan for restoring the dependence of America on Great Britain to a state of perfection* (London, 1774).

[Almon, John], *A Collection of the most interesting tracts, lately published in England and America, on . . . taxing the American Colonies . . .* (John Almon, pub., 6 vols., London, 1766–79); *Biographical, Literary and Political Anecdotes . . .* (John Almon, pub., 3 vols., London, 1797); and *The History of the Late Minority . . .* (London, 1766).

[Anderson, James], *Free Thoughts on the American Contest* (Edinburgh, 1776).

Bancroft, Edward, *Remarks on the Review of the Controversy between Great Britain and her Colonies* (London, 1769).

Bernard, Sir Francis, *Select Letters on the trade and government of America . . .* (London, 1774).

[Blacklock, Dr.], *Remarks on the Nature and Extent of Liberty* (Edinburgh, 1776).

Bollan, William, *A Succinct View of the Origin of our Colonies . . .* (London, 1766).

Boucher, Rev. Jonathan, *A View of the Causes and Consequences of the American Revolution* (London, 1797). Views of a Southern Loyalist in thirteen discourses.

Burgh, James, *Political Disquisitions* (2 vols., London, 1774).

Burnaby, Archdeacon Andrew, *Travels through the Middle Settlements in North America . . .* (London, 1775).

Claim of the Colonies to an Exemption from Internal Taxes Imposed by Authority of Parliament Examined. In a Letter from a Gentleman [William Knox?] in London to his Friend in America, The (London, 1765).

Considerations on the American Stamp Act, and on the Conduct of the Minister who Planned It (London, 1766).

Considerations on the American War. Addressed to the People of England (London, 1776). Very hostile to the conduct of the Americans.

Constitutional Right of the Legislature of Great Britain, to Tax the British Colonies in America, Impartially Stated, The (London, 1768). Colonial interests must not transcend those of the mother country.

[Cooper, Samuel], *The Crisis. Or a Full Defence of the Colonies* (London, 1766).

Crowley, Thomas, *Letters and Dissertations on Various Subjects* (London, 1776). For an imperial Parliament.

Cunningham, J., *An Essay on Trade and Commerce . . . with . . . Reflections on the Importance of our Trade to America* (London, 1770).

Cunningham, T., *The History of our Customs, Aids, Subsidies, National Debts and Taxes* (London, 1761).

[Dempster, George], *Letters of George Dempster* [Member of Parliament] *to Sir Adam Ferguson, 1756–1813* (ed. J. Ferguson, London, 1934).

Eddis, William, *Letters from America . . . from 1769 to 1777 . . .* (London, 1792).

Estwick, Samuel, *A Letter to the Reverend Josiah Tucker . . . in which the present War against America Is Shewn to be The Effect, Not of the Causes assigned by him and Others, but of a fixed Plan of Administration . . .* (London, 1776).

Evelyn, Captain W. G., *Memoir and Letters . . . from North America, 1774–1776* (ed. G. D. Scull, Oxford, 1879).

Fothergill, John, *Considerations Relative to the North American Colonies* (London, 1765).

Graham, Catherine M., *Observations on . . . Thoughts on the Cause of the present discontents* (London, 1770); *Address to the People of England, Scotland, and Ireland . . .* (London, 1775).

[Grenville, George], *The Regulations Lately Made Concerning the Colonies, and the Taxes Imposed upon Them, considered* (London, 1765, 1775); and also (with William Knox) *The Present State of the Nation . . .* (London, 1768; pub. anon.); also their acknowledged *An Appendix to the Present State of the Nation . . .* (London, 1769).

Hollis, Thomas, *The true sentiments of America contained in a collection of letters* (London, 1768).

Home, M. J., *A Letter from an Officer Retired, to his Son in Parliament* (London, 1776). Americans lean on nonexistent rights.

[Huske, John], *Copy of a Letter from John Huske to the Committee of Merchants in Boston* (London, 1764).

Hutchinson, Thomas, *The History of the Province of Massachusetts Bay from the Year 1749, until June, 1774* (London, 1828).

Importance of the British Dominion in India, compared with that in America, The (London, 1770). India of greater value than the Colonies.

Interests of the Merchants and Manufacturers of Great Britain in the Present Contest with the Colonies, Stated and Considered, The (London, 1774).

Jenkinson Papers, 1760–1776, The (ed. Ninetta S. Jucker, London, 1949).

Jenyns, Soame, *The Objections to Taxation of our American Colonies, by the Legislature of Great Britain, briefly considered* (London, 1765).

Johnson, Samuel, *Taxation no Tyranny . . .* (London, 1775).

[Junius, pseud.], *The Letters of Junius* (ed. Woodfall, London, 2 vols., 1902).

Justice and Necessity of Taxing the American Colonies Demonstrated. Together with a Vindication of the Authority of Parliament, The (London, 1766).

Keith, Sir William, *Two Papers on the Subject of Taxing the British Colonies in America* (London, 1767).

Knox, William, *The Present State of the Nation . . .* (London, 1768); *The Controversy between Great Britain and her Colonies Reviewed* (London, 1769); and *The Justice and Policy of the late Act of Parliament for Making More Effectual Provision for the Government of the Province of Quebec . . .* (London, 1774).

Late Occurrences in North America, and [the] Policy of Great Britain Considered, The (London, 1766).

[Lee, Arthur (?)], *An Appeal to the Justice and Interests of the People of Great Britain . . . By an Old Member of Parliament* (London, 1774); *A true state of the proceedings in the Parliament . . . and in . . . Massachusetts Bay* (London, 1774).

Letter to a Member of Parliament, wherein the Power of the British Legislature, and the Case of the Colonists are briefly and impartially Considered, A (London, 1765).

Letter to the Gentlemen of the Committee of London Merchants, Trading to North America, A (London, 1766). The right of taxing the colonies stressed.

[Lind, J.], *Remarks on the Principal Acts of the Thirteenth Parliament of Great Britain . . .* (London, 1775).

Lloyd, Charles, *Conduct of the late Administration examined* (London, 1767). Relative to the American Stamp Act.

"London Merchants on the Stamp Act repeal," printed documents in Mass. Hist. Soc., *Proc.,* LV (1923).

Lyttelton, Thomas, *A Letter . . . to . . . [the] Earl of Chatham, on the Quebec Bill* (London, 1774).

[MacPherson, J.?], *The Rights of Great Britain Asserted . . .* (London, 1776).

Maseres, Francis, *Considerations on the Expediency of Admitting Representatives from the American Colonies into the British House of Commons* (London, 1770).

McCulloh (MacCulloh), Henry, *Miscellaneous Representations Relative to our Concerns in America . . .* (London, 1761; reissued, ed. W. A. Shaw, London, 1905).

[Mitchell, John], *The present state of Great Britain and North America . . .* (London, 1767).

Necessity of Repealing the American Stamp-Act Demonstrated, The (London, 1766).

New and Impartial Collection of Interesting Letters, . . . September 1765, to May 1767, A (2 vols., London, 1767).

Nicholls, J., *Recollections and reflections . . .* (2 vols., London, 1820–22).

Plain and Seasonable Address to the Freeholders of Great Britain on the Present Posture of Affairs in America, A (London, 1766). On the impossibility of appeasing the Americans.

Plain Question upon the present Dispute with our American Colonies, The (London, 1776).

Pownall, Thomas, *The Administration of the Colonies* (4th ed., London, 1768).

Price, Richard, *Observations on the Nature of Civil Liberty . . .* (London, 1776).

Priestley, Joseph, *The Present State of Liberty in Great Britain and her Colonies* (London, 1769); *An Address to Protestant Dissenters* [unsigned] (London, 1774).

Pulteney, William, *Thoughts on the Present State of Affairs with America* (London, 1778).

Ramsay, Allan, *Thoughts on the Origin and Nature of Government* (London, 1769); *Letters on the present disturbances in Great Britain and her American Provinces [1771 and 1775]* (London, 1777); and *A Plan of Reconciliation between Great Britain and her Colonies . . .* (London, 1776).

Ray, Nicholas, *The Importance of the Colonies of North America* (London, 1766). To treat the colonies not as dependents but allies.

Reflexions on Representation in Parliament (London, 1766). Americans entitled to parliamentary representation.

[Rowe, John], *Letters and Diary of John Rowe, Boston Merchant* (ed. Anne R. Cunningham, Boston, 1903).

Sharp, Granville, *Declaration of the People's Natural right to a share in the legislature . . .* (London, 1774).

Shipley, Jonathan, Bishop of St. Asaph, *A Speech Intended to have been Spoken on the Bill for Altering the Charters of the Colony of Massachusetts Bay . . .* (London, 1774). Favorable to the colonies.

Smith, Adam, *Wealth of Nations . . .* (London, 1776). For colonial parliamentary representation and imperial federation.

Some Reasons for Approving of the Dean of Gloucester's Plan . . . (London, 1775).

[Steele, Joshua], *An Account of a Late Conference on the Occurrences in America* (London, 1766). Englishmen would oppose parliamentary representation for Americans.

Supremacy of the British Legislature over the Colonies Candidly discussed, The (London, 1775). The war with France fought for the colonies, but the chief cost of it laid on the English taxpayers.

[Toplady, A. M.], *An Old Fox Tarr'd and feather'd* . . . (London, 1775). A reply to John Wesley's *A Calm Address*.

True Interest of Great Britain, with respect to her American Colonies, Stated and Impartially Considered . . ., The (London, 1766).

Tucker, Josiah, *A Letter from a Merchant in London to his Nephew in North America* (London, 1766); *The True Interest of Great Britain, set forth in regard to the Colonies* (London, 1774, and Philadelphia, 1776); and *A Letter to Edmund Burke, Esq.* (Gloucester, Eng., 1775).

Wesley, John, *A Calm Address to our American Colonies* (London, 1775), and *Some Observations on Liberty* (London, 1776). In defense of the Quebec Act.

Whately, Thomas, *Considerations on the trade and finances of this Kingdom* (London, 1769).

Published in America

Additional Observations to a short Narrative of the Horrid Massacre (Boston, 1770).

American Alarm . . . By a British Bostonian, The (Boston, 1773). Opposes any subordination to Parliament.

[Aplin, John], *Verses on Doctor Mayhew's Book . . . on . . . the Society for the Propagation of the Gospel . . . by a Gentleman of Rhode Island* (Providence, 1763).

Appleton, Rev. Nathaniel, *Thanksgiving Sermon on the Total Repeal of the Stamp-Act* (Boston, 1766).

Association, etc. of the Delegates of the Colonies, at the Grand Congress . . . By Bob Jingle, Esq., The ([Philadelphia], 1774).

[Barker, John], *The British in Boston, being the diary of Lieutenant John Barker . . . [for the years 1774–1776]* (Cambridge, Mass., 1924).

Bland, Richard, *An Enquiry into the Rights of the British Colonies . . .* (Williamsburg and London, 1766; ed. E. G. Swem, Richmond, 1922). On the pernicious effects of the Navigation Acts.

Boston under Military Rule [1768–1769] as revealed in a Journal of the Times (ed. O. M. Dickerson, Boston, 1936).

Boucher, Jonathan, *Reminiscences of an American loyalist, 1738–1789 . . .* (ed. J. Boucher, Boston, 1925); "The Letters of Jonathan Boucher," *Md. Hist. Mag.,* VII–IX.

Boyle, John, ". . . Journal of occurrences in Boston, 1759–1778," *New Eng. Hist. and Geneal. Mag.,* LXXXV (1931).

[Brush, Crean], *The Speech of a Member of the General Assembly of New York* (New York, 1775). On the usurpations of the Continental Congress.

Candidus [pseud.], *Plain Truth; Addressed to the Inhabitants of America,*

Containing Remarks on a Late Pamphlet, entitled Common Sense . . . (Philadelphia, 1776).

Caroline and Southampton Counties, Va. *Proceedings of the Committees of Safety . . . 1774–1776* (Richmond, 1929).

Carroll, Charles, of Carrollton, *Correspondence of "First Citizen"—Charles Carroll of Carrollton, and "Antilon," Daniel Dulany, Junior* (pub., 1776; repub., ed. E. S. Riley, Baltimore, 1902); "Extracts from the Carroll Papers in the year 1774," *Md. Hist. Mag.,* XVI (1921); also *Unpublished Letters of Charles Carroll of Carrollton* (ed. T. M. Field, New York, 1902).

Carter, Landon, "Diary," *Wm. and Mary Quar.,* 2nd ser., vols. XIII-XVIII.

Cartwright, John, *American Independence The Interest and Glory of Great Britain* (Philadelphia, 1776).

"Case of the *Good Intent,* 1770, The," *Md. Hist. Mag.,* XVI (1921). Involving violation of the nonimportation agreement.

Champion, Richard, *The American Correspondence of a Bristol Merchant, 1766–1776* . . . (ed. G. H. Guttridge, Berkeley, 1934).

[Chandler, Thomas Bradbury?], *A Friendly address to all reasonable Americans* . . . (New York, 1774). Great Britain not guilty of tyranny. Also *What Think Ye of the Congress Now? Or, An Enquiry, how far the Americans are Bound to Abide by and Execute the Decisions of the late Congress?* (New York, 1775).

Chauncy, Rev. Charles, *A Discourse on "The Good News from a Far Country"* (Boston, 1766) and *A Letter to a Friend. Giving a Concise, but Just, Representation of the Hardships and Sufferings the Town of Boston is Exposed to . . . By T. W. A Bostonian* (Boston, 1774).

Church, Benjamin, *An Address to a Provincial Bashaw, O Shame! Where is thy Blush?* (Boston, 1769).

Connecticut Assembly, *Reasons Why the British Colonies Should not be charged with Internal Taxes* (New Haven, 1764).

Considerations on Slavery, and the Expediency of its Abolition (Burlington, N.J., 1773).

Considerations on the present state of Virginia [1774]; attributed to John Randolph, attorney general; and *Considerations on the present state of Virginia examined, by Robert Carter Nicholas* [1774], (ed. E. G. Swem, New York, 1919).

Considerations Upon The Act of Parliament Whereby A Duty is laid . . . on Molasses, and . . . on Sugar of foreign Growth, imported into any of the British Colonies (Boston, 1764).

Considerations upon the Rights of the Colonists . . . (New York, 1766).

[Cooper, Dr. Myles, Pres. of King's College], *The American Querist, or some questions proposed relative to the present disputes* . . . (New York, 1774).

[Cooper, Samuel], "Letters of Samuel Cooper to Thomas Pownall, 1769–1777," ed. F. Tuckerman, *Amer. Hist. Rev.*, VIII (1903).

[Cushing, Thomas], "Letters of Thomas Cushing from 1767 to 1775," Mass. Hist. Soc., *Coll.*, 4th ser., IV.

[Deane, Silas], *Correspondence of Silas Deane . . . 1774–76* (Hartford, 1870).

Discourse Addressed to the Sons of Liberty, At a Solemn Assembly, near Liberty-Tree, in Providence, February 14, 1766, A (Providence, 1766).

[Downer, Silas], *Discourse Delivered in Providence . . . at the Dedication of the Tree of Liberty . . . By a Son of Liberty* (Providence, 1768).

[Drayton, W. H.?], *A Letter from Freeman of South Carolina, to the Deputies of North-America* (Charleston, 1774). Offering a plan of union.

Duché, Rev. Jacob, *Observations . . .* (Philadelphia, 1774); *The Duty of Standing Fast in our Spiritual and Temporal Liberties . . . 1775* (Philadelphia, 1775).

[Dulany, Daniel], *Considerations on the Propriety of Imposing Taxes in the British Colonies* (Annapolis and London, 1766?). A very able essay.

Elegy to the Infamous Memory of Sir F[rancis] B[ernard], An (Boston[?], 1769).

Englishman's Answer to the Address from the Delegates, An (New York, 1775).

Essay on the Trade of the Northern Colonies of Great Britain in North America, An (Philadelphia and London, 1764).

Essay upon Government . . . Wherein the Lawfulness of Revolutions, are Demonstrated . . ., An (Philadelphia, 1775).

First Book of . . . American Chronicles . . ., The (Boston, 1775). An attack on General Gage.

[Fithian, Philip Vickers], *Journal & Letters of Philip Vickers Fithian, 1773–1774 . . .* (ed. H. D. Farish, Williamsburg, 1943).

Force, Peter, *Tracts . . . relating . . . to the origin, settlement, and progress of the Colonies in North America* (4 vols., Washington, 1836–46).

[Galloway, Joseph], *A Candid Examination of the Mutual Claims of Great Britain, and the Colonies: with a plan of Accommodation, on constitutional principles* (New York, 1775).

[Gordon, Harry], "Captain [Harry] Gordon's views of the British military establishment in America" [1766], *Miss. Valley Hist. Rev.*, XV (1928).

Gordon, Rev. William, *A Discourse preached December 15, 1774. Religions and Civil Liberty . . .* (Boston, 1775).

[Gray, Harrison], *A Few Remarks Upon Some of the . . . Resolutions of the Continental Congress* (Boston, 1775).

[Harrower, John], "Diary of John Harrower, 1773–1776," *Amer. Hist. Rev.*, VI (1900).

[Henshaw, John], "Letters of Joshua Henshaw . . . in 1768," *Jour. Am. Hist.*, XVIII (1924). On political disturbances in Boston.

[Hopkins, Stephen], *The Rights of Colonies Examined* . . . (Providence, 1765; repr. in London in 1766 under title, *The Grievances of the American Colonies Candidly Examined*).

[Howard, Martin], *A defence of the letter from a gentleman at Halifax* (Newport, 1765); also *A letter from a gentleman at Halifax to his friend in Rhode-Island* (Newport, 1765), a reply to Hopkins's *The Rights of the colonies*. Howard in turn was answered by Otis's *A Vindication*.

[Hulton, Ann], *Letters of a loyalist lady* . . . *Ann Hulton, sister of Henry Hulton, Commissioner of customs at Boston, 1767–1776* (Cambridge, Mass., 1927).

Hunt, Isaac, *The Political Family: or* . . . *Advantages which Flow from an Uninterrupted Union between Great Britain and her American Colonies* . . . (Philadelphia, 1775).

Hutchinson, Thomas, *A Brief Statement of the Claims of the Colonies* (Boston, 1764); *Copy of Letters Sent to Great Britain, by His Excellency Thomas Hutchinson* . . . *and several other persons* . . . (Boston, 1773).

Inglis, Charles, *The true interest of America impartially stated* (Philadelphia, 1776). A tract against Paine's *Common Sense*.

[Johnson, S.], *Some Important Observations* (Newport, 1766).

Johnson, Rev. Samuel, *A Candid Examination of Dr. Mayhew's Observations* (Boston, 1763).

Jones, David, *Defensive War in a Just Cause Sinless* . . . (Philadelphia, 1775).

"Journal of a French Traveller in the Colonies, 1765," *Amer. Hist. Rev.*, XXVI (1921) and XXVII (1921).

[Laird, John?], *An Englishman's Answer, to the Address, from the Delegates, to the People of Great Britain* . . . (New York, 1775).

Lathrop, Rev. John, *Innocent Blood Crying to God from the Streets of Boston* (Boston and London, 1771).

[Lee, Charles], *Strictures upon* . . . *"a Friendly Address to all Reasonable Americans* . . .*"* (Philadelphia and New York, 1774). A reply to Dr. Myles Cooper of King's College.

[Leonard, Daniel], *Massachusettensis: or, a Series of Letters* . . . *[on] the present troubles in the Province of Massachusetts-Bay* (Boston and London, 1776). Letters from a prominent loyalist, to which John Adams replied in his "Novanglus" letters in the Boston *Gazette*.

Letters on the American Revolution, 1774–1776 (ed. Margaret W. Willard, Boston, 1925).

Letters to the Rt. Hon. the Earl of Hillsborough, from Governor Bernard, General Gage [and others] (Boston, 1769).

"Liberty Pole on the Commons, The," New York, *Hist. Soc., Bul.,* III (1920). Contemporary documents for the years 1766–1770.

Livingston, Philip, *The other side of the question . . . In answer to a late Friendly Address* (New York, 1774). An answer to President Cooper's *A Friendly Address. . . .*

"London Merchants on the Stamp Act repeal," Mass. Hist. Soc., *Proc.,* LV (1922).

[Mauduit, Jasper], *Jasper Mauduit, Agent in London for the Province of the Massachusetts Bay, 1762–1765* (ed. C. G. Washburn, Boston, 1918). Documents concerning Mauduit's activities.

Maury, Ann, *Memoirs of a Huguenot Family* (New York, 1853). For Rev. James Maury's memoirs.

Mayhew, Rev. Jonathan, *Observations on the Character and Conduct of the Society for the Propagation of the Gospel in Foreign Parts* (Boston, 1763). The Society blamed for the sale of arms by Albany traders to Indians in order to slaughter New England people. See also *Remarks on an Anonymous Tract* (Boston, 1764) and *Popish Idolatry* (Boston, 1765), both against Catholic influences in England; and *The Snare Broken* (Boston, 1766), warning Americans against the powers of the Crown.

Mecklenburg County declarations of July 29, 1774, in "An Interesting Colonial Document," ed. Archibald Henderson, *Va. Mag. Hist.,* XXVIII (1920).

Mein, John, *Sagittarius's Letters and Political Speculations* (Boston, 1775).

Ministerial Catechise, Suitable to be Learned by all Modern Provincial Governors, Pensioners, Placemen, etc. Dedicated to T[homas] H[utchinson], Esq., A (Boston, 1771).

"Minutes of the Tea Meetings, 1773," Mass. Hist. Soc., *Proc.,* XX (1884).

Moore, Maurice, *The Justice . . . of Taxing the American Colonies . . . considered . . .* (Wilmington, N.C., 1765; and repr. in W. K. Boyd, *Some Eighteenth Century Tracts Concerning North Carolina,* Raleigh, 1927).

"Philadelphia Tea-party—1773" (ed. R. W. Kelsey), Friends' Hist. Soc., *Bul.,* X (1921).

Quincy, Josiah, *Observations on the . . . Boston Port Bill* (Boston, 1774).

[Robertson, Archibald], "Archibald Robertson . . . his diaries and sketches in America, 1762–1780," ed. H. M. Lydenberg, N.Y. Pub. Lib., *Bul.,* XXXVII (1933).

[Robinson, Matthew], *Considerations on the Measures Carrying on with respect to the British Colonies . . .* (London, Philadelphia, Boston, 1774).

[Schaw, Janet], *Journal of a Lady of Quality; being the narrative of a journey . . . to the West Indies, North Carolina . . . 1774–1776* (ed. Evangeline W. and C. M. Andrews, New Hav., 1921).

Seabury, Samuel, *Letters of a Westchester farmer [1774–1775] by the Rev.*

Samuel Seabury . . ., ed. C. H. Vance, Westchester Co. Hist. Soc., *Pub.*, VIII (1930).

[Sewell, Jonathan], "Letters of Jonathan Sewell," Mass. Hist. Soc., *Proc.*, 2nd ser., X (1896); *The Americans Roused, in a Cure for the Spleen* (pub. anon., Boston, 1775, repr. in *Mag. of Hist.*, 1922).

Short Narrative of the Horrid Massacre in Boston, A (Boston, 1770).

Some Chapters of the Book of Chronicles of Isaac the Scribe . . . (New York, n.d.). An attack on Governor Sir Henry Moore.

"Some Letters of 1775," ed. W. C. Ford, Mass. Hist. Soc., *Proc.*, LIX (1926).

[Stiles, Ezra], *Literary Diary of Ezra Stiles* . . . (ed. F. B. Dexter, New York, 1901).

Tea-leaves, being a collection of letters and documents . . . *1773* . . . (comp. F. S. Drake, Boston, 1884).

Thatcher, Oxenbridge, *The Sentiments of a British American* (Boston, 1764).

Three letters written by British Officers from Boston, 1774 and 1775 (ed. A. Shuttleworth and I. R. Till), Bostonian Soc., *Proc.*, 1919.

Virginia Committee of Correspondence, "Proceedings . . . 1759–1770," *Va. Mag. of Hist. and Biog.*, X–XII.

Warren-Adams Letters . . . *1743–1777,* Mass. Hist. Soc., *Coll.*, LXXII (Boston, 1917).

[Wilkes, John, *et al.*], "John Wilkes and Boston," Mass. Hist. Soc., *Proc.*, XLVII (1914).

V. NEWSPAPERS

The student needing aid with this most important source of information should consult the exhaustive work of Clarence S. Brigham, *History and Bibliography of American Newspapers, 1690–1820* (2 vols., Worcester, Mass., 1947).

VI. REGIONAL, STATE AND LOCAL HISTORIES

New England

Among the great number of regional, state, and local histories, the following, beginning with New England, are especially useful: J. G. Palfrey, *A compendious history of New England* . . . (4 vols., Boston, 1884); James Truslow Adams, *Revolutionary New England, 1691–1776* (Boston, 1923); J. Belknap, *The History of New Hampshire* . . . (3 vols., Philadelphia, 1813); W. H. Fry, *New Hampshire as a Royal Province* (New York, 1908); R. F. Upton, *Revolutionary New Hampshire* . . . (Hanover, 1936); G. R. Minot, *Continuation of the History of the Province of Massachusetts Bay* . . . [*to 1765*] (2 vols., Boston, 1798–1803); Alden Bradford, *History of Massachusetts*

(3 vols., Boston, 1822–29); J. S. Barry, *The History of Massachusetts* (3 vols., Boston, 1855–57); H. A. Cushing, *History of the Transition from Province to Commonwealth in Massachusetts* (New York, 1896); *Commonwealth History of Massachusetts* (ed. A. B. Hart, New York, 1928), vol. II; Josiah Quincy, Jr., *Reports of Cases . . . in the Superior Court of Judicature of the Province of Massachusetts Bay* (Boston, 1865); Justin Winsor (ed.), *Memorial History of Boston* (a cooperative work, 4 vols., Boston, 1880–81); S. G. Arnold, *History of the State of Rhode Island and Providence Plantations* (2 vols., New York, 1859–60); F. G. Bates, *Rhode Island and the Formation of the Union* (New York, 1898); G. H. Hollister, *History of Connecticut . . .* (2 vols., Hartford, 1857); Benjamin Trumbull, *Complete History of Connecticut . . . to 1764* (2 vols., New London, 1898); Alexander Johnston, *Connecticut; A Study of a Commonwealth Democracy* (Boston, 1903); Edith A. Bailey, *Influences toward Radicalism in Connecticut, 1754–1775* (Northampton, Mass., 1920); Oscar Zeichner, *Connecticut's Years of Controversy, 1750–1776* (Raleigh, N.C., 1949).

The Middle Colonies

Turning now to the Middle Colonies, the following histories may be especially recommended: Thomas Jones, *History of New York during the Revolutionary War . . .* (New York, 1879), vol. I; James Sullivan, *History of the State of New York* (New York, 1927), vol. III; *History of the State of New York* (ed. A. C. Flick, New York, 1933), vol. III, *Whig and Tory,* another large cooperative work; C. L. Becker, *The History of Political Parties in the Province of New York, 1760–1776* (Madison, Wis., 1909); C. H. Levermore, "The Whigs in Colonial New York," *Amer. Hist. Rev.,* I (1896); H. M. Morais, "The Sons of Liberty in New York," in *Era of the American Revolution* (New York, 1939); Irving Mark, *Agrarian Conflicts in Colonial New York, 1711–1775* (New York, 1940); T. J. Wertenbaker, *Father Knickerbocker Rebels* (New York, 1948); G. W. Edwards, *New York as an Eighteenth-Century Municipality, 1731–1776* (New York, 1917); Wilbur C. Abbott, *New York in the American Revolution* (New York, 1929); E. J. Fisher, *New Jersey as a Royal Province, 1738–1776* (New York, 1911); D. L. Kemmerer, *Path to Freedom; The Struggle for Self-Government in Colonial New Jersey, 1703–1776* (Princeton, 1940); Leonard Lundin, *Cockpit of the Revolution: The War for Independence in New Jersey* (Princeton, 1940); Robert Proud, *History of Pennsylvania . . . till after the Year 1742, [supplemented by] a description [of Pennsylvania] between the years 1760 and 1770* (2 vols., Philadelphia, 1797–98); W. R. Shepherd, *History of the Proprietary Government in Pennsylvania* (New York, 1896); Isaac Sharpless, *A History of Quaker Government in Pennsylvania* (2 vols., Philadelphia, 1899); W. T. Root, *The Relations of Pennsylvania with the British Government, 1696–1765* (New

York, 1912); C. H. Lincoln, *Revolutionary Movement in Pennsylvania* (Philadelphia, 1901); E. L. Pennington, "The Anglican Clergy of Pennsylvania in the American Revolution," *Pa. Mag. of Hist. and Biog.*, LXIII (1939); W. R. Smith, "Sectionialism in Pennsylvania during the Revolution," *Pol. Sci. Quar.*, XXIV (1909); J. F. Watson, *Annals of Philadelphia, and Pennsylvania, in the Olden Time* (2 vols., Philadelphia, 1857); and J. T. Scharf and T. Westcott, *History of Philadelphia* . . . (3 vols., Philadelphia, 1884).

The South

For the southern colonies the following works have merit: J. T. Scharf, *History of Maryland* . . . (3 vols., Baltimore, 1879), to be used with caution; N. D. Mereness, *Maryland as a Proprietary Province* (New York, 1901); M. P. Andrews, *History of Maryland: Province and State* (New York, 1929); Charles A. Barker, "Maryland before the Revolution," *Amer. Hist. Rev.*, XLVI (1940), and *The Background of the Revolution in Maryland* (New Haven, 1940); B. C. Steiner, *Western Maryland in the Revolution*, in Johns Hopkins Univ., *Studies*, XX, (1902); J. D. Burk's, *History of Virginia* . . . *to the Present Day* [*1775*] (3 vols., Petersburg, 1804–5); Charles Campbell, *History of the Colony and Ancient Dominion of Virginia* (Philadelphia, 1860); P. S. Flippin, *Royal Government in Virginia, 1624–1775* (New York, 1919); H. J. Eckenrode, *The Revolution in Virginia* (Boston, 1916); Isaac S. Harrell, "Some Neglected Phases of the Revolution in Virginia," *Wm. and Mary Quar.*, 2nd ser., V (1925); C. R. Lingley, *The Transition in Virginia from Colony to Commonwealth* (New York, 1910); C. S. Sydnor, *Gentlemen Freeholders: Political Practices in Washington's Virginia* (Chapel Hill, N.C., 1952); S. Kercheval, *A History of the Valley of Virginia* . . . (Strasburg, Va., 1925); T. P. Abernethy, *Western Lands and the American Revolution* (New York, 1937); John W. Moore, *History of North Carolina; from the Earliest Discoveries to the Present Time* (2 vols., Raleigh, N.C., 1880); C. L. Raper, *North Carolina; A Study in English Colonial Government* (New York, 1904); M. D. Haywood, *Governor William Tryon, and His Administration in the Province of North Carolina, 1765–1771* (Raleigh, N.C., 1903); E. W. Sikes, *Transition of North Carolina from Colony to Commonwealth*, Johns Hopkins Univ., *Studies*, XVI, Nos. 10 and 11 (1898); Samuel A'Court Ashe, *History of North Carolina* (Greens., N.C., 1908), vol. I; A. Henderson, *North Carolina* . . . (5 vols., Chicago, 1941); David Ramsay, *The History of South-Carolina* . . . (2 vols., Charleston, 1809), of value only when the work becomes contemporary history; John Drayton, *Memoirs of the American Revolution* . . . *to the year 1776* . . . *as relating to the State of South-Carolina* . . . (2 vols., Charleston, 1821); Edward McCrady, *The History of South Carolina under the Royal Government, 1719–1776* (New York, 1899); W. R. Smith, *South Carolina as a Royal Province, 1719–1776* (New

York, 1903); D. D. Wallace, *History of South Carolina* (4 vols., New York, 1934); R. L. Meriwether, *The Expansion of South Carolina, 1729–1865* (Kingsport, Tenn., 1940); W. B. Stevens, *A History of Georgia* . . . (2 vols., New York, 1847); C. C. Jones, *History of Georgia* (2 vols., Boston, 1883); P. S. Flippin, "The royal government in Georgia, 1752–1776," *Ga. Hist. Quar.* VIII, IX, XII; Marjorie M. Daniel, *The Revolutionary Movement in Georgia, 1763–1777* (Chicago, 1937); Burton Barrs, *East Florida in the American Revolution* (Jackson, 1932); C. L. Mowat, *East Florida as a British Province, 1763–1784* (Berkeley, 1943); Cecil Johnson, *British West Florida, 1763–1783* (New Haven, 1943); and C. N. Howard, *The British Development of West Florida* (Berkeley, 1947).

Canada and the West Indies

Since certain parts of the present British Empire and Commonwealth were very closely related to the Thirteen Colonies during the period under consideration, reference should be made to at least a few works of especial importance to students of American colonial history. Among these are A. L. Burt, *The Old Province of Quebec* (Toronto and Minneapolis, 1933); V. Coffin, *The Province of Quebec and the Early American Revolution* (Madison, 1896); J. B. Brebner, *The Neutral Yankees of Nova Scotia* (New York, 1937); H. C. Wilkinson, *Bermuda in the Old Empire* (London, 1950); W. B. Kerr, *Bermuda and the American Revolution, 1760–1783* (Princeton, 1936); F. W. Pitman, *The Development of the British West Indies, 1700–1763* (New Haven, 1917); Bryan Edwards, *The History, Civil and Commercial of the British Colonies in the West Indies* (3 vols., London, 1793–1801); [E. Long], *The History of Jamaica* (3 vols., London, 1774); L. M. Penson, "The London West India Interest in the Eighteenth Century," *Eng. Hist. Rev.*, XXXVI (1921); L. T. Ragatz, *The Fall of the Planter Class in the British Caribbean, 1763–1833* (New York, 1928); H. H. Wrong, *Government of the West Indies* (Oxford, 1923); C. S. S. Higham, "The General Assembly in the Leeward Islands," *Eng. Hist. Rev.*, XLI (1926); and Agnes M. Whitson, "The Outlook of the Continental American Colonies on the West Indies, 1760–1775," *Pol. Sci. Quar.*, XLV (1930).

VII. BIOGRAPHIES

British Leaders

Lord Jeffery Amherst: A Soldier of the King (New York, 1933), by John C. Long.

Political Life of W. Wildman, Viscount Barrington . . . (London, 1814), by Shute Barrington, Bishop of Durham.

Among the biographies of Burke, the following may be mentioned: *Memoir of the Life and Character of Edmund Burke* . . . (London, 1824), by Sir James Prior; *Edmund Burke* (London, 1873), by John Morley; *The Political Philosophy of Edmund Burke* (London, 1913), by John MacCunn; *The Early Life, Correspondence and Writings of Edmund Burke* (London, 1923), by A. P. I. Samuel; *Edmund Burke and his Kinsmen* (Boulder, Col., 1939), by Dixon Wecter; *Our Eminent Friend Edmund Burke* (New Haven, 1949), by T. W. Copeland.

Life and Administration of Sir Robert Eden [Governor of Maryland], (Baltimore, 1898), by B. C. Steiner.

Dr. John Fothergill and his friends . . . (London, 1919), by R. H. Fox.

Life and Times of C. J. Fox (3 vols., London, 1859–66), by Lord John Russell; *Charles James Fox, a Political Study* (London, 1903), by J. L. Hammond; *Early History of Charles James Fox* . . . (London, 1908), by Sir G. O. Trevelyan; and *Charles James Fox* (New York, 1928), by John Drinkwater.

General Gage in America . . . (Baton Rouge, 1948), by J. R. Alden.

Memoirs of the Life and Reign of . . . *George III* (3 vols., London, 1867), by J. H. Jesse; *Farmer George* (2 vols., London, 1907), by L. Melville (pseud. for L. S. Benjamin); *George III as Man, Monarch and Statesman* (London, 1907), by Beckles Willson; and *George the Third; a record of a King's Reign* (London, 1936), by J. D. G. Davies.

The Life of Lord Chancellor Hardwicke . . . (3 vols., London, 1847), by George Harris; *Life and Correspondence of Philip Yorke, Earl of Hardwicke* . . . (Cambridge, Eng., 1913), by P. C. Yorke.

Thomas Pelham-Hollis, Duke of Newcastle . . . (Philadelphia, 1931), by S. H. Nulle, which deals, however, with only the earlier years of Newcastle.

Lord North, Second Earl of Guilford, 1732–1792 (2 vols., London, 1913), by Reginald Lucas.

A History of the Right Honourable William Pitt, Earl of Chatham (2 vols., London, 1827), by Rev. Francis Thackeray; *Pitt* (London, 1891), by Lord Rosebery; *Chatham* (London, 1905), by Frederick Harrison; *William Pitt, Earl of Chatham* (3 vols., London, 1907), by Albert von Ruville; *Life of William Pitt, Earl of Chatham* (2 vols., London, 1913), by Basil Williams; and *Mr. Pitt and America's Birthright* (New York, 1940), by John C. Long.

Thomas Pownall . . . (London, 1908), by C. A. W. Pownall; and *Thomas Pownall, British Defender of American Liberty* . . . (Glendale, Calif., 1951), by J. A. Schutz.

Memoirs of the Marquis of Rockingham and his Contemporaries (2 vols., London, 1852), by George Thomas Keppel, Earl of Albemarle.

Life of William, Earl of Shelburne (3 vols., London, 1875–76), by Lord Edmond Fitzmaurice.

Charles Townshend (London, 1866), by Percy Fitzgerald.

"Barlow Trecothick," by T. D. Jervey, in *S.C. Mag. Hist.*, XXXII (1931).

Life of John Wilkes (New York, 1917), by Horace Bleackley; *That Devil Wilkes* (New York, 1929), by R. W. Postgate.

American Leaders [1]

Life of John Adams (2 vols., Philadelphia, 1871), by C. F. Adams; *John Adams, the Statesman of the American Revolution* (Boston, 1898), by Mellen Chamberlain; *John Adams* (Boston, 1898), by J. T. Morse, Jr.; *Political Science of John Adams* (New York, 1915), by Correa M. Walsh; *Honest John Adams* (Boston, 1933), by G. Chinard; and *John Adams and the American Revolution* (Boston, 1950), by Catherine D. Bowen.

The Life and Public Service of Samuel Adams (3 vols., Cambridge, Mass., 1866), by W. V. Wells; *Samuel Adams, the Man of the Town Meeting* (Baltimore, 1884), by J. K. Hosmer; *Samuel Adams, Promoter of the American Revolution* (New York, 1923), by R. V. Harlow; *Sam Adams: Pioneer in Propaganda* (Boston, 1936), by John C. Miller.

Benjamin Chew, 1722–1810, Head of the Pennsylvania Judiciary System . . . (Philadelphia, 1932), by B. A. Konkle.

Silas Deane . . . (New York, 1913), by G. L. Clark.

The Life and Times of John Dickinson (Philadelphia, 1891), by C. J. Stillé; *John Dickinson, the Author of the Declaration on Taking Up Arms in 1775* (New York, 1890) by G. H. Moore; and "The Disputed Authorship of The Declaration on the Causes and Necessity of Taking Up Arms, 1775," by J. P. Boyd, in *Pa. Mag. of Hist. and Biog.*, LXXIV (1950).

"Eliphalet Dyer: Connecticut Revolutionist," by George C. Groce, Jr., in *Era of the American Revolution* (New York, 1939).

Among the many lives of Franklin the following should be mentioned: *Life and Times of Benjamin Franklin* (2 vols., Boston, 1864), by James Parton; *Benjamin Franklin as a Man of Letters* (Boston, 1887), by J. B. McMaster; *Benjamin Franklin* (Boston, 1889), by J. T. Morse, Jr.; *The True Benjamin Franklin* (Philadelphia, 1889), by S. G. Fisher; *The Many-sided Franklin* (New York, 1899), by P. L. Ford; *The Amazing Benjamin Franklin* (New York, 1929), by J. H. Smythe; *Benjamin Franklin* (New York,

---

[1] In this connection the student should consult the *Dictionary of American Biography* (ed. Allen Johnson and Dumas Malone, 20 vols., New York, 1928–36).

1938), by Carl Van Doren; and *Benjamin Franklin—Englishman and American* (Providence, 1936), by V. W. Crane.

Joseph Galloway, the Loyalist Politician (Philadelphia, 1902), by E. H. Baldwin.

The Life of Nathanael Greene (3 vols., New York, 1867–71), by G. W. Greene.

Life of Captain Nathan Hale (Hartford, 1856), by I. W. Stuart.

The Life of Alexander Hamilton (2 vols., New York, 1834), by J. C. Hamilton; *The Life of Alexander Hamilton* (2 vols., Boston, 1876), by J. T. Morse, Jr.; *Alexander Hamilton* (Boston, 1882), by H. C. Lodge; *Alexander Hamilton* (Boston, 1901), by James Schouler; *The Intimate Life of Alexander Hamilton* (London, 1910), by Allan M. Hamilton; *Alexander Hamilton* (New York, 1920), by H. J. Ford.

John Hancock and his Times (Boston, 1891), by W. C. Burrage; *John Hancock, the Picturesque Patriot* (Boston, 1912), by Lorenzo Sears; *John Hancock, Patriot in Purple* (New York, 1948), by H. S. Allan; *The House of Hancock* (Cambridge, Mass., 1945), by W. T. Baxter.

Joseph Hawley, Colonial Radical (New York, 1931), by Ernest F. Brown.

Sketches of the Life and Character of Patrick Henry (Philadelphia, 1817), by William Wirt; *Patrick Henry* (Boston, 1887), by M. C. Tyler; *Patrick Henry, Life, Correspondence and Speeches* (3 vols., New York, 1891), by W. W. Henry; *The True Patrick Henry* (Philadelphia, 1907), by George Morgan.

Stephen Hopkins, A Rhode Island Statesman. A Study in the Political History of the Eighteenth Century (*R.I. Hist. Tracts, No. XIX,* Providence, 1884), by W. E. Foster.

The Life of Thomas Hutchinson . . . (Boston, 1896), by J. K. Hosmer.

Jared Ingersoll: A Study of American Loyalism in Relation to British Colonial Government (New Haven, 1920), by L. H. Gipson.

As Jefferson has been honored with many biographies, only the following need be mentioned: *Life of Thomas Jefferson* (2 vols., Philadelphia, 1837), by George Tucker; *Life of Thomas Jefferson* (Boston, 1874), by James Parton; *Thomas Jefferson* (Boston, 1883), by J. T. Morse, Jr.; *The Life of Thomas Jefferson* (3 vols., Philadelphia, 1888), by H. S. Randall; *Thomas Jefferson: The Apostle of Americanism* (Boston, 1929), by G. Chinard; *The Young Jefferson* (Boston, 1945), bý C. G. Bowers; *Jefferson and His Time* (Boston, 1948), by Dumas Malone, vol. I, *Jefferson the Virginian.*

The Life of Thomas Johnson (New York, 1927), by E. S. Delaplaine.

Life and Times of Sir William Johnson (2 vols., Albany, 1865), by W. L. Stone; *Sir William Johnson and the Six Nations* (New York, 1891), by W. E. Griffis; *Sir William Johnson* (New York, 1903), by A. C. Buell.

William Samuel Johnson. A Maker of the Constitution (New York, 1937), by G. C. Groce.

Life of Arthur Lee (2 vols., Boston, 1829), by R. H. Lee; *A Vindication of Arthur Lee* (Richmond, 1894), by C. H. Lee.

General Charles Lee . . . (Baton Rouge, 1951), by J. R. Alden.

Memoir of the Life of Richard Henry Lee (2 vols., Philadelphia, 1825), by R. H. Lee.

The Livingstons of Livingston Manor (New York, 1910), by E. B. Livingston, for the biographies of Peter van Brugh Livingston and Philip Livingston.

James Madison (Boston, 1850), by J. J. Adams; *. . . James Madison* (3 vols., Boston, 1859–68), by W. C. Rives; *James Madison* (Boston, 1884), by S. H. Gay; *. . . James Madison* (New York, 1902), by Gaillard Hunt; *James Madison: The Virginia Revolutionist* (Indianapolis, 1941), by I. Brant.

Life of George Mason, 1725–1792 (2 vols., New York, 1892), by Kate M. Rowland; *George Mason, Constitutionalist . . .* (Cambridge, Mass., 1938), by Helen D. Hill.

Memoirs of the Life and Writings of the Rev. Jonathan Mayhew (Boston, 1838), by Alden Bradford.

Gouverneur Morris (Boston, 1898), by Theodore Roosevelt.

Robert Morris, Patriot and Financier (New York, 1903), by E. P. Oberholtzer.

Life of Major-General Peter Muhlenberg of the Revolutionary Army (Philadelphia, 1849), by H. A. Muhlenberg; *The Muhlenbergs of Pennsylvania* (Philadelphia, 1949), by P. A. W. Wallace, for lives of Frederick and Henry Ernest, as well as Peter, Muhlenberg.

The Life of James Otis of Massachusetts (Boston, 1823), by William Tudor; *Life of James Otis* (Boston, 1864), by Francis Bowen, in J. Sparks, *Library of American Biography;* "James Otis," by J. H. Ellis, *Amer. Law Rev.,* July, 1869.

Life of Thomas Paine (New York, 1809), by James Cheetham; *Life of Thomas Paine* (2 vols., New York, 1862), by M. D. Conway; *Damaged Souls* (Boston, 1923), by Gamaliel Bradford; *Thomas Paine, Prophet and Martyr of Democracy* (New York, 1927), by Mary A. Best.

Israel Pemberton, King of the Quakers (Philadelphia, 1943), by Theodore Thayer.

Richard Peters, Provincial Secretary and Cleric, 1704–1776 (Philadelphia, 1944), by Hubertis Cummings.

Life of Timothy Pickering (4 vols., Boston, 1867–73), by Octavius Pickering and C. W. Upham.

Israel Putnam (New York, 1901), by W. F. Livingston.

Life and Correspondence of Joseph Reed (2 vols., Philadelphia, 1847), by W. B. Reed.

The Life of Colonel Paul Revere (2 vols., Boston, 1891), by E. H. Goss; *Paul Revere and the World He Lived In* (Boston, 1942), by Esther Forbes.

Benjamin Rush, Physician and Citizen, 1746–1813 (Philadelphia, 1934), by N. G. Goodman.

The Life and Times of Philip Schuyler (New York, 1860), by B. J. Lossing; *Colonial New York, Philip Schuyler and his Family* (New York, 1885), by G. W. Schuyler; *Life of General Philip Schuyler* (New York, 1903), by Bayard Tuckerman.

Life and Correspondence of the Right Reverend Samuel Seabury (Boston, 1881), by E. E. Beardsley.

William Smith, Educator and Churchman, 1727–1803 (Philadelphia, 1943), by A. F. Gegenheimer.

John Stuart and the Southern Colonial Frontier . . . 1754–1775 (Ann Arbor, 1944), by J. R. Alden.

The Life of Charles Thomson (Philadelphia, 1900), by L. R. Harley.

The Life of Jonathan Trumbull, Sr. (Boston, 1859), by I. M. Stuart; *Jonathan Trumbull . . .* (Boston, 1919), by Jonathan Trumbull.

The Life and Times of Joseph Warren (Boston, 1865), by Richard Frothingham, Jr.

Only a few of the many lives of Washington can be mentioned: *The True George Washington* (Philadelphia, 1896), by P. L. Ford; *George Washington* (2 vols., Boston, 1898), by H. C. Lodge; *George Washington* (2 vols., New York, 1900), by W. C. Ford; *George Washington, the Rebel and Patriot* (New York, 1927), by Rupert Hughes; *George Washington* (2 vols., New York, 1940), by N. W. Stephenson and W. H. Dunn; and *George Washington: A Biography* (New York, 1948), by D. S. Freeman, vols. I and II, *Young Washington*.

John Wentworth, Governor of New Hampshire, 1767–1775 (Cambridge, Mass., 1921), by L. S. Mayo.

VIII. GENERAL HISTORIES COVERING THE PERIOD

Abernethy, T. P., *Western Lands and the American Revolution* (Charlottesville, 1937).

Adams, James Truslow, *Building the British Empire. To the End of the First Empire* (New York, 1938), and *Revolutionary New England* (Boston, 1923).

Alvord, C. W., *The Mississippi Valley in British Politics* (2 vols., Cleveland, 1917).

Andrews, C. M., *The Colonial Period of American History* (New Haven, 1938), vol. IV.

Avery, E. M., *History of the United States* . . . (7 vols., Cleveland, 1904–10).

Bancroft, George, *History of the United States* (10 vols., Boston, 1834–75). A work with a wealth of detail but to be used with caution.

Becker, C. L., *The Eve of the Revolution: A Chronicle of the Breach with England* (New Haven, 1918).

Brebner, J. B., *North Atlantic Triangle; The Interplay of Canada, the United States and Great Britain* (New Haven, 1945).

Cambridge History of the British Empire (Cambridge, Eng., 1929), vol. I.

Chalmers, George, *An Introduction to the History of the Revolt of the American Colonies* (2 vols., London, 1782 and 1845).

Channing, Edward, *A History of the United States* (New York, 1912), vol. III.

Chase, Ellen, *The Beginnings of the American Revolution Based on Contemporary Letters, Diaries and Other Documents* (2 vols., New York, 1910).

Coleman, R. V., *Liberty and Property* (New York, 1951).

Doyle, J. A., *The English in America* (5 vols., London, 1882–1907).

Fisher, S. G., *The True History of the American Revolution* (Philadelphia, 1902), and *The Struggle for American Independence* . . . (2 vols., London, 1908).

Fiske, John, *The American Revolution* (2 vols., Boston, 1891).

Frothingham, Richard, *The Rise of the Republic of the United States* (Boston, 1890).

Gershoy, Leo, *From Despotism to Revolution, 1763–1789* (New York, 1944).

Gipson, L. H., *The British Empire Before the American Revolution* (Caldwell, Ida., and New York, 1936), vols. I–III.

Hacker, L. M., *The Triumph of American Capitalism* . . . (New York, 1940).

Heckscher, E. F., *Mercantilism* (2 vols., London, 1934).

Hertz [Hurst], G. B., *British Imperialism in the Eighteenth Century* (London, 1908), and *The Old Colonial System* (Manchester, 1905).

Hildreth, Richard, *History of the United States* (rev. ed., 6 vols., New York, 1880).

Howard, G. E., *Preliminaries of the Revolution, 1763–1775* (New York, 1905).

Hunt, William, *The Political History of England* . . . *1760–1801* (London, 1905).

Keith, A. B., *Constitutional History of the First British Empire* (Oxford, 1930).

Lecky, W. E. H., *A History of England in the Eighteenth Century* (8 vols., London, 1878–1890).

Lodge, H. C., *The Story of the Revolution* (2 vols., New York, 1898).

Mahon, Lord, *History of England, 1713–1783* (3rd rev. ed., 7 vols., Boston, 1853–54).

Massey, W. N., *History of England during the Reign of George the Third* (4 vols., London, 1855–63).

May, T. E., *Constitutional History of England . . .* (3 vols., London, 1882).

Miller, J. C., *Origins of the American Revolution* (Boston, 1943).

Mullett, C. F., *The British Empire* (New York, 1938).

Namier, L. B., *England in the Age of the American Revolution* (London, 1930).

Nettels, C. P., *The Roots of American Civilization* (New York, 1938).

Osgood, H. L., *The American Colonies in the Eighteenth Century* (4 vols., New York, 1924). Useful largely for background materials.

Palfrey, J. G., *History of New England* (5 vols., Boston, 1858–90).

Pitkin, Timothy, *Political and Civil History of the United States* (2 vols., New Haven, 1828).

Robertson, C. G., *England under the Hanoverians* (New York, 1911).

Seeley, Sir J. R., *The Expansion of England* (London, 1883).

Semple, E. C., *American History and Its Geographic Conditions* (Boston, 1903).

Trevelyan, Sir G. O., *The American Revolution . . .* (6 vols., London, 1905–16).

Tyler, M. C., *The Literary History of the American Revolution 1763–1783* (2 vols., New York, 1897).

Van Tyne, C. H., *The Causes of the War of Independence, Being the First Volume of a History of the Founding of the American Republic* (Boston, 1922); *England and America, Rivals in the American Revolution* (Cambridge, Eng., 1927).

Warren, Mercy O., *History of the Rise, Progress, and Termination of the American Revolution* (3 vols., Boston, 1805).

Williamson, J. A., *A Short History of British Expansion* (London, 1930).

Winsor, Justin, *Narrative and Critical History of America* (8 vols., Boston, 1884–89).

IX. SPECIAL STUDIES AND OTHER SPECIAL WORKS

Government of Great Britain

Adams, G. B., *Constitutional History of England* (rev. R. L. Schuyler, New York, 1934).

Anson, Sir W. R., *The Law and Custom of the Constitution* (2 vols., Oxford, 1922–35).

Barnes, Donald, "The Myth of an Eighteenth Century Whig Oligarchy," A.H.A., Pacific Branch, *Proc.*, 1929.

Blauvelt, Mary T., *The Development of Cabinet Government in England* (London, 1902).

Butler, Sir G. G., *The Tory Tradition* . . . (London, 1914).

Dicey, A. V., *Introduction to the Study of the* . . . *Constitution* (9th ed., London, 1939).

Feiling, K. G., *The Second Tory Party, 1714–1832* (London, 1938).

Jenks, Edward, *Parliamentary England; the Evolution of the Cabinet System* (London, 1903).

Maitland, F. W., *The Constitutional History of England* . . . (Cambridge, Eng., 1908).

Namier, L. B., *Structure of Politics at the Accession of George III* (2 vols., London, 1929).

Pares, Richard, *King George III and the Politicians* (Oxford, 1953).

Porritt, Edward, *The Unreformed House of Commons* . . . (2 vols., Cambridge, Eng., 1903).

Temperley, H. W. V., "Inner and Outer Cabinet and Privy Council, 1679–1783," *Eng. Hist. Rev.*, XXVII (1912).

Trevelyan, G. M., *The two-party system in English political history* (Oxford, 1926).

Turberville, A. S., *The House of Lords in the XVIII century* (Oxford, 1927).

Turner, E. R., *The Cabinet Council in England in the Seventeenth and Eighteenth Centuries, 1622–1784* (2 vols., Baltimore, 1930–32), and *The Privy Council of England in the Seventeenth and Eighteenth Centuries, 1603–1784* (2 vols., Baltimore, 1927–28).

Winstanley, D. A., *Personal and Party Government* . . . *1760–1766* (Cambridge, Eng., 1910), and *Lord Chatham and the Whig Opposition* (Cambridge, Eng., 1912).

Witmer, Helen E., *The Property Qualifications of Members of Parliament* (New York, 1943).

Wolkins, G. G., "Writs of Assistance in England," Mass. Hist. Soc., *Proc.*, LXVI (1942).

British Colonial Government

Albion, R. G., *Forests and Seapower; the Timber Problem of the Royal Navy, 1652–1862* (Cambridge, Mass., 1926).

Andrews, C. M., "The Royal Disallowance," Amer. Antiq. Soc., *Proc.*, 1914;

List of Commissions, Instructions, and Additional Instructions Issued to Royal Governors and others in America (Washington, 1913); and *List of Reports and Representations of the . . . Board of Trade, 1696–1782 . . .* (Washington, 1915).

Appleton, Marguerite, "The Agents of the New England Colonies in the Revolutionary Period," *New Eng. Quar.,* VI (1933).

Atkinson, C. T., "British Forces in North America, 1774–1781: Their Distribution and Strength,' Soc. Army Hist. Research, *Jour.,* XVI (1937).

Barker, C. A., "Property Rights in Provincial Maryland," *Jour. of South. Hist.,* II (1936).

Barnes, Viola F., "Frances Legge, Governor of Loyalist Nova Scotia, 1773–1776," *New Eng. Quar.,* IV (1931).

Basye, A. H., *The Lords Commissioners of Trade and Plantations, 1748–1782* (New Haven, 1925), and "The Secretary of State for the Colonies, 1768–1782," *Amer. Hist. Rev.,* XXVIII (1922).

Bining, A. C., *British Regulation of the Colonial Iron Industry* (Philadelphia, 1933).

Bishop, C. F., *History of Elections in the American Colonies* (New York, 1893).

Bond, B. W., Jr., "The Colonial Agent as a Popular Representative," *Pol. Sci. Quar.,* XXXV (1920).

Burns, J. F., *Controversies between Royal Governors and their Assemblies in the Northern American Colonies* (2 vols., Boston, 1923).

Carpenter, A. H., "Naturalization in England and in the American Colonies," *Am. Hist. Rev.,* IX (1904).

Carter, C. E., "The Significance of the Military Office in America, 1763–1775," *Amer. Hist. Rev.,* XXVIII (1923); and "The Office of Commander in Chief: A Phase of Imperial Unity on the Eve of the Revolution," in *The Era of the American Revolution* (New York, 1939).

Clark, Dora M., "The American Board of Customs, 1767–1783," *Am. Hist. Rev.,* XLV (1940); and "The British Treasury and the Administration of Military Affairs in America," *Pa. Hist.,* II (1935).

Clarke, Mary P., *Parliamentary Privilege in the American Colonies* (New Haven, 1943).

Coupland, R., *The Quebec Act: A Study in Statesmanship* (Oxford, 1925).

Curtis, E. E., *The Organization of the British Army in the American Revolution* (New Haven, 1926).

Dickerson, O. M., *American Colonial Government, 1696–1765* (Cleveland, 1912).

Dorland, A. G., *The Royal Disallowance in Massachusetts,* Queen's Univ., Can., Bull. No. 22 (1917).

Dunbar, Louise B., "The Royal Governors in the Middle and Southern Colonies on the Eve of the Revolution: A Study in Imperial Personnel," in *The Era of the American Revolution* (New York, 1939).

Fortescue, Sir J. W., *History of the British Army* (London, 1903), vol. III; and *British Regiments* (London, 1934).

Gipson, L. H., "Acadia and the Beginnings of Modern British Imperialism," in *Essays in Modern English History* . . . (Cambridge, Mass., 1944).

Gray, Horace, "Writs of Assistance," in Josiah Quincy's *Reports of Cases* . . . (Boston, 1865), Appendix.

Greene, E. B., *The Provincial Governor in the English Colonies of North America* (New York, 1898).

Hall, Hubert, "Chatham's Colonial Policy," *Amer. Hist. Rev.,* V (1900).

Hickman, Emily, "Colonial Writs of Assistance," *New Eng. Quar.,* V (1932).

Hotblack, Kate, *Chatham's Colonial Policy* . . . (London, 1917).

Humphreys, R. A., "Lord Shelburne and a Projected Recall of Colonial Governors in 1767," *Am. Hist. Rev.,* XXXVII (1932); "Lord Shelburne and the Proclamation of 1763," *Eng. Hist. Rev.,* XLIX (1939).

Keith, A. B., *Constitutional History of the First British Empire* (Oxford, 1930).

Kellogg, Louise P., "A Footnote to the Quebec Act," *Can. Hist. Rev.,* XIII (1932).

Labaree, L. W., *Royal Government in America* (New Haven, 1930); *Royal Instructions to British Colonial Governors, 1670–1776* (2 vols., New York, 1935).

Lewis, Sir G. C., *An Essay on the Government of Dependencies* (ed. C. P. Lucas, Oxford, 1891).

Lilly, E. P., *The Colonial Agents of New York and New Jersey* (Washington, 1936).

Lonn, Ella, *The Colonial Agents of the Southern Colonies* (Chapel Hill, 1945).

Martin, Chester, *Empire and Commonwealth* (Oxford, 1929).

McKinley, A. E., *The Suffrage Franchise in the Thirteen English Colonies in America* (Philadelphia, 1905).

Metzger, C. H., *The Quebec Act; a Primary Cause of the American Revolution* (New York, 1936).

Namier, L. B., "Charles Garth and his Connections," *Eng. Hist. Rev.,* LIV (1939).

Penson, L. M., *The Colonial Agents of the British West Indies* (London, 1924).

Russell, E. B., *The Review of American Colonial Legislation by the King in Council* (New York, 1915).

Schlesinger, A. M., *Colonial Appeals to the Privy Council* (2 vols., New York, 1913).

J. H. Smith, *Appeals to the Privy Council from the American Plantations* (New York, 1950).

Smith, W., *The History of the Post Office in British North America, 1639–1870* (Cambridge, Eng., 1920).

Spector, Margaret M., *The American Department of the British Government, 1768–1782* (New York, 1940).

Tanner, E. P., "Colonial Agencies in England during the Eighteenth Century," *Pol. Sci. Quar.,* XVI (1901).

Washburne, G. W., *Imperial Control of the Administration of Justice in the Thirteen Colonies, 1684–1776* (New York, 1923).

Wolkins, G. G., "Daniel Malcom and Writs of Assistance," Mass. Hist. Soc., *Proc.,* LVIII (1924); and "Bollan on Writs of Assistance," *ibid.,* LIX (1926).

The American Revolutionary Movement *

Adams, R. G., *Political Ideas of the American Revolution . . . 1765–1775* (Durham, N.C., 1922); "The Legal Theories of James Wilson," *Univ. Pa. Law Rev.,* LXVIII (1920); and "The Olive Branch Petition," *D.A.R. Mag.,* LXVI (1932).

Alvord, C. W., "Mississippi Valley Problems and the American Revolution," *Minn. Hist. Bull.,* IV, and "The Imperial Issue," *Landmark,* VIII (1926).

Andrews, C. M., "The American Revolution: An Interpretation," *Am. Hist. Rev.,* XXXI (1926); and *The Colonial Background of the American Revolution; Four Essays in American Colonial History* (rev. ed., New Haven, 1931).

Baldwin, Alice M., *The New England Clergy and the American Revolution* (Durham, N.C., 1928).

Bartlett, J. R., *History of the Destruction of . . . the Gaspee . . .* (Providence, 1861).

Bassett, J. S., *The Regulators of North Carolina, 1756–1771* (Washington, 1894).

Becker, C. L., "Growth of Revolutionary Parties and Methods in New York Province, 1765–1774," *Am. Hist. Rev.,* VII (1901); *The Declaration of Independence* (New York, 1922); and *The Spirit of '76* (Washington, 1927).

Boyd, J. P., *Anglo-American Union: Joseph Galloway's Plans to Preserve the British Empire, 1774–1788* (Philadelphia, 1941).

Brown, W. A., *Empire or Independence: A Study in the Failure of Reconciliation, 1774–1783* (Baton Rouge, 1941).

* In addition to the general works already listed, the following should be consulted.

Chamberlain, Mellon, "The Revolution Impending," in Winsor's *Narrative and Critical History* (Boston, 1884–89), vol. IV.

Clark, Dora M., *British Opinion and the American Revolution* (New Haven, 1930).

Connor, R. D. W., "Josiah Tucker; or Cassandra picks the pocket of Mars," *World Affairs*, CIII (1940).

Coupland, R., *The American Revolution and the British Empire* (London, 1930); "The Truth about the American Revolution," *Landmark*, V (1923).

Darling, A. B., *A Historical Introduction to the Declaration of Independence* (New Haven, 1932); *Our Rising Empire, 1763–1803* (New Haven, 1940).

Davidson, Philip, "The Southern Backcountry on the Eve of the Revolution," in *Essays in Honor of William E. Dodd* (Chicago, 1935); "Whig Propagandists of the American Revolution," *Am. Hist. Rev.*, XXXIX (1934); and *Propaganda and the American Revolution, 1763–1783* (Chapel Hill, 1941).

Davitt, L. J., *A Re-study of the Movement toward American Independence, 1760–1778* (Washington, 1929).

Dickerson, O. M., *The Navigation Acts and the American Revolution* (Philadelphia, 1951); and "Writs of Assistance as a Cause of the Revolution," in *The Era of the American Revolution* (New York, 1939).

Dutcher, G. M., "The Rise of Republican Government in the United States," *Pol. Sci. Quar.*, LV (1940).

Eckenrode, H. J., *The Revolution in Virginia* (Boston, 1916).

Egerton, H. E., *The Causes and Character of the American Revolution* (Oxford, 1923).

Ericson, F. J., "British Motives for Expansion in 1763: Territory, Commerce, or Security," Mich. Acad. of Science, Arts, and Letters, *Papers*, XXVII (1942); *The British Colonial System and the Question of Change of Policy on the Eve of the American Revolution* (Chicago, 1943).

Ewing, J., "The Constitution of the Empire—from Bacon to Blackstone," chap. XXI of *The Cambridge History of the British Empire* (Cambridge, Eng., 1929), vol. I.

Farrand, Max, "The West and the Principles of the Revolution," *Yale Review*, c.ser., XVII (1908).

Fitzpatrick, J. C., *The Spirit of the Revolution* . . . (Boston, 1924).

Ford, P. L., *Josiah Tucker and His Writings: An Eighteenth Century Pamphleteer on America* (Chicago, 1894).

Franklin, W. N., "Some Aspects of Representation in the American Colonies," *N.C. Hist. Rev.*, VI (1929).

Friedenwald, Herbert, *The Declaration of Independence* . . . (New York, 1904).

Frothingham, T. G., "The Military Test of the Spontaneous American Revolution," Mass. Hist. Soc., *Proc.*, LVIII (1925).

Gipson, L. H., "Some Reflections upon the American Revolution," *Pa. Hist.*, IX (1942); "The Art of Preserving an Empire," *Wm. and Mary Quar.*, 3rd ser., II (1945); "The American Revolution as an Aftermath of the Great War for the Empire," *Pol. Sci. Quar.*, LXV (1950).

Guttridge, G. H., "English Liberty and the American Revolution," A.H.A., Pacific Branch, *Proc.*, 1930; *English Whiggism and the American Revolution* (Berkeley, 1942).

Harvey, R. S., "Some Legal and Historical Phases of the American Revolution," *Georgetown Law Jour.*, XV (1927).

Hatch, Mary R. P., "Colonial Newspapers . . . on the Eve of the Revolution," *Jour. Amer. Hist.*, XX (1926).

Hazelton, J. H., *The Declaration of Independence, Its History* (New York, 1906).

Heatley, D. P., *Studies in British History and Politics* (London, 1913).

Henderson, Archibald, "The Origin of the Regulation in North Carolina," *Amer. Hist. Rev.*, XXI (1916).

Hinkhouse, F. J., *The Preliminaries of the American Revolution as Seen in the English Press, 1763–1775* (New York, 1926).

Humphreys, R. A., "British Colonial Policy and the American Revolution," *History,* n.ser., XIX (1934).

Jameson, F. J., *The American Revolution Considered as a Social Movement* (Princeton, 1926).

Jensen, Merrill, *The Articles of Confederation: An Interpretation of the Social-Constitutional History of the American Revolution, 1774–1781* (Madison, 1940).

Johnston, Arthur, *Myths and Facts of the American Revolution* (Toronto, 1908).

Knorr, Klaus E., *British Colonial Theories, 1570–1850* (Toronto, 1944).

Laprade, W. T., "The Stamp Act in British Politics," *Amer. Hist. Rev.*, XXXV (1930).

Laub, C. H., "Revolutionary Virginia and the Crown Lands," *Wm. and Mary Quar.*, 2nd ser., XI (1931).

Leake, J. M., *The Virginia Committee System and the American Revolution* (Baltimore, 1917).

Leffmann, Henry, "The Real Declaration of Independence: A Study of Colonial History under a Modern Theory," *Pa. Mag. Hist.*, XLVII (1923).

Levermore, C. H., "The Whigs of Colonial New York," *Amer. Hist. Rev.*, I (1896).

Longley, R. S., "Mob Activities in Revolutionary Massachusetts," *New Eng. Quar.*, VI (1933).

McCormac, E. I., *Colonial Opposition to Imperial Authority during the French and Indian War* (Berkeley, 1914).

McCrady, Edward, *The History of South Carolina in the Revolution, 1775–1780* (New York, 1901).

McIlwain, C. H., *The American Revolution: A Constitutional Interpretation* (New York, 1923).

McLaughlin, A. C., *America and Britain* (New York, 1918); "Some Reflections on the American Revolution," in *Aspects of the Social History of America* (Chapel Hill, 1931); *The Foundations of American Constitutionalism* (New York, 1932); *A Constitutional History of the United States* (New York, 1935).

Merriam, C. E., *History of American Political Theories* (New York, 1903).

Meyer, J. C., *Church and State in Massachusetts from 1740 to 1833; A Chapter in the History of the Development of Individual Freedom* (Cleveland, 1930).

Miller, J. C., "The Massachusetts Convention, 1768," *New Eng. Quar.,* VII (1934).

Morris, R. B., "Legalism versus Revolutionary Doctrine in New England," *New Eng. Quar.,* IV (1931).

Mullett, C. F., *Colonial Claims to Home Rule (1764–1775): An Essay in Imperial Politics* (Columbia, Mo., 1927); *Fundamental Law and the American Revolution, 1760–1776* (New York, 1933); and "Tory Imperialism on the Eve of the Declaration of Independence," *Can. Hist. Rev.,* XII (1931).

Osgood, H. L., "The American Revolution," *Pol. Sci. Quar.* (1898).

Parrington, V. L., *Main Currents of American Thought* (New York, 1927), vol. I, *The Colonial Mind, 1620–1800.*

Pate, J. E., "Richard Bland's Inquiry into the Rights of the British Colonies," *Wm. and Mary Quar.,* 2d ser., XI (1931).

Peabody, A. P., "Boston Mobs before the Revolution," *Atlantic Monthly,* LXII (1888).

Perry, R. B., *Puritanism and Democracy* (New York, 1944).

Pomerantz, S. I., "The Patriot Newspaper and the American Revolution," in *The Era of the American Revolution* (New York, 1939).

Rossiter, Clinton, *Seedtime of the Republic* (New York, 1953).

Roth, P. A., *Masonry in the Formation of our Government* (Milwaukee, 1927).

Russell, J. A., "The Influence of Indian Confederations on the Union of the American Colonies," *Jour. Amer. Hist.,* XXII, no. 1 (1928).

Salley, A. S., Jr., "The Mecklenberg Declaration," *Amer. Hist. Rev.,* XIII (1907).

Sanders, J. B., "Thomas Burke in the Continental Congress," *N.C. Hist. Rev.*, IX (1932).

Savelle, Max, *Seeds of Liberty: the Genesis of the American Mind* (New York, 1948); "The American Balance of Power and European Diplomacy, 1713–78," in *The Era of the American Revolution* (New York, 1939).

Schlesinger, A. M., "The American Revolution Reconsidered," *Pol. Sci. Quar.*, XXXIV (1919); "Politics, Propaganda and the Philadelphia Press, 1767–1770," *Pa. Mag. Hist.*, LX (1936); "Propaganda and the Boston Newspaper Press, 1767–1770," Col. Soc. Mass., *Pub.*, XXXII (1937); "Liberty Tree: A Genealogy," *New Eng. Quar.*, XXV (1952).

Schuyler, R. L., "The Britannic Question and the American Revolution," *Pol. Sci. Quar.*, XXXVIII (1923); *Parliament and the British Empire: Some Constitutional Controversies Concerning Imperial Legislative Jurisdiction* (New York, 1929).

Scott, A. P., "The Parson's Cause," *Pol. Sci. Quar.*, XXXI (1916).

Silver, J. A., *The Provisional Government of Maryland (1774–1777)* (Baltimore, 1895).

Staples, W. R., *Documentary History of the Destruction of the Gaspee* (Providence, 1845).

Stark, W., *America: Ideal and Reality: The United States of 1776 in Contemporary European Diplomacy* (London, 1947).

Stourzh, Gerald, *Benjamin Franklin and American Foreign Policy* (Chicago, 1954).

Thornton, J. W., *The Pulpit of the American Revolution* (Boston, 1860).

Turner, F. J., *The Frontier in American History* (New York, 1921).

Van Tyne, C. H., "The Influence of the Clergy, and of Religious and Sectarian Forces in the American Revolution," *Amer. Hist. Rev.*, XIX (1913); "Sovereignty in the American Revolution," *Amer. Hist. Rev.*, XII (1907).

Wagner, D. O., "Some Antecedents of the American Doctrine of Judical Review," *Pol. Sci. Quar.*, XL (1925).

Williams, Basil, "Chatham and the Representation of the Colonies in the Imperial Parliament," *Eng. Hist. Rev.*, XXII (1907).

Winsor, Justin, "Virginia and the Quebec Bill," *Amer. Hist. Rev.*, I (1896).

Winstanley, D. A., *Lord Chatham and the Whig Opposition* (Cambridge, Eng., 1912).

Wolkins, G. G., "The Seizure of John Hancock's Sloop 'Liberty,' " Mass. Hist. Soc., *Proc.*, LV (1922).

Wright, B. F., Jr., *American Interpretations of Natural Law* (Cambridge, Mass., 1931).

Wrong, G. M., *Canada and the American Revolution . . .* (New York, 1935).

Loyalism and Conservatism in America

DeMond, R. O., *The Loyalists in North Carolina* . . . (Durham, 1940).

Flick, A. C., *Loyalism in New York during the American Revolution* (New York, 1901).

Gilbert, G. A., "Connecticut Loyalists," *Amer. Hist. Rev.,* IV (1899).

Gipson, L. H., *Jared Ingersoll: A Study of American Loyalism in Relation to British Colonial Government* (New Haven, 1920).

Hancock, H. B., *The Delaware Loyalists* (Wilmington, 1940).

Harrell, I. S., *Loyalism in Virginia: Chapters in the Economic History of the Revolution* (Durham, N.C., 1926); and "North Carolina Loyalists," *N.C. Hist. Rev.,* III (1926).

Jones, E. A., *The Loyalists of New Jersey, Their Memorials, Petitions, Claims, etc., from English records* (Newark, N.J., 1927); *The Loyalists of Massachusetts* . . . (London, 1930).

Labaree, L. W., *Conservatism in Early American History* (New York, 1948).

Peck, E., *The Loyalists of Connecticut* (New Haven, 1934).

Ryerson, E., *The Loyalists of America and their Times* . . . (2 vols., Toronto, 1880).

Sabine, Lorenzo, *Biographical Sketches* . . . *of the American Revolution* (2 vols., Boston, 1864).

Siebert, W. H., *The Flight of American Loyalists to the British Isles* (Columbus, 1911); "The Dispersion of American Tories," *Miss. Val. Hist. Rev.,* I (1914); *The Loyalists and Six Nations* . . ., Royal Soc. of Can., *Trans.,* 3rd ser. (1914), VIII; *The Loyalist Refugees of New Hampshire,* Ohio State Univ., *Bull.,* XXI (1916), No. 2; "The Loyalists of West Florida . . .," *Miss. Val. Hist. Rev.,* II (1916); *The Refugee Loyalists of Connecticut,* Royal Soc. of Can., *Trans.,* 3rd ser. (1916), VIII; *The Loyalists of Pennsylvania,* Ohio State Univ., *Bull.* (1920); and *East Florida as a Refuge of Southern Loyalists, 1774–1785* (Worcester, Mass., 1928). The late Professor Siebert also published other brief studies on the Loyalists which chiefly bear on the post-American Revolutionary War period.

Stark, J. H., *The Loyalists of Massachusetts* . . . (2 vols., Boston, 1910).

Sullivan, James, *Loyalism in New York* (New York, 1901).

Tyler, M. C., "The Party of the Loyalists in the American Revolution," *Amer. Hist. Rev.,* I (1895).

Van Tyne, C. H., *The Loyalists in the American Revolution* (New York, 1902).

Walker, Mabel G., "Sir John Johnson, Loyalist," *Miss. Val. Hist. Rev.,* III (1916).

The Commerce of the Colonies and Commercial Policy

Andrews, C. M., *The Colonial Period of American History* (New Haven, 1938), vol. I, *England's Commercial and Colonial Policy;* "The Boston Merchants and the Non-importation Movement," Col. Soc. Mass., *Pub.,* XIX (1917).

Baxter, W. T., *The House of Hancock: Business in Boston, 1724–1775* (Cambridge, Mass., 1945).

Beer, G. L., *The Commercial Policy of England toward the American Colonies* (New York, 1893); *British Colonial Policy, 1754–1765* (New York, 1907).

Bell, H. C., "The West India Trade before the American Revolution," *Am. Hist. Rev.,* XXII (1917).

Beyer, R. L., "American Colonial Commerce and British Protection," *Jour. Am. Hist.,* XXII (1928).

Bigelow, B. M., "Aaron Lopez, Merchant of Newport," *New Eng. Quar.,* IV (1931).

Bradlee, F. B. C., *Colonial Trade and Commerce, 1733–1774* (Salem, Mass., 1927).

Brunhouse, R. I., "The Effect of the Townshend Acts in Pennsylvania," *Pa. Mag. Hist. and Biog.,* LIV (1930).

Crittenden, C. C., *The Commerce of North Carolina, 1763–1789* (New Haven, 1936).

Donnan, Elizabeth, "Eighteenth-Century English Merchants: Micajah Perry," *Jour. Econ. and Bus. His.,* IV (1932); and *Documents Illustrative of the Slave Trade to America* (4 vols., Washington, 1930–35).

Ford, W. C., "Colonial Commerce in 1774–1776," Mass. Hist. Soc., *Proc.* LIX (1926).

Giesecke, A. A., *American Commercial Legislation before 1789* (New York, 1910).

Hacker, L. M., "The First American Revolution," *Columbia Univ. Quar.,* XXVII (1935).

Harper, L. A., *The English Navigation Laws* . . . (New York, 1939); "The Effect of the Navigation Acts on the Thirteen Colonies," in *The Era of the American Revolution* (New York, 1939).

Harrington, Virginia D., *The New York Merchant on the Eve of the Revolution* (New York, 1935).

Hedges, James B., *The Browns of Providence Plantations* (Cambridge, Mass., 1952).

Johnson, Emory R., Van Metre, T. W., *et al., History of Domestic and Foreign Commerce of the United States* (Washington, 1915), vol. I.

McClellan, W. S., *Smuggling in the American Colonies at the Outbreak of the Revolution, with Special reference to the West India Trade* (New York, 1912).

Morison, S. E., "The Commerce of Boston on the Eve of the Revolution," Am. Antiq. Soc., *Proc.*, n.ser., XXXII (1922).

Packard, L. B., *The Commercial Revolution, 1400–1776. Mercantilism—Colbert—Adam Smith* (New York, 1927).

Phillips, J. D., *Salem in the Eighteenth Century* (Boston, 1937).

Phillips, U. B., *A History of Transportation in the Eastern Belt to 1860* (New York, 1908).

Schlesinger, A. M., *The Colonial Merchants and the American Revolution, 1763–1776* (New York, 1918).

Schuyler, R. L., *The Fall of the Old Colonial System . . . 1770–1870* (New York, 1945).

Sellers, Leila, *Charleston Business on the Eve of the American Revolution* (Chapel Hill, 1934).

Smith, G. C., "An Era of Non-importation Associations, 1768–1773," *Wm. and Mary Quar.*, 2nd ser., XX (1940).

Wiener, F. B., "The Rhode Island Merchants and the Sugar Act," *New Eng. Quar.*, III (1930).

Williams, Justin, "English Mercantilism and Carolina Naval Stores, 1705–1776," *Jour. South. Hist.*, I (1935).

Williamson, A. S., *Credit Relations between Colonial and English Merchants in the Eighteenth Century* (Iowa City, 1832).

Colonial Money, Finance, and Revenue

Bolles, A. S., *The Financial History of the United States, from 1774–1789 . . .* (New York, 1879).

Bond, B. W., *The Quit-Rent System in the American Colonies* (New Haven, 1919).

Chalmers, R., *A History of Currency in the British Colonies* (London, 1893).

Connolly, J. C., "Quit-Rents in Colonial New Jersey as a Contributing Cause for the American Revolution," N.J. Hist. Soc., *Proc.*, n.ser., VII (1922).

Davis, A. M., *Provincial Banks: Land and Silver,* Col. Soc. Mass., *Pub.*, III (1900).

Dewey, D. R., *Financial History of the United States* (New York, 1903).

Douglas, C. H. J., *Financial History of Massachusetts Bay . . . to the American Revolution* (New York, 1892).

Farrand, Max, "The Taxation of Tea, 1767–1773," *Amer. Hist. Rev.*, III (1898).

Felt, J. B., *An Historical Account of Massachusetts Currency* (Boston, 1839).

Flippin, P. S., *The Financial Administration of the Colony of Virginia* (Baltimore, 1915).

Gipson, L. H., "Taxation of the Connecticut Towns, 1750–1775," in *Essays in Colonial History* . . . (New Haven, 1931); "Connecticut Taxation and Parliamentary Aid Preceding the Revolutionary War," *Amer. Hist. Rev.*, XXXVI (1931).

Gould, C. P., *Money and Transportation in Maryland, 1720–1765* (Baltimore, 1915).

Kemmerer, D. L., "The Colonial Loan-Office System in New Jersey," *Jour. Pol. Econ.*, XLVII (1939).

Parker, Coralie, *History of Taxation in North Carolina* (New York, 1928).

Phillips, Henry, *Historical Sketches of the Paper Currency of the American Colonies* (Roxbury, Mass., 1865).

Potter, E. R., and Rider, P. S., *Some Account of Bills of Credit . . . of Rhode Island* (*R. I. Hist. Tracts,* No. VIII, Providence, 1880).

Ripley, W. Z., *The Financial History of Virginia, 1609–1776* (New York, 1893).

Rodney, R. S., *Colonial Finances in Delaware* (Wilmington, 1928).

Sioussat, S. G. L., "The Breakdown of the Royal Management of Lands in the Southern Provinces, 1773–1775," *Agri. Hist.* III (1929).

Economic and Social Conditions in the Colonies *

Andrews, C. M., *Colonial Folkways* (New Haven, 1919).

Bidwell, P. W., and Falconer, J. I., *History of Agriculture in the Northern United States, 1620–1860* (Washington, 1925).

Bishop, J. L., *History of American Manufacturing from 1608 to 1860* (3 vols., Philadelphia, 1868).

Boston, C. A., "Some Glimpses of Colonial History," Pa. Bar Assoc., *Rep.*, 37th Annual Meeting, 1931.

Bridenbaugh, Carl, *Myths and Realities: Societies of the Colonial South* (Baton Rouge, 1952).

Callender, G. S., *Selections from the Economic History of the United States, 1765–1860* (Boston, 1909).

Clark, V. S., *History of Manufactures in the United States, 1607–1860* (Washington, 1916).

Cross, A. L., *The Anglican Episcopate and the American Colonies* (New York, 1902).

Cunningham, W., *The Growth of English Industry and Commerce* (2 vols., Cambridge, Eng., 1890–92).

* Only a few works dealing primarily with American colonial economic and social conditions can be presented here.

Davidson, P., "The Southern Backcountry on the Eve of the Revolution," in *Essays in Honor of W. E. Dodd* (Chicago, 1935).

Gewehr, W. M., *The Great Awakening in Virginia, 1740–1790* (Durham, N.C., 1930).

Greene, E. B., and Harrington, V. D., *American Population before the Federal Census of 1790* (New York, 1932).

Hamilton, J. G. de R., "Southern Members of the Inns of Court," *N.C. Hist. Rev.,* X (1933).

Kraus, Michael, *Intercolonial Aspects of American Culture on the Eve of the Revolution* . . . (New York, 1928); *The Atlantic Civilization* (Washington, 1949).

Lord, E. L., *Industrial Experiments in the British Colonies of North America* (Baltimore, 1898).

Morais, H. M., *Deism in Eighteenth Century America* (New York, 1934).

Morris, R. B., *Studies in the History of American Law* (New York, 1930); "Labor and Mercantilism in the Revolutionary Era," in *The Era of the American Revolution* (New York, 1939); and *Government and Labor in Early America* (New York, 1946).

Phillips, U. B., *Life and Labor in the Old South* (Boston, 1929).

Singleton, Esther, *Social New York under the Georges, 1714–1776* . . . (New York, 1902).

Spiegel, Käthe, *Kulturgeschichtliche Grundlagen der Amerikanischen Revolution* (New Haven, London, and Munich, 1931).

Spruill, Julia C., "Women's Life and Work in the Southern Colonies," *N.C. Hist. Rev.,* XVI (1939).

Thomas, I., *The History of Printing in America* . . . (2 vols., Albany, 1874).

Weeden, W. B., *Economic and Social History of New England, 1620–1789* (2 vols., Boston, 1890).

Wertenbaker, T. J., *The Founding of American Civilization: The Middle Colonies* (New York, 1938); *The Old South* (New York, 1942); and *The · Puritan Oligarchy* (New York, 1947).

Wright, L. B., *The Atlantic Frontier: Colonial American Civilization, 1607–1763* (New York, 1947).

Racial and Social Groups *

Ballagh, J. C., *White Servitude in the Colony of Virginia* (Baltimore, 1895); *A History of Slavery in Virginia* (Baltimore, 1902).

Bassett, J. S., *Slavery and Servitude in the Colony of North Carolina* (Baltimore, 1896).

* Here again only a few works out of many can be mentioned.

Brackett, J. R., *The Negro in Maryland* (Baltimore, 1889).

Donnan, Elizabeth, "The Slave Trade in South Carolina before the Revolution," *Amer. Hist. Rev.,* XXXIII (1928).

Dunaway, W. F., *The Scotch-Irish of Colonial Pennsylvania* (Chapel Hill, 1944).

Faust, A. B., *The German Element in the United States* (2 vols., Boston, 1909).

Flanders, R. B., *Plantation Slavery in Georgia* (Chapel Hill, 1933).

Ford, H. J., *The Scotch-Irish in America* (Princeton, 1915).

Geiser, K. F., *Redemptioners and Indentured Servants in Pennsylvania,* Yale Rev., Suppl., 1901.

Græff, A. D., *The Relations between the Pennsylvania Germans and the British Authorities (1750–1776),* Pa. Ger. Soc., *Proc.,* XLVII (1939).

Greene, G. W., *The German Element in the War of American Independence* (New York, 1876).

Greene, L. J., *The Negro in Colonial New England, 1620–1776* (New York, 1942).

Hamer, Marguerite B., "A Century before Manumission . . . in Mid-Eighteenth Century South Carolina," *N.C. Hist. Rev.,* XVII (1940).

Harr, C. M., "White Indentured Servants in Colonial New York," *Americana,* XXXIV (1940).

Herrick, C. A., *White Servitude in Pennsylvania* . . . (Philadelphia, 1926).

Jernegan, M. W., *Laboring and Dependent Classes in Colonial America, 1607–1783* . . . (Chicago, 1931); "Slavery and the Beginnings of Industrialism in the American Colonies," *Amer. Hist. Rev.,* XXV (1920).

McCormac, E. I., *White Servitude in Maryland, 1634–1820* (Baltimore, 1904).

McCrady, E., "Slavery in . . . South Carolina (1670–1770)," A.H.A., *Rep.,* 1895.

Morris, R. B., *Government and Labor in Early America* (New York, 1946).

Phillips, U. B., *American Negro Slavery* . . . (New York, 1918).

Smith, A. E., *Colonists in Bondage: White Servitude and Convict Labor in America, 1607–1776* (Chapel Hill, 1947).

Turner, E. R., *The Negro in Pennsylvania* . . . *1639–1861* (Washington, 1911).

Wayland, J. W., *The German Element in the Shenandoah Valley* (Charlottesville, 1907).

The Stamp Act

While many of the general and special works deal with the Stamp Act crisis in detail, a few studies particularly concerned with phases of it should be mentioned: G. P. Anderson's "Ebenezer Mackintosh: Stamp Act Rioter and Patriot" and "A Note on Ebenezer Mackintosh," Col. Soc. of Mass., *Pub.*, XXVI (1927); J. C. Connolly's "The Stamp Act and New Jersey's Opposition to It," N.J. Hist. Soc., *Proc.*, n.ser., IX (1924); P. G. Davidson's "Sons of Liberty and Stamp Act Men," *N.C. Hist. Rev.*, IX (1932); F. J. Ericson's "The Contemporary British Opposition to the Stamp Act, 1764–1765," Mich. Acad. of Science, Arts, and Letters, *Pap.*, XXIX (1944); P. H. Giddens's "Maryland and the Stamp Act Controversy," *Md. Hist. Mag.*, XXVII (1932); Helen H. Hodge's "The Repeal of the Stamp Act," *Pol. Sci. Quar.*, XIX (1904); and A. M. Schlesinger's "The Colonial Newspapers and the Stamp Act," *New Eng. Quar.*, VIII (1935). E. S. and Helen M. Morgan's study on *The Stamp Act Crisis* (Chapel Hill, 1953) that has lately appeared from the press is the best study of the topic.

The Boston Massacre

In addition to Frederick Kidder's . . . *The Boston Massacre* . . . (Albany, 1870), a work hitherto not mentioned, there is R. G. Adams's *New Light on the Boston Massacre* (Worcester, Mass., 1938); Emil Bænesch's *A Boston Boy, the First Martyr to American Liberty* (Manitowoc, Wis., 1924); and Wade Millis's "A Monument to the American Sense of Justice," *Mich. Law Rev.*, XXV (1926). The trial of the soldiers is presented in P. W. Chandler's *American Criminal Trials* (Boston, 1841), vol. I.

The Crisis of 1773–75

The events of the years 1773–75 are very fully covered by works previously cited. Reference, however, may be made to the following studies: Richard Frothingham's "The Boston Tea-Party," Mass. Hist. Soc., *Proc.*, XIII (1875); W. P. Parker's "Some Facts About the Boston Tea Party," Nantucket Hist. Assoc., *Proc.*, XXVIII; P. L. Ford's "The Association of the First Congress," *Pol. Sci. Quar.*, VI (1891); Harold Murdock's *The Nineteenth of April 1775* (Boston, 1923); and Allen French's *The First Year of the American Revolution* (Boston, 1934).

Index

harper ✦ torchbooks

HUMANITIES AND SOCIAL SCIENCES

American Studies: General

THOMAS C. COCHRAN: The Inner Revolution. *Essays on the Social Sciences in History* TB/1140
EDWARD S. CORWIN: American Constitutional History. *Essays edited by Alpheus T. Mason and Gerald Garvey* △ TB/1136
CARL N. DEGLER, Ed.: Pivotal Interpretations of American History TB/1240, TB/1241
A. HUNTER DUPREE: Science in the Federal Government: *A History of Policies and Activities to 1940* TB/573
A. S. EISENSTADT, Ed.: The Craft of American History: *Recent Essays in American Historical Writing* Vol. I TB/1255; Vol. II TB/1256
CHARLOTTE P. GILMAN: Women and Economics: *A Study of the Economic Relation between Men and Women as a Factor in Social Evolution. ‡ Ed. with an Introduction by Carl N. Degler* TB/3073
OSCAR HANDLIN, Ed.: This Was America: *As Recorded by European Travelers in the Eighteenth, Nineteenth and Twentieth Centuries. Illus.* TB/1119
MARCUS LEE HANSEN: The Atlantic Migration: 1607-1860. *Edited by Arthur M. Schlesinger* TB/1052
MARCUS LEE HANSEN: The Immigrant in American History. TB/1120
JOHN HIGHAM, Ed.: The Reconstruction of American History △ TB/1068
ROBERT H. JACKSON: The Supreme Court in the American System of Government TB/1106
JOHN F. KENNEDY: A Nation of Immigrants. △ *Illus.* TB/1118
LEONARD W. LEVY, Ed.: American Constitutional Law: *Historical Essays* TB/1285
RALPH BARTON PERRY: Puritanism and Democracy TB/1138
ARNOLD ROSE: The Negro in America TB/3048
MAURICE R. STEIN: The Eclipse of Community. *An Interpretation of American Studies* TB/1128
W. LLOYD WARNER and Associates: Democracy in Jonesville: *A Study in Quality and Inequality* ¶ TB/1129
W. LLOYD WARNER: Social Class in America: *The Evaluation of Status* TB/1013

American Studies: Colonial

BERNARD BAILYN, Ed.: Apologia of Robert Keayne: *Self-Portrait of a Puritan Merchant* TB/1201
BERNARD BAILYN: The New England Merchants in the Seventeenth Century TB/1149
JOSEPH CHARLES: The Origins of the American Party System TB/1049

LAWRENCE HENRY GIPSON: The Coming of the Revolution: 1763-1775. † *Illus.* TB/3007
LEONARD W. LEVY: Freedom of Speech and Press in Early American History: *Legacy of Suppression* TB/1109
PERRY MILLER: Errand Into the Wilderness TB/1139
PERRY MILLER & T. H. JOHNSON, Eds.: The Puritans: *A Sourcebook of Their Writings*
Vol. I TB/1093; Vol. II TB/1094
EDMUND S. MORGAN, Ed.: The Diary of Michael Wigglesworth, 1653-1657: *The Conscience of a Puritan* TB/1228
EDMUND S. MORGAN: The Puritan Family: *Religion and Domestic Relations in Seventeenth-Century New England* TB/1227
RICHARD B. MORRIS: Government and Labor in Early America TB/1244
KENNETH B. MURDOCK: Literature and Theology in Colonial New England TB/99
WALLACE NOTESTEIN: The English People on the Eve of Colonization: 1603-1630. † *Illus.* TB/3006
LOUIS B. WRIGHT: The Cultural Life of the American Colonies: 1607-1763. † *Illus.* TB/3005

American Studies: From the Revolution to 1860

JOHN R. ALDEN: The American Revolution: 1775-1783. † *Illus.* TB/3011
MAX BELOFF, Ed.: The Debate on the American Revolution, 1761-1783: *A Sourcebook* △ TB/1225
RAY A. BILLINGTON: The Far Western Frontier: 1830-1860. † *Illus.* TB/3012
W. R. BROCK: An American Crisis: *Congress and Reconstruction, 1865-67* ° △ TB/1283
EDMUND BURKE: On the American Revolution: *Selected Speeches and Letters. ‡ Edited by Elliott Robert Barkan* TB/3068
WHITNEY R. CROSS: The Burned-Over District: *The Social and Intellectual History of Enthusiastic Religion in Western New York, 1800-1850* △ TB/1242
GEORGE DANGERFIELD: The Awakening of American Nationalism: 1815-1828. † *Illus.* TB/3061
CLEMENT EATON: The Freedom-of-Thought Struggle in the Old South. *Revised and Enlarged. Illus.* TB/1150
CLEMENT EATON: The Growth of Southern Civilization: 1790-1860. † *Illus.* TB/3040
LOUIS FILLER: The Crusade Against Slavery: 1830-1860. † *Illus.* TB/3029
DIXON RYAN FOX: The Decline of Aristocracy in the Politics of New York: 1801-1840. ‡ *Edited by Robert V. Remini* TB/3064
FELIX GILBERT: The Beginnings of American Foreign Policy: *To the Farewell Address* TB/1200
FRANCIS GRIERSON: The Valley of Shadows: *The Coming of the Civil War in Lincoln's Midwest: A Contemporary Account* TB/1246

---

† The New American Nation Series, edited by Henry Steele Commager and Richard B. Morris.

‡ American Persectives series, edited by Bernard Wishy and William E. Leuchtenburg.

* The Rise of Modern Europe series, edited by William L. Langer.

¶ Researches in the Social, Cultural, and Behavioral Sciences, edited by Benjamin Nelson.

§ The Library of Religion and Culture, edited by Benjamin Nelson.

Σ Harper Modern Science Series, edited by James R. Newman.

° Not for sale in Canada.

△ Not for sale in the U. K.

W. O. HASSALL, Ed.: Medieval England: *As Viewed by Contemporaries* △ TB/1205
DENYS HAY: Europe: The Emergence of an Idea TB/1275
DENYS HAY: The Medieval Centuries ᵒ △ TB/1192
J. M. HUSSEY: The Byzantine World △ TB/1057
ROBERT LATOUCHE: The Birth of Western Economy: *Economic Aspects of the Dark Ages.* ᵒ △ *Intro. by Philip Grierson* TB/1290
FERDINAND LOT: The End of the Ancient World and the Beginnings of the Middle Ages. *Introduction by Glanville Downey* TB/1044
G. MOLLAT: The Popes at Avignon: 1305-1378 △ TB/308
CHARLES PETIT-DUTAILLIS: The Feudal Monarchy in France and England: *From the Tenth to the Thirteenth Century* ᵒ △ TB/1165
HENRI PIRENNE: Early Democracies in the Low Countries: *Urban Society and Political Conflict in the Middle Ages and the Renaissance. Introduction by John H. Mundy* TB/1110
STEVEN RUNCIMAN: A History of the Crusades. △
Volume I: *The First Crusade and the Foundation of the Kingdom of Jerusalem. Illus.* TB/1143
Volume II: *The Kingdom of Jerusalem and the Frankish East, 1100-1187. Illus.* TB/1243
FERDINAND SCHEVILL: Siena: *The History of a Medieval Commune. Intro. by William M. Bowsky* TB/1164
SULPICIUS SEVERUS et al.: The Western Fathers: *Being the Lives of Martin of Tours, Ambrose, Augustine of Hippo, Honoratus of Arles and Germanus of Auxerre.* △ *Edited and trans. by F. O. Hoare* TB/309
HENRY OSBORN TAYLOR: The Classical Heritage of the Middle Ages. *Foreword and Biblio. by Kenneth M. Setton* TB/1117
F. VAN DER MEER: Augustine The Bishop: *Church and Society at the Dawn of the Middle Ages* △ TB/304
J. M. WALLACE-HADRILL: The Barbarian West: *The Early Middle Ages, A.D. 400-1000* △ TB/1061

History: Renaissance & Reformation

JACOB BURCKHARDT: The Civilization of the Renaissance in Italy. △ *Intro. by Benjamin Nelson & Charles Trinkaus. Illus.* Vol. I TB/40; Vol. II TB/41
JOHN CALVIN & JACOPO SADOLETO: A Reformation Debate. *Edited by John C. Olin* TB/1239
ERNST CASSIRER: The Individual and the Cosmos in Renaissance Philosophy. △ *Translated with an Introduction by Mario Domandi* TB/1097
FEDERICO CHABOD: Machiavelli and the Renaissance △ TB/1193
EDWARD P. CHEYNEY: The Dawn of a New Era, 1250-1453. * *Illus.* TB/3002
G. CONSTANT: The Reformation in England: *The English Schism, Henry VIII, 1509-1547* △ TB/314
R. TREVOR DAVIES: The Golden Century of Spain, 1501-1621 ᵒ △ TB/1194
G. R. ELTON: Reformation Europe, 1517-1559 ᵒ △ TB/1270
DESIDERIUS ERASMUS: Christian Humanism and the Reformation: *Selected Writings. Edited and translated by John C. Olin* TB/1166
WALLACE K. FERGUSON et al.: Facets of the Renaissance TB/1098
WALLACE K. FERGUSON et al.: The Renaissance: *Six Essays. Illus.* TB/1084
JOHN NEVILLE FIGGIS: The Divine Right of Kings. *Introduction by G. R. Elton* TB/1191
JOHN NEVILLE FIGGIS: Political Thought from Gerson to Grotius: 1414-1625: *Seven Studies. Introduction by Garrett Mattingly* TB/1032
MYRON P. GILMORE: The World of Humanism, 1453-1517. * *Illus.* TB/3003
FRANCESCO GUICCIARDINI: Maxims and Reflections of a Renaissance Statesman (Ricordi). *Trans. by Mario Domandi. Intro. by Nicolai Rubinstein* TB/1160
J. H. HEXTER: More's Utopia: *The Biography of an Idea. New Epilogue by the Author* TB/1195

HAJO HOLBORN: Ulrich von Hutten and the German Reformation TB/1238
JOHAN HUIZINGA: Erasmus and the Age of Reformation. △ *Illus.* TB/19
JOEL HURSTFIELD, Ed.: The Reformation Crisis △ TB/1267
ULRICH VON HUTTEN et al.: On the Eve of the Reformation: *"Letters of Obscure Men." Introduction by Hajo Holborn* TB/1124
PAUL O. KRISTELLER: Renaissance Thought: *The Classic, Scholastic, and Humanist Strains* TB/1048
PAUL O. KRISTELLER: Renaissance Thought II: *Papers on Humanism and the Arts* TB/1163
NICCOLÒ MACHIAVELLI: History of Florence and of the Affairs of Italy: *from the earliest times to the death of Lorenzo the Magnificent. Introduction by Felix Gilbert* △ TB/1027
ALFRED VON MARTIN: Sociology of the Renaissance. *Introduction by Wallace K. Ferguson* TB/1099
GARRETT MATTINGLY et al.: Renaissance Profiles. △ *Edited by J. H. Plumb* TB/1162
MILLARD MEISS: Painting in Florence and Siena after the Black Death: *The Arts, Religion and Society in the Mid-Fourteenth Century.* △ *169 illus.* TB/1148
J. E. NEALE: The Age of Catherine de Medici ᵒ △ TB/1085
ERWIN PANOFSKY: Studies in Iconology: *Humanistic Themes in the Art of the Renaissance.* △ *180 illustrations* TB/1077
J. H. PARRY: The Establishment of the European Hegemony: 1415-1715: *Trade and Exploration in the Age of the Renaissance* △ TB/1045
J. H. PLUMB: The Italian Renaissance: *A Concise Survey of Its History and Culture* △ TB/1161
A. F. POLLARD: Henry VIII. ᵒ △ *Introduction by A. G. Dickens* TB/1249
A. F. POLLARD: Wolsey. ᵒ △ *Introduction by A. G. Dickens* TB/1248
CECIL ROTH: The Jews in the Renaissance. *Illus.* TB/834
A. L. ROWSE: The Expansion of Elizabethan England. ᵒ △ *Illus.* TB/1220
GORDON RUPP: Luther's Progress to the Diet of Worms ᵒ △ TB/120
FERDINAND SCHEVILL: The Medici. *Illus.* TB/1010
FERDINAND SCHEVILL: Medieval and Renaissance Florence. *Illus.* Volume I: *Medieval Florence* TB/1090
Volume II: *The Coming of Humanism and the Age of the Medici* TB/1091
G. M. TREVELYAN: England in the Age of Wycliffe, 1368-1520 ᵒ △ TB/1112
VESPASIANO: Renaissance Princes, Popes, and Prelates: *The Vespasiano Memoirs: Lives of Illustrious Men of the XVth Century. Intro. by Myron P. Gilmore* TB/1111

History: Modern European

FREDERICK B. ARTZ: Reaction and Revolution, 1815-1832. * *Illus.* TB/3034
MAX BELOFF: The Age of Absolutism, 1660-1815 △ TB/1062
ROBERT C. BINKLEY: Realism and Nationalism, 1852-1871. * *Illus.* TB/3038
ASA BRIGGS: The Making of Modern England, 1784-1867: *The Age of Improvement* ᵒ △ TB/1203
CRANE BRINTON: A Decade of Revolution, 1789-1799. * *Illus.* TB/3018
D. W. BROGAN: The Development of Modern France. ᵒ △
Volume I: *From the Fall of the Empire to the Dreyfus Affair* TB/1184
Volume II: *The Shadow of War, World War I, Between the Two Wars. New Introduction by the Author* TB/1185
J. BRONOWSKI & BRUCE MAZLISH: The Western Intellectual Tradition: *From Leonardo to Hegel* △ TB/3001
GEOFFREY BRUUN: Europe and the French Imperium, 1799-1814. * *Illus.* TB/3033
ALAN BULLOCK: Hitler, A Study in Tyranny. ᵒ △ *Illus.* TB/1123

E. H. CARR: German-Soviet Relations Between the Two World Wars, 1919-1939   TB/1278
E. H. CARR: International Relations Between the Two World Wars, 1919-1939 ° △   TB/1279
E. H. CARR: The Twenty Years' Crisis, 1919-1939: An Introduction to the Study of International Relations ° △   TB/1122
GORDON A. CRAIG: From Bismarck to Adenauer: Aspects of German Statecraft. Revised Edition   TB/1171
WALTER L. DORN: Competition for Empire, 1740-1763. * Illus.   TB/3032
FRANKLIN L. FORD: Robe and Sword: The Regrouping of the French Aristocracy after Louis XIV   TB/1217
CARL J. FRIEDRICH: The Age of the Baroque, 1610-1660. * Illus.   TB/3004
RENÉ FUELOEP-MILLER: The Mind and Face of Bolshevism: An Examination of Cultural Life in Soviet Russia. New Epilogue by the Author   TB/1188
M. DOROTHY GEORGE: London Life in the Eighteenth Century △   TB/1182
LEO GERSHOY: From Despotism to Revolution, 1763-1789. * Illus.   TB/3017
C. C. GILLISPIE: Genesis and Geology: The Decades before Darwin §   TB/51
ALBERT GOODWIN: The French Revolution △   TB/1064
ALBERT GUÉRARD: France in the Classical Age: The Life and Death of an Ideal △   TB/1183
CARLTON J. H. HAYES: A Generation of Materialism, 1871-1900. * Illus.   TB/3039
J. H. HEXTER: Reappraisals in History: New Views on History and Society in Early Modern Europe △
                                                         TB/1100
STANLEY HOFFMANN et al.: In Search of France: The Economy, Society and Political System in the Twentieth Century   TB/1219
A. R. HUMPHREYS: The Augustan World: Society, Thought, & Letters in 18th Century England ° △
                                                         TB/1105
DAN N. JACOBS, Ed.: The New Communist Manifesto and Related Documents. Third edition, revised
                                                         TB/1078
HANS KOHN: The Mind of Germany: The Education of a Nation △   TB/1204
HANS KOHN, Ed.: The Mind of Modern Russia: Historical and Political Thought of Russia's Great Age TB/1065
WALTER LAQUEUR & GEORGE L. MOSSE, Eds.: International Fascism, 1920-1945. ° △ Volume I of Journal of Contemporary History   TB/1276
WALTER LAQUEUR & GEORGE L. MOSSE, Eds.: The Left-Wing Intelligentsia between the Two World Wars. ° △ Volume II of Journal of Contemporary History
                                                         TB/1286
FRANK E. MANUEL: The Prophets of Paris: Turgot, Condorcet, Saint-Simon, Fourier, and Comte TB/1218
KINGSLEY MARTIN: French Liberal Thought in the Eighteenth Century: A Study of Political Ideas from Bayle to Condorcet   TB/1114
L. B. NAMIER: Facing East: Essays on Germany, the Balkans, and Russia in the 20th Century △ TB/1280
L. B. NAMIER: Personalities and Powers: Selected Essays △   TB/1186
L. B. NAMIER: Vanished Supremacies: Essays on European History, 1812-1918 °   TB/1088
JOHN U. NEF: Western Civilization Since the Renaissance: Peace, War, Industry, and the Arts TB/1113
FRANZ NEUMANN: Behemoth: The Structure and Practice of National Socialism, 1933-1944   TB/1289
FREDERICK L. NUSSBAUM: The Triumph of Science and Reason, 1660-1685. * Illus.   TB/3009
DAVID OGG: Europe of the Ancien Régime, 1715-1783 ° △
                                                         TB/1271
JOHN PLAMENATZ: German Marxism and Russian Communism. ° △ New Preface by the Author   TB/1189
RAYMOND W. POSTGATE, Ed.: Revolution from 1789 to 1906: Selected Documents   TB/1063

PENFIELD ROBERTS: The Quest for Security, 1715-1740. * Illus.   TB/3016
PRISCILLA ROBERTSON: Revolutions of 1848: A Social History   TB/1025
GEORGE RUDÉ: Revolutionary Europe, 1783-1815 ° △
                                                         TB/1272
LOUIS, DUC DE SAINT-SIMON: Versailles, The Court, and Louis XIV. ° △ Introductory Note by Peter Gay
                                                         TB/1250
ALBERT SOREL: Europe Under the Old Regime. Translated by Francis H. Herrick   TB/1121
N. N. SUKHANOV: The Russian Revolution, 1917: Eyewitness Account. △ Edited by Joel Carmichael
                    Vol. I TB/1066; Vol. II TB/1067
A. J. P. TAYLOR: From Napoleon to Lenin: Historical Essays ° △   TB/1268
A. J. P. TAYLOR: The Habsburg Monarchy, 1809-1918: A History of the Austrian Empire and Austria-Hungary ° △   TB/1187
G. M. TREVELYAN: British History in the Nineteenth Century and After: 1782-1919. ° △ Second Edition TB/1251
H. R. TREVOR-ROPER: Historical Essays ° △   TB/1269
ELIZABETH WISKEMANN: Europe of the Dictators, 1919-1945 ° △   TB/1273
JOHN B. WOLF: The Emergence of the Great Powers, 1685-1715. * Illus.   TB/3010
JOHN B. WOLF: France: 1814-1919: The Rise of a Liberal-Democratic Society   TB/3019

Intellectual History & History of Ideas

HERSCHEL BAKER: The Image of Man: A Study of the Idea of Human Dignity in Classical Antiquity, the Middle Ages, and the Renaissance   TB/1047
R. R. BOLGAR: The Classical Heritage and Its Beneficiaries: From the Carolingian Age to the End of the Renaissance △   TB/1125
RANDOLPH S. BOURNE: War and the Intellectuals: Collected Essays, 1915-1919. △ ‡ Edited by Carl Resek
                                                         TB/3043
J. BRONOWSKI & BRUCE MAZLISH: The Western Intellectual Tradition: From Leonardo to Hegel △ TB/3001
ERNST CASSIRER: The Individual and the Cosmos in Renaissance Philosophy. △ Translated with an Introduction by Mario Domandi   TB/1097
NORMAN COHN: The Pursuit of the Millennium: Revolutionary Messianism in Medieval and Reformation Europe △   TB/1037
C. C. GILLISPIE: Genesis and Geology: The Decades before Darwin §   TB/51
G. RACHEL LEVY: Religious Conceptions of the Stone Age and Their Influence upon European Thought. △ Illus. Introduction by Henri Frankfort   TB/106
ARTHUR O. LOVEJOY: The Great Chain of Being: A Study of the History of an Idea   TB/1009
FRANK E. MANUEL: The Prophets of Paris: Turgot, Condorcet, Saint-Simon, Fourier, and Comte △ TB/1218
PERRY MILLER & T. H. JOHNSON, Editors: The Puritans: A Sourcebook of Their Writings
                    Vol. I TB/1093; Vol. II TB/1094
MILTON C. NAHM: Genius and Creativity: An Essay in the History of Ideas   TB/1196
ROBERT PAYNE: Hubris: A Study of Pride. Foreword by Sir Herbert Read   TB/1031
RALPH BARTON PERRY: The Thought and Character of William James: Briefer Version   TB/1156
GEORG SIMMEL et al.: Essays on Sociology, Philosophy, and Aesthetics. ¶ Edited by Kurt H. Wolff TB/1234
BRUNO SNELL: The Discovery of the Mind: The Greek Origins of European Thought △   TB/1018
PAGET TOYNBEE: Dante Alighieri: His Life and Works. Edited with Intro. by Charles S. Singleton △ TB/1206
ERNEST LEE TUVESON: Millennium and Utopia: A Study in the Background of the Idea of Progress. ¶ New Preface by the Author   TB/1134
PAUL VALÉRY: The Outlook for Intelligence △   TB/2016

5

Political Science & Government

Psychology

8

Christianity: General

Christianity: Origins & Early Development

Christianity: The Middle Ages and The Reformation

Christianity: The Protestant Tradition

10